REA

ACPL ITEM

DISCARDED

3 1833 02460 8074

Y0-BSF-555

268

Tarbell's teacher's guide

TARBELL'S

Teacher's Guide

to the International Sunday School Lessons

Includes the RSV and KJV

Dr. William P. Barker

David C. Cook Church Ministries
Elgin, Illinois/Weston, Ontario

This volume is based on the International Sunday School Lessons; the International Bible Lessons for Christian Teaching, copyright © 1990 by the committee on the Uniform Series.

The text of the Revised Standard Version of the Bible and quotations therefrom are copyright © 1946 and 1952 by the Division of Christian Education, National Council of Churches, and used by permission.

Unless otherwise identified, biblical quotations in the material used by the author to illustrate the lesson are from the Revised Standard Version of the Bible.

Allen County Public Library
900 Webster Street
PO Box 2270
Fort Wayne, IN 46801-2270

COPYRIGHT © 1994 DAVID C. COOK PUBLISHING CO.
All rights reserved—no part of this book may be reproduced in any form without permission in writing from the publisher.

Published by David C. Cook Church Ministries
850 North Grove Avenue
Elgin, Illinois 60120
Cable address: DCCOOK
Printed in the United States of America
ISBN 0-7814-4995-2

CONTENTS

LIST OF LESSONS

SEPTEMBER—NOVEMBER 1994
FROM THE CONQUEST TO THE KINGDOM

DECEMBER 1994—FEBRUARY 1995
JESUS THE FULFILLMENT (THE GOSPEL OF MATTHEW)

MARCH—MAY 1995
CHRISTIAN LIVING IN COMMUNITY

JUNE—AUGUST 1995
A NATION TURNS TO GOD

A WORD TO THE TEACHER

Some unknown soul wrote a list of what every successful teacher needs:
- The education of a college president,
- The executive ability of a financier,
- The humility of a deacon,
- The adaptability of a chameleon,
- The hope of an optimist,
- The courage of a hero,
- The wisdom of a serpent,
- The gentleness of a dove,
- The patience of Job,
- The grace of God, and
- The persistence of the devil.

As a teacher, you undoubtedly are smiling—and agreeing with the anonymous author of that list! You also probably realize that you could use an additional helping of each of these traits as you prepare to teach this year.

Do you remember the sequence in *All in the Family* a few years ago in which Archie Bunker was debating religion with his son-in-law, "Meathead"? Archie was growing increasingly exasperated at Meathead for his agnostic remarks. Archie is finally silenced for a few moments when Meathead asks if there is a God when there is so much suffering in the world. Archie pauses in bewilderment, then shouts at his wife, "Edith, would you get in here and help me? I'm having to defend God all by myself."

But you never have to defend God all by yourself. In spite of your flaws and inadequacies, God is in your classroom with you. Through the Holy Spirit, He presents the good news of Jesus Christ as you serve faithfully in His name.

Go into your church class each Sunday this year with the awareness that the Lord is using you as a special instrument for His work. Most of all, teach each lesson with the knowledge that the risen, living Lord stands beside you, using your efforts—feeble and fumbling though they may seem sometimes—to present His eternal message of salvation!

Your colleague always in His service,

William F. Barker

Use Tarbell's with Material from These Publishers

Sunday school materials from the following denominations and publishers follow the International Sunday School Lesson outlines (sometimes known as the Uniform Series). Because Tarbell's Teacher's Guide follows the same ISSL outlines, you can use Tarbell's as an excellent teacher resource to supplement the materials from these publishing houses.

Denominational:

Advent Christian General Conference—*Adult*
American Baptist (Judson Press)—*Adult*
Church of God in Christ (Church of God in Christ Publishing House)—
   Adult
Church of Christ Holiness—*Adult*
Church of God (Warner Press)—*Adult*
Church of God by Faith—*Adult*
National Baptist Convention of America (Boyd)—*All ages*
National Primitive Baptist Convention—*Adult*
Progressive National Baptist Convention—*Adult*
Presbyterian Church (U.S.A.) (*Bible Discovery Series*—Presbyterian
   Publishing House or P.R.E.M.)—*Adult*
Southern Baptist (Baptist Sunday School Board)—*All ages*
Union Gospel Press—*All ages*
United Holy Church of America—*Adult*
United Methodist Church (Cokesbury)—*All ages*

Nondenominational:

David C. Cook Church Ministries—*Adult*
Echoes Sunday School Literature—*Adult*
Standard Publishing—*Adult*
Urban Ministries—*All ages*

SEPTEMBER, OCTOBER, NOVEMBER 1994

FROM THE CONQUEST TO THE KINGDOM

LESSON 1—SEPTEMBER 4

SPYING OUT JERICHO

Background Scripture: Joshua 1—2
Devotional Reading: Joshua 1:1-9

KING JAMES VERSION	REVISED STANDARD VERSION

KING JAMES VERSION

JOSHUA 2:1 And Joshua the son of Nun sent out of Shittim two men to spy secretly, saying, Go view the land, even Jericho. And they went, and came into an harlot's house, named Rahab, and lodged there.

8 And before they were laid down, she came up unto them upon the roof;

9 And she said unto the men, I know that the Lord hath given you the land, and that your terror is fallen upon us, and that all the inhabitants of the land faint because of you.

10 For we have heard how the Lord dried up the water of the Red sea for you, when ye came out of Egypt; and what ye did unto the two kings of the Amorites, that were on the other side Jordan, Sihon and Og, whom ye utterly destroyed.

11 And as soon as we had heard these things, our hearts did melt, neither did there remain any more courage in any man, because of you: for the Lord your God, he is God in heaven above, and in earth beneath.

12 Now therefore, I pray you, swear unto me by the Lord, since I have shewed you kindness, that ye will also shew kindness unto my father's house, and give me a true token:

13 And that ye will save alive my father, and my mother, and my brethren, and my sisters, and all that they have, and deliver our lives from death.

14 And the men answered her, Our life for your's, if ye utter not this our business. And it shall be, when the Lord hath given us the land, that we will deal kindly and truly with thee.

22 And they went, and came unto the mountain, and abode there three days, until the pursuers were returned: and the pursuers sought them throughout all the way,

REVISED STANDARD VERSION

JOSHUA 2:1 And Joshua the son of Nun sent two men secretly from Shittim as spies, saying, "Go, view the land, especially Jericho." And they went, and came into the house of a harlot whose name was Rahab, and lodged there.

8 Before they lay down, she came up to them on the roof, 9 and said to the men, "I know that the Lord has given you the land, and that the fear of you has fallen upon us, and that all the inhabitants of the land melt away before you. 10 For we have heard how the Lord dried up the water of the Red Sea before you when you came out of Egypt, and what you did to the two kings of the Amorites that were beyond the Jordan, to Sihon and Og, whom you utterly destroyed. 11 And as soon as we heard it, our hearts melted, and there was no courage left in any man, because of you; for the Lord your God is he who is God in heaven above and on earth beneath. 12 Now then, swear to me by the Lord that as I have dealt kindly with you, you also will deal kindly with my father's house, and give me a sure sign, 13 and save alive my father and mother, my brothers and sisters, and all who belong to them, and deliver our lives from death." 14 And the men said to her, "Our life for yours! If you do not tell this business of ours, then we will deal kindly and faithfully with you when the Lord gives us the land."

22 They departed, and went into the hills, and remained there three days, until the pursuers returned; for the pursuers had made search all along the way and found nothing. 23 Then the two men came down again from the hills, and passed over and came to Joshua the son of Nun; and they told him all that had befallen them. 24 And

but found them not.

23 So the two men returned, and descended from the mountain, and passed over, and came to Joshua the son of Nun, and told him all things that befell them:

24 And they said unto Joshua, Truly the Lord hath delivered into our hands all the land; for even all the inhabitants of the country do faint because of us.

they said to Joshua, "Truly the Lord has given all the land into our hands; and moreover all the inhabitants of the land are fainthearted because of us."

KEY VERSE: Truly the Lord has given all the land into our hands. Joshua 2:24a.

HOME DAILY BIBLE READINGS

Aug 29	M.	Psalm 105:37-45	*Praise for God's Leading*
Aug. 30	T.	Deuteronomy 31:14-23	*Joshua's Commissioning to Lead the People*
Aug. 31	W.	Joshua 1:1-9	*God Encourages Joshua to be Courageous*
Sept. 1	T.	Joshua 1:10-18	*Joshua Organizes to Cross the Jordan*
Sept 2	F	Joshua 2:1-7	*Joshua's Spies Are Hidden by Rahab*
Sept. 3	S.	Joshua 2:8-14	*The Promise to Protect Rahab's Family*
Sept 4	S.	Joshua 2:15-24	*The Spies Report to Joshua*

BACKGROUND

Anyone wanting to understand the United States must know something of American history. George Washington and Thomas Jefferson, Valley Forge and Yorktown define the early days of the nation. Other personalities and events—Andrew Jackson, Abraham Lincoln, Robert E. Lee, the Alamo, the Civil War, the Spanish-American War, the two World Wars, the Depression, the Cold War, the assassinations of the Kennedys and Martin Luther King, Jr., Vietnam, Watergate, the presidencies of powerful national leaders—all must be studied if one is to understand the American people.

Likewise, a person must read the Old Testament story in order to comprehend more fully the significance of the New Testament. This quarter's lessons center on the key period from the conquest of the Promised Land under Joshua to the establishment of the Kingdom under David and Solomon. These lessons draw from the books of Joshua, Judges, I and II Samuel, and I Kings, focusing on the most significant events and persons in Israel's history from the time of Joshua to the reign of Solomon.

We start today with the preparations by Joshua to conquer the land. Previously, the Israelites had been miraculously delivered from slavery in Egypt. The next forty years under Moses' leadership were a period of testing and toughening. During those years, God sealed His covenant relationship with the Israelites and gave them the Ten Commandments. Finally, Moses died and Joshua assumed leadership.

Joshua gathered his forces on the east side of the Jordan river. Before attempting an invasion, however, he needed valuable information about the forces he would encounter. Earlier, he and eleven other representatives of the twelve tribes had spied out the land of Canaan (see Num. 13). Joshua and Caleb pressed for an invasion, but the rest of the spies had given such a pessimistic report that the people of Israel trembled at the prospect of trying to conquer the Canaanites. Joshua realized that he still had to have detailed, up-to-date intelligence on the opposition.

Jericho guarded the entrance to the Promised Land. Since this great city straddled the key trade routes, Joshua would have to capture it before advancing into Canaanite territory. His spies risked their lives by sneaking into the powerful fortress-city. Knowing that they would need local aid and protection, they sought out the person who was most likely to feel alienated from the community—the local prostitute, Rahab. The spies' visit to Rahab was not for sexual pleasure but to secure a military ally. Thanks to Rahab's courage and ingenuity, the spies survived to return to Joshua with valuable military information.

NOTES ON THE PRINTED TEXT

Go, view the land, especially Jericho (2:1). Israel was advancing into Canaan toward Jericho, the oldest known city in the world. The city had an abundant water supply and plenty of food; anyone planning to conquer Canaan had to secure this key site. In order to do this, Joshua needed information. He sent spies to Jericho to survey the city's defenses.

When the spies arrived in Jericho, they stayed in the home of Rahab. Rahab was a prostitute, perhaps connected with a fertility cult within the Canaanite religion. Her profession enabled her to come into contact with many of the city's men. She would be able to provide the spies with details of the city's defenses and descriptions of the fighting force's morale—information that was vital to Joshua. Also, since they were entering the house of a prostitute, the spies would encounter little risk of being noticed.

With Joshua's army nearby, the city was alert and vigilant. When the king of Jericho received information that Rahab was harboring spies, he demanded she bring the men to him. But Rahab deliberately misled the king, responding that the spies had departed at nightfall but could still be overtaken and captured. In the meantime, she had hidden the two spies on her flat roof under stalks of drying flax. The deception succeeded; an armed force left the city to pursue the spies.

Later, on the roof, Rahab outlined to the spies the fear and faintheartedness of the people. Having received reports of Israel's powerful Lord, the morale of the enemy was low. *I know that the Lord has given you the land, and that the fear of you has fallen upon us, and that all the inhabitants of the land melt away before you. For we have heard how the Lord dried up the water of the Red Sea . . . and what you did to the two kings of the Amorites. . . . And as soon as we heard it our hearts melted, and there was no courage left . . . for the Lord your God is he who is God* (2:9-11).

Rahab's aid and information came with a price. She asked the spies for protection for herself and her family when the Israelites conquered the land. *Swear to me by the Lord that as I have dealt kindly with you, you also will deal kindly with my father's house . . . and deliver our lives from death* (2:12, 13). The two men agreed. For her silence, they promised, *Our life for yours! If you do not tell this business of ours, then we will deal kindly and faithfully with you when the Lord gives us the land* (2:14). A scarlet cord tied outside her window would be a sign to the attacking Israelites to spare the inhabitants of her house. Rahab ordered the spies to hide for three days in the hills and then she lowered them by rope through a window built into the wall.

Archaeological evidence suggests that Rahab lived in the poor quarter of Jericho. On the north side of the city, a fifteen-foot-high, mud-brick wall surrounded the city. This was the city's first line of defense (though it was rather flimsy, since it was only one mud-brick thick). Remains of houses on the inside of the wall have been unearthed. Rahab probably lived in such a location.

The spies followed Rahab's instructions in every detail, departing and going into the hills. They hid for three days, dodging their pursuers, who were carrying out a thorough search. Three days later they returned to Joshua and reported that the situation was perfect for an attack. God had given the land to the Israelites. *Truly the Lord has given all the land into our hands; and moreover all the inhabitants of the land are fainthearted because of us* (2:24).

SUGGESTIONS TO TEACHERS

Every military leader knows that accurate, advanced intelligence is essential for a successful operation. Joshua was no exception. Today's lesson describes the exciting, secret mission of Joshua's agents, who were sent to spy on Jericho's defenses.

On one level, this material from the opening chapters of the Book of Joshua is part of the body of great spy literature. However, the Scripture writers were not interested in merely recording a good spy story. The narrative about Joshua's secret service operatives demonstrated that God would keep His promise to give the land to His people, the Israelites. Therefore, remember that the Lord, not the spies or Rahab, must remain in the spotlight throughout this lesson.

1. COMMAND OF THE LORD. Joshua wisely realized that he would have to depend totally on the Lord for guidance and for power. Human wisdom and human strength would never be sufficient to accomplish the invasion of Canaan. Joshua knew that God gives what humans need to carry out His plans. Such help starts with an awareness that God addresses those who listen faithfully and obediently. "The Lord said to Joshua . . ." reminds us that our God communicates His will to those who intend to serve Him.

2. COMMITMENT OF JOSHUA. Joshua agreed to carry out God's orders. "Commitment" is not always a popular idea in our culture. Whether undertaking a military campaign, as in Joshua's case, or determining to maintain a marriage, or making a financial pledge to the church, the personal commitment is crucial. Ask your group members to talk about commitments they have found difficult to keep. For God's people, commitment starts with determining to serve the Lord at all costs and in all situations.

3 1833 02460 8074

3. CONFIDENCE OF THE PEOPLE. Many observers of our culture in the mid-1990s point to the lack of trust among us today. People seem to have little confidence in the promises of leaders or institutions. With little sense of community, self-interest reigns. Some who note these flaws in our society speak of a "crisis of confidence." But confidence comes from faith in God. Explore with your group members how greater trust may be developed in your church and in your community.

4. COURAGE OF RAHAB. God sometimes astonishes us by using unexpected agents for His purposes. Here is Rahab, probably dismissed as an unsavory outcast by the respectable people of Jericho, or tolerated as a sex object but kept on the fringe on society. Her courage in the face of immense danger came from acknowledging the God of the Israelites.

Perhaps some in your class think they have little significance in God's plans. Remind them that even Rahab was important in the Lord's work.

TOPIC FOR ADULTS
PREPARING FOR VICTORY

Still Practicing at 100. The great cellist Pablo Casals continued to perform concerts into his old age, living to be almost 100 years old. He disciplined himself with hours of practice every morning, as he prepared for his outstanding performances. It is reported that on the day he died, Casals was downstairs at 6:00 a.m., holding his bow and going over his practice exercises with his cello. This artist knew that he had to prepare for victory in the concert hall, and he disciplined himself accordingly.

We need to be ready to take up various forms of preparation in our service to God, as well. Joshua and the Israelites prepared for victory by carefully spying out Jericho. We, too, must prepare for the various ministry roles God marks out for us.

Supported by Faith-filled Congregation. The father of the modern missions movement was a young shoemaker-cobbler in England named William Carey. He was a lay person with little education. Nevertheless, he sensed God's call to go to India to share the Christian faith.

The powerful East India Company said Carey was a fool and tried to prevent him from considering such a venture. In May, 1792, he preached a sermon to the Nottingham Association in England, sharing his missionary vision. On the basis of that sermon, the Nottingham Congregation took an offering and sent William Carey to India. There, the little cobbler began an astounding work that awakened others to the call to missions work overseas. All this happened because a congregation in Nottingham had the willingness to support William Carey initially.

God's work requires the assistance and cooperation of us all! Loners cannot bring God's plans to fruition; it takes the effort of a community of believers, just as it did in Joshua's time.

Essential Ingredient of Trust. A friend describes visiting the circus in Boston as a child. He marveled at the trapeze artists, soaring impossibly through space, always catching the flying swing from each other.

"Aren't they scared?" he whispered to his mother.

A man in the row ahead turned to answer. "They aren't scared, son," he said gently. "They trust each other."

"That man used to be on the high wires himself," someone whispered.

Whenever my friend thinks of trusting people, he remembers those fly-ing figures, a hairbreadth from death, each making a place of safety for the other. He is reminded that, for all their courage and training, their successful, breathtaking performance could not have been carried out without one essential ingredient: Trust.

Questions for Students on the Next Lesson. 1. What were God's instruc-tions to Joshua about how the people were to cross the Jordan? 2. What was the ark of the covenant? 3. What similarities do you see between Joshua and the people crossing the Jordan, and Moses and the people crossing the Red Sea? 4. What risks have you taken because of your faith in Christ? 5. Have you ever faced danger and uncertainty in your life? How did your faith help you handle the situation?

TOPIC FOR YOUTH
FACING HARD CHALLENGES

Battle of Wills. Mona, a gifted teenager at a Youth Guidance Camp, had the reputation of relating well to children. Lucinda was assigned to Mona at the start of the new camping period.

Lucinda's life had been miserable, and she seemed to want other peo-ple's lives to be as miserable as her own. She hated her fellow campers as well as the camp's authority figures, which included her new camp coun-selor, Mona. Lucinda used every possible means to express her dislike, saving her most ingenious methods for night time. Mona had assigned Lucinda the bunk above her own in order to keep an eye on Lucinda. During the night, Lucinda would drop objects off her bed that would crash to the floor and wake Mona up.

Mona knew a huge battle of wills was developing and she resolved to win this battle by showing and telling Lucinda about the message of God's saving love. For several days, in every circumstance, Mona showed the rebellious teenager God's grace and favor.

The barrage at night continued, but with a difference. Pieces of paper now fell to the floor. Mona got ready to reprimand Lucinda, but paused to read one of the papers. Scrawled on the paper were the words: "I LOVE YOU." The story of God's love and care had finally touched Lucinda's heart.

Like Mona, Israel had to face a difficult task. The challenge seemed impossible, yet Israel resolved to follow God's guidance. Ultimately, in each instance, the challenge was met successfully.

Climbing for the Challenge. George Willig, 27, began climbing at 6:00 a.m. Wearing an orange backpack that contained a long coil of blue nylon rope, George drew the attention of a window washer. Casually, George said he was just taking a walk. Then he climbed straight up! By 10:30 a.m. he had completed his climb of the 110-story World Trade Center in Lower Manhattan.

During the first few minutes, spectators, television crews, and the police had arrived. Some of the police officers decided to ride up the build-ing in a window washer's scaffold beside George and finally acted as guides for his difficult ascent to the roof. A police helicopter hovered nearby, and police mobilized to handle the huge traffic jams and crowds that George drew. Thousands of jubilant people cheered and blew their horns when George reached the top, where he was arrested on charges of criminal trespass, reckless endangerment, and disorderly conduct. The city wanted to fine him $250,000 to cover the costs of the police force.

However, because of George's instant popularity, the city canceled its law suit. George was fined a mere $1.10, a penny for each floor!

Why did George climb? It was an awesome challenge to his ingenuity and endurance, he claimed. Perhaps Joshua would have understood. God gave him what seemed to be a huge challenge. With resourcefulness, ingenuity, and God's help, he knew he could triumph. Rather than breaking the law with his skills, Joshua fulfilled God's will.

Risk Brought Satisfaction. In Steven Spielberg's film *Empire of the Sun* Christopher Bale plays a young James Graham, the eleven-year-old son of an English merchant in Shanghai at the outbreak of World War II. James is separated from his parents in the panic of the attempted escape from Shanghai. He eventually becomes one of the millions interned by the Japanese during the war. James suffers the adversity of an internment camp alone, except for the aid of a scruffy American sailor.

James is asked by the American to crawl under the camp's barbed-wire fence and set a series of snares to trap pheasants to supplement their meager food rations. The task was both difficult and dangerous; the risks enormous. To be caught outside the perimeter fence meant brutal punishment or death. It was a terribly hard decision for James. Ultimately, he accepted the challenge and the risk. James felt a sense of relief when the job was completed and he was satisfied when he ate the fruits of his labors.

Like James, perhaps you experience a sense of relief and satisfaction when you have successfully completed a difficult task. Certainly, Joshua's spies must have felt the "joy of completion" upon their return to Joshua and the people.

Questions for Students on the Next Lesson. 1. Why would God promise to exalt Joshua? 2. What instructions did God give to Joshua? 3. What was the ark of the covenant? 4. Why was the crossing of the Jordan River a miraculous event? 5. What did Joshua and the people do to commemorate this event?

LESSON 2—SEPTEMBER 11

ACTING ON FAITH

Background Scripture: Joshua 3—4
Devotional Reading: Hebrews 11:23-24

KING JAMES VERSION	REVISED STANDARD VERSION

KING JAMES VERSION

JOSHUA 3:7 And the Lord said unto Joshua, This day will I begin to magnify thee in the sight of all Israel, that they may know that, as I was with Moses, so I will be with thee.

8 And thou shalt command the priests that bear the ark of the covenant, saying, When ye are come to the brink of the water of Jordan, ye shall stand still in Jordan.

9 And Joshua said unto the children of Israel, Come hither, and hear the words of the Lord your God.

10 And Joshua said, Hereby ye shall know that the living God is among you, and that he will without fail drive out from before you the Canaanites, and the Hittites, and the Hivites, and the Perizzites, and the Girgashites, and the Amorites, and the Jebusites.

11 Behold, the ark of the covenant of the Lord of all the earth passeth over before you into Jordan.

12 Now therefore take you twelve men out of the tribes of Israel, out of every tribe a man.

13 And it shall come to pass, as soon as the soles of the feet of the priests that bear the ark of the Lord, the Lord of all the earth, shall rest in the waters of Jordan, that the waters of Jordan shall be cut off from the waters that come down from above; and they shall stand upon an heap.

14 And it came to pass, when the people removed from their tents, to pass over Jordan, and the priests bearing the ark of the covenant before the people;

15 And as they that bare the ark were come unto Jordan, and the feet of the priests that bare the ark were dipped in the brim of the water, (for Jordan overfloweth all his banks all the time of harvest,)

16 That the waters which came down from above stood and rose up upon an heap very far from the city Adam, that is beside Zaretan: and those that came down toward the sea of the plain, even the salt sea, failed, and were cut off: and the people passed over right against Jericho.

17 And the priests that bare the ark of the covenant of the Lord stood firm on dry

REVISED STANDARD VERSION

JOSHUA 3:7 And the Lord said to Joshua, "This day I will begin to exalt you in the sight of all Israel, that they may know that, as I was with Moses, so I will be with you. 8 And you shall command the priests who bear the ark of the covenant, 'When you come to the brink of the waters of the Jordan, you shall stand still in the Jordan.' " 9 And Joshua said to the people of Israel, "Come hither, and hear the words of the Lord your God." 10 And Joshua said, "Hereby you shall know that the living God is among you, and that he will without fail drive out from before you the Canaanites, the Hittites, the Hivites, the Perizzites, the Girgashites, the Amorites, and the Jebusites. 11 Behold, the ark of the covenant of the Lord of all the earth is to pass over before you into the Jordan. 12 Now therefore take twelve men from the tribes of Israel, from each tribe a man. 13 And when the soles of the feet of the priests who bear the ark of the Lord, the Lord of all the earth, shall rest in the waters of the Jordan, the waters of the Jordan shall be stopped from flowing, and the waters coming down from above shall stand in one heap."

14 So, when the people set out from their tents, to pass over the Jordan with the priests bearing the ark of the covenant before the people, 15 and when those who bore the ark had come to the Jordan, and the feet of the priests bearing the ark were dipped in the brink of the water (the Jordan overflows all its banks throughout the time of harvest), 16 the waters coming down from above stood and rose up in a heap far off, at Adam, the city that is beside Zarethan, and those flowing down toward the sea of the Arabah, the Salt Sea, were wholly cut off; and the people passed over opposite Jericho. 17 And while all Israel were passing over on dry ground, the priests who bore the ark of the covenant of the Lord stood on dry ground in the midst of the Jordan, until all the nation finished passing over the Jordan.

ground in the midst of Jordan, and all the Israelites passed over on dry ground, until all the people were passed clean over Jordan.

KEY VERSE: The priests who bore the ark of the covenant of the Lord stood on dry ground in the midst of the Jordan, until all the nation finished passing over the Jordan. Joshua 3:17b.

HOME DAILY BIBLE READINGS

Sept.	5	M.	Hebrews 11:23-31	*They Acted by Faith*
Sept.	6	T.	Joshua 3:1-6	*Instructions to Follow the Ark*
Sept.	7	W.	Joshua 3:7-13	*The Jordan Will Stop Flowing*
Sept.	8	T.	Joshua 3:14—4:7	*Israel Crosses over the Jordan*
Sept.	9	F.	Joshua 4:8-14	*Twelve Stones Carried with Them*
Sept.	10	S.	Joshua 4:15-24	*Stones for Remembering the Crossing*
Sept.	11	S.	Isaiah 43:1-7	*God Offers Restoration and Protection*

BACKGROUND

Joshua was the George Washington of Israel. Against near-impossible odds, this great general engineered the conquest of the promised land. However, Joshua and the biblical writers insisted that God be given the credit and glory for this wonderful event. They realized that the intervention of the Lord, not mere human might or generalship, brought success.

Today's lesson underscores the fact that it was the Lord who brought the Israelites safely across the Jordan. The details of the episode emphasize the work of God. The ark, the sacred box symbolizing the presence of the Lord, was deliberately carried by the priests before the people. God was leading His chosen ones.

Rains had swelled the Jordan River. In the view of the pagan inhabitants of Canaan, the rains had fallen at the command of the god Baal. But the miracle by which the Israelites crossed the Jordan indicated to everyone that the Lord God of Israel was victorious over the local weather deity and all other foreign gods.

There are records of the Jordan River being temporarily blocked by mud slides or by collapsing banks due to heavy flooding, allowing people to cross on the river bed for a brief time. Yet the Bible writers and the Israelites under Joshua never regarded the crossing as merely a fortunate event brought about by natural causes. To these faith-filled people, crossing the Jordan indicated the miraculous intervention of the Lord. Just as God had parted the waters of the Red Sea in Moses' time, so now the Lord parted the waters of Jordan in Joshua's time. God alone brought deliverance. His people, in turn, were called to respond with trust in His power.

NOTES ON THE PRINTED TEXT

Under Joshua's command, all Israel mobilized and advanced from Shittim. The nation camped on the Plains of Moab near the major ford of the Jordan River, a few miles north of the Dead Sea.

The Lord said to Joshua, "This day I will begin to exalt you in the sight of all Israel, that they may know that, as I was with Moses, so I will be with you" (3:7). At the Lord's command, Moses had chosen Joshua as his successor. While he had assumed the role of the leader for the nation, Israel had to know and understand that God was with him. Now God promised His help. He would exalt Joshua in the people's eyes.

The people were to be told that God was about to act. *Hereby you shall know that the living God is among you, and that he will without fail drive out from before you the Canaanites, the Hittites, the Hivites, the Perizzites, the Girgashites, the Amorites, and the Jebusites* (3:10). The Canaanites were the inhabitants of the plains. Scattered throughout the Canaanite population were small colonies of Hittites from Syria and Asia Minor. The Hivites were a small clan located near Shechem and in the four Gibeonite cities. The Amorites tended to live in the hill country while the Jebusites occupied Jerusalem. Nothing is known of the other two peoples. Only the true Sovereign, *the Lord of all the earth* (3:11), could, in such a mighty manner, dispose of a portion of His world.

One other preparation remained: the choosing of twelve men. Each tribe was to select one man. *Take twelve men from the tribes of Israel, from each tribe a man* (3:12). Then Joshua told the people that if they followed God's instructions, God would stop the waters of the Jordan River, and the people would be able to cross safely. *The Lord of all the earth, shall rest in the waters of the Jordan, [and] the waters of the Jordan shall be stopped from flowing* (3:13).

While the Jordan had a fertile floodplain suitable for agriculture, it was unlike the Nile River. It did not flood at the right time in late summer and early autumn. The Jordan flooded at the wrong time, at harvest time, during late winter and early spring. *The Jordan overflows all its banks throughout the time of harvest* (3:15). Since it was harvest time, the fords would be impassable.

The procession began with the priests carrying the ark of the covenant, followed at a distance by the people. As the priests carrying the ark stepped into the Jordan, the river stopped flowing. *The waters coming down from above stood and rose up in a heap far off* (3:16). With the waters blocked, the nation walked across the still wet stones lying in the now rapidly drying river bed.

The Jordan River has been blocked numerous times as a result of earthquake activity. In A.D. 1267, a mud slide fell into the river at Damiya. No water flowed for eight hours. In 1546, water ceased to flow for two days. In 1906, the waters stopped for ten hours. In 1927, a section of a cliff, 150 feet high, collapsed near the river as a result of an earthquake and blocked the river for twenty-one hours. The same happened in 1956, and again in 1970, when a 900-foot-long embankment collapsed. Other stoppages were recorded in 1160 and in 1834. In the biblical account, however, the nation's crossing in the midst of the Jordan River on dry land was surely a miracle.

The priests stood on dry ground in the middle of the Jordan until all the people had crossed. Once everyone had crossed, Joshua took the twelve stones that had been removed from the river and stood them in a circle to commemorate the miraculous event.

SUGGESTIONS TO TEACHERS

Try to imagine how the Israelites must have felt when they stood on the bank of the Jordan. A raging stream at flood level surged before them. On the other side, in the distance, stood the great fortress walls of Jericho, guarding the entry into the Promised Land. Cross that river and invade that country? Every practical-thinking person would have dismissed the idea as impossible.

But God had promised Abraham and his descendants that they would be delivered by divine intervention and would have a homeland. The Israelites faced the decision: Do we act according to our human, practical-minded ideas, or do we act out of trust in God's promise? This question is at the core of today's lesson.

Remember that this lesson is not meant to be only an excursion back to the times of Joshua. The lesson can help all of us face the same decision and reach the same conclusion as Joshua's people did. We, too, must learn to act on faith every day.

1. MANDATE FROM THE LORD. The Israelites under Joshua no doubt sensed that they were carrying out God's purposes and glorifying Him. They were participants in the great drama of history being directed by the Lord. Do you and your class members believe the same? Does not every believer live with the mandate to "glorify God and enjoy him forever," as the old catechism stated?

2. MIRACULOUS CROSSING. True, some scholars have offered natural explanations for the Jordan's waters dropping. The account in Joshua 3, however, stresses that the Lord was with His people and that His power alone delivered them. Ask your students to reflect on their personal histories with this same powerful Lord. All should be able to recall occasions in which they experienced God's presence and power. The life of a believer does not unfold by luck or happenstance in a jumble of meaningless episodes. Rather, God guides us in His perfect plans by His constant presence.

3. MEANING IN CELEBRATING. The Israelites celebrated their miraculous passage across the Jordan, but the jubilation was more than a victory blast. Joshua and the people erected a memorial for future generations to learn about God's actions on behalf of His people. The stone piling was to be a sign "so that when your children ask in time to come, 'What do these stones mean to you?' then you shall tell them" about God's miraculous work (4:6). In what ways are you and your congregation helping the coming generation to learn how God has been at work in history and in your lives? What signs of strong faith do young people see in your life?

TOPIC FOR ADULTS
ACTING ON FAITH

Ring the Bell for Abreus. Some years ago, in 1935, a severe hurricane swept through Cuba, hitting the village of Abreus and destroying the small Methodist Church building. The people, dazed from the tragedy, tried to rebuild their own homes. But no money was available to erect a new church structure. Two women from the congregation, the Valero sisters, gathered what they could find of their beloved church from the rubble. They took home a couple of battered benches, a communion set, the tattered pulpit Bible, and the bell from the tower. For twenty years, the Valero women carefully guarded these remnants from their church. "We shall not die," they said,"until we hear the bell ring again from the church tower."

Most people in the village scoffed. Living in a poor area where money was scarce, the townspeople viewed the Valero sisters' faith as ridiculous. However, the sisters persuaded a Methodist missionary to visit Abreus and they shared their story. They assured him that they would live to see the bell ring again from the church in Abreus. Together, they began to visit others in the village. The missionary wrote letters to the United States. Only a few of the old members were still living, but they caught the Valero sisters' vision. These faithful few made the sisters' prayer their own: "O Lord, let us live long enough to hear the bell ring from the church tower."

Finally, a new church building began to rise from its new foundations. At the close of the dedication service, the Valero sisters proudly rang the bell. The villagers wept for joy. Everyone wanted to pull the bell rope, so each member, in turn, was given that marvelous privilege.

Belief Still Alive in "ME Generation." "My generation came of age in the Vietnam era and during Watergate. When we were in elementary school, everyone told us how great we would be simply because we were enjoying the best life has to offer. We have been called the 'ME Generation,' with the explanation that we were all so self-centered. Now we are written off as the worst of cynics and skeptics.

"Yet we have gone on to assume public roles, to take jobs in all sorts of business and to raise the next generation of human beings. For me that spells faith in something greater than ourselves . . . . Somehow we believe."—Nancy D. Lindell

Genius. How would you define a genius? Here is Meredith Wilson's definition. Note how it fits Joshua.

"A genius," said Wilson, "is one who makes the illogical seem inevitable." Joshua faced the Jordan at floodtide and commanded His people to capture Jericho. He was able to make the Israelites realize that with God the illogical was inevitable.

Questions for Students on the Next Lesson. 1. Why did the Israelites have to capture Jericho? 2. Why were Rahab and her family spared? 3. What were God's specific instructions to Joshua and the people about how to seize Jericho? 4. How has the faith of believers enabled your congregation to overcome obstacles? 5. What part does obedience play in faith?

TOPIC FOR YOUTH
ACTING ON FAITH

Follow the Instructions. Could you build a bulldozer? You would probably answer: "No!" Assembling the steel motor, body, and caterpillar tracks;

attaching the blade; and installing the hydraulic system would seem impossible to most people.

Bob Borland bought a miniature, fully operable, riding bulldozer to clean out the manure from the family barn. The only catch was that the bulldozer arrived in a box, as a kit to be assembled! The task seemed monumental.

Each evening Bob sat in the corner of the barn under a bank of fluorescent lights. On the work bench in front of him was the instruction manual. Patiently and carefully Bob followed the instructions for almost three months. Gradually, the pile of pieces began to diminish, and a miniature bulldozer took shape. Finally, it was completed.

To no one's surprise, the bulldozer actually worked. And it finally fulfilled the purpose for which it had been created—it cleaned the barn.

Like Bob, Joshua, and others, you can accomplish huge tasks on your own when you follow instructions. For Joshua, the task ahead of him seemed enormous. Yet he followed God's instructions and accomplished the task.

Follow the Leader. The twenty boys, aged seven to thirteen, were sent to the Mel Blount Youth Home in Taylortown, Pennsylvania, by the Children and Youth Services' personnel. All were inner-city boys who had never seen a farm. The slums, their filthy homes, and dirty beds were all behind them. Now they faced three log cabins, a white barn, desks with Bibles on them, and basements filled with weight-lifting equipment and pool tables. Their responsibility was to keep the cabins spotlessly clean, go to school, learn how to look others in the eye, converse, farm, and care for the farm's livestock. They also ran sprints on a hill with the home's founder, former Pittsburgh Steeler Mel Blount, a man they revered and admired.

The boys' dedication did not wane even when things got tough: when the state reviewed the financial operations of the home, when the Ku Klux Klan burned several crosses and rallied against the project, and when licensing procedures bogged down and threatened to close the home. Even though the home's future was uncertain, the boys did not waver in their respect for their gentle giant, the man they referred to as "Mr. Mel."

Israel's future must have seemed uncertain in the days when Joshua took the reins of leadership. Yet by following Joshua, a leader the nation trusted every bit as much as the twenty boys trusted Mel Blount, the Hebrew people could look forward to years of blessing under God's care.

Follow in Faith. A friend tells of serving in the Gulf War in the Middle East a few years ago. He and a few buddies were assigned to proceed to a certain location in Kuwait near the Iraqi border. The area had been sown with mines by the retreating Iraqi forces. However, the leader of my friend's patrol had been given a map and a detailed briefing describing the zigzag pathway through the minefield. My friend knew that to step away from the lines laid out by the leader would bring instant death or injury from an exploding mine. He also realized that he had to trust the leader and follow in faith.

The experience that day in the minefield taught him what it means to act as a Christian when the Lord commands a follower to come to Him in trust. My friend, relying on the instructions of the leader, safely traversed that deadly minefield. He also now tries to act in faith when His supreme Commander, Jesus, calls him to follow.

Questions for Students on the Next Lesson. 1. Why would Israel attack Jericho first? 2. What battle plans did God reveal to Joshua? 3. Who was Rahab? Why was she chosen? 4. Why was Rahab spared when Jericho was destroyed? 5. Why does the Book of Joshua insist that God alone gave Israel the victory?

LESSON 3—SEPTEMBER 18

WINNING THE BATTLE

Background Scripture: Joshua 6
Devotional Reading: Psalm 149

KING JAMES VERSION

JOSHUA 6:1 Now Jericho was straitly shut up because of the children of Israel: none went out, and none came in.

2 And the Lord said unto Joshua, See, I have given into thine hand Jericho, and the king thereof, and the mighty men of valour.

3 And ye shall compass the city, all ye men of war, and go round about the city once. Thus shalt thou do six days.

4 And seven priests shall bear before the ark seven trumpets of rams' horns: and the seventh day ye shall compass the city seven times, and the priests shall blow with the trumpets.

5 And it shall come to pass, that when they make a long blast with the ram's horn, and when ye hear the sound of the trumpet, all the people shall shout with a great shout; and the wall of the city shall fall down flat, and the people shall ascend up every man straight before him.

15 And it came to pass on the seventh day, that they rose early about the dawning of the day, and compassed the city after the same manner seven times: only on that day they compassed the city seven times.

16 And it came to pass at the seventh time, when the priests blew with the trumpets, Joshua said unto the people, Shout; for the Lord hath given you the city.

17 And the city shall be accursed, even it, and all that are therein, to the Lord: only Rahab the harlot shall live, she and all that are with her in the house, because she hid the messengers that we sent.

18 And ye, in any wise keep yourselves from the accursed thing, lest ye make yourselves accursed, when ye take of the accursed thing, and make the camp of Israel a curse, and trouble it.

19 But all the silver, and gold, and vessels of brass and iron, are consecrated unto the Lord: they shall come into the treasury of the Lord.

20 So the people shouted when the priests blew with the trumpets: and it came to pass, when the people heard the sound of the trumpet, and the people shouted with a great shout, that the wall fell down flat, so

REVISED STANDARD VERSION

JOSHUA 6:1 Now Jericho was shut up from within and from without because of the people of Israel; none went out, and none came in. 2 And the Lord said to Joshua, "See, I have given into your hand Jericho, with its king and mighty men of valor. 3 You shall march around the city, all the men of war going around the city once. Thus shall you do for six days. 4 And seven priests shall bear seven trumpets of rams' horns before the ark; and on the seventh day you shall march around the city seven times, the priests blowing the trumpets. 5 And when they make a long blast with the ram's horn, as soon as you hear the sound of the trumpet, then all the people shall shout with a great shout; and the wall of the city will fall down flat, and the people shall go up every man straight before him."

15 On the seventh day they rose early at the dawn of day, and marched around the city in the same manner seven times: it was only on that day that they marched around the city seven times. 16 And at the seventh time, when the priests had blown the trumpets, Joshua said to the people, "Shout; for the Lord has given you the city. 17 And the city and all that is within it shall be devoted to the Lord for destruction; only Rahab the harlot and all who are with her in her house shall live, because she hid the messengers that we sent. 18 But you, keep yourselves from the things devoted to destruction, lest when you have devoted them you take any of the devoted things and make the camp of Israel a thing for destruction, and bring trouble upon it. 19 But all silver and gold, and vessels of bronze and iron, are sacred to the Lord; they shall go into the treasury of the Lord." 20 So the people shouted, and the trumpets were blown. As soon as the people heard the sound of the trumpet, the people raised a great shout, and the wall fell down flat, so that the people went up into the city, every man straight before him, and they took the city.

that the people went up into the city, every
man straight before him, and they took the
city.

KEY VERSE: *Joshua said to the people, "Shout; for the Lord has given you
the city." Joshua 6:16b.*

HOME DAILY BIBLE READINGS

Sept.	12	M.	Joshua 5:10-15	*Joshua's Preparation for Battle*
Sept.	13	T.	Psalm 145:14-20	*The Lord Is Nigh*
Sept.	14	W.	Joshua 6:1-5	*God's Promise to Joshua*
Sept.	15	T.	Joshua 6:6-11	*Beginning the March around Jericho*
Sept.	16	F.	Joshua 6:12-20	*The Fall of Jericho*
Sept.	17	S.	Joshua 6:21-25	*Rahab's Family Is Spared*
Sept.	18	S.	Psalm 98:1-6	*God Gives Victory*

BACKGROUND

The defenders of Jericho assumed that no one would attack during the
flood stage of the Jordan River. The melting snow from the mountains in
the north and the heavy, late winter rains sometimes made the river a
mile wide. No one had ever tried to invade at the height of the flood season.

Joshua and the Israelites surprised Jericho's smug force. The God of
Israel had obviously proved His superiority to Canaan's Baal, the heralded
storm god who was supposed to control the rains, snows, and floods. The
awed defenders in the fortress were further demoralized when the
Israelites' priests marched triumphantly around the city walls, day after
day, for six days. The priests must have been impressive as they blew
their horns while the rest of the invading force followed in disciplined
ranks.

The biblical narrative repeatedly uses the number seven: seven days'
trips around the city, seven priests, seven trumpets, seven times circling
the city on the seventh day. The number seven was understood to be
sacred, signifying completeness and perfection, and therefore, belonging to
God.

As promised by God, the walls collapsed after the seventh circuit on the
seventh day. Earthquake? The Israelites say nothing about any geological
disturbances. The fall of the great walls came about as a result of God's
power. Although archaeologists have carefully excavated the site of
ancient Jericho, they find nothing that conclusively explains the crash of
the walls of Jericho. The Lord made possible a stupendous and unexpected
victory for His people. The Lord may be trusted to keep His word!

NOTES ON THE PRINTED TEXT

With the spies having provided valuable information on the stronghold
and its inhabitants, Joshua and his army advanced on Jericho, preparing
to besiege the city. First the Israelites surrounded the city and threw up
their lines, preparing to starve the city into submission. *Jericho was shut
up from within and from without because of the people of Israel; none went*

out, and none came in (6:1).

The tactic could have resulted in a stalemate since the attackers might have suffered like the defenders. But God had a declaration for Joshua: Victory! *See, I have given into your hand Jericho, with its king and mighty men of valor* (6:2).

God then gave Joshua specific instructions about the way to capture Jericho. The methods were certainly unique in the annals of warfare. *You shall march around the city, all the men of war going around the city once. Thus shall you do for six days* (6:3). The Israelites were to walk the circumference of the city wall each day for six successive days. After the encircling maneuver, the army would retire to its camp. Perhaps the strategy was to distract the enemy, or perhaps it was a tactic known as "conditioning." By repeating the same field exercise in the open, the Israelites would lull the enemy until its vigilance was relaxed and a decisive strike could follow.

The seven priests were to lead the march, carrying the ark of the covenant and blowing the trumpets of rams' horns. *And seven priests shall bear seven trumpets of rams' horns before the ark; and on the seventh day you shall march around the city seven times, the priests blowing the trumpets* (6:4). The trumpet was the *shofar [SHOW-far]*, a type of musical instrument made from a ram's horn.

God's instructions were specific. For six days the priests were to carry the ark around the walls as the army followed. On the seventh day, the procession was to march the circuit seven times blowing the trumpets. Then the army was to shout loudly and witness the collapse of the city's walls. If the people followed these instructions, the walls would fall down. For six days, Israel carried out God's directives.

On the seventh day the army rose at dawn and walked the circuit of the city silently, seven times. However, just as the trumpets blew, Joshua issued some additional instructions. While the city and its people were to be slaughtered, God ordered the Israelites to spare the house of Rahab, who had helped the Israelite spies. *And the city and all that is within it, shall be devoted to the Lord for destruction; only Rahab the harlot and all who are with her in her house shall live, because she hid the messengers that we sent* (6:17). The population was sinful and impure. Rather than endanger Israel through temptation, it had to be removed. Therefore, the taking of booty and spoils was also forbidden. *Keep yourselves from the things devoted to destruction, lest when you have devoted them you take any of the devoted things and make the camp of Israel a thing for destruction, and bring trouble upon it* (6:18). Only the silver, gold, bronze, and iron were to be saved and placed in the treasury of the Lord. *All silver and gold, and vessels of bronze and iron, are sacred to the Lord; they shall go into the treasury of the Lord* (6:19).

Enthused by the sound of the trumpets, the Israelites gave a great shout, and the massive walls tumbled down, leaving the city defenseless. Possibly the earth shook under the Jordan Valley, crumbling the massive stone wall and the mud-brick wall on top of it. As the wall tumbled, the homes between this inner wall and the lower, outer mud-brick wall must have collapsed, forming a ramp that allowed the attackers to go directly into the exposed city.

SUGGESTIONS TO TEACHERS

Some of your class members may smile and dismiss the story of the fall of Jericho as nothing more than quaint lyrics for the old spiritual, "Joshua Fit the Battle of Jericho." Scripture was handed down to us, however, to introduce us to the Lord and His involvement in human history. The spectacular tumbling of Jericho's walls vividly emphasizes that involvement.

1. ACKNOWLEDGMENT OF THE LORD. We may recoil from the gory details of the capture of Jericho as recounted in the Book of Joshua, but we must acknowledge that God was central in the lives of those Israelites. We may have difficulty dealing with the picture of God that sometimes seems to emerge through this account. However we must remember that God's character is holy and just. But we must note how intentionally the people under Joshua sought to serve their Lord.

So often, for us, God is allowed only in the margins of our lives. God becomes merely an unimportant "extra" rather than the central focus of our lives. Discuss with your students how faith in God can influence such matters as making a budget, considering a job, planning a career, choosing a life partner for marriage, joining a service club, and selecting a group of social acquaintances.

2. ADHERENCE TO ORDERS. The remarkable discipline of Joshua's people, keeping silent for the six days' circuits of the wall by the priests, shows a willingness to obey. These people willingly put their personal inclinations aside for the good of the community. They even abstained from grabbing loot for themselves after the fall of the city. In light of the modern emphasis on "doing your own thing," you may wish to comment on the need for balancing individual rights with the responsibility to care for one another in community.

3. ADVANCE ON THE CITY. Don't try to come up with natural explanations for the sudden collapse of Jericho's walls. Even the brightest archaeologists can't offer a completely satisfactory explanation. Remember, the point of the narrative is that the Lord delivered Jericho into Joshua's hands so that the promise of God for a homeland could be fulfilled.

4. APPRECIATION OF RAHAB. In the midst of the slaughter of the inhabitants of Jericho, we read that Rahab and her family were spared as promised. The invading force under Joshua remembered this valiant woman's help in providing intelligence and hiding the spies. Do we always remember the persons who have helped us in the past?

TOPIC FOR ADULTS
OBEYING GOD

Tuning. A well-known piano tuner states that an expert can best tune a piano by using a tuning fork. He reports that it is nearly impossible to tune one piano by listening to a previously tuned piano. Tuning one piano with the tuning fork, then the second, he can get both instruments to be in perfect pitch with each other. The tuning fork assures that the two pianos will adhere to the same standards of pitch.

Only when Christians are tuned to God's commands, and not to the vibrations and pitch of the surrounding culture, can they work harmoniously. This means being obedient to God's will. Only when Joshua and each Israelite invader realized that they had to be attuned to the detailed orders of the Lord to carry out the seven-day circuits of Jericho could they succeed in capturing the city. Likewise, for believers today, obedience to God, rather than to other competing voices, is the key to significant service.

Eyes Fixed on One. The composer Giuseppe Verdi stood in the shadows of the concert hall in Florence listening to the performance of his first opera. At the close, the audience applauded and cheered. Verdi, however, waited. His eyes were fixed on one person—his mentor, Gioacchino Rossini. Verdi didn't care whether the audience cheered or jeered. He wanted only the approval of the master, Rossini. A faint smile of relief broke over the young composer's face as he saw the nod of affirmation and encouragement from Rossini.

Obedient living means keeping one's attention fixed on Christ. Christians learn to care little whether the crowds cheer or jeer as they seek only the approval of The Master.

Percentage of Obedience. Several years ago, a cartoon showed a businessman sitting at his desk in an office. On the desk was an engraved name plate identifying the man as "John T. Hale." Below the name some additional lines read:

> 45 percent Presbyterian,
> 28 percent Republican,
> 15 percent Businessman,
> 9 percent Golfer,
> 3 percent Manwich.

The cartoonist deftly illustrated these claims of John T. Hale. Significantly, even his church got less than half of his loyalty. The Lord Himself was not even mentioned. As Dietrich Bonhoeffer stated, "When Christ calls a man, he calls him to die." The Lord demands complete obedience, not meager percentages.

Questions for Students on the Next Lesson. 1. Why did Joshua feel it was necessary to gather all the tribes at Shechem? 2. What was the main point of Joshua's speech to the tribes? 3. What did Joshua challenge the people to do? 4. What faith-challenging choices do you face today? 5. What are the hardest long-term commitments for you to make and keep?

TOPIC FOR YOUTH
OBEYING ORDERS

Obeyed the Doctor's Orders. Little Wilma was born in 1940 in Clarksville, Tennessee. Before her fifth birthday, she had had double pneumonia, scarlet fever, and polio. The polio left her with a twisted left foot. She had to wear a brace with corrective shoes for several years.

As impossible as it seemed, her parents believed that she would learn to walk normally some day. Twice a week, Wilma and her mother climbed on a bus and made the hundred-mile bus trip to a clinic in Nashville, where Wilma underwent physical therapy.

Wilma did learn to walk. At twelve she gave up her leg brace. She also began to run. By the ninth grade, she was actually winning races. In the tenth grade, she was invited to a track competition at Tennessee State University. At sixteen, she was running in the 1956 Olympic Games at Melbourne, Australia, where she won a bronze medal. In 1960, Wilma Rudolph won three gold medals in track!

As impossible as the doctor's orders seemed, she had followed them. She did all the exercises for her legs and overcame the battle against polio. And as improbable as God's orders sounded to Joshua and the people, they carried them out. Ultimately, their obedience to God's orders won the battle.

Listening and Doing. A sixty-three-year-old man died in New York City. He had never worked a day in his life! His adult life had been spent in college. Over those years, he had acquired more academic degrees than anyone could ever need.

When the man was a child, a wealthy relative died, naming him the beneficiary of a huge sum of money. But the man was to be given only enough of the money, in installments, to support him every year that he was in school. As soon as his education was completed, the support was to be discontinued.

The gift was abused, wasn't it? The man technically met the terms of the will by remaining in school indefinitely. The will provided him with a steady lifetime income, something it was never intended to do by the man's beneficiary. The man spent thousands of dollars simply listening, but never really doing anything.

God called His people to listen, and then to act. They were to carry out His orders. Listening without acting results in a wasted life.

Sight, Not Senses. When a student is learning to fly, the instructor often induces vertigo and then turns over the plane's controls to the student. Invariably, the student's inner sense of direction is contrary to the instruments' readings. Yet the student tends to put his trust in his senses rather than in the instruments. His incorrect reaction can have dire consequences; he must learn to be disciplined and operate the aircraft in accord with the data given on the instrument panel.

Obedience to God calls for the same kind of discipline. It requires more than just maintaining the right feelings. It means carrying out God's will even when we understand the full consequences. Thus, Joshua trusted in God's orders, not in his own senses.

Questions for Students on the Next Lesson. 1. Where was Shechem? What was it? Why was it important? 2. Can you identify the people of Canaan that Israel conquered? 3. Who provided Israel's power and success in the conquest of the land? How is He described? 4. What gods tempted the fathers of Israel? 5. What important decision did Israel eventually make before Joshua and the Lord?

LESSON 4—SEPTEMBER 25

CHOOSING TO SERVE GOD

Background Scripture: Joshua 24
Devotional Reading: Psalm 116:12-19

KING JAMES VERSION

JOSHUA 24:1 And Joshua gathered all the tribes of Israel to Shechem, and called for the elders of Israel, and for their heads, and for their judges, and for their officers; and they presented themselves before God.

2 And Joshua said unto all the people, Thus saith the Lord. . . .

11 And ye went over Jordan, and came unto Jericho: and the men of Jericho fought against you, the Amorites, and the Perizzites, and the Canaanites, and the Hittites, and the Girgashites, the Hivites, and the Jebusites; and I delivered them into your hand.

12 And I sent the hornet before you, which drave them out from before you, even the two kings of the Amorites; but not with thy sword, nor with thy bow.

13 And I have given you a land for which ye did not labour, and cities which ye built not, and ye dwell in them; of the vineyards and oliveyards which ye planted not do ye eat.

14 Now therefore fear the Lord, and serve him in sincerity and in truth: and put away the gods which your fathers served on the other side of the flood, and in Egypt; and serve ye the Lord.

15 And if it seem evil unto you to serve the Lord, choose you this day whom ye will serve; whether the gods which your fathers served that were on the other side of the flood, or the gods of the Amorites, in whose land ye dwell: but as for me and my house, we will serve the Lord.

16 And the people answered and said, God forbid that we should forsake the Lord, to serve other gods. . . .

22 And Joshua said unto the people, Ye are witnesses against yourselves that ye have chosen you the Lord, to serve him. And they said, We are witnesses.

23 Now therefore put away, said he, the strange gods which are among you, and incline your heart unto the Lord God of Israel.

24 And the people said unto Joshua, The Lord our God will we serve, and his voice will we obey.

25 So Joshua made a covenant with the

REVISED STANDARD VERSION

JOSHUA 24:1 Then Joshua gathered all the tribes of Israel to Shechem and summoned the elders, the heads, the judges, and the officers of Israel; and they presented themselves before God. 2 And Joshua said to all the people, "Thus says the Lord. . . ."

11 "'And you went over the Jordan and came to Jericho, and the men of Jericho fought against you, and also the Amorites, the Perizzites, the Canaanites, the Hittites, the Girgashites, the Hivites, and the Jebusites; and I gave them into your hand. 12 And I sent the hornet before you, which drove them out before you, the two kings of the Amorites; it was not by your sword or by your bow. 13 I gave you a land on which you had not labored, and cities which you had not built, and you dwell therein; you eat the fruit of vineyards and oliveyards which you did not plant.'

14 "Now therefore fear the Lord, and serve him in sincerity and in faithfulness; put away the gods which your fathers served beyond the River, and in Egypt, and serve the Lord. 15 And if you be unwilling to serve the Lord, choose this day whom you will serve, whether the gods your fathers served in the region beyond the River, or the gods of the Amorites in whose land you dwell; but as for me and my house, we will serve the Lord."

16 Then the people answered, "Far be it from us that we should forsake the Lord, to serve other gods. . . ."

22 Then Joshua said to the people, "You are witnesses against yourselves that you have chosen the Lord, to serve him." And they said, "We are witnesses." 23 He said, "Then put away the foreign gods which are among you, and incline your heart to the Lord, the God of Israel." 24 And the people said to Joshua, "The Lord our God we will serve, and his voice we will obey." 25 So Joshua made a covenant with the people that day, and made statutes and ordinances for them at Shechem.

people that day, and set them a statute and
an ordinance in Shechem.

*KEY VERSE: Choose this day whom you will serve . . . but as for me and
my house, we will serve the Lord. Joshua 24:15b.*

HOME DAILY BIBLE READINGS

Sept	19	M.	Psalm 116:12-19	*Praise for God's Care*
Sept.	20	T.	Joshua 23:1-8	*Joshua's Reminder of God's Protection*
Sept.	21	W.	Joshua 23:9-11, 14-16	*Joshua's Charge to Remain Faithful*
Sept.	22	T.	Joshua 24:5-13	*Israel's Deliverance History*
Sept.	23	F.	Joshua 24:14-21	*Joshua's Call for Commitment*
Sept.	24	S.	Joshua 24:22-28	*The Stone of Witness*
Sept.	25	S.	Joshua 24:29-31	*The Death of Joshua*

BACKGROUND

Joshua's winning campaign against the Canaanites enabled the
Israelites to possess the land God had promised them. His military genius
continues to be acknowledged. (For example, the British Army in the
Middle East during World War I, and the Israeli troops in 1947, studied
Joshua's strategy and tactics with great benefit). With a blend of speed
and surprise, Joshua's desert-trained warriors swept up the canyons and
passes of the high spine of the land between the Jordan and the
Mediterranean, seizing key citadels from the Canaanites. Finally, the con-
quest was completed. The tribes of Israel secured themselves in the
Promised Land.

Joshua, however, was more than a military leader. As Moses' under-
study in the desert, Joshua had learned that he had to be a civil leader
and maker of religious policy, as well. Significantly, Joshua was one of the
rare geniuses who was equally successful in times of peace as in times of
war.

His sound judgment came through in the way he distributed the land to
the various tribes after the successful military campaign. Joshua placed
each of the conquering tribes in a natural geographic area, thus preventing the bloody civil wars that so often follow such military conquests.
Although some of the tribal boundaries shifted a bit at different times in
later history, the overall geographic picture remained relatively the same
throughout the following centuries—a tribute to Joshua's wise leadership.

Joshua never allowed success to go to his head. He remained a devoted
servant of the Lord, accepting the burden of serving as the Israelites' religious leader. Yet Joshua was also growing old. Furthermore, he knew that
many of those who had ventured across the Jordan with him were aging
and dying. The great generation of those who had obeyed God and experienced His deliverance was passing from the scene. Would their children
realize that God had given them this land? Would the coming generation
remember that the Lord had brought victory?

Joshua's final act as leader was to convene the people of the twelve tribes for a great meeting at Shechem. There he called for covenant renewal. "Choose!" he demanded. Serving God faithfully, he knew, meant deliberately siding with God's chosen leader and keeping His covenant.

NOTES ON THE PRINTED TEXT

Joshua gathered all the tribes of Israel to Shechem, and summoned the elders, the heads, the judges, and the officers of Israel; and they presented themselves before God (24:1). Shechem, one of the most important cities in Canaan, lay near a major east-west pass cutting through the massive central highlands that formed the backbone of central Canaan. Joshua stood in the mountain pass before the people, the twelve tribes gathered on the flanks of the mountain pass, with Mt. Gerizim to the southeast and Mt. Ebal to the northwest. The nation's leaders had been summoned to ratify a sacred covenant.

Joshua reminded the people of all that God had done for them in the conquest of the land. *You went over the Jordan and came to Jericho, and the men of Jericho fought against you* (24:11). Joshua also reminded his listeners of the various military campaigns against *the Amorites, the Perizzites, the Canaanites, the Hittites, the Girgashites, the Hivites, and the Jebusites* (24:11). Through God's direction and might, the land had been conquered. The Lord was like a bee or a hornet. Fear of Him paralyzed the land, particularly the *two kings of the Amorites* (24:12), likely Og, King of Bashan, and Sihon. *It was not by your sword or by your bow* (24:12) or your bravery that the land was conquered, Joshua reminded his listeners. The Lord Himself had provided success. He gave them the land they had not farmed, the cities they had not built, and the fruit of the vineyards they had not planted. Joshua told the people that God had blessed them with an abundant land whose riches they received without working for them.

In the ancient world, when a people entered a new land, they placed themselves under the jurisdiction of the local deity. Now was the time to make such a choice. Joshua invited his listeners, *Now therefore fear the Lord, and serve him in sincerity and in faithfulness; put away the gods which your fathers served beyond the River, and in Egypt, and serve the Lord* (24:14). The people had to choose between the Lord or the gods of Mesopotamia, Egypt, and Canaan. Joshua's challenge made it clear that there could be no compromise. *If you be unwilling to serve the Lord, choose this day whom you will serve* (24:15). He explicitly exhorted them to serve God sincerely and faithfully. Finally Joshua announced his own choice. *As for me and my house, we will serve the Lord* (24:15).

The people declared that they would worship the Lord, but Joshua had some misgivings. He reminded the listeners that the Lord would tolerate no divided loyalty; they must give total obedience. The people again responded to Joshua's challenge by stating their intention to worship and serve God always.

You are witnesses against yourselves that you have chosen the Lord, to serve Him (24:22). Joshua warned the people that they would be held accountable for their choices and actions. Anyone who violated the commitment would be condemned. The people acknowledged their accountability. *We are witnesses* (24:22).

Once again Joshua demanded that the people remove and bury their foreign gods. *Then put away the foreign gods which are among you, and incline your heart to the Lord, the God of Israel* (24:23). The nation again reaffirmed its intention to commit itself to God's service. *The Lord our God we will serve, and his voice we will obey* (24:24). Joshua then made a covenant with the people, erecting a stone as a witness to the nation's commitment.

In modern times, a standing stone almost five feet tall and and sixteen inches thick has been unearthed at Shechem and re-erected in its stone base and socket. This stone may have been the one described by Joshua as the "witness" to Israel's covenant.

SUGGESTIONS TO TEACHERS

A well-known actress and her current live-in boyfriend recently became parents. The baby was her second child out of wedlock—each by different fathers—and his third by different women. No, the actress and her current sex partner had no intentions of marrying. "We don't like to make long-term commitments," she stated.

Long-term commitments, however, are what God demands, whether to Him, to a spouse in marriage, to the community of faith, to the planet, or to life itself. As believers, we make commitments to God in response to God's prior commitment to us. Through the covenants with our spiritual ancestors, and, finally, through Jesus Christ, God has given His word that He remains committed to us.

Today's lesson focuses on commitments and our responsibility to keep them. Using the twenty-fourth chapter of Joshua, we will gain new insights into God's long-term commitment to us and our responsibility to choose to serve Him.

1. DETAILS OF DELIVERANCE. Joshua retold the story of God's marvelous acts. His sermon at Shechem reminded everyone that God had rescued Israel from defeat and despair and had brought them safely to the Promised Land.

Human memory is frail, quickly forgetting what God has done. Invite your class members to consider the value of regular, weekly worship and regular, daily Bible reading and prayer. Through these means believers recall the details of God's involvement and continuing presence with them. Long-term commitments to the Lord are made and kept as we recall His goodness and nearness in our spiritual journeys.

2. DEMAND FOR A DECISION. Joshua correctly insists that the people must make a firm choice to serve God. A decision to serve God cannot be put off or evaded. Here you may ask students to share about some of the excuses people give to avoid making a commitment to the Lord. Have you, as a teacher, and those in your class made a definite decision to serve Jesus Christ? What does this mean, in practical terms today?

3. DESTRUCTION FROM DISLOYALTY. Joshua bluntly told his people that lack of commitment to God brings destruction, personally and corporately. In this age of "Feel-Good Religion," many in our society turn away from such warnings. We want to hear nice things; we crave a sooth-

ing spirituality. The word of Scripture, however, remains before us: Not choosing God means refusing God, and without God no one can survive.

4. DEDICATION OF THE DETERMINED. The very word *religion* comes from the Latin word meaning "to bind." The heart of true faith is to bind oneself to the Lord. The covenant ceremony at Shechem under Joshua was such a binding event, a bonding of God and His people. Help your group members realize that this is the same kind of relationship God desires with His people today.

TOPIC FOR ADULTS
MAKING CHOICES

Nation's Choice. Nations as well as individuals must choose to serve God. The United States and other countries need to remember that God is supreme and that He calls them to develop policies that conform to His values. As in Joshua's time, peoples can decide to act as God's subjects.

In calling for a national day of prayer during the Civil War, Abraham Lincoln wrote: "We have been the recipients of the choicest bounties of heaven. We have been preserved, these many years, in peace and prosperity. We have grown in numbers, wealth, and power, as no other nation has grown. But we have forgotten God. We have forgotten the gracious hand which preserved us in peace and multiplied and enriched and strengthened us; and we have vainly imagined . . . that all these blessings were produced by some superior wisdom and virtue of our own. Intoxicated with unbroken success, we have become too self-sufficient to feel the necessity of redeeming and preserving grace, too proud to pray to the God that made us! It behooves us, then, to humble ourselves before the offended Power, to confess our national sins, and to pray for clemency and forgiveness."

Salt of the Earth. Young Steve Robbins and his father and brother are lobstermen in Stonington, Maine. They work hard, often battling forces beyond their control, including the weather, water temperatures, the price of lobsters, and the numbers in their catch.

One day, teenager Steve Robbins was called upon to sell some lobsters to a group "from away" (the term Maine folks use to refer to anyone from out of state). The visitors who had called Steve were from an expensive yacht club far to the south and were enjoying cocktails on the fantail of a fancy yacht. Young Steve Robbins realized that he could easily cheat the wealthy visitors a bit on the weight since it was left to him to make an estimate. But Steve chose not to take advantage of the well-to-do boaters. The yachtsman, who hailed from the cut-throat world of urban businessmen, thought about Steve and others like him. "These people are the salt of the earth," he said.

The visitor's comment about Steve Robbins' choice to practice integrity inspired a video about Robbins with the title, "Salt of the Earth." The point is that choices for God and for right confront us each day in the working world. God calls each to be "salt of the earth" at each point of decision.

Beyond Personal Gain. A couple of years ago, Will Steger, along with five companions from five different countries and thirty-six sled dogs, braved the elements to cross Antarctica. The journey took seven months, with the crew enduring ice storms, whiteouts, and wind-chill temperatures of 110 degrees below zero.

Steger's purpose was to focus attention on the fragility of the Antarctic and the need to preserve it in a virgin state as a world park. His venture covered a staggering 3,741 miles, twice the distance achieved by any other polar foot traveler. He disclosed important information, such as the fact that 70 percent of the world's fresh water is in the Antarctic icecap. Hoping to preserve the Antarctic and the planet earth, Steger later sent a message to the students at his alma mater, the College of St. Thomas in St. Paul, Minnesota. His words echo those of Joshua in calling for choices:

"Your generation must reverse the tide of destruction and strive to preserve the future. As I learned anew in crossing Antarctica, the only limit to achievement is the limit you place on your own dreams. As you seek your own way in the world, look beyond personal gain to your responsibility as God's stewards of the earth. Let your vision be guided by hope, your path be adventurous, and the power of your thoughts be directed toward the betterment of tomorrow."

Questions for Students on the Next Lesson. 1. Why was God displeased with Israel? 2. What was the result of the Israelites' disobedience? 3. What, exactly, was Baal worship? 4. What was the role of a "judge" in this period of Israel's history? 5. What examples can you find of disobedience by God's people today?

TOPIC FOR YOUTH
MAKING WISE CHOICES

How Committed? The building in the center of the small village of Pennyghael, on the Isle of Mull, in Scotland, was obviously constructed as a church. The pointed Gothic arches on the three windows on each side, the small belfry, and the overall architectural design show that the structure was intended to serve as a place of worship. Oldtimers in the village admit that it once was a church. But no congregation gathers there today.

The building is neatly kept, boasting a new roof and fresh paint. But the sign in front does not give the time of Sunday worship; rather, it advertises: "BED and BREAKFAST." The man who now owns the former church building laughs and boasts that the place is busier now as a small inn than it ever was as a place of worship. Apparently the people in the congregation grew careless about attending and serving. The lure of other activities on Sunday and the appeal of the city gradually caused the numbers to dwindle. Finally, an enterprising buyer's offer to take over the property proved irresistible. The church members were pleased at the prospect of the money. And the little church became merely another quaint guest house profiting its owner. The gods of the culture prevailed.

Discovered the Past. When Maria Parker Pascua was a girl, she wondered about her ancestors. She lived then, as now, in a village of Neah Bay on the Olympic Peninsula in the state of Washington. She knew that her great-grandfather and his ancestors were powerful men in the Makah tribe, but she knew little more about them.

In January, 1970, a Pacific storm exposed the ancient village of Ozette, thirty miles from Maria's village (a tremendous mud slide had buried

Ozette in A.D. 1500). As an employee of the Makah Cultural and Research Center, Maria was able to discover interesting information about her ancestors as the archaeologists from Washington State University conducted a decade of excavations.

Maria learned of the British and Spanish explorers who had made contact with the villagers at the end of the eighteenth century. She discovered that by the mid-1800s, two-thirds of the Makah tribe had died from smallpox, measles, and other diseases that the traders and missionaries had brought with them. By the 1890s, Makah children were forced to attend school in Neah Bay, where efforts were made to suppress the traditional language and culture of the tribe.

Today, Maria Parker Pascua is a devout Christian. She is not sorry that the missionaries came, but she does wish they had let the people gradually change their lives without imposing western culture on them. Maria feels she lost much of her heritage, but she is again discovering it so that it may live again.

Some of today's young people have little knowledge of, or interest in, their historical roots. They are much like the children of the biblical Hebrews in certain periods of their history. So Joshua insisted that young and old alike recall the nation's history with God, recognizing all that God had done on their behalf. We, too, must understand our heritage and what God has done for us through Jesus Christ.

Priorities. Even in the modern world, individuals still struggle with destructive ancient traditions. Recently, in Kenya, there has been a resurgence of oath-taking, in which persons and families pledge their ultimate loyalty to a particular tribe.

Yet many families have refused to take an oath of loyalty to their tribes. These men, women, and children have put their loyalty to Christ first. Some have been killed by the tribes for their unwillingness to compromise.

Do you have trouble making choices? Could you make the same decision as these families did? We often face difficult choices that call us to show our true loyalties. At those times we must place God first, Joshua told his listeners. The Lord must be our first priority.

Questions for Students on the Next Lesson. 1. What actions of Israel led God to punish the nation? 2. How did God punish the nation? 3. Why did God punish the nation? 4. What was the role of a "judge" during this period of Israel's history? 5. What happened after each judge died?

LESSON 5—OCTOBER 2

ISRAEL'S TRAGIC PATTERN OF LIFE

Background Scripture: Judges 2:6—3:6
Devotional Reading: Psalm 81:6-16

KING JAMES VERSION

JUDGES 2:11 And the children of Israel did evil in the sight of the Lord, and served Baalim:

12 And they forsook the Lord God of their fathers, which brought them out of the land of Egypt, and followed other gods, of the gods of the people that were round about them, and bowed themselves unto them, and provoked the Lord to anger.

13 And they forsook the Lord, and served Baal and Ashtaroth.

14 And the anger of the Lord was hot against Israel, and he delivered them into the hands of spoilers that spoiled them, and he sold them into the hands of their enemies round about, so that they could not any longer stand before their enemies.

15 Whithersoever they went out, the hand of the Lord was against them for evil, as the Lord had said, and as the Lord had sworn unto them: and they were greatly distressed.

16 Nevertheless the Lord raised up judges, which delivered them out of the hand of those that spoiled them.

17 And yet they would not hearken unto their judges, but they went a whoring after other gods, and bowed themselves unto them: they turned quickly out of the way which their fathers walked in, obeying the commandments of the Lord; but they did not so.

18 And when the Lord raised them up judges, then the Lord was with the judge, and delivered them out of the hand of their enemies all the days of the judge: for it repented the Lord because of their groanings by reason of them that oppressed them and vexed them.

19 And it came to pass, when the judge was dead, that they returned, and corrupted themselves more than their fathers, in following other gods to serve them, and to bow down unto them; they ceased not from their own doings, nor from their stubborn way.

REVISED STANDARD VERSION

JUDGES 2:11 And the people of Israel did what was evil in the sight of the Lord and served the Baals; 12 and they forsook the Lord, the God of their fathers, who had brought them out of the land of Egypt; they went after other gods, from among the gods of the peoples who were round about them, and bowed down to them; and they provoked the Lord to anger. 13 They forsook the Lord, and served the Baals and the Ashtaroth. 14 So the anger of the Lord was kindled against Israel, and he gave them over to plunderers, who plundered them; and he sold them into the power of their enemies round about, so that they could no longer withstand their enemies. 15 Whenever they marched out, the hand of the Lord was against them for evil, as the Lord had warned, and as the Lord had sworn to them; and they were in sore straits.

16 Then the Lord raised up judges, who saved them out of the power of those who plundered them. 17 And yet they did not listen to their judges; for they played the harlot after other gods and bowed down to them; they soon turned aside from the way in which their fathers had walked, who had obeyed the commandments of the Lord, and they did not do so. 18 Whenever the Lord raised up judges for them, the Lord was with the judge, and he saved them from the hand of their enemies all the days of the judge; for the Lord was moved to pity by their groaning because of those who afflicted and oppressed them. 19 But whenever the judge died, they turned back and behaved worse than their fathers, going after other gods, serving them and bowing down to them; they did not drop any of their practices or their stubborn ways.

KEY VERSE: The people of Israel did what was evil in the sight of the Lord and served the Baals; and they forsook the Lord. Judges 2:11, 12.

34

HOME DAILY BIBLE READINGS

Sept.	*26*	*M.*	Psalm 81:6-16	*God's Goodness Calls for Faithful Response*
Sept.	*27*	*T.*	Judges 2:6-13	*After Joshua's Death, Israel Forsook God*
Sept.	*28*	*W.*	Judges 2:14-19	*The Lord Raises Up Judges*
Sept.	*29*	*T.*	Judges 2:20—3:6	*A Time of Testing*
Sept.	*30*	*F.*	Judges 3:7-11	*Another Cycle of Apostasy and Deliverance*
Oct.	*1*	*S.*	Judges 4:4-10	*Again God Rescues a Wayward People*
Oct.	*2*	*S.*	Isaiah 30:8-14	*Israel Known as a Rebellious People*

BACKGROUND

Edward Gibbon completed his monumental *The Rise and Fall of the Roman Empire* in 1788. Since then, several outstanding studies, such as Paul Kennedy's *The Rise and Fall of the Great Powers*, in 1987, have traced the ascendancy and waning of other nations. The history books of the Hebrew Bible could collectively be called *The Rise and Fall of Israel.* Today's lesson material from Judges presents this theme in condensed form.

We have been studying the historic steps leading up to the establishment of the Israelite nation, culminating in the successful conquest of Canaan under Joshua. We've seen that those who carried out the invasion insisted that the Lord had given them the victory. Last week we learned of the covenant at Shechem, in which the Israelites gave their word that they would obey only God and serve Him faithfully.

Alas, a few years later, the people of Israel seemed to have forgotten their promise to the Lord. They had once been desert nomads. Now settled in Canaan, they quickly discovered that their Canaanite neighbors had a superior material culture in many regards. For one thing, they observed that the Canaanites were successful farmers and herdsmen. The Israelites were told that the nature deities, the Baals, had blessed the people with their fine crops and herds. The Israelite invaders heard that the Baals must be placated in order for the rains to fall, the barley to ripen, the grapes to grow, and the livestock to reproduce. Before long, the younger generation of Israelites joined the Canaanites in paying respect to these fertility gods. So the Israelites soon found themselves involved in ceremonies that combined superstition with sexual ritual. The God with whom the Hebrews and their parents had covenanted, the Lord of all creation, who had delivered them to the promised land, was gradually forgotten.

NOTES ON THE PRINTED TEXT

The Book of Judges reveals the same basic depressing pattern, the fortune of the nation following the same repetitive cycle. Israel leaves Yahweh, the Lord, for other gods; God allows the nation to suffer at the hands of various enemies; Israel then cries to the Lord for help; God then raises up a deliverer in response. The nation usually remains committed to God until the deliverer dies. Then the same old cycle of rebellion-to-repentance-to-restoration begins again. This pattern comes through clearly in Judges 2, today's lesson Scripture.

After making the covenant, Joshua dismissed the people to take possession of the land of Canaan. The first generation served the Lord and was obedient, but the second generation's commitment wavered. *And the people of Israel did what was evil in the sight of the Lord and served the Baals* (2:11). The people once again became unfaithful. They first deserted the one true God for Baal, the Canaanite storm-god who supposedly showered life and fertility upon all vegetation and humankind. Baal was said to provide the rain and the growth of crops, herds, and flocks.

Israel also pursued other local gods. *They forsook the Lord, the God of their fathers, who had brought them out of the land of Egypt; they went after other gods, from among the gods of the peoples who were round about them, and bowed down to them* (2:12).

Finally, the nation settled on the worship of Baal and his consort, Astarte. *They forsook the Lord, and served the Baals and the Ashtaroth* (2:13). Astarte was the warlike sister and wife of Baal, and one of the leading fertility goddesses. She was the inspiration for every form of passion, making this religion highly sensuous in its rituals. The Canaanite temples offered male and female prostitutes and every sort of sexual excess to its worshiper.

So the anger of the Lord was kindled against Israel, and he gave them over to plunderers (2:14). God judged the people's unfaithfulness, allowing the nation to suffer under the hands of its enemies. Whenever the nation resisted and fought, it was defeated. *Whenever they marched out, the hand of the Lord was against them* (2:15). None of this was unexpected; God had warned the nation and had vowed to punish disobedience. *The Lord had warned . . . the Lord had sworn to them* (2:15). The writer of Judges summed up the situation in a single statement: *They were in sore straits* (2:15).

Then the Lord raised up judges, who saved them out of the power of those who plundered them (2:16). When the people of Israel cried out because of their oppression, God raised up judges to deliver them. These judges were not the legal experts that we think of when we hear the word "judge" today. Rather, they were men and women with special gifts dedicated to upholding God's covenant. These dynamic individuals arose to deal with the spiritual crisis of faith and to deliver the nation from foreign oppression as temporary rulers. *Whenever the Lord raised up judges for them, the Lord was with the judge, and he saved them from the hand of their enemies all the days of the judge; for the Lord was moved to pity by their groaning because of those who afflicted and oppressed them* (2:18). God was with the judges to grant freedom. However, when the judge died, or the crisis passed, the people returned to idol worship. The whole tragic pattern began again.

Literally, the nation prostituted itself to the Baals. *Whenever the judge died, they turned back and behaved worse than their fathers, going after other gods, serving them and bowing down to them; they did not drop any of their practices or their stubborn ways* (2:19). With each generation, the level of Israel's disobedience increased.

SUGGESTIONS TO TEACHERS

Henry Ford might have been an engineering genius, but he was pathetically mistaken when he proclaimed: "History is bunk!" Ford sniffed at the need to reflect on the rise and fall of empires. Yet his own automobile empire, over which he intended his family dynasty to rule personally, had to be run by hired managers after it experienced serious decline in Ford's old age. Philosopher George Santayana was right when he said that those who forget the past are in danger of repeating it. This is why we are studying the story of ancient Israel.

Today, you and your students will receive an overview of the sad and tragic pattern of spiritual rebellion. The themes of this lesson recur with dismal regularity throughout the history of Israel—and other nations. We'll no doubt notice many parallels with modern nations, including our own.

1. THE PERIL OF FORGETTING. "The next generation forgot the Lord and what he had done for Israel" (Judg. 2:10, TEV). How important it is to remember the past and what God has done! Will the coming generation remember what God has done in years gone by? What steps are you taking to help the younger generation remember God? Remind your students of Santayana's words.

2. THE PRACTICE OF FOOLISHNESS. Israel was constantly tempted to neglect its covenant with the Lord. Forgetting to acknowledge and serve God as the supreme Lord inevitably brings spiritual disaster. Human knowledge, human plans, human goals are always flawed. Substituting them for the Lord's will never results in lasting happiness.

3. THE PATTERN OF FAILURE. The Israelites decided to adopt the customs and culture of Canaan. Perhaps wanting to "fit in" with Canaanite society, the sons and daughters of those who had invaded the land with Joshua began to blend their neighbors' life-styles with their own. The people ignored the judges God provided and "played the harlot after other gods and bowed down to them" (2:17). Strong words!

Bring your lesson down to our day. What gods does our society seem intent on having affairs with? What are some of the lesser deities we lust after? Violence? Sexual gratification without caring and commitment? Greedy exploitation of the earth's resources? What others?

4. THE PATIENCE OF THE FATHER. Throughout the ups and downs of the nation of Israel, the Lord patiently and persistently called His people to settled faithfulness. And God continues to do this with us today. Bring in the Gospel message to your students here. Through Jesus Christ, God has made His judgment and mercy known in terms we must not ignore.

TOPIC FOR ADULTS
CHOICES HAVE CONSEQUENCES

Consequences in Chaco Canyon. For several centuries, the Anasazi Indian community thrived in Chaco Canyon, in what is now New Mexico. Until recently, scientists and historians were perplexed as to why this community disintegrated about eight hundred years ago. Recently, however, Julio Betancourt, of the U.S. Geological Survey, and Thomas Van Devender, of the Arizona-Sonora Desert Museum, have explained the departure of the Anasazi Indians from Chaco Canyon.

By studying middens (ancient refuse heaps) that showed 11,000 years of vegetation change in the canyon, Betencourt and Van Devender discovered that the Indians eventually used up all the surrounding pine trees for their dwellings and firewood, depleting the woodland and eroding the farmland vital to the tribe's survival.

Thus, we might make this general statement about life: Inevitable consequences follow when any people continues to live irresponsibly.

Somalian Tragedy. An old Somalian saying states: "I and Somalia against the world. I and my clan against Somalia. I and my family against the clan. I and my brother against the family. I against my brother." Not surprisingly, Somalia has been wracked with an appallingly brutal civil war and caught in the throes of grim famine.

Twentieth-Century Object Lesson. History presents many object lessons showing what happens when people choose pure self-interest as a guiding principle. Until well into the twentieth century, for instance, Argentina was one of the richest nations in the world.

Endowed with a country of ample resources, favorable climate, and rich soil, Argentineans enjoyed a high living standard and a promising future. But several decades ago, none of the people in the country—the landed gentry, the laborers, the middle class, the bankers—were willing to make sacrifices to keep the country growing. The economy weakened, then collapsed, under the weight of all their demands upon it. The refusal of the various Argentinean factions to subordinate their own interests to the common good wrecked the nation's economy and caused great social misery. For a time, Argentine ebbed between violent anarchy and brutal dictatorship. The Me-first and I-don't-care-about-God attitude always brings dire consequences; it nearly ruined Argentina.

Questions for Students on the Next Lesson. 1. What was Gideon doing when God called him? 2. Why did God instruct Gideon to pare down the size of his army? 3. Who were the Midianites? 4. What are the details of the startling victory over the Midianite encampment? 5. Does God still call persons for tasks which appear to be beyond their capabilities? Give a personal example.

TOPIC FOR YOUTH
FOLLOWING A DOWNWARD PATH

Modern Parallel. A French-built car pulled alongside Thomas Sutherland's car in 1985. As the car sideswiped his automobile, two other cars pulled up. Eight youths with machine guns jumped out and began firing at the pavement.

That was the beginning of captivity for the professor of agriculture at American University in Beirut, Lebanon. Sutherland was held hostage for six and a half years. He spent his first twenty-eight days in solitary confinement in a six-by-six-foot cell, blindfolded, with no sunshine, little fresh air, and fifteen minutes once a day to use the bathroom. Then Sutherland was placed in a cell with Reverend Ben Wier, a Presbyterian minister, and Father Martin Jenco, a Catholic priest. Later Terry Anderson and David Jacobson would join them.

Sutherland had once been a church goer, but his commitment had lapsed fifteen years earlier. Captivity, though, renewed his faith. Wier and Martin conducted worship services, and the men spoke of their faith. Sutherland began to hear God's call once again. Ultimately, the terrible ordeal of captivity forced Sutherland back into a close relationship with God.

Sutherland's experience parallels Israel's cycle of rebellion and restoration. Why not stay in a close relationship with God rather than keeping the cycle going?

Remembered. Outside Stratford-on-Avon, England, stands Warwick Castle. In the dungeon of the castle is the *oubliette.* This is a tiny pit beneath the floor of the dungeon where the poor wretch who had been judged and condemned was thrown. There he would (just as the name was translated) be forgotten.

The story of Judges reminds us that although the nation was judged, condemned, and punished, God never forgot His people. Unlike the forgotten prisoners of Warwick Castle, God heard the cries of His people and acted to save them. He raised up others to help the people and He calls us to do the same today.

Square and True. Jean Travaglio's father was a master carpenter. He was regarded as one of the best in the county, particularly when it came to installing hardwood floors. Jean, who had once asked her father what his most important tool was, expected him to respond that it was his saw or his hammer. Instead, the man showed his daughter his square. This tool allowed all his other tools to work true.

God gave the people of Israel commandments that would help the nation stay true to Him. Instead, the nation deviated from the truth presented in those commandments and followed other gods. Spiritual darkness and sadness resulted. Will we choose to view the commandments as valuable guides to Christian joy?

Questions for Students on the Next Lesson. 1. Why did the Lord insist that Gideon reduce the size of his army? 2. What steps did Gideon follow to fulfill the Lord's commands? 3. How did Gideon defeat the Midianites? 4. Can people succeed in life without God's help? 5. Is physical strength or numbers always the deciding factor in military victory? Explain.

LESSON 6—OCTOBER 9

DELIVERANCE BY GOD'S HAND

Background Scripture: Judges 6:1—8:21
Devotional Reading: Psalm 33:10-22

KING JAMES VERSION

JUDGES 7:2 And the Lord said unto Gideon, The people that are with thee are too many for me to give the Midianites into their hands, lest Israel vaunt themselves against me, saying, Mine own hand hath saved me.

3 Now therefore go to, proclaim in the ears of the people, saying, Whosoever is fearful and afraid, let him return and depart early from mount Gilead. And there returned of the people twenty and two thousand; and there remained ten thousand.

4 And the Lord said unto Gideon, The people are yet too many; bring them down unto the water, and I will try them for thee there: and it shall be, that of whom I say unto thee, This shall go with thee, the same shall go with thee; and of whomsoever I say unto thee, This shall not go with thee, the same shall not go.

5 So he brought down the people unto the water: and the Lord said unto Gideon, Every one that lappeth of the water with his tongue, as a dog lappeth, him shalt thou set by himself; likewise every one that boweth down upon his knees to drink.

6 And the number of them that lapped, putting their hand to their mouth, were three hundred men: but all the rest of the people bowed down upon their knees to drink water.

7 And the Lord said unto Gideon, By the three hundred men that lapped will I save you, and deliver the Midianites into thine hand: and let all the other people go every man unto his place.

19 So Gideon, and the hundred men that were with him, came unto the outside of the camp in the beginning of the middle watch; and they had but newly set the watch: and they blew the trumpets, and brake the pitchers that were in their hands.

20 And the three companies blew the trumpets, and brake the pitchers, and held the lamps in their left hands, and the trumpets in their right hands to blow withal: and they cried, The sword of the Lord, and of Gideon.

21 And they stood every man in his place round about the camp; and all the host ran, and cried, and fled.

REVISED STANDARD VERSION

JUDGES 7:2 The Lord said to Gideon, "The people with you are too many for me to give the Midianites into their hand, lest Israel vaunt themselves against me, saying, 'My own hand has delivered me.' 3 Now therefore proclaim in the ears of the people, saying, 'Whoever is fearful and trembling, let him return home.'" And Gideon tested them; twenty-two thousand returned, and ten thousand remained.

4 And the Lord said to Gideon, "The people are still too many; take them down to the water and I will test them for you there; and he of whom I say to you, 'This man shall go with you,' shall go with you; and any of whom I say to you, 'This man shall not go with you,' shall not go." 5 So he brought the people down to the water; and the Lord said to Gideon, "Every one that laps the water with his tongue, as a dog laps, you shall set by himself; likewise every one that kneels down to drink." 6 And the number of those that lapped, putting their hands to their mouths, was three hundred men; but all the rest of the people knelt down to drink water. 7 And the Lord said to Gideon, "With the three hundred men that lapped I will deliver you and give the Midianites into your hand; and let all the others go every man to his home."

19 So Gideon and the hundred men who were with him came to the outskirts of the camp at the beginning of the middle watch, when they had just set the watch; and they blew the trumpets and smashed the jars that were in their hands. 20 And the three companies blew the trumpets and broke the jars, holding in their left hands the torches, and in their right hands the trumpets to blow; and they cried, "A sword for the Lord and for Gideon!" 21 They stood every man in his place round about the camp, and all the army ran; they cried out and fled.

KEY VERSE: Arise; for the Lord has given the host of Midian into your hand. Judges 7:15b.

HOME DAILY BIBLE READINGS

Oct.	3	M.	Judges 6:1-10	*A Faithless People Cry for Help*
Oct.	4	T.	Judges 6:11-18	*Gideon's Call to Lead the Israelites*
Oct.	5	W.	Judges 6:19-24	*A Sign to Reassure Gideon*
Oct.	6	T.	Judges 6:25-32	*Gideon Destroys the Altar of Baal*
Oct.	7	F.	Judges 6:33-40	*Two More Signs Affirm God's Call*
Oct.	8	S.	Judges 7:2-14	*The Selection of Gideon's Army*
Oct.	9	S.	Judges 7:15-21	*The Enemy Flees from Gideon's Army*

BACKGROUND

In the desert, only a few pieces of land can be tilled, and the desert-dwelling Israelite tribesmen knew little of raising crops. After settling in Canaan, however, these tribesmen found themselves in an agricultural society. They had to learn farming from their Canaanite neighbors. They heard that successful farming, however, was closely tied to the worship of the Canaanite fertility gods and goddesses. Their agricultural advisors insisted that participating in the Baal cults insured that the crops would grow, the weather would be favorable, the rains would come, and the harvest would be bountiful. Consequently, the Israelite farmers began to take part in the ceremonies at the hilltop shrines of the heathen deities. These cults, scholars point out, were disgustingly depraved, usually involving sex orgies and often even child sacrifice.

A period of decline would follow Israel's involvement with Baal worship. After allowing a series of dismal defeats, God would raise up a temporary leader, called a judge, to rally the Israelite tribes. A period of repentance would set in, followed finally by a military victory over the oppressive pagan powers.

But the old cycle would start over after a period of faithfulness to the Lord. Once again, the people would drift away from God, and hardship would come. God's judgment on the rebelliousness and disobedience of His people always followed. This cycle of sin and salvation formed the historical backdrop within which the judges operated. The judges were not courtroom figures, as our word might imply, but political-military-spiritual leaders for the crisis period.

Today's lesson describes a deeper crisis for the Israelites—facing the dreaded Midianite oppressors. This vicious tribe had revolutionized warfare by introducing the camel into military action. Swooping across the Jordan valley from the desert on their fast-moving camels, these tough warriors repeatedly raided the farms and villages of the Israelites in lightning-swift invasions. Since a camel can bear up to five hundred pounds or more, the Midianites were able to carry off enormous quantities of loot on the backs of these unusual steeds.

Though the Israelites seemed helpless, once again God heard their cries and raised up a new deliverer. As was often the case, God designated an unlikely person to act as His agent. In this situation, it was Gideon.

NOTES ON THE PRINTED TEXT

The people's evil ways resulted in God's judgment: The Midianites invaded the land. Midian comprised an area in the Arabian Desert, southeast of the Dead Sea, beyond Moab. These camel-riding bedouins from the east swept through southern Israel, spreading terror and stealing the produce Israel had raised. People hid in caves and dens in the mountains to hide from the Midianites' raids. Others, such as Gideon, were forced to hide when they threshed their meager supply of wheat.

God called Gideon to lead Israel out of Midianite oppression. Although Gideon initially hesitated, he eventually rallied his people to fight the invaders. However, too many men responded to his call to arms. Some 32,000 came and encamped in the Jezreel Valley. God said that Gideon's army was so large the people would take credit for their victory. *The people with you are too many for me to give the Midianites into their hand, lest Israel vaunt themselves against me, saying, "My own hand has delivered me"* (7:2).

The Lord had a solution. *Proclaim in the ears of the people, saying, "Whoever is fearful and trembling, let him return home"* (7:3). God instructed Gideon to let those who were afraid go home. Some 22,000 lacked the courage for the fight and departed. This left 10,000 soldiers. But even 10,000 men were still too many. Once again God proposed a method to determine which men would fight.

Gideon was to take the men to a nearby stream. (The Kishon River flows through the Jezreel Valley. It is well fed by a number of streams.) The Lord commanded Gideon to watch the men drink. *Every one that laps the water with his tongue, as a dog laps, you shall set by himself; likewise every one that kneels down to drink* (7:5). Three hundred men drank their water by cupping a hand and bringing it up to their mouths. The remainder knelt or laid down and lapped their water like dogs.

The test was one of alertness. Those who cupped their water and brought it to their mouths were more vigilant, constantly alert for any emergency or an attack. Those who laid or knelt down relaxed their vigilance. These men were ordered home. God declared, *With the three hundred men . . . I will deliver you and give the Midianites into your hand* (7:7).

The Lord assured Gideon of victory. The Lord also suggested that Gideon spy on the enemy. That night, Gideon and his servant surveyed the Midianite lines. The flickering campfires revealed a huge tent city and numerous camels. The two overheard a Midianite soldier describing his dream and realized that morale was low and that the enemy had no courage to fight. The two returned to camp and quickly outlined a plan.

The handpicked warriors were divided into three companies. Each man was to carry a trumpet and also a torch, which was to be kept inside an earthenware jar. When Gideon blew his trumpet, the warriors were to do the same.

Gideon's forces arrived at the beginning of the middle watch, or in the middle of the night, gathering around the edges of the Midianite camp. Gideon and his men blew their trumpets, smashed their jars, held the torches aloft, and shouted, *"A sword for the Lord and for Gideon!"* (7:20).

The Midianites were suddenly awakened by the noise. Seeing their camp surrounded by torches, they assumed they were being attacked by a huge army. Panic and confusion resulted. Fleeing, they were trapped and slaughtered by Gideon's men and by a group of Ephraimites who had belatedly joined the battle. Gideon and his army of three hundred men defeated the Midianites as God had promised.

SUGGESTIONS TO TEACHERS

"Defeat is an orphan, but victory has many fathers," the saying goes. Everyone wants to claim credit for a win. The Scriptures, however, insist that the victories won by the Israelites were fathered by God and God only. The story of Gideon and his three hundred warriors underscores this point.

1. RESULTS OF REBELLIOUSNESS. The Bible insists that God holds nations as well as individuals accountable for their actions. Furthermore, the Scriptures report that failure to be accountable to God brings judgment, whether the subject be a solitary person or an immense empire. Actions do have consequences. In the case of ancient Israel, refusal to live responsibly before God brought defeat by enemies and times of severe trial and testing. The Midianites' invasion, recorded in today's lesson, was an example of divine displeasure and judgment. Ask your students to think about what it means to "rebel" against God today. Try to put this in very practical terms; ask for personal examples.

2. RELUCTANCE OF THE RESCUER. Look closely at the call of Gideon. Note his reluctance to respond. Remark on Gideon's demand for proofs that God's call was authentic. This episode offers an opportunity to discuss the way God has called each member of your class to serve Him. Through Christ, every Christian has been "called." In what ways is our task of discerning God's will like, and unlike, Gideon's?

3. RECOVERY OF REPENTANCE. The people of Israel finally turned back to the Lord. Repentance means turning back to God, a daily discipline for every believer. Consider how we sometimes associate repentance only with revivalism, thinking that only a hardened sinner can come to repentance. In truth, each Christian must return to God again and again, in attitude and action, throughout the course of daily living.

4. ROUT BY A REMNANT. The thrilling rout of the Midianite hordes by Gideon's small force of elite commandos makes for exciting battle drama. In our era of big numbers, large institutions, and massive power, the victory of Gideon's three hundred reminds us that the Lord delights in using a small core of faithful people to accomplish His great deeds.

Your congregation, for instance, may be quite small. But with dedication on the part of all, in spite of the relatively small force, you may effectively serve your community and the area beyond in astonishing ways. After all, Jesus started with just twelve.

5. RECOGNITION OF REALITY. The glorious defeat of the great

Midianite army by Gideon's three hundred may lead a casual observer to give the glory to Gideon. Make sure, however, that your class realizes that the details of the account have been arranged to give the Lord the credit for the victory. Invite your students to share about times in their own lives when no other explanation—except for the supernatural working of God—could explain the unfolding of events.

TOPIC FOR ADULTS
GOD CHOOSES AND EMPOWERS

Unlikely Instruments. Some of the greatest contributors to humanity have come from unlikely backgrounds. Booker T. Washington was born in a one-room log cabin; his mother was a slave, his father unknown. Marian Anderson's father died when she was twelve years old, and her mother worked in a department store to keep food on the table and a roof over their heads. Albert Einstein was so slow in learning to talk that his parents thought he was abnormal and his teachers were sure he would be a poor student. Hans Christian Anderson was born into poverty; Robert Louis Stevenson struggled with pain and disease; John Keats had tuberculosis when he was twenty and died at twenty-six. The list could go on and on.

In the same way, the Scriptures show us how God often chooses the least likely to carry out His will—not just for humanity, but for the advancement of His eternal Kingdom.

No Fear. Fear can hinder any person, young or old, from being a part of an important action. Gideon's soldiers were no different than the ones gathered around General "Stonewall" Jackson one evening in the Shenandoah Valley. The General had outlined a daring raid with his senior officers. The odds against the raid's success were very high, but the potential gains enormous. When asked for their comments, one of the officers timidly said, "Sir, I'm afraid of this. I fear we can't carry it off."

Jackson placed his hand on the subordinate's shoulder. Looking at him he said, "Never take counsel of your fears, Major. Never take counsel of your fears."

Fortunately, this was the advice Gideon followed. Even though the odds were against him, he listened to God's voice and did not take counsel of his fears. God had chosen him for the mission, and God would empower him to carry it out.

Fulfilling the Mission. Lt. Clebe McClary fought with the United States Marines in Vietnam. During his tour of duty, he lost one of his eyes and his left arm, and he underwent thirty-three operations to mend the rest of his body.

Now McClary travels as an evangelist. He proclaims his personal faith in Jesus Christ and describes his life as a member of the Lord's army. McClary is fond of pointing out that he still fulfills the vow he took when he joined the Marines: that any mission that is assigned he will accomplish in an exemplary manner, no matter what the obstacles.

Clebe understands the story of Gideon. God calls everyone to be like Gideon. We are to act in courage even when circumstances seem so desperate. The same Lord commands us to fulfill His mission in an exemplary manner, no matter what the obstacles, because it is God's strength that empowers us.

Questions for Students on the Next Lesson. 1. Why did the Israelites want a king? 2. Why did Samuel have such strong misgivings about kings? 3. Why weren't Samuel's sons suitable to succeed him? 4. What warnings did Samuel give the people when the Lord allowed a king to be anointed? 5. How was the king of Israel different from kings of other nations?

TOPIC FOR YOUTH
GETTING READY FOR ACTION

Preparation of a Hero. Dr. Benjamin Carson, Director of Pediatric Neurosurgery at the Johns Hopkins Children's Center in Baltimore, is widely known for his remarkable surgical skills. Described as a "miracle worker" by the news media after performing a brain operation that saved the life of a hydrocephalic baby still in the womb, Dr. Carson more recently headed the team that successfully separated Siamese twins. The twins were born joined at the skull and they shared a brain and a blood system.

Dr. Carson is the winner of two of the most prestigious awards in surgery. He is also the most unlikely of heroes. Growing up as a poor black youngster in a tough, poverty-stricken neighborhood of Detroit, young Benjamin Carson had what he describes as a "pathological temper." His anger flared out of control whenever he felt anyone had slighted him. He fought with fists, broken bottles, rocks, hammers, knives—whatever came to hand.

One day, in his teens, Carson ran after another teenager and tried to stab him with a large hunting knife. Fortunately, the other boy was wearing a heavy metal belt buckle that deflected the blow and broke the knife. Ben Carson went home, realizing that he could have killed the other youth and landed in prison for most of his life. Sitting for hours alone on the edge of the bathtub, Carson thought about his situation. Then he prayed, asking the Lord to take away his temper.

With the help of God and the encouragement of his mother, who held two and sometimes three jobs to keep the family going, Carson began the uphill task of finishing high school in the face of tremendous peer pressure to drop out, do drugs, and get into crime. Eventually he won a scholarship to Yale and went on to medical school.

In spite of the honors he received, Dr. Carson humbly states that the Lord gave him surgical abilities. He knows that speaking out so candidly and clearly about his Christian faith is unusual in the academic and hospital center where he works. But this unlikely hero is convinced that God prepared him to serve others.

Ready for the Future? On April 10, 1912, the largest, most expensive, and most luxurious oceangoing vessel ever constructed sailed from Southampton, England. The ship was said to be unsinkable.

Four days later, at 11:40 p.m., the ship struck an iceberg just off the Newfoundland coast. The 2,207 passengers and crew, many celebrating, were hardly aware of the seriousness of the accident. They trusted in the sheer size of the ship and in its reputation. Although lifeboats were launched (the ship carried only enough boats for 1,200 individuals), three hours later, the unsinkable Titanic slid beneath the ocean's surface, claiming 1,522 lives.

Young people sometimes feel self-sufficient and have an excessive sense of pride. Surely, the sinking of the *Titanic* stands as one of the great reminders of humankind's monumental neglect of true readiness for action. No matter how carefully we try to engineer our lives, we are not ready for our future until we place it in God's hands.

Questions for Students on the Next Lesson. 1. Who ruled Israel between the days of Joshua and Samuel? 2. Why did the people of Israel want a king? 3. Why did Samuel protest Israel's request? 4. How do you react to Samuel's description of life under a king? 5. What was the significance of the thunderstorm?

LESSON 7—OCTOBER 16

ISRAEL DEMANDS A KING

Background Scripture: I Samuel 7:15—8:22; 12:19-25
Devotional Reading: Psalm 47:1-9

KING JAMES VERSION

I SAMUEL 8:4 Then all the elders of Israel gathered themselves together, and came to Samuel unto Ramah,

5 And said unto him, Behold, thou art old, and thy sons walk not in thy ways: now make us a king to judge us like all the nations.

6 But the thing displeased Samuel, when they said, Give us a king to judge us. And Samuel prayed unto the Lord.

7 And the Lord said unto Samuel, Hearken unto the voice of the people in all that they say unto thee: for they have not rejected thee, but they have rejected me, that I should not reign over them.

8 According to all the works which they have done since the day that I brought them up out of Egypt even unto this day, wherewith they have forsaken me, and served other gods, so do they also unto thee.

9 Now therefore hearken unto their voice: howbeit yet protest solemnly unto them, and shew them the manner of the king that shall reign over them.

19 Nevertheless the people refused to obey the voice of Samuel; and they said, Nay; but we will have a king over us;

12:19 And all the people said unto Samuel, Pray for thy servants unto the Lord thy God, that we die not: for we have added unto all our sins this evil, to ask us a king.

20 And Samuel said unto the people, Fear not: ye have done all this wickedness: yet turn not aside from following the Lord, but serve the Lord with all your heart;

21 And turn ye not aside: for then should ye go after vain things, which cannot profit nor deliver; for they are vain.

22 For the Lord will not forsake his people for his great name's sake: because it hath pleased the Lord to make you his people.

23 Moreover as for me, God forbid that I should sin against the Lord in ceasing to pray for you: but I will teach you the good and the right way:

24 Only fear the Lord, and serve him in truth with all your heart: for consider how great things he hath done for you.

25 But if ye shall still do wickedly, ye shall be consumed, both ye and your king.

REVISED STANDARD VERSION

I SAMUEL 8:4 Then all the elders of Israel gathered together and came to Samuel at Ramah, 5 and said to him, "Behold, you are old and your sons do not walk in your ways; now appoint for us a king to govern us like all the nations." 6 But the thing displeased Samuel when they said, "Give us a king to govern us." And Samuel prayed to the Lord. 7 And the Lord said to Samuel, "Hearken to the voice of the people in all that they say to you; for they have not rejected you, but they have rejected me from being king over them. 8 According to all the deeds which they have done to me, from the day I brought them up out of Egypt even to this day, forsaking me and serving other gods, so they are also doing to you. 9 Now then, hearken to their voice; only, you shall solemnly warn them, and show them the ways of the king who shall reign over them."

19 But the people refused to listen to the voice of Samuel; and they said, "No! but we will have a king over us, . . ."

12:19 And all the people said to Samuel, "Pray for your servants to the Lord your God, that we may not die; for we have added to all our sins this evil, to ask for ourselves a king." 20 And Samuel said to the people, "Fear not; you have done all this evil, yet do not turn aside from following the Lord, but serve the Lord with all your heart; 21 and do not turn aside after vain things which cannot profit or save, for they are vain. 22 For the Lord will not cast away his people, for his great name's sake, because it has pleased the Lord to make you a people for himself. 23 Moreover as for me, far be it from me that I should sin against the Lord by ceasing to pray for you; and I will instruct you in the good and the right way. 24 Only fear the Lord, and serve him faithfully with all your heart; for consider what great things he has done for you. 25 But if you still do wickedly, you shall be swept away, both you and your king."

KEY VERSE: Appoint for us a king to govern us like all the nations.
I Samuel 8:5b.

HOME DAILY BIBLE READINGS

Oct.	10	M.	I Samuel 7:12-17	Peace under Samuel's Leadership
Oct.	11	T.	I Samuel 8:1-9	Israel Asks for a King
Oct.	12	W.	Psalm 47	God Reigns over All the Earth
Oct.	13	T.	I Samuel 8:10-22	Rejection of Samuel's Warning about a King
Oct.	14	F.	I Samuel 12:1-5	Samuel Defends His Own Leadership
Oct.	15	S.	I Samuel 12:6-18	Samuel Pleads for God's Kingship
Oct.	16	S.	I Samuel 12:19-25	Samuel Appeals for Faithfulness to God

BACKGROUND

The history of the tribes of Israel after Joshua unfolded in a series of dismal cycles. Each cycle followed the same pattern: 1) A new generation forgets and forsakes God; 2) the people serve the Canaanite fertility gods and goddesses; 3) the Lord allows His people to fall into the hands of oppressive raiders and local overlords; 4) the Israelites finally cry to God for help; 5) God raises up a judge or deliverer.

The vicious cycle began again when the Philistines appeared. Seafaring warriors who migrated from the Aegean to the coastal area of Palestine around 1300 B.C., the Philistines quickly became rivals to the Israelites. One reason for the military and economic success of the Philistines was their superior technology in metallurgy. For some time, they jealously guarded the secret of smelting iron. Iron swords and spears, and iron plows and hoes are much stronger than bronze weapons and implements. The Philistine rulers exploited this advantage in war and business.

With their superior equipment, the Philistine army slaughtered an Israelite army and destroyed Shiloh and its tabernacle. Shiloh had been the one shrine of the Lord that each of the twelve tribes held sacred. At Shiloh, the priesthood of Aaron presided over the sacrificial ceremonies of all the tribes. When the Philistines obliterated Israel's central sanctuary and carried away the box containing the sacred tablets, the ark of the covenant, the Philistines reasoned that Israelite resistance would collapse.

But God raised up a new leader for his people. Under the energetic leadership of Samuel, a brief season of spiritual springtime followed a long winter of discord and disobedience. Samuel's circuit judgeship began to centralize the government of the tribes. In spite of the grievous loss of Shiloh and the capture of the sacred ark of the covenant, Samuel managed to rally the people.

The people pleaded for a dictator like the Philistines had, however. The clamor for a king grew so insistent that when he grew old, and his sons proved to have none of the required leadership qualities to succeed him, Samuel finally agreed to anoint a king of Israel.

NOTES ON THE PRINTED TEXT

Behold, you are old and your sons do not walk in your ways; now appoint for us a king to govern us like all the nations (8:5). Samuel was a judge called by God, but he attempted to institutionalize the office. His method was hereditary succession. He appointed his sons as assistant judges in the southernmost sanctuary of Israel, Beersheba; however, the boys proved unworthy. Because Samuel's sons took bribes, perverted justice, and violated the laws of God, the elders of the twelve tribes wanted change. The old way of raising up judges had disadvantages; other countries had kings and were prospering.

The thing displeased Samuel (8:6). The demand for a king flew in the face of Samuel's beliefs. Asking for a king was blasphemy. God was the nation's king on earth and in heaven.

Samuel turned to the Lord and prayed for guidance. God first told Samuel not to take the elders' request personally. The people were not rejecting him; they were rejecting the Lord as their ruler. *They have not rejected you, but they have rejected me from being king over them* (8:7). God also reminded Samuel that the elders' request was characteristic of Israel. During its whole history the nation had forsaken the Lord as its ruler. *According to all the deeds which they have done to me, from the day I brought them up out of Egypt even to this day, forsaking me and serving other gods, so they are also doing to you* (8:8).

While God did not endorse the request, He did not reject it either. Instead, Samuel was to warn Israel of what it could expect from a king. *Warn them, and show them the ways of the king who shall reign over them* (8:9). Samuel warned the people of all that they would suffer if a king ruled over them. Sons would be conscripted into the army, individuals would be forced to work on the king's lands and build weapons, and the king would take over their farms and claim their harvests. A king would impose taxes, and the nation would become a kingdom of slaves.

The people rejected Samuel's predictions and disregarded the potential cost of a king. They increased their demands. *The people refused to listen to . . . Samuel; and they said, "No! but we will have a king over us"* (18:19).

Preparing to depart from Mizpah, Samuel offered a farewell. He reviewed Israel's history and the people's failure to do the Lord's will. His sermon was powerfully aided by a thunderstorm, which Samuel said proved the people's wickedness. Standing in the midst of the terrible storm, the people realized their sin against God, and in fear and repentance they begged Samuel, *Pray for your servants to the Lord your God, that we may not die; for we have added to all our sins this evil, to ask for ourselves a king* (12:19).

Samuel assured the nation of God's faithfulness. *The Lord will not cast away his people, for his great name's sake, because it has pleased the Lord to make you a people for himself* (12:22). The assurance came packaged with two demands. First, the people must serve the Lord with all their heart (12:20). In addition, the people must not follow false gods. *Do not turn aside after vain things which cannot profit or save* (12:21).

The old judge also assured the frightened people that he would continue to pray for the people and to instruct them. *Far be it from me that I should sin against the Lord by ceasing to pray for you; and I will instruct you in the good and the right way* (12:23).

Israel's faithfulness would bring the blessing of God. The old prophet again summoned the rain-soaked listeners to be faithful. *Only fear the Lord, and serve him faithfully with all your heart; for consider what great things he has done for you* (12:24). Samuel concluded with one final warning: *If you still do wickedly, you shall be swept away, both you and your king* (12:25).

SUGGESTIONS TO TEACHERS

When life's circumstances become more difficult than usual, people long for someone who will solve their problems. No human leader, of course, can fulfill all our needs or expectations, but the illusion persists that a political leader with a firm hand and clear vision can make everything perfect.

1. WARNINGS AGAINST MONARCHS. Samuel faced the demand that he anoint a king. The problem was that the people wanted a dictatorial ruler similar to the Philistines' kings. Samuel's words of caution (see I Sam. 8:10-18) apply today. Political rulers will always have a tendency to seek absolute power, perhaps trampling on the rights of others. A "Jehovah complex" easily afflicts kings and presidents, even church leaders of every stripe.

The concept of the "divine right of kings" persisted in western Europe up to the American revolution and continues to be held in various circles even now. Samuel's key point was that monarchs will always be inclined to displace the Lord. Supreme allegiance belongs solely to God. Everyone, kings included, is accountable to the Lord.

2. WILLFULNESS BY THE PEOPLE. Ask your students why people are apt to expect the impossible from their leaders in times of trouble. Is it not because people often refuse to accept personal responsibility for their own lives? Use some of your session time to consider what we ought to look for in our leaders: in the church, in the community, and in the nation.

3. WARRANT BY GOD. Look closely at I Samuel 12:22-24, which shows God making a solemn promise to His people. God vows that He will not abandon them but calls them to live faithfully and obediently. Invite student response to this question: In what practical ways are believers called to obedience today?

4. WATCHFULNESS AGAINST IDOLATRY. Hero worship can be harmful to one's health! Idolatry is not limited to the act of worshiping in front of a stone statue. Whenever we give any cause, any leader, any ideology, any institution, any scheme—anything—priority over God, we succumb to a form of *idolatry*. We must maintain constant vigilance, lest any unworthy "ism"—even a good cause—begins to usurp God's place of pre-eminence in our lives.

TOPIC FOR ADULTS
ACCEPTING RESPONSIBILITY

Nation's Real Line of Defense. In the ancient world, the great Babylonian Empire was thought to be invincible. Its capital, Babylon, was apparently impregnable to enemy attackers, with thick walls that could withstand any siege. No foreign power could topple mighty Babylon, ruler of the world. In 539 B.C., however, Cyrus the Great conquered the city without breaching those thick walls.

How did he do it? A few months earlier, Cyrus had come disguised as a visitor's servant and had bribed a greedy money lender to show him the city. Cyrus returned home quietly. The waters of the Euphrates mysteriously lowered. When the river was only knee-deep, Cyrus led his army under the wall one night and seized the city without a fight. Instead of attacking the city walls directly, Cyrus had learned from the greedy Babylonian money lender that he could divert the waters of the Euphrates into a huge, abandoned reservoir.

A nation's real strength lies not in its military might but in its respect for God's commandments. Words such as "morality" and "responsibility" and "duty" are not in vogue these days, but they describe how citizens maintain God's values in society. The people who personally live by such values are the true line of defense of a nation. A country can flourish when its citizens forsake greed and comfort and accept personal responsibility.

Recalling Our Heritage. The belief in personal responsibility to God and others has formed the ethical foundation for the United States of America from the days of the earliest New England settlers. The New England Confederation opens with the words, "Wherefore as we all came into these parts of America with one and the same end and aim, namely, to advance the kingdom of our Lord Jesus Christ. . . ." The first election held on American soil was in Salem on July 20, 1629. The Pastor and the teacher were elected, only after praise, prayer, and Scripture study.

If we could go back in time to August, 1629, in Salem, we would see the people gather and "covenant with the Lord and one with another and . . . bind ourselves in the presence of God to walk together in all his ways according as He is pleased to reveal Himself to us in His blessed Word."

Avoiding Cynicism and Fanaticism. Let us acknowledge the ultimate Ruler beyond all earthly rulers as the source and center of our life as a nation. Governments are held accountable to the Lord of all.

William Penn, a century before the creation of the Declaration of Independence, said it clearly: "Those people who will not be governed by God will be ruled by tyrants." One of the reasons the early colonists rebelled was the assumption on the part of the English king that he had the "divine right" of rulership. Divine right is reserved only for the Lord.

Apart from God, there will be tyranny. Apart from God, something or someone will be given the place of lordship: It may be a king, or a creed, or a sacred object such as a flag, or a myth, or a dictator. An anemic faith results in a sick patriotism.

Without God at the center of the life of a people, fanaticism or cynicism flourishes. Both "isms" are twisted forms of human good: fanaticism demands zeal without the possibility of doubt in mere human wisdom. Cynicism lifts human doubt to center stage, leaving divine guidance in the background.

Questions for Students on the Next Lesson. 1. What did it mean to "anoint" a king? 2. Why was Saul such an attractive candidate for kingship? 3. What was Saul's reaction when he was revealed as king? 4. Have you sometimes resisted accepting significant responsibilities? 5. What should we expect from our national leaders today?

TOPIC FOR YOUTH
WE WANT A HERO!

Desire to Follow. Pepe Jeans, a blue jeans manufacturing company, administered a thirty-minute questionnaire to eight hundred teenagers in malls in three different cities across the country. The firm also organized focus groups so young people could discuss their feelings about life . . . and jeans. The company even sent trained researchers to study the clothing in twenty typical teenagers' closets to find out what students owned and wore, why they wore particular garments, and how they felt about those clothes. All of this research was part of an attempt to understand what teenagers preferred in clothing.

Teenage Research Unlimited in Chicago questioned two thousand teenagers every six months so that it could tell clients such as Coke, Levi Strauss, and Frito-Lay what was in style. Similarly, Xtreme in New York, handling clients such as Pepsi, Nike, and J. Walter Thompson, made in-depth studies of young people's preferences.

These companies and their researchers understand that youth want to fit in with the culture around them and follow the fashion trends. Israel wanted to follow cultural trends, too. The Hebrew people wanted a king just like all the surrounding nations. Yet Samuel knew that Israel could easily slide away from its reliance on the Lord. Israel had to be unique. The nation had to follow its true Hero—the Lord God.

Heroes. Every year, researchers for the Gallup Youth Survey poll teenagers between the ages of 13 and 17 to find out which individual they most admire. In 1982, the most admired individuals were predominantly politicians. They included (in order of preference): Ronald Reagan, Jesse Jackson, Pope John Paul II, Jimmy Carter, and George Bush. In 1992, the top five still included three politicians. The most admired individuals were: George Bush, Jesse Jackson, Ronald Reagan, Michael Jordan, and Donald Trump.

Obviously, young people are aware of the influence political leaders have on their lives. Samuel points out for us, though, that the greatest quality of leadership is a reliance on God. The real leader must be one who follows the directions of the true King, Jesus Christ.

Fallout. On April 26, 1986, the Chernobyl nuclear power plant in the republic of the Ukraine suffered a near-meltdown. Large amounts of nuclear radiation were released from the burning reactor and carried downwind.

As predicted, the cancer rate among the people in the vicinity increased rapidly. Sadly, many cases were found in children. Childhood thyroid cancer skyrocketed from an average of four cases a year to sixty. Children are especially susceptible because the thyroid glands concentrate iodine, and huge amounts of radioactive iodine were released in the accident. The consequences of nuclear energy affected an entire nation.

In the same manner, the sin of disobedience spreads a kind of spiritual disease among a people. Samuel saw the potential consequences of rebellion affecting the whole nation. The people's demand for a king and the rejection of God would produce a fallout the people would never suspect. Samuel's warnings still stand as a reminder to us about what happens when God is replaced by someone or something else as leader.

Questions for Students on the Next Lesson. 1. Who was Israel's first king? 2. What is the purpose of anointing? 3. How was Saul actually chosen as king? 4. Why did Saul hide? 5. What characteristics should a leader possess?

LESSON 8—OCTOBER 23

SAUL'S OPPORTUNITY AS KING

Background Scripture: I Samuel 9:15—10:1a, 20-24
Devotional Reading: Psalm 106:40-48

KING JAMES VERSION

I SAMUEL 9:15 Now the Lord had told Samuel in his ear a day before Saul came, saying,

16 To morrow about this time I will send thee a man out of the land of Benjamin, and thou shalt anoint him to be captain over my people Israel, that he may save my people out of the hand of the Philistines: for I have looked upon my people, because their cry is come unto me.

17 And when Samuel saw Saul, the Lord said unto him, Behold the man whom I spake unto thee of! this same shall reign over my people.

10:1 Then Samuel took a vial of oil, and poured it upon his head, and kissed him, and said, Is it not because the Lord hath anointed thee to be captain over his inheritance?

20 And when Samuel had caused all the tribes of Israel to come near, the tribe of Benjamin was taken.

21 When he had caused the tribe of Benjamin to come near by their families, the family of Matri was taken, and Saul the son of Kish was taken: and when they sought him, he could not be found.

22 Therefore they enquired of the Lord further, if the man should yet come thither. And the Lord answered, Behold he hath hid himself among the stuff.

23 And they ran and fetched him thence: and when he stood among the people, he was higher than any of the people from his shoulders and upward.

24 And Samuel said to all the people, See ye him whom the Lord hath chosen, that there is none like him among all the people? And all the people shouted, and said, God save the king.

REVISED STANDARD VERSION

I SAMUEL 9:15 Now the day before Saul came, the Lord had revealed to Samuel: 16 "Tomorrow about this time I will send to you a man from the land of Benjamin, and you shall anoint him to be prince over my people Israel. He shall save my people from the hand of the Philistines; for I have seen the affliction of my people, because their cry has come to me" 17 When Samuel saw Saul, the Lord told him, "Here is the man of whom I spoke to you! He it is who shall rule over my people."

10:1 Then Samuel took a vial of oil and poured it on his head, and kissed him and said, "Has not the Lord anointed you to be prince over his people Israel? And you shall reign over the people of the Lord and you will save them from the hand of their enemies round about.

20 Then Samuel brought all the tribes of Israel near, and the tribe of Benjamin was taken by lot. 21 He brought the tribe of Benjamin near by its families, and the family of the Matrites was taken by lot; finally he brought the family of the Matrites near man by man, and Saul the son of Kish was taken by lot. But when they sought him, he could not be found. 22 So they inquired again of the Lord, "Did the man come hither?" and the Lord said, "Behold, he has hidden himself among the baggage." 23 Then they ran and fetched him from there; and when he stood among the people, he was taller than any of the people from his shoulders upward. 24 And Samuel said to all the people, "Do you see him whom the Lord has chosen? There is none like him among all the people." And all the people shouted, "Long live the king!"

KEY VERSE: *Samuel . . . said, "Has not the Lord anointed you to be prince over his people Israel?"* I Samuel 10:1a.

HOME DAILY BIBLE READINGS

Oct.	17	M.	I Samuel 9:1-10	*Saul Seeks Help from a Seer*
Oct.	18	T.	I Samuel 9:11-21	*Saul Comes to Samuel*
Oct.	19	W.	I Samuel 9:22—10:1	*Samuel Anoints Saul to Be King*
Oct.	20	T.	I Samuel 10:2-8	*Signs to Confirm Saul's Appointment*
Oct.	21	F.	I Samuel 10:9-16	*Saul's Heart Is Changed*
Oct.	22	S.	I Samuel 10:17-26	*Saul's Kingship Affirmed by Israel*
Oct.	23	S.	I Samuel 11	*Saul's Victory over Israel's Enemy*

BACKGROUND

What the Israelites had really asked for was a military dictatorship like the Philistines had. "Now appoint for us a king to govern us like all the nations," they demanded. Samuel took their plea to the Lord.

God denied the request for an absolute dictator but did grant Israel a constitutional monarch. However, God reserved the right to choose His own leader and stated that this new king was to be anointed by His special representative, Samuel. The Lord also, in effect, added to the Law of Moses an important amendment: King as well as people must obey God! This was a "first" in human history. Previously, kings and people assumed that rulers' powers were absolute and that kings were not accountable to anyone.

Samuel set out to find the candidate God would select. The old prophet undoubtedly felt some personal disappointment because his own sons had turned out to be such greedy incompetents rather than worthy successors. But Samuel obeyed God. When he finally encountered the young giant, Saul, it appeared that God's choice was at hand. Samuel secretly anointed Saul. (Interestingly, the Hebrew term for "anointed one" [that is, "Messiah"] means the same as the Greek term *Christos*. Both terms have been used as titles for Jesus.)

If ever a man seemed to have all the attributes for a great king, it was Saul. He started his career as one of the most gifted and promising personalities in the Bible. A giant in every way, Saul towered head and shoulders above everyone else. He had a heart to match his size. For example, when one group refused to give him allegiance at his coronation and acted sourly toward him, Saul showed great restraint and attempted no personal vengeance (I Sam. 10:27).

Saul was refreshingly self-effacing in an age when humility was little practiced. When singled out and pressed to accept the kingship, he protested his unworthiness by reminding everyone of his humble background. Once crowned, however, Saul quickly distinguished himself. When messengers told him that Jabesh-Gilead was being attacked, Saul was busy plowing. No regal airs here! Yet Saul moved decisively. Summoning all able-bodied men in his realm, he repelled the invaders and saved the city of Jabesh-Gilead. This brawny giant was an inspired choice, everyone agreed.

NOTES ON THE PRINTED TEXT

Israel's elders stood by their demand for a king in spite of Samuel's ominous prediction. Samuel sent them away, promising them that he would find them a king. Returning home, he waited for a sign from the Lord. Soon, God told Samuel that He was sending him a man who would lead the people to victory over the Philistines. The man would come from the smallest of Israel's twelve tribes, Benjamin. *Tomorrow about this time I will send to you a man from the land of Benjamin, and you shall anoint him to be prince over my people Israel. He shall save my people from the hand of the Philistines* (9:16).

In the meantime, for three days Saul and a servant had been fruitlessly searching for some lost donkeys. Unable to find them, Saul planned to give up the search and return home. The servant, though, advised Saul to speak with Samuel. Perhaps the old prophet and seer could tell them where to look for the donkeys. The servant even offered to pay.

Here is the man of whom I spoke to you! He it is who shall rule over my people (9:17). Samuel was on his way to the high place to make a sacrifice. When Samuel met Saul, the Lord told him that Saul was the one who would rule over Israel. Saul was to be anointed as Israel's liberator. *Then Samuel took a vial of oil and poured it on his head, and kissed him* (10:1).

In an old Middle Eastern ritual, Samuel anointed Saul as king. The mixture used for the anointing was typically a fine grade of olive oil, frequently scented with herbs and perfumes. Often it was poured from a horn-shaped vessel. (One such vessel with its cup banded in gold was unearthed at Megiddo by modern-day archaeologists.) Perhaps Saul was anointed from this type of vessel or from a small earthen flask similar to the modest five-inch clay vessel wrapped in palm fibers found in a cave near Qumran. The flask contained a thick vegetable oil with a honey-like consistency that may have been a fragrant balsam oil or the oil of a persimmon plant. Because the flask had been carefully hidden and buried in a pit three feet deep, and because the flask contained an unidentifiable oil, archaeologists believe the oil may have been used to anoint the ancient kings of Israel.

The anointing was done in secret. Saul returned home but said nothing about being anointed king. One week later, Samuel gathered the twelve tribes together at Mizpah. He planned to announce the name of Israel's first king, confirming Saul publicly.

Surprisingly, the new king could not be found. *When they sought him, he could not be found* (10:21). Saul was nervous and reticent; he had hidden himself. The expectant crowd, eager to see its new king, had to ask God for his whereabouts! The Lord instructed the people that Saul was hiding among the people's baggage.

Saul was found and his height made a great impression. *When he stood among the people, he was taller than any of the people from his shoulders upward* (10:23). He literally stood head and shoulders above others!

Samuel presented Saul to the people. *Do you see him whom the Lord has chosen?* (10:24). Before them stood God's picked candidate. The people joyfully shouted and cried. *Long live the king!* (10:24). They enthusiastically acknowledged their allegiance.

SUGGESTIONS TO TEACHERS

Imagine being a reporter interviewing young Saul when Samuel anointed him king. What a glowing article you would write! You would no doubt comment on his looks and mannerisms. You would state that the country surely had a promising future with such an impressive man in leadership.

Setting up an imaginary interview with new King Saul might be a good way to get into the lesson with your students. Here are some of the important points that might be covered in such an interview:

1. APPEALING. Saul certainly *looked* like a king. His commanding presence because of his towering height seemed to make Saul the perfect candidate. But looks aren't everything. Although Saul was endowed with physical attributes that made him appear regal, he eventually proved to be morally, emotionally, and spiritually flawed. Remind your group members that, in spite of all our modern-day advertising about the importance of attractiveness, outward appearance is not the most essential matter in God's view.

2. ACCLAIMED. Saul was chosen by Samuel, who acted on the Lord's instructions. Yet Saul declined when Samuel first confronted him with the task of serving as Israel's first king. When we are presented with challenges to serve God, we also may try to back away. Point out that, like Saul, each member of Christ's body has been chosen by God. Is not baptism, for instance, similar to anointing in that it declares one's identification with the Lord's royal family?

3. ACCEPTABLE. Emphasize Saul's humility at the time he was chosen. Saul would not boast about his family or his background (see I Sam. 9:21). Later, when the time for his coronation arrived, Saul hid himself out of reluctance to push his candidacy. Discuss with your students the practical nature of true Christian humility. Be sure to refer to the humility exhibited by Jesus. Ask students to share about contemporary examples of genuine humility they have witnessed.

4. ANOINTED. Saul was given great opportunity when he was anointed as king. His anointing and coronation were not intended to elevate him to a superior status, but to position him for God's service.

For us, too, the opportunities to carry out the Lord's purposes are more abundant for than we may realize. Talk about the kinds of opportunities to serve that might be overlooked. Remind your students that they are "anointed" for daily service.

TOPIC FOR ADULTS
OVERCOMING RELUCTANCE TO LEAD

Don't Feel Like It? The woman's voice from downstairs in the kitchen was insistent. "Johnny! Get up! It's time to get ready for Sunday school and church!"

A sleepy voice replied, "Aw, I'm too tired."

The woman called back, "Come on, Johnny. You have to get up."

Upstairs, the whining answer came, "But I don't feel like it today."

The next sound was the firm footsteps of the woman of the house tramping up the stairs. She threw open the bedroom door and called. "Johnny! Get up at once! You are forty-two years old. And besides, you are the minister of the church!"

Like Johnny, we do not always feel like carrying out our responsibilities. Most of us don't jump to accept difficult leadership tasks. But God gives us all important assignments in His Kingdom work. We may feel reluctant, we may make excuses, but we have been chosen to serve Him.

Mark of a World Leader. When you go through the speeches and letters of Lincoln you may find the word "responsibility" about as often as you find the word "freedom." Lincoln wanted freedom, for all men, everywhere. He has become a world figure, in a certain sense, adopted by the whole family of humankind because of what he represented in the name of human freedom. Yet we will have to go far to find any human struggler so keenly and so sincerely weighted down by the burden of personal responsibility that he assumed on his own as a volunteer, as a citizen free and willing.—Carl Sandburg

Humility. Broadcast journalist David Brinkley is honest and humble enough to tell this story on himself: Once, while Brinkley was co-anchoring the news with Chet Huntley, a woman approached him. "Aren't you Chet Huntley?" she asked. To avoid embarrassing her, Brinkley smiled and said that he was.

"Well," she continued, "I like *you*. But how can you put up with that idiot Brinkley?"

Few famous persons display the virtue of genuine humility. Saul showed a humble spirit at the start of his reign, but few others can.

Questions for Students on the Next Lesson. 1. What made the Philistines such powerful adversaries? 2. What was Saul's primary sin? 3. In what ways did Saul disobey God? 4. How did Saul try to justify himself? 5. Have you ever grown impatient with God and tried to take matters into your own hands? What happened?

TOPIC FOR YOUTH
ME? A LEADER?

Not Luck, but Choice. Casino managers provided high roller Debra Kim Cohen with free VIP perks such as free meals, limo service, and rooms. They were unconcerned that Debra was only seventeen, four years under New Jersey's legal gambling age. The owners maintained that she was an exception and had great luck! However, she did not. Debra, one of a million teenaged compulsive gamblers, eventually lost thousands of dollars at the blackjack tables at various casinos in Atlantic City.

Christians believe that God controls the world; not chance or luck. Belief in luck denies the dominion of God. It substitutes pure chance as the supreme power in life, thereby undermining God's rule.

Saul's choice as king was not by luck. God chose Saul, and it was God's will that Samuel anoint Saul. The same God has chosen you to lead in His Kingdom causes. Allow Him to use you.

True Leader. Eighteen-year-old Shannon Huddleston won the Louis Caplan Human Relations Award from the Pittsburgh Chapter of the American Jewish Committee. Through her efforts, UNITY was organized at Mt. Lebanon High School. UNITY was created to foster racial harmony and to promote tolerance and a greater appreciation of differences.

The interracial group of thirty-five young people researched the human relations contributions of famous African-Americans and developed a showcase of civil rights-era highlights. They brought in speakers, sponsored field trips to galleries featuring black art, and invited an African dance group to entertain the students and community residents.

Although Shannon never experienced any racially motivated problems or prejudice, she was aware that many of the white students held wrong perceptions of black people. She wanted them to see the positive side of black culture. She knew she had to start somewhere. Organizing a group of interracial students was one way to make a difference.

Shannon discovered that she was a willing and capable leader. She was able to form a model interracial program that brought her honor and a scholarship. Here is a young woman who sensed that God had chosen her to act as a leader.

Leadership Qualities. He failed the sixth grade; no one expected much from him. However, Winston Churchill went on to become England's greatest Prime Minister, spending sixty years as a member of the House of Commons and leading his nation through World War II.

Another man entered the Black Hawk War as a captain and was released as a private. He failed later in almost a dozen business ventures. Yet Abraham Lincoln went on to become America's sixteenth president and to lead the nation through the Civil War.

If you doubt that you have leadership potential, look at these stories or at Saul's story. God transforms ordinary individuals into exceptional leaders. He takes the ordinary and creates new powerful men and women to lead! He did it with Saul, and He can do it with you.

Questions for Students on the Next Lesson. 1. Early in his reign, what did Saul do that angered Samuel? 2. What explanation did Saul offer to Samuel? 3. What was Samuel's judgment upon Saul? 4. Do you think this was fair? Why, or why not? 5. Have you ever been unfairly judged for a decision that you made? Describe the incident.

LESSON 9—OCTOBER 30

KING SAUL DISOBEYS GOD

Background Scripture: I Samuel 13
Devotional Reading: I Samuel 15:22-26

KING JAMES VERSION

I SAMUEL 13:5 And the Philistines gathered themselves together to fight with Israel, thirty thousand chariots, and six thousand horsemen, and people as the sand which is on the sea shore in multitude: and they came up, and pitched in Michmash, eastward from Bethaven.

6 When the men of Israel saw that they were in a strait, (for the people were distressed,) then the people did hide themselves in caves, and in thickets, and in rocks, and in high places, and in pits.

7 And some of the Hebrews went over Jordan to the land of Gad and Gilead. As for Saul, he was yet in Gilgal, and all the people followed him trembling.

8 And he tarried seven days, according to the set time that Samuel had appointed: but Samuel came not to Gilgal; and the people were scattered from him.

9 And Saul said, Bring hither a burnt offering to me, and peace offerings. And he offered the burnt offering.

10 And it came to pass, that as soon as he had made an end of offering the burnt offering, behold, Samuel came; and Saul went out to meet him, that he might salute him.

11 And Samuel said, What hast thou done? And Saul said, Because I saw that the people were scattered from me, and that thou camest not within the days appointed, and that the Philistines gathered themselves together at Michmash;

12 Therefore said I, The Philistines will come down now upon me to Gilgal, and I have not made supplication unto the Lord: I forced myself therefore, and offered a burnt offering.

13 And Samuel said to Saul, Thou hast done foolishly: thou hast not kept the commandment of the Lord thy God, which he commanded thee: for now would the Lord have established thy kingdom upon Israel for ever.

14 But now thy kingdom shall not continue: the Lord hath sought him a man after his own heart, and the Lord hath commanded him to be captain over his people, because thou hast not kept that which the Lord commanded thee.

REVISED STANDARD VERSION

I SAMUEL 13:5 And the Philistines mustered to fight with Israel, thirty thousand chariots, and six thousand horsemen, and troops like the sand on the seashore in multitude; they came up and encamped in Michmash, to the east of Bethaven. 6 When the men of Israel saw that they were in straits (for the people were hard pressed), the people hid themselves in caves and in holes and in rocks and in tombs and in cisterns, 7 or crossed the fords of the Jordan to the land of Gad and Gilead. Saul was still at Gilgal, and all the people followed him trembling.

8 He waited seven days, the time appointed by Samuel; but Samuel did not come to Gilgal, and the people were scattering from him. 9 So Saul said, "Bring the burnt offering here to me, and the peace offerings." And he offered the burnt offering. 10 As soon as he had finished offering the burnt offering, behold, Samuel came; and Saul went out to meet him and salute him. 11 Samuel said, "What have you done?" And Saul said, "When I saw that the people were scattering from me, and that you did not come within the days appointed, and that the Philistines had mustered at Michmash, 12 I said, 'Now the Philistines will come down upon me at Gilgal and I have not entreated the favor of the Lord'; so I forced myself, and offered the burnt offering." 13 And Samuel said to Saul, "You have done foolishly; you have not kept the commandment of the Lord your God, which he commanded you; for now the Lord would have established your kingdom over Israel for ever." 14 But now your kingdom shall not continue; the Lord has sought out a man after his own heart; and the Lord has appointed him to be prince over his people, because you have not kept what the Lord commanded you."

KEY VERSE: Your kingdom shall not continue . . . because you have not kept what the Lord commanded you. I Samuel 13:14.

HOME DAILY BIBLE READINGS

Oct.	24	M.	I Samuel 13:1-7a	*Saul Battles the Philistines*
Oct.	25	T.	I Samuel 13:7b-14	*Samuel Condemns Saul's Offering and Leadership*
Oct.	26	W.	I Samuel 13:15-22	*Saul's Army Lacks Weapons*
Oct.	27	T.	I Samuel 14:52—15:9	*Saul Disobeys God's Command*
Oct.	28	F.	I Samuel 15:10-19	*Samuel Disregards Saul's Excuses*
Oct.	29	S.	I Samuel 15:20-29	*God Rejects Saul as King*
Oct.	30	S.	I Samuel 15:34—16:3	*Samuel's Commission to Anoint Another King*

BACKGROUND

The story of Saul's life seemed to unfold like a Shakespearean tragedy. Endowed with immense potential to become a superb ruler of God's people, Saul eventually disintegrated into a murderous psychotic.

Divinely appointed and divinely empowered at the start of his reign, Saul apparently had a bright future ahead. The Scriptures state that "God gave him another heart" and "the spirit of God came mightily upon him" (I Sam. 10:9, 10). The one-time farm boy was God's man. A good organizer, he managed to put together the necessary financial, military, legal, and judicial structures to govern the new nation. Personally brave, he led his forces and drubbed any desert tribes who threatened his people.

Saul's downfall began when he presumed he could take over for the Lord. Instead of continuing to see himself as God's servant, Saul gave in to the fatal error of imagining that he was the Lord's equal or even God's superior. The relationship between king and Creator became estranged as Saul began to do as he wished. Finally, "the Spirit of the Lord departed from Saul" (I Sam. 16:14).

Saul's case fascinates certain psychiatrists. His dark, destructive moods led to attempted murder. Suspicious of everyone, Saul could not trust anyone and became alienated from the human race as well as from God. Saul's life seems to be the story of a person who tried to kill off God in his life, tried to kill others who crossed him, and eventually succeeded in killing himself.

Today's lesson tells about Saul taking over the priestly office. The Israelites were battling for independence against the Philistines, and though the Philistines had superior technology, holding a monopoly on iron weapons manufacturing, the Israelites understood from Samuel that they were led by the Lord. God's guidance, Saul and his nation knew, was what would bring them victory over the stronger, better armed Philistines. Nevertheless, Saul took matters into his own hands, disobeying God and displaying a pattern of willfulness that would culminate in his own death.

NOTES ON THE PRINTED TEXT

Saul, Israel's new king, focused his attention on Israel's enemy, the Philistines. He gathered three thousand soldiers and assigned them to their stations. Saul's son, Jonathan, commanded one thousand soldiers at Gibeah while Saul commanded two thousand, half of which were in Michmash (a small Benjamite village) and the remainder spread throughout the hills around Bethel. After Jonathan's victory at Geba, Saul mobilized all of Israel to fight the Philistines.

The Philistines mustered to fight with Israel, thirty thousand chariots, and six thousand horsemen, and troops like the sand on the seashore (13:5). Because the Philistines had initially discounted the importance of Israel, especially its new king, they did not move quickly to destroy Saul. Perhaps Saul's action of dispersing his followers to their homes had lulled the Philistines into a false sense of security. Their hesitation allowed Israel under Jonathan to win the first victory. Quickly, the Philistines mustered their forces with precision. Heavily armed, better equipped, well supplied and disciplined, the Philistines marched. Their enormous and overwhelming forces encamped at Michmash.

When the men of Israel saw that they were in straits . . . the people hid themselves (13:6). Israel's initial joy quickly turned to fear. Caves in the limestone hills began to fill with frightened people. The bell-shaped cisterns that normally caught precious rain water became hiding places; along with various holes, and even tombs. Other people fled across the Jordan River seeking refuge. Still others ran trembling to Gilgal where their new king followed Samuel's instructions and waited.

He waited seven days, the time appointed by Samuel; but Samuel did not come to Gilgal, and the people were scattering from him (13:8). Saul tried to rally the volunteer militia and maintain its loyalty, but each day the sight of the massive Philistine army took its toll on the Israelites' morale. At night, Saul's army diminished as men deserted *en masse* and slipped across the river or into the hills. Still, Samuel did not arrive. Saul was desperate.

"Bring the burnt offering here to me, and the peace offerings." And he offered the burnt offering (13:9). Finally, Saul offered the sacrifice himself, an act to remind the army of God's presence and commitment to the war. It was designed to rally the troops. Saul did what he felt was necessary since Samuel never specifically prohibited him from making the sacrifice. However, Saul was a king and a soldier, and Samuel had not authorized him to make the sacrifice.

What have you done? (13:11). When Samuel finally did arrive, Saul had just finished the sacrifice. Poor Saul innocently went to welcome and greet the old prophet. Literally, he went to bless him. Samuel, however, was furious, bitterly accusing Saul of gross disobedience.

Seeking to justify himself, Saul explained the reason for his action. He protested that Samuel's delay was nearly fatal. Of the three thousand men only six hundred remained. *The people were scattering from me* (13:11). He also added that the Philistines were deploying their troops and securing the area. He did not want to start the battle without the appropriate religious sacrifice. Saul told Samuel that since he was so late, he had to force himself to offer the sacrifice. He maintained he did not want to usurp

Samuel's power nor did he perform the sacrifice out of greed. He had made the sacrifice out of necessity.

You have done foolishly; you have not kept the commandment of the Lord your God (13:13). Samuel condemned Saul's action as a violation of God's command. The specific commandment was not mentioned. Then Samuel announced to Saul that as a result of his action, his kingdom would *not continue* (13:14).

As if all this judgment were not enough, another harsh announcement followed. God had chosen someone else to be ruler over Israel. *The Lord has sought out a man after his own heart; and . . . appointed him to be prince over his people, because you have not kept what the Lord commanded you* (13:14). Then Samuel departed angrily.

SUGGESTIONS TO TEACHERS

You don't have to hold a degree in psychiatric medicine to discuss the case of King Saul. His career is a tragic example of a person who refuses to obey God and ends by trying to murder God in his life, murder others, and finally, murder himself.

Although today's lesson covers only one episode in Saul's life, you may wish to read several chapters that follow chapter 13 in order to trace the rest of Saul's sad story. This will put the material in I Samuel 13 in proper context.

1. PRESUMPTUOUS DEFICIENCY. Saul disobeyed, wrongfully deciding to act as a priest. This act, while it may seem innocent to us, was a deliberate flaunting of God's instructions as given by Samuel. Naturally, Saul thought he had good reasons; he could rationalize his behavior. Part of the insidious nature of sin is the way we humans can find ways of exonerating ourselves from guilt. Saul's action showed him to be an impatient, untrusting leader who thought that God could be manipulated. Is this not the problem with each sinner?

2. PROMISED DESTRUCTION. Allow your group members plenty of time to examine Saul's character and his flaws. Note details of Saul's thinking and behavior at Gilgal. Foundational to everything that happened that day was Saul's rebelliousness against the authority of the Lord.

For some in your class, the word "sin" may mean merely sexual misdemeanor. Help your class to understand that sin is "any want [or lack] of conformity unto, or transgression of, the law of God," as the old Shorter Catechism stated it. Rejection of the Lord brings the destruction of a personality.

3. PREDICTABLE DECLINE. Sin also has corporate effects. It is never "merely a personal matter." Samuel warned Saul that his refusal to heed God's instructions would have dire consequences within his own family and within the nation. This point needs to be taken most seriously by your students. The prevailing philosophy of our day proclaims that "I have the right to be happy." Our culture trumpets distrust of all authority, including God's, encouraging each person to follow his or her own whims and wishes in the pursuit of personal pleasure. Families and nations decline and fall when individuals leave moral absolutes behind.

TOPIC FOR ADULTS
CONSEQUENCES OF DISOBEDIENCE

Cost: Two Runs. Dave Cone was pitching for the New York Mets one afternoon in 1990. In a game against the Atlanta Braves, the batter hit a ball to the first baseman and Cone ran to cover first base, where he apparently put the runner out. The umpire, however, ruled that the runner was safe, stating that Cone's foot had not touched the bag. Cone protested, yelling and arguing with the umpire. Meanwhile, Cone's teammates were yelling at him to throw the ball. Cone, still holding the ball, continued his angry shouting match with the umpire. While Cone ignored the infield to protest the call—disobeying all the instructions of his coaches—two Atlanta runners raced safely home!

Costly Blunder. Field Marshall Bernard Montgomery wanted a British masterstroke to end the war in Europe in 1944. He decided to launch a British attack on Arnhem, in German-occupied Holland. However, many other officers, including his intelligence officer, Brian Urquhart, and the officer put in charge of the operation against Arnhem, General Browning, advised Montgomery that the operation, called "Market Garden," would end disastrously.

Montgomery's plan called for airborne troops to land sixty miles ahead of ground troops in order to take out three main bridges over three wide rivers.Then the relieving ground troops would move across low country, and the 1st Airborne Division would land in the area where two of the best Panzer divisions in the German Army, the 9th and 10th S.S. Panzer Divisions, were refitting. The complex plan seemed hopeless to Montgomery's staff, but Montgomery overruled all objections. Going against all advice, General Montgomery insisted on carrying out his pet scheme, "Market Garden." The consequences of this action cost the lives of 12,000 Allied men, and, according to some experts, significantly prolonged the war.

Dictator's Disobedience. Napoleon strutted proudly as a mighty emperor in the early nineteenth century. Disdaining to have a representative of the church preside at his lavish coronation, Napoleon even insisted on placing the crown on his head himself. The proud master of France and most of the Continent felt no need to obey anyone, not even God. He twisted the ministry of the Christian church in his realm into a civil religion glorifying him and the state. Perhaps Napoleon's greatest conceit was decreeing that his birthday, August 15, be celebrated as the Feast of St. Napoleon everywhere in his realm.

God demands that dictators obey him. Ultimately, He will bring about the downfall of even the most daring and despotic who insist on defying Him.

Questions for Students on the Next Lesson. 1. How did David come to be anointed as king? 2. Why did David want to build a temple? 3. What was Nathan's message to David regarding the plan to build the temple? 4. In II Samuel 7 what are the two meanings of the word "house" ? 5. What was the substance of God's promise to David?

TOPIC FOR YOUTH
AM I TO BLAME?

Excuses Won't Work. Young John Rosano, Jr., was stopped by the Massachusetts State Police. A trooper had clocked Rosano's speed at 120 MPH. Rosano explained to the startled policeman that he had just purchased a hot roast-beef sandwich and wanted to get home to eat it before it got cold!

Like Rosano, many young people try to justify their actions when called to account by others. Saul was no different; he offered an excuse, too. Samuel saw through that ancient deception as clearly as the state trooper saw through the modern-day excuse. Deception fails.

Not to Blame. Ryan White, 18, died on April 8, 1990, after a five-year battle with AIDS. The whole American nation mourned. Ryan showed a stunned nation that not all cases of AIDS stem from immoral behavior.

When White was 13, he was diagnosed with the disease and subsequently barred from his school near Kokomo, Indiana. School officials simply rejected the health authorities' claims that AIDS could not be spread through casual contact, and Ryan was attacked viciously by other students. "Ryan White jokes" poked fun at him. Rumors circulated that he was spitting on vegetables at the local supermarket. Students at school spray-painted obscenities on his locker. Finally, the Whites moved and were welcomed in nearby Arcadia. Ryan was befriended by students at Hamilton Heights High School.

Was Ryan to blame for his disease? No! He had not used illegal drugs, nor had he been involved in casual sex. He had contracted the disease through a blood-clotting agent used to treat his hemophilia.

In the midst of his terrible situation, Ryan became an inspiration to many who suffer terminal illnesses. He also stood for greater Christian compassion toward those who have contracted AIDS, whether through blood transfusions or through promiscuous sex. Ryan knew that he was not to blame for his situation, as so many are by their foolish actions. He used his illness to reach out to others. As Christians we are called to reach out in compassion while modeling the risk-free biblical standard: sexual abstinence before marriage.

Fatal Consequences. Jack Liebmann and George Taylor were classmates. On September 30, 1991, the two were "horsing around" in Pittsburgh's Allderdice High School's shop class. When they walked out of the classroom into the hallway, Taylor struck Liebmann on the side of the jaw. Liebmann fell, got up, then fell again. Paramedics were called to treat the collapsed youth. They took the teenager to the hospital, where he was pronounced dead! Taylor was arrested and charged with criminal homicide (which was later, after an investigation, changed to involuntary manslaughter).

Taylor expressed extraordinary remorse as he underwent psychotherapy. He, like the two families, was grief-stricken over the death of his friend. There simply was no way to justify his actions. It had all been in fun, he thought. One wrong decision had brought a terrible consequence.

Saul, too, made a wrong decision and suffered the consequences for his wrongdoing. His kingdom would not continue because God had chosen another ruler.

Questions for Students on the Next Lesson. 1. Why did David want to build a temple? 2. Why did God not permit David to build the temple? 3. What promise did God make to David? 4. Did God fulfill His promise? 5. In what ways have you seen God's involvement in your own life?

LESSON 10—NOVEMBER 6

DAVID CLAIMS GOD'S PROMISE

Background Scripture: II Samuel 7
Devotional Reading: Psalm 86:1-12

KING JAMES VERSION

II SAMUEL 7:18 Then went king David in, and sat before the LORD, and he said, Who am I, O Lord God? and what is my house, that thou hast brought me hitherto?

19 And this was yet a small thing in thy sight, O Lord God; but thou hast spoken also of thy servant's house for a great while to come. And is this the manner of man, O Lord God?

20 And what can David say more unto thee? for thou, Lord God, knowest thy servant.

21 For thy word's sake, and according to thine own heart, hast thou done all these great things, to make thy servant know them.

22 Wherefore thou art great, O Lord God: for there is none like thee, neither is there any God beside thee, according to all that we have heard with our ears.

23 And what one nation in the earth is like thy people, even like Israel, whom God went to redeem for a people to himself, and to make him a name, and to do for you great things and terrible, for thy land, before thy people, which thou redeemedst to thee from Egypt, from the nations and their gods?

24 For thou hast confirmed to thyself thy people Israel to be a people unto thee for ever: and thou, Lord, art become their God.

25 And now, O Lord God, the word that thou hast spoken concerning thy servant, and concerning his house, establish it for ever, and do as thou hast said.

26 And let thy name be magnified for ever, saying, The Lord of hosts is the God over Israel: and let the house of thy servant David be established before thee.

27 For thou, O Lord of hosts, God of Israel, hast revealed to thy servant, saying, I will build thee an house: therefore hath thy servant found in his heart to pray this prayer unto thee.

28 And now, O Lord God, thou art that God, and thy words be true, and thou hast promised this goodness unto thy servant:

29 Therefore now let it please thee to bless the house of thy servant, that it may continue for ever before thee: for thou, O Lord God, hast spoken it: and with thy blessing let the

REVISED STANDARD VERSION

II SAMUEL 7:18 Then King David went in and sat before the Lord, and said, "Who am I, O Lord God, and what is my house, that thou hast brought me thus far? 19 And yet this was a small thing in thy eyes, O Lord God; thou has spoken also of thy servant's house for a great while to come, and has shown me future generations, O Lord God! 20 And what more can David say to thee? For thou knowest thy servant, O Lord God! 21 Because of thy promise, and according to thy own heart, thou has wrought all this greatness, to make thy servant know it. 22 Therefore thou art great, O Lord God; for there is none like thee, and there is no God besides thee, according to all that we have he70 ard with our ears. 23 What other nation on earth is like thy people Israel, whom God went to redeem to be his people, making himself a name, and doing for them great and terrible things, by driving out before his people a nation and its gods? 24 And thou didst establish for thyself thy people Israel to be thy people for ever; and thou, O Lord, didst become their God. 25 And now, O Lord God, confirm for ever the word which thou hast spoken concerning thy servant and concerning his house, and do as thou hast spoken; 26 and thy name will be magnified for ever, saying, 'The Lord of hosts is God over Israel,' and the house of thy servant David will be established before thee. 27 For thou, O Lord of hosts, the God of Israel, hast made this revelation to thy servant, saying, 'I will build you a house'; therefore thy servant has found courage to pray this prayer to thee. 28 And now, O Lord God, thou art God, and thy words are true, and thou hast promised this good thing to thy servant; 29 now therefore may it please thee to bless the house of thy servant, that it may continue for ever before thee; for thou, O Lord God, hast spoken, and with thy blessing shall the house of thy servant be blessed for ever."

house of thy servant be blessed for ever.

KEY VERSE: O Lord God, confirm for ever the word which thou hast spoken concerning thy servant and concerning his house, and do as thou hast spoken. II Samuel 7:25.

HOME DAILY BIBLE READINGS

Oct.	31	M.	II Samuel 5:1-10	*David Becomes King and Captures Jerusalem*
Nov.	1	T.	Psalm 89:1-8	*God's Covenant with David*
Nov.	2	W.	Psalm 89:19-27	*God Will Exalt David*
Nov.	3	T.	Psalm 89:28-37	*David's Line Will Endure Forever*
Nov.	4	F.	II Samuel 7:1-7	*David Wishes to Build a Temple*
Nov.	5	S.	II Samuel 7:8-17	*David's Son Will Build the Temple*
Nov.	6	S.	II Samuel 7:18-29	*Prayer for Blessing on David's House*

BACKGROUND

In contrast to King Saul, David was "a man after [God's] own heart" (I Sam. 13:14). Although David had been chosen during the early part of Saul's reign and anointed as king by Samuel, he would not step forward to claim his throne while Saul, God's anointed, was still alive. In fact, David refrained from taking Saul's life when opportunities arose. When Saul finally met his end, David mourned. Even then, David carefully refrained from taking over until he had asked the Lord whether he should make any political moves.

At first David ruled only over Judah. The northern tribes were not ready to accept his claims. Because David showed great statesmanship and diplomacy, he eventually won over all the Israelite tribes.

David's military abilities matched his governing skills. The Philistines realized the threat of this energetic young commander and suddenly attacked. Their attempt to squash David's kingdom before he could consolidate his power failed. David's brilliant campaign brought an end to Philistine military domination forever. By about 1000 B.C., David had secured his throne.

David's newly united nation needed a capital that would be neither in the southern realm of Judah nor in the northern area of the ten tribes of Israel. He shrewdly selected Jerusalem, situated in neutral ground, and developed this city as the focal point for the nation's government, religion, and business. Saul had murdered most of the priestly line of Aaron, but David collected the survivors of the massacre and assigned them to serve in the tabernacle in Jerusalem.

Out of the ruins of Saul's realm, David built the nation of Israel into one of the superpowers of the day. He extended the nation's boundaries nearly from the Euphrates in the north to the borders of Egypt. Briefly, Israel stood as the dominant power on the international scene. Military conquests brought commercial success as Israel profited by trade with conquered powers. The country also reaped the benefits from the iron industry that it now controlled. With better implements to use, especially in farming, food production increased, and the nation's population doubled.

With Israel's great golden age bringing peace and prosperity, David evaluated his capital at Jerusalem. Knowing the city was headquarters for both church and state, David determined to provide religion with a building as magnificent as his personal palace. The idea seemed to appeal to everyone. Everyone, that is, except the Lord! To David's intense disappointment, God refused to allow David to build the temple. However, the Lord would use David to provide an even greater "house." From the house of David, we remember, came Jesus!

NOTES ON THE PRINTED TEXT

Once David had conquered Jerusalem, he made plans to build a temple. This was David's dream, and the prophet Nathan initially agreed with his plans. However, God did not! Nathan quickly told David that the Lord desired no plush, holy structure. Instead of a house for the Lord, God would build David a dynasty. A warrior who had shed blood should not build the Lord's house. So David laid aside his plans for the shrine. *King David went in and sat before the Lord* (7:18). David entered the tent that housed the ark of the covenant. Since sitting was not normally a posture for prayer, David likely either knelt or laid down.

Who am I, O Lord God, and what is my house, that thou hast brought me thus far? (7:18). So close was David's relationship with God that he could speak God's awesome name. David prayed gratefully, aware of God's action in his life. He thought over his life, recalling God's involvement in it. He was astonished that God would have noticed an insignificant shepherd boy and would make him king. His greatness seemed insignificant compared to God's. Everything that happened to him was a result of God's graciousness. So David thanked God for the great things He had done and had promised to do in the future.

And yet this was a small thing in thy eyes, O Lord God; thou hast spoken also of thy servant's house for a great while to come, and hast shown me future generations, O Lord God! (7:19). The Lord had shown David the future, and David was thankful for God's promise of future involvement with his family. Overwhelmed by God's goodness and graciousness to him, David could only ask, *And what more can David say to thee? For thou knowest thy servant, O Lord God!* (7:20).

Reflecting on his life, David saw God's word and promise. Now he understood it to be a sign of God's warm and close relationship with him. *Because of thy promise, and according to thy own heart, thou hast wrought all this greatness, to make thy servant know it* (7:21).

Overwhelmed by God's greatness, David offered praise. *Thou art great, O Lord God; for there is none like thee, and there is no God besides thee, according to all that we have heard with our ears* (7:22).

In addition, David was aware of God's long relationship with Israel. He marveled that God had chosen Israel, had freed it from slavery, and had made a place for it by driving out other nations and their gods. Gladly he acknowledged God's involvement in the life of the country. *What other nation on earth is like thy people Israel, whom God went to redeem to be his people, making himself a name, and doing for them great and terrible things, by driving out before his people a nation and its gods? And thou didst establish for thyself thy people Israel to be thy people for ever; and thou, O Lord, didst become their God* (7:23, 24).

David was not embarrassed at all to pray, asking God to keep His promise to lift up the house of David forever. *And now, O Lord God, confirm for ever the word which thou hast spoken concerning thy servant and concerning his house, and do as thou hast spoken* (7:25).

David promised that he and the people of Israel would praise and magnify the name of God together. *Thy name will be magnified for ever, saying, "The Lord of hosts is God over Israel"* (7:26). David concluded by requesting that the Lord would fulfill His promise and bless David's house forever. *Now therefore may it please thee to bless the house of thy servant, that it may continue for ever before thee* (7:29).

SUGGESTIONS TO TEACHERS

Today's lesson is based on the time in history when David was at his most glorious. His nation, spanning the area from modern Iraq through Syria to Egypt, stood tall and secure. His plan to build a magnificent edifice for the Lord would also be a monument to David's power and piety. But God vetoed David's plan.

1. DREAM HOUSE. The idea of a lovely temple seemed good and right. After all, David's city of Jerusalem was the center of worship and held many grandiose buildings, including David's own palace. David set his heart on constructing a proper place for the Lord. His motives seemed pure and admirable. Yet God turned down David's plan.

This would be a good time to discuss with your students the occasions when God seems to say "No!" to us. We may feel disappointed, even angry at God when He refuses to go along with our dreams and plans. Invite your group members to tell about times when God seemed to block their plans. How did they handle those situations?

2. DISSENTING HEARER. Bring the prophet Nathan to center stage for a time. Notice how he listened to the Lord, and not just to his "boss," David. Nathan had the courage to go against King David's wishes! He probably knew that building the planned temple would bring great satisfaction to David. He also realized that it is not always wise or healthy to oppose the rich and powerful. But Nathan took the risk, standing up for God. Focus part of your lesson on the need for God's people to be prophetic even today.

3. DIFFERENT HOUSE. Help your students appreciate the play on words with the term *house*. "House" can mean both a building and a dynasty (or one's descendants). David learned that God had in mind a different kind of house than the one proposed. The Lord told David that he wouldn't erect a house of stone and wood, but he would found a house that will live on. Remind your class that Jesus descended from the lineage of David. God kept His promise to David about a "house."

4. DEMONSTRATED HUMILITY. David accepted God's refusal to erect

a house for worship in Jerusalem and trusted God's promise to have a house for posterity through his descendants. David's beautiful prayer should be studied as a model of good praying. Help your students see that David's prayer includes gratitude and acceptance. Such humility, the opposite of pride, must permeate all prayer.

TOPIC FOR ADULTS
CLAIMING GOD'S PROMISE

Unwanted Answer. Have you heard the story of the little boy whose mother found him on his knees beside his bed one evening, mumbling, "Tokyo! Tokyo, Tokyo—please, God." His mother finally asked what the meaning of the youngster's prayer was.

"Well, on the geography test today," the boy replied, "they asked the capital of France, and I put Tokyo. I'm praying to ask God to change the capital of France before my teacher sees my paper."

We don't like to hear anyone say "No" to us. It's hard to get turned down, and it's especially difficult to receive a refusal from God. Yet sometimes our prayers must inevitably bring "No" for an answer—particularly when our requests intend to fulfill selfish purposes or manipulate God in some way.

King David, cherishing his dreams to build a temple for the Lord, prepared to transfer his ideas to the drawing board. But God said "No."

"No" to David? Not build a place of worship? Not erect a soaring masterpiece of stone, with enormous walls and imposing towers, all for the glory of God? David felt this was not fair. He had been a man after God's heart; he had consulted with the Lord during every step of his rise from shepherd boy to king. Was David not God's anointed? Had he not prayed and composed those magnificent psalms, those devotional jewels that are regularly recited even today?

God had better plans. He wanted David to be remembered for an even greater "house"!

Humble General. Few great leaders can willingly step aside for someone else. David accepted God's insistence that David's dreams for a great house for the Lord be set aside. Not many have that humility. General Theodore Roosevelt, Jr., was one who also showed such a flash of greatness. On one occasion, Gen. Roosevelt was waiting at an airport during World War II. He overheard a young sailor talking to the airline agent at the ticket counter. "Please," pleaded the ordinary seaman, "I want to get home to see my mother before I'm shipped out. There's only a few days."

"Sorry," the woman behind the counter said. "There is simply no more space on a flight to your city. All the seats have been booked and taken."

Striding to the ticket counter, the General instructed the ticket agent to give the young seaman his place on the flight. An aide to the General saw and heard what was happening, and asked, "But General Roosevelt, aren't you in a hurry, too?"

Roosevelt answered, "It's a matter of rank. I'm only a general. This boy is a son."

Who Am I? As David prayed, he marveled at God's involvement in his own life. Have you ever wondered about God's role in the creation of your own body? You have an average of 750 movable muscles, 500 of which work in pairs. Your skin covers an area of 20 square feet. A postage-stamp sized piece of skin contains four yards of nerves, over a hundred sweat glands, fifteen oil glands, a yard of blood vessels, and over three million assorted cells. God's power created you. His power will continue to be at work in your life as it was in David's.

Questions for Students on the Next Lesson. 1. How did Nathan respond to David's sin? 2. What was the parable that Nathan told? 3. How did David respond to Nathan's parable? 4. Was David able to be forgiven? 5. How do you define sin?

TOPIC FOR YOUTH
CLAIMING PROMISES

The True Promise. Twenty-five years ago, in August, 1969, youth gathered on a farm in upstate New York for the Woodstock Music Festival. For the thousands who jammed the muddy fields, the weekend was to be a time that would be free from hypocrisy and the shams of life.

The young people expressed their deepest longings. They asked probing questions. Many were hungering for something authentic, sensing in their lives a spiritual vacuum that needed filling. They wanted joy and meaning in their lives. Unfortunately, the music, sex, drugs, and togetherness did not provide a lasting answer. They left the fields and returned to the same world they had tried so desperately to escape.

Like David, look at what God has done for you in Jesus Christ. He has been with you. Above all, He has redeemed you from sin through Jesus Christ. Claim the promise of true and lasting freedom that God has provided you.

Claiming Wellness. Dr. Brown, eminent plastic surgeon of St. Louis, told of a young lad who had come to his office. The boy had lost his hand at the wrist. Dr. Brown said that, as he sat down to talk with the boy, he said to the young man: "Tell me about your handicap." The boy responded quickly: "I don't have a handicap, Sir. I just don't have a right hand." As they talked together, Dr. Brown learned that this young man was one of the leading scorers on his high school football team.

Fulfilled Promise. Olympic diving champion Greg Louganis was spotted diving at the age of thirteen by Dr. Sammy Lee, himself a former Olympic champion. Dr. Lee approached the teenager and offered him the promise that one day Louganis would stand on the top of the Olympic victory platform, just as Lee had done.

Louganis trusted that promise and built his hopes on its fulfillment. Eventually, Dr. Lee's promise was indeed fulfilled.

God's promises may seem remote or unlikely at the moment. Throughout his life David learned that God's promises could be trusted. He knew God's promise of a "house" would be fulfilled and that his family line would continue.

Questions for Students on the Next Lesson. 1. What was David's sin? 2. Why did Nathan utilize a parable to confront David? 3. How did David respond to Nathan's story? 4. What was the judgment against David? 5. How did David handle his guilt?

LESSON 11—NOVEMBER 13

DAVID SINS AGAINST GOD

Background Scripture: II Samuel 11:1—12:19
Devotional Reading: 1 John 1:5-10

KING JAMES VERSION

II SAMUEL 12:1 And the Lord sent Nathan unto David. And he came unto him, and said unto him, There were two men in one city; the one rich, and the other poor.

2 The rich man had exceeding many flocks and herds:

3 But the poor man had nothing, save one little ewe lamb, which he had bought and nourished up: and it grew up together with him, and with his children; it did eat of his own meat, and drank of his own cup, and lay in his bosom, and was unto him as a daughter.

4 And there came a traveller unto the rich man, and he spared to take of his own flock and of his own herd, to dress for the wayfaring man that was come unto him; but took the poor man's lamb, and dressed it for the man that was come to him.

5 And David's anger was greatly kindled against the man; and he said to Nathan, As the Lord liveth, the man that hath done this thing shall surely die:

6 And he shall restore the lamb fourfold, because he did this thing, and because he had no pity.

7 And Nathan said to David, Thou art the man. Thus saith the Lord God of Israel, I anointed thee king over Israel, and I delivered thee out of the hand of Saul;

8 And I gave thee thy master's house, and thy master's wives into thy bosom, and gave thee the house of Israel and of Judah; and if that had been too little, I would moreover have given unto thee such and such things.

9 Wherefore hast thou despised the commandment of the Lord, to do evil in his sight? thou hast killed Uriah the Hittite with the sword, and hast taken his wife to be thy wife, and hast slain him with the sword of the children of Ammon.

10 Now therefore the sword shall never depart from thine house; because thou hast despised me, and hast taken the wife of Uriah the Hittite to be thy wife.

13 And David said unto Nathan, I have sinned against the Lord. And Nathan said unto David, The Lord also hath put away thy sin; thou shalt not die.

REVISED STANDARD VERSION

II SAMUEL 12:1 And the Lord sent Nathan to David. He came to him, and said to him, "There were two men in a certain city, the one rich and the other poor. 2 The rich man had very many flocks and herds; 3 but the poor man had nothing but one little ewe lamb, which he had bought. And he brought it up, and it grew up with him and with his children; it used to eat of his morsel, and drink from his cup, and lie in his bosom, and it was like a daughter to him. 4 Now there came a traveler to the rich man, and he was unwilling to take one of his own flock or herd to prepare for the wayfarer who had come to him, but he took the poor man's lamb, and prepared it for the man who had come to him." 5 Then David's anger was greatly kindled against the man; and he said to Nathan, "As the Lord lives, the man who has done this deserves to die; 6 and he shall restore the lamb fourfold, because he did this thing, and because he had no pity."

7 Nathan said to David, "You are the man. Thus says the Lord, the God of Israel, 'I anointed you king over Israel, and I delivered you out of the hand of Saul; 8 and I gave you your master's house, and your master's wives into your bosom, and gave you the house of Israel and of Judah; and if this were too little, I would add to you as much more. 9 Why have you despised the word of the Lord, to do what is evil in his sight? You have smitten Uriah the Hittite with the sword, and have taken his wife to be your wife, and have slain him with the sword of the Ammonites. 10 Now therefore the sword shall never depart from your house, because you have despised me, and have taken the wife of Uriah the Hittite to be your wife.'

13 David said to Nathan, "I have sinned against the Lord." And Nathan said to David, "The Lord also has put away your sin; you shall not die."

KEY VERSE: David said to Nathan, "I have sinned against the Lord."
II Samuel 12:13a.

HOME DAILY BIBLE READINGS

Nov.	7	*M.*	II Samuel 11:1-13	*David's Sin*
Nov.	8	*T.*	II Samuel 11:14-25	*David Causes Uriah's Death*
Nov.	9	*W.*	II Samuel 11:26—12:9	*Nathan Rebukes David*
Nov.	10	*T.*	II Samuel 12:10-14	*God's Judgment and Forgiveness*
Nov.	11	*F.*	Psalm 51:1-14	*A Prayer of Repentance*
Nov.	12	*S.*	Psalm 32:1-7	*Thanksgiving for Forgiveness*
Nov.	13	*S.*	II Samuel 12:15-23	*Death of the Child*

BACKGROUND

After a long struggle, David had developed his nation into a strong, stable power. David stood at the pinnacle of his career. He had overcome every setback and finally found himself without terrible pressures and worries. A splendid organizer, he had delegated responsibilities to capable subordinates. He had turned over the policing and peacekeeping to a tough old professional soldier, Joab, and no longer needed to be personally involved in the constant border skirmishes.

At that point in his life, David allowed himself to fall into an affair with the attractive wife of one of his army officers. What followed was a chain reaction of events that turned David's final years into a series of nightmarish family problems.

Some scholars suggest that the woman, Bathsheba, made a play for David by deliberately and provocatively bathing where she knew she would be observed by the king. After all, the royal palace was always higher than any other residence, and perhaps Bathsheba knew that the view from David's roof would reveal her bathing. This, of course, even if true, would not excuse David. Although other kings could give vent to their lustful impulses with any woman they wanted, Israel's kings were responsible to God and His standards of holiness.

When Bathsheba announced that she was pregnant, David tried to cover up the sordid affair by bringing her husband, Uriah, back from the frontier so that he would appear to have fathered the baby. David's ploy failed when Uriah insisted on maintaining his army discipline by not sleeping with his wife while on active duty. David then sank to the unspeakable depth of contriving to have the innocent, valiant Uriah picked off and killed in a minor military operation.

In any other kingdom and culture of the time, David might have gotten away with his deeds. But not in God's realm, or in God's nation. The Lord's spokesman, Nathan, boldly confronted the mighty David. Using a parable as his means of portraying David as the sinner he was, Nathan convicted King David of sinning against God. David recognized his sin, and showed remorse. However, the damage had been done, and David's reign became filled with intrigue, jealousies, and even a rebellion by a son.

NOTES ON THE PRINTED TEXT

David desired Bathsheba, the wife of Uriah the Hittite. In order to have her, he deliberately arranged Uriah's death. Perhaps David believed he had done nothing wrong, and he surely believed no one knew what he had done. He failed to face the fact that God knew.

The Lord sent Nathan to David (12:1). The Lord had sent Nathan to speak with David about David's actions. Obviously, Nathan had been a frequent visitor, a trusted adviser to the king, so he had no trouble gaining entry. Nathan announced that he knew of a situation that required David's attention. As the high court judge, David sat and listened.

There were two men in a certain city, the one rich and the other poor (12:1). Of the two men Nathan described, one was rich. This rich man had everything, but, like most people of his day, his wealth was tied up in the form of livestock. *The rich man had very many flocks and herds* (12:2). In contrast, *the poor man had nothing but one little ewe lamb, which he had bought* (12:3). The poor man had only one female lamb. With great difficulty, this poor man had saved his money and bought the lamb, raising and nurturing the little animal along with raising his children. The lamb was part of the family; the man had even fed the lamb food and drink from his table, and often it slept securely in his arms. This one little lamb was like his daughter. *And he brought it up, and it grew up with him and with his children; it used to eat of his morsel, and drink from his cup, and lie in his bosom, and it was like a daughter to him* (12:3).

A traveler arrived at the rich man's house, and custom dictated that the host feed his guest. However, the rich man was so greedy that he did not want to slaughter even one of his many sheep to feed his visitor. Crudely ingenious, the rich man took the poor man's lamb, prepared it, served it, and ate it with his guest. *Now there came a traveler to the rich man, and he was unwilling to take one of his own flock or herd to prepare for the wayfarer who had come to him, but he took the poor man's lamb, and prepared it for the man who had come to him* (12:4).

Listening to Nathan's story, David became incensed. Such injustice, such selfishness, such greed could not go unpunished! Accustomed to hearing cases and offering indictments and sentences, David offered his judgment. Furious, he said to Nathan, *As the Lord lives, the man who has done this deserves to die* (12:5). While the death sentence was in order, David had something else in mind: restitution. Some reparation had to be made. *He shall restore the lamb fourfold, because he did this thing and because he had no pity* (12:6).

You are the man (12:7). Having been drawn into the story and forced to offer judgment, David now heard that he had pronounced a judgment upon himself. Nathan had successfully addressed the king (a risky business at anytime when truth must speak to power). David could have easily had Nathan killed. However, the stunned David was speechless. Overwhelmed by the moment, David silently listened to Nathan speak God's judgment.

Nathan reviewed God's past graciousness. The Lord had chosen and anointed David. God was with David when Saul pursued him and when David eventually replaced Saul. God gave Saul's wives to David and all the female members of Saul's house. God gave David the whole kingdom of Israel and Judah. *I anointed you king over Israel, and I delivered you out of the hand of Saul; and I gave you your master's house, and your master's wives into your bosom, and gave you the house of Israel and of Judah; and if this were too little, I would add to you as much more* (12:7, 8).

Why have you despised the word of the Lord? (12:9). As king, perhaps David imagined himself above God's laws. Why had he disregarded the commandments God had given? The Lord reviewed the indictment against David. David had broken three commandments: he had coveted Uriah's wife; he had committed adultery; and he had murdered by arranging the death of Uriah the Hittite.

The Lord passed sentence. *Therefore the sword shall never depart from your house, because you have despised me* (12:10). David's punishment was that his family would never be free from conflict and trouble for the entire future!

I have sinned against the Lord (12:13). David repented and confessed his sinfulness, acknowledging his guilt. He admitted that he, the king, also stood under God and the covenant's law. After David confessed his sins, Nathan assured him of God's forgiveness. *The Lord also has put away your sin; you shall not die* (12:13). David would experience God's mercy. He would be allowed to live.

SUGGESTIONS TO TEACHERS

David's affair with Bathsheba unfolds like a modern soap opera. David might have lived three thousand years ago, but his schemes and excuses are still being used today.

As teacher, your big temptation in this lesson will be to dwell on the lurid details of David's carryings-on with Bathsheba. But emphasize the key point of the Scripture passage: Sin is more than a naughty affair; it is rebelling against God!

1. SINFUL SECRET. "Nobody will ever know." "It's our business only, nobody else's." How often these words have been used to justify an illicit sexual relationship! But sin is never "private." Point to the words, "You did it secretly . . ." (II Sam. 12:12) and the following phrases, which stress that wrongdoing affects everyone. God sees and knows. Supposedly "secret sins" flaunt God's rule.

2. SORDID STRATEGY. We sometimes hear people "explain away" sinful behavior with phrases like, "If things can be fixed so nobody gets into trouble, everything is okay." David thought he was clever enough to arrange a cover-up for his sin by having Uriah appear to be the father of Bathsheba's child. But even he as king couldn't "fix things up"—either with Uriah or Bathsheba, his own family, and especially with God! Sin can never be resolved merely by trying to make things look good.

3. SCANDALOUS SCHEME. David's original, lustful pursuit led him into deeper and darker paths of wrongdoing. His actions resulted finally in having Uriah slaughtered. The shabby excuse, "Everything's all right as long as nobody gets hurt," simply is not true. In the end, sin means people do get hurt. In the case of David, sin led to a murder plot against an innocent man.

4. SEVERE SENTENCE. Bring Nathan into the lesson. His words are the key to understanding the biblical passage. David finally learns: "I am the man Nathan is talking about in the parable." And he responds, "I have

sinned against the Lord" (II Sam. 12:13). Here is the essence of sin—acting "against the Lord." This is the heart of today's lesson, so make sure your class members comprehend that sin means alienation from God. But also make sure people remember that through Jesus Christ, our sin is forgiven.

5. SAD SITUATION. Divine forgiveness does not mean that suddenly everything will be cleared up and be rosy, that no consequences of our actions will follow. The fallout of sin in David's case was a host of family problems in the future. If time permits, you may touch on some of these problems, such as the death of the baby conceived by David and Bathsheba.

TOPIC FOR ADULTS
ACKNOWLEDGING OUR SIN

The Man He Used to Be. Emile Verhaeren fought in the trenches of World War I in Europe. He recalled the hatred he experienced and the cruelties he inflicted. He later also remembered how his conscience became diminished. With great pain, he realized that the beliefs he had held before he allowed himself to be degraded by combat had eroded. Verhaeren, with emotion and disillusionment as he acknowledged what he had done, dedicated the pages of his memoirs "to the man I used to be."

David must have felt great remorse when he was confronted with his sin. He could recall the person he used to be and knew he must acknowledge true guilt if he were to move back into fellowship with God.

Spreading Effects. Over a century ago, an exposition at New Orleans' horticultural hall featured a lovely, fragrant blossom from Venezuela. The plant grew in water, and was called a "Water Hyacinth." No one in North America had ever seen anything like the pretty, orchid-like flowers. Everyone agreed the water hyacinths had a beautiful aroma as well as a gorgeous bloom. Unfortunately, many visitors secretly snipped off small pieces of the roots to take home and plant in swampy areas of the South. These clips of hyacinths flourished, and within a few years, the transplantings began to take over all water channels. Eventually, many streams and rivers were clogged with the plant. It was later discovered that each plant brings forth shoots producing a thousand new plants every two months. The original plants stolen from the exposition in New Orleans were bringing ruin to America's southern waterways.

This is the way sin operates. It seems innocent and attractive at first, but the acts eventually produce unbelievably destructive effects. David's affair with Bathsheba ultimately spread ruinous results in his own life, in Bathsheba's and Uriah's lives, and in the lives of his family members. Let's recognize sin's consequences!

Truth Will Out! This amusing story comes from the days before refrigeration, when the corner butcher shop kept freshly-dressed chickens in a barrel of ice. One Saturday night, a customer came into the shop and asked to buy a chicken. The butcher rummaged around in the barrel and found the one remaining bird, plopped it on the scale, and announced the price as 43 cents. The woman customer paused, then stated that she wanted a bird slightly larger. Without hesitating, the butcher returned the chicken to the barrel, and made a great pretense of searching for a larger one. A few moments later, he triumphantly removed the same chicken, placed it on the scale, but secretly rested his thumb lightly on the scale, too. "Ah, that will be 51 cents," he announced.

"Good," replied the delighted woman. "I'll take both of them."

All attempts to deceive God or others about our wrongdoing will eventually come to light—on earth, or at the final judgment. Sin is never secret.

Questions for Students on the Next Lesson. 1. What outstanding gifts did Solomon display? 2. What example can you find of Solomon's genuine faith when the temple was completed? 3. What was the Queen of Sheba's opinion of Solomon? 4. What is wisdom, according to the Scriptures? 5. In your opinion, how important is personal achievement?

TOPIC FOR YOUTH
ADMITTING OUR WRONG

Second Chance. He had been accused of hitting others and starting fights on the school bus. His reputation was School Bus Bully. Actually, school administrators had only a few stories about the twelve-year-old terror, but no hard evidence, since the child denied ever bullying anyone.

The school bus contractor had invested in a new system marketed by a Texas firm. The system placed cameras in the school buses and secretly videotaped the riders from a camera mounted above the driver's rearview mirror. This hidden camera captured the twelve year old bullying, roughhousing, and vandalizing school property.

The school confronted the boy and his parents again with his wrongdoing. The boy vehemently denied doing anything wrong. The boy then watched silently as the videotape rolled. Finally, he had to admit his wrongdoing. The administrators, the guidance counselors, and the boy's parents all listened to his promise to change his behavior.

David and the boy thought no one knew their sin. Confronted with the evidence, each admitted their wrongs. Each was judged and given another opportunity to make the best of the second chance that arose from the judgment. You, too, have that opportunity. God has forgiven you in Christ. Make the most of the new opportunities provided to you.

Reexamination. In 1992, the United States was caught up in celebrating the 500th anniversary of Columbus' discovery of the Americas. However, not everyone celebrated. Many native Americans pointed to the tremendous changes that Columbus' arrival brought to them and their culture. These individuals helped Americans and other colonizing nations to understand the destruction that occurred. The colonizers had brought death by disease and slavery, and the ruin of much of the Native American culture.

Some people denounced these critics, labeling them "Columbus bashers." However, no one can deny that genocide, destruction, and kidnapping did occur. Even the most ardent supporters of Columbus recognized that these critics were properly incensed by the injustices brought about by Columbus' "discovery."

David grew angry over an imaginary story. Surely, we as Americans should be equally incensed over a true historical story that has been told to us. Can we not use Columbus Day each year to reexamine the so-called benefits that Europe brought to the new world?

Acting His Faith. For over fifty years, J. Edgar Hoover, former Director of the Federal Bureau of Investigation, promoted himself as America's chief guardian of the law. He had once considered becoming a minister before being recruited by the Justice Department. Throughout his entire career, however, Hoover carefully presented an outward image of piety.

However, the real Hoover was quite different from this outward appearance. He would never admit he was wrong. He never forgave. He decorated his house at government expense. He accepted free vacations. He maintained a private, confidential file of derogatory information about public officials and celebrities. This information, often unsubstantiated, consisted largely of details about minor misdeeds, petty sins, rumors, and tidbits of gossip. Hoover used these files as leverage with politicians to influence their votes, particularly when an issue would affect the bureau in any way. The files sometimes managed to discredit individuals, such as "Wild Bill" Donovan, head of the Office of Strategic Services (the CIA's predecessor), or to slander innocent persons, such as former first lady Eleanor Roosevelt. Hoover died without ever admitting that his files were a mistake and a liability.

Hoover discredited himself by treating those around him unjustly. His example shows that outward piety is not enough, just as King David learned when Nathan sternly warned him.

Questions for Students on the Next Lesson. 1. What was built during Israel's "Golden Age of Solomon?" 2. What is consecration? How was God involved in this action? 3. Who was the Queen of Sheba? From where did she come? 4. What was her intention? 5. What conclusion did she reach after her visit? Was it justified?

LESSON 12—NOVEMBER 20

SOLOMON'S GLORIOUS REIGN

Background Scripture: I Kings 9:1-9; 10:1-24
Devotional Reading: Proverbs 3:5-15

KING JAMES VERSION

I KINGS 9:1 And it came to pass, when Solomon had finished the building of the house of the Lord, and the king's house, and all Solomon's desire which he was pleased to do,

2 That the Lord appeared to Solomon the second time, as he had appeared unto him at Gibeon.

3 And the Lord said unto him, I have heard thy prayer and thy supplication, that thou hast made before me: I have hallowed this house, which thou hast built, to put my name there for ever; and mine eyes and mine heart shall be there perpetually.

10:1 And when the queen of Sheba heard of the fame of Solomon concerning the name of the Lord, she came to prove him with hard questions.

2 And she came to Jerusalem with a very great train, with camels that bare spices, and very much gold, and precious stones: and when she was come to Solomon, she communed with him of all that was in her heart.

3 And Solomon told her all her questions: there was not any thing hid from the king, which he told her not.

4 And when the queen of Sheba had seen all Solomon's wisdom, and the house that he had built,

5 And the meat of his table, and the sitting of his servants, and the attendance of his ministers, and their apparel, and his cupbearers, and his ascent by which he went up unto the house of the Lord; there was no more spirit in her.

6 And she said to the king, It was a true report that I heard in mine own land of thy acts and of thy wisdom.

7 Howbeit I believed not the words, until I came, and mine eyes had seen it: and, behold, the half was not told me: thy wisdom and prosperity exceedeth the fame which I heard.

23 So king Solomon exceeded all the kings of the earth for riches and for wisdom.

24 And all the earth sought to Solomon, to hear his wisdom, which God had put in his heart.

REVISED STANDARD VERSION

I KINGS 9:1 When Solomon had finished building the house of the Lord and the king's house and all that Solomon desired to build, 2 the Lord appeared to Solomon a second time, as he had appeared to him at Gibeon. 3 And the Lord said to him, "I have heard your prayer and your supplication, which you have made before me; I have consecrated this house which you have built, and put my name there for ever; my eyes and my heart will be there for all time."

10:1 Now when the queen of Sheba heard of the fame of Solomon concerning the name of the Lord, she came to test him with hard questions. 2 She came to Jerusalem with a very great retinue, with camels bearing spices, and very much gold, and precious stones; and when she came to Solomon, she told him all that was on her mind. 3 And Solomon answered all her questions; there was nothing hidden from the king which he could not explain to her. 4 And when the queen of Sheba had seen all the wisdom of Solomon, the house that he had built, 5 the food of his table, the seating of his officials, and the attendance of his servants, their clothing, his cupbearers, and his burnt offerings which he offered at the house of the Lord, there was no more spirit in her.

6 And she said to the king, "The report was true which I heard in my own land of your affairs and of your wisdom, 7 but I did not believe the reports until I came and my own eyes had seen it; and, behold, the half was not told me; your wisdom and prosperity surpass the report which I heard.

23 Thus King Solomon excelled all the kings of the earth in riches and wisdom. 24 And the whole earth sought the presence of Solomon to hear his wisdom, which God had put into his mind.

KEY VERSE: King Solomon excelled all the kings of the earth in riches and in wisdom. I Kings 10:23.

HOME DAILY BIBLE READINGS

Nov.	*14*	*M.*	I Kings 1:28-40	*Solomon Is Made King*
Nov.	*15*	*T.*	I Kings 9:1-9	*God's Blessing and Promise*
Nov.	*16*	*W.*	I Kings 9:10-19	*Solomon's Building Projects*
Nov.	*17*	*T.*	I Kings 9:20-28	*Solomon's Prosperity*
Nov.	*18*	*F.*	I Kings 10:1-5	*The Queen of Sheba Visits Solomon*
Nov.	*19*	*S.*	I Kings 10:6-13	*Praise and Gifts from the Queen*
Nov.	*20*	*S.*	I Kings 10:14-29	*Solomon's Greatness in Riches and Wisdom*

BACKGROUND

Although Solomon was David's son through the sinful marriage to Bathsheba, Solomon was also David's handpicked successor to the throne. The young king quickly showed exceptional abilities. At the start of his reign, he also prayed movingly, "O Lord my God, thou has made thy servant king . . . although I am but a little child. . . . Give thy servant therefore an understanding mind to govern thy people, that I may discern between good and evil" (I Kings 3:7-9). Here was a man of genuine faith.

Solomon's wisdom is still respected among all populations in the Middle East to this day. His literary gifts are disclosed in the great number of proverbs ascribed to him. The Book of Proverbs, in fact, is a kind of manual on how to live the godly life. Solomon could express great truths in dramatic epigrams.

During his long reign, Solomon carried out an enormous series of building programs. His most famous project was the great temple in Jerusalem. This magnificent edifice became one of the architectural marvels of the ancient world, admired by everyone. Nor did Solomon neglect his own royal buildings; his palace, armory, and throne room were lavishly constructed and decorated.

Solomon's organizational skills make him sound strikingly modern. He divided the country into twelve administrative districts, each with its own capital, governmental buildings, and military barracks. Excavations at Megiddo have revealed the grand scale of his chariot depots. For example, the Megiddo army headquarters, one of twelve, had stalls for 450 horses, a huge parade ground, and elaborate fortifications.

Master-builder Solomon was a master politician as well. His diplomacy won him valuable trade pacts with such foreign powers as the Queen of Sheba. These shrewd business arrangements brought great wealth to Israel. Solomon also controlled the caravan routes from the desert's edge at Palmyra down to Aqabah on the Red Sea. Even Egypt was forced to pay taxes to Solomon for goods transported through his kingdom.

No wonder this great ruler was remembered with awe by later generations. Even Jesus alluded to him: "Even Solomon in all his glory . . ." (Matt. 6:29).

NOTES ON THE PRINTED TEXT

When Solomon had finished building the house of the Lord and the king's house and all that Solomon desired to build, the Lord appeared to Solomon (9:1, 2a). Solomon's temple was laid out in a rectangle measuring 90 feet long and 30 feet wide, with a height of 45 feet. Several small rooms supported the massive roof. The temple stood on a nine-foot-high terrace. Huge doors opened to reveal the nave, which measured 60 by 30 by 45 feet, the largest room in the temple. It was lighted by eight or ten recessed windows. Beyond the nave and up a short flight of steps was the holy of holies, a 30-foot cube.

Skilled craftsmen constructed the building out of cut stone. They made the floors out of cypress, with the lintels, doors, and doorposts of olive wood. Costly cedarwood covered the walls, and gold was inlaid in those walls and in the doors. Mammoth pillars stood on either side of the front door. Builders labored for seven years to complete the structure.

Solomon's palace took thirteen years to build. It consisted of a complex of five major buildings. The House of the Forest of Lebanon had forty-five pillars of cedar and was the largest single room in the palace, measuring roughly 150 feet by 75 feet by 45 feet. Adjacent to this room was The Hall of Pillars. The Hall of Judgment was where Solomon kept his throne, which was made of ivory overlaid with gold. It had carved lions on each side. Six steps raised the throne above the level of the floor. Soaring porches decorated with carvings and bronze-cast statues, made by the finest craftsmen, contributed to the palace's fame throughout the world.

I have heard your prayer . . . I have consecrated this house which you have built, and put my name there for ever; my eyes and my heart will be there for all time (9:3). God assured Solomon that He had heard his dedicatory prayer. In response, the Lord had consecrated the temple by His presence.

Now when the queen of Sheba heard of the fame of Solomon . . . she came to test him with hard questions (10:1). What magnificence Solomon bestowed upon Jerusalem! Even the Queen of Sheba made a long and difficult trip to meet him, hearing of his reputation for great knowledge and wisdom. Solomon had studied a wide variety of subjects, ranging from human psychology to natural science. He was also reputed to have collected over three thousand proverbs.

The queen also came to Solomon in order to discuss trading arrangements. Solomon's fleet brought in cargoes of almug (perhaps black coral), sandalwood, gold, precious stones, silver, ivory, apes, monkeys, and peacocks from as far away as Somaliland in Africa. His wisdom and his wealth intrigued the queen. She wanted to meet him and ask tough questions.

She came to Jerusalem with a very great retinue, with camels bearing spices, and very much gold, and precious stones (10:2). The Queen of Sheba had made the long and difficult trip through the Negev, laden with treasure. Her trading empire was built largely on the transportation of luxury items, exotic animals, and above all, frankincense and myrrh production. She had profited immensely from these resources used to make perfume. The meager supply of aromatic material extracted from the plants, the complicated processing operation, and the heavy shipping expenses made her very wealthy.

The report was true which I heard in my own land of your affairs and of your wisdom, but I did not believe the reports until I came and my own eyes had seen it; and, behold, the half was not told me; your wisdom and prosperity surpass the report which I heard (10:6, 7). After visiting Solomon, the queen conceded that all she had heard concerning Solomon's wealth and wisdom was indeed true. She had been unable to best him at matching wits and riddles. She was literally breathless from viewing his wealth, his elegant life-style, and his piety.

Thus King Solomon excelled all the kings of the earth in riches and in wisdom (10:23). Jerusalem became a center of considerable wealth and prosperity, no other king surpassing Solomon in wealth and wisdom. In fact, people all over the earth sought Solomon's God-given wisdom. And the whole earth sought the presence of Solomon to hear his wisdom, which God had put in his mind (10:24). Truly Solomon's reign was glorious.

SUGGESTIONS TO TEACHERS

When Solomon began his long and glorious reign, he prayed one of the most moving prayers ever recorded: "O Lord my God, thou has made thy servant king in place of David my father, although I am but a little child; I do not know how to go out or come in . . . . Give thy servant therefore an understanding mind to govern thy people, that I may discern between good and evil. . ." (I Kings 3:7-9). No wonder this passage was read to young Victoria by Lord Melbourne when it was announced she was to be Queen of England in 1837. And not surprisingly, this same prayer was spoken by Harry S. Truman on hearing that he was to succeed Franklin D. Roosevelt, who had just died. Solomon's prayer seemed to be answered. His nation flourished until his death.

Your lesson develops around the personality of this extraordinary ruler. Remember, of course, that God is the central character. And keep in mind that Solomon, like all humans, had his flaws.

1. APPEARANCE AND INSTRUCTIONS. David had been forbidden to build the temple in Jerusalem, but Solomon proceeded to carry out the project. When completed, the temple stood as one of the most magnificent structures ever erected. Look at the dedication service in I Kings 9. Focus on the call to Solomon to serve God with honesty and justice.

2. ALLEGIANCE AND INTEGRITY. God demanded Solomon's personal allegiance. In other nations, the king could place himself above all restraints and responsibilities. In some cultures, such as Egypt, in fact, the ruler was held to have divine status. Not so in Israel. Even the king had to bow to God. And so with all of us.

3. AMAZEMENT AND IMPRESSIONS. Take a few minutes to look at the report of the visit by the Queen of Sheba. This wealthy woman was astonished at Solomon's wisdom and his wealth. As a person who was renowned for her own wealth and wisdom, this ruler recognized that Solomon was superior to anyone she had ever encountered. Examine some examples of Solomon's wisdom within a few of the sections of the Book of Proverbs.

4. APES AND IVORY. The wealth of Solomon's court astounded every-one. Exotic imports came in from distant lands: Africa, the Arabian penin-sula, and beyond. However, none of these treasures remain. Archaeologists can point to examples of a few of Solomon's massive build-ing programs, but Solomon left all his wealth behind at his death. Suggest to your students that all possessions are on loan, so to speak, and intended to be used responsibly until they are given back to their Owner. Perhaps your church has been conducting its annual stewardship campaign. The close of this lesson, which surveys Solomon's great wealth, could comple-ment your church's message about the wise use of money.

TOPIC FOR ADULTS
LIVING WISELY

Proper Perspective. William Beebe, the naturalist, made many visits to the home of Theodore Roosevelt, himself something of a naturalist. After an evening's conversation, the two men would go outdoors, gaze up at the sky, and see who could first detect the faint speck of light-mist beyond the lower left-hand corner of the Great Square of Pegasus, and then one or the other would recite: "That is the Spiral Galaxy in Andromeda. It is as large as our Milky Way. It is one of a hundred million galaxies. It is 750,000 light-years away. It consists of one hundred billion suns, each larger than our sun." Whereupon, Beebe reports, Roosevelt would grin at him and say: "Now I think we are small enough. Let's go to bed."

Solomon had that kind of perspective at the start of his reign. He real-ized that he was not the center of the universe, and that the Lord was far greater than he. As his proverbs illustrate, Solomon's recognition of God's greatness was the source of his wisdom.

Exemplum. Medieval dictionaries defined the word *exemplum* as "a clearing in the woods." Our words "example" and "exemplar" come from the root word which originally referred to taking out the trees and brush so that the sun could shine through in a clearing. In the midst of the dark-ness and tangle, the sun could stream in, bringing warmth and light.

The person who lives wisely allows the light and warmth of God to shine through, creating a clearing of hope and growth in the midst of a jungle of despair and death. Those who are truly wise live as "exem-plums". Solomon was such a person in the early years of his long reign.

Self-Esteem through Success. Popular wisdom these days teaches that self-esteem and personal fulfillment are the be-all and end-all of life. For example, one school now has a program called "Very Important Kids" for children three to six years old. The program teaches the children to hold a very high view of themselves and their abilities.

But in a recent international test of mathematical skills, American grade school pupils ranked far above Oriental children in their *assessment* of their own abilities, but far below in actual *performance!*

Some advocates of self-esteem training conclude that people feel badly about themselves simply because they have not received enough verbal affirmation. Not so! Self-esteem does not follow merely from verbal praise; it develops as people are given the opportunities for accountability and responsibility and they successfully follow through. In short, to develop self-esteem, learn to work hard. This requires competing and sometimes failing. No amount of hollow praise can substitute for the esteem that comes from striving for personal excellence within the context of an objective assessment of one's gifts and limitations.

Questions for Students on the Next Lesson. 1. How did Solomon disobey the Lord? 2. What did Solomon's wives do to cause such problems? 3. What was God's punishment for Solomon's disobedience? 4. What most influences your own moral decisions? 5. What pressures does our culture put on people trying to live by God's values?

TOPIC FOR YOUTH
SHOWING WISDOM

Acquiring Wisdom. During the coronation of Queen Elizabeth II on June 2, 1953, the future queen put on several pieces of special coronation vestments. Along with the crown, the ring, the staff, and the scepter, the future queen put on an ancient pair of ceremonial bracelets called armills. These were the bracelets of "sincerity and wisdom."

How wonderful it would be if sincerity and wisdom were acquired as easily as putting on a bracelet! Remember, though, that in the Bible, true wisdom requires respect for God. Solomon understood this truth and placed God above everything else in his kingdom. So must we.

Priorities. A survey by the New Hampshire Department of Employment Security found that seven out of ten teenagers surveyed held jobs. It also discovered that eight out of ten high school students worked and almost half of those who worked put in more than twenty hours per week. Interestingly, the survey further discovered that these young people used most of their earnings to buy cars, automobile insurance, gasoline, clothing, and concert tickets. Few indicated that they saved their money.

Wisdom, for Solomon, was getting life's priorities straight and placing God before everything else. In our culture, we are told that wisdom means preferring cars, fancy clothing, and amusement. Solomon, though, put God first; after the Lord came everything else. That was true wisdom.

Knowing Where to Turn. Ken Griffey, Jr., centerfielder for the Seattle Mariners, was in a batting slump. He needed help, and he knew where to turn for advice. He asked his father, Ken Griffey, Sr., what to do.

Ken Griffey, Jr., knew there was a lot he could learn by seeking his dad's advice. His dad had played fifteen years of major league baseball. He had gotten more than two thousand hits in his career and had been named the Most Valuable Player in an All-Star Game. He had also played on two world championship teams.

Fathers can offer sound advice. A truly smart person doesn't mind turning to someone with experience and wisdom for guidance. An even smarter person turns to God for advice, too.

Questions for Students on the Next Lesson. 1. How did Solomon disobey the Lord's commandments? 2. What were the consequences of Solomon's actions for the nation? 3. What was God's judgment upon Solomon? 4. What happened to Solomon's sons? 5. How might disobeying God's commands bring judgment upon us today?

LESSON 13—NOVEMBER 27

SOLOMON TURNS FROM GOD

Background Scripture: I Kings 11
Devotional Reading: Proverbs 16:1-7

KING JAMES VERSION

I Kings 11:1 But king Solomon loved many strange women, together with the daughter of Pharaoh, women of the Moabites, Ammonites, Edomites, Zidonians, and Hittites:

2 Of the nations concerning which the Lord said unto the children of Israel, Ye shall not go in to them, neither shall they come in unto you: for surely they will turn away your heart after their gods: Solomon clave unto these in love.

3 And he had seven hundred wives, princesses, and three hundred concubines: and his wives turned away his heart.

4 For it came to pass, when Solomon was old, that his wives turned away his heart after other gods: and his heart was not perfect with the Lord his God, as was the heart of David his father.

5 For Solomon went after Ashtoreth the goddess of the Zidonians, and after Milcom the abomination of the Ammonites.

6 And Solomon did evil in the sight of the Lord, and went not fully after the Lord, as did David his father.

7 Then did Solomon build an high place for Chemosh, the abomination of Moab, in the hill that is before Jerusalem, and for Molech, the abomination of the children of Ammon.

8 And likewise did he for all his strange wives, which burnt incense and sacrificed unto their gods.

9 And the Lord was angry with Solomon, because his heart was turned from the Lord God of Israel, which had appeared unto him twice,

10 And had commanded him concerning this thing, that he should not go after other gods: but he kept not that which the Lord commanded.

11 Wherefore the Lord said unto Solomon, Forasmuch as this is done of thee, and thou hast not kept my covenant and my statutes, which I have commanded thee, I will surely rend the kingdom from thee, and will give it to thy servant.

12 Notwithstanding in thy days I will not do it for David thy father's sake: but I will rend it out of the hand of thy son.

REVISED STANDARD VERSION

I KINGS 11:1 Now King Solomon loved many foreign women: the daughter of Pharaoh, and Moabite, Ammonite, Edomite, Sidonian, and Hittite women, 2 from the nations concerning which the Lord had said to the people of Israel, "You shall not enter into marriage with them, neither shall they with you, for surely they will turn away your heart after their gods"; Solomon clung to these in love. 3 He had seven hundred wives, princesses, and three hundred concubines; and his wives turned away his heart. 4 For when Solomon was old his wives turned away his heart after other gods; and his heart was not wholly true to the Lord his God, as was the heart of David his father. 5 For Solomon went after Ashtoreth the goddess of the Sidonians, and after Milcom the abomination of the Ammonites. 6 So Solomon did what was evil in the sight of the Lord, and did not wholly follow the Lord, as David his father had done. 7 Then Solomon built a high place for Chemosh the abomination of Moab, and for Molech the abomination of the Ammonites, on the mountain east of Jerusalem. 8 And so he did for all his foreign wives, who burned incense and sacrificed to their gods.

9 And the Lord was angry with Solomon, because his heart had turned away from the Lord, the God of Israel, who had appeared to him twice, 10 and had commanded him concerning this thing, that he should not go after other gods; but he did not keep what the Lord commanded. 11 Therefore the Lord said to Solomon, "Since this has been your mind and you have not kept my covenant and my statutes which I have commanded you, I will surely tear the kingdom from you and will give it to your servant. 12 Yet for the sake of David your father I will not do it in your days, but I will tear it out of the hand of your son. 13 However I will not tear away all the kingdom; but I will give one tribe to your son, for the sake of David my servant and for the sake of Jerusalem which I have chosen."

13 Howbeit I will not rend away all the
kingdom; but will give one tribe to thy son
for David my servant's sake, and for
Jerusalem's sake which I have chosen.

*KEY VERSE: Solomon did what was evil in the sight of the Lord, and did
not wholly follow the Lord. I Kings 11:6a.*

HOME DAILY BIBLE READINGS

Nov.	21	M.	Ecclesiastes 2:4-9	*Solomon's Achievements*
Nov.	22	T.	Proverbs 16:1-9	*God Sees into the Heart*
Nov.	23	W.	I Kings 11:1-8	*Solomon Disobeys God's Command*
Nov.	24	T.	I Kings 11:9-13	*Solomon's Kingdom Will End*
Nov.	25	F.	I Kings 11:14-22	*Edomite Foes Organize against Solomon*
Nov.	26	S.	I Kings 11:23-26	*Other Adversaries Take Action*
Nov.	27	S.	I Kings 11:28-40	*Ahijah's Prophecy about Jeroboam's Reign*

BACKGROUND

Solomon's glory ended in tragedy. After his great start with a deep faith
in God, he allowed himself to stray from keeping the covenant and observing the commandments. He wrote memorable proverbs about serving the
Lord, but in the end he failed to practice what he preached.

Solomon the politician entered into alliances with numerous foreign
powers. In those times, such alliances were normally sealed with political
marriages, and Solomon's harem grew because of these ties. It was diplo-
matic custom to grant such foreign wives the privilege of continuing to
observe their own religions, so most of these women brought their pagan
worship practices to Jerusalem with them. Solomon indulged these wives
in their loyalty to other gods and goddesses and even accompanied some of
them in their worship. With seven hundred wives and three hundred concubines, Solomon eventually not only set a bad example as king but also
peppered the kingdom with scores of pagan shrines. By the end of his
reign, Solomon abandoned his first love for the Lord.

Gradually turning from the Lord, Solomon indulged himself increasingly in his own luxurious tastes. Although it had taken seven years to erect
the temple, so ornate and expensive was Solomon's own palace that it took
thirteen years to build. Solomon lived in staggering magnificence. Even
his throne was made of ivory and covered with pure gold. He accumulated
immense wealth and power and embarked on an ambitious—and costly—
series of building projects. Remnants of his water systems, stables, provincial palaces, and fortresses may be seen to this day.

Unfortunately, Solomon failed to see that there had to be limits to his
expensive building programs. Although Solomon was himself rich, most of
his subjects were peasants who had barely progressed from being desert
nomads to simple farmers. Solomon levied heavy taxes—driving his country toward bankruptcy—in order to support his ambitious projects, his

enormous bureaucracy, his great personal escort and staff, and his own costly whims and pageants. When Solomon finally resorted to forcing Israelite subjects to serve as slave laborers, the people became increasingly discontented. A couple of popular uprisings fizzled, but a day of reckoning was inevitable. Solomon, the man who once talked wisdom, ended by practicing foolishness in his neglect of God.

NOTES ON THE PRINTED TEXT

For all the greatness and glory associated with Solomon's reign, one activity proved to be unpopular and disastrous. The king had a harem of one thousand wives and concubines. *Now King Solomon loved many foreign women: the daughter of Pharaoh, and Moabite, Ammonite, Edomite, Sidonian, and Hittite women* (11:1). The ancient and modern East celebrated the virility of the ruler. Unfortunately, the enormous number of women meant that a very high percentage of the population of Jerusalem was associated in some manner, either as members of, or as servants to, Solomon's harem. A host of bureaucrats swarmed around Solomon. The worship of these foreigners offended the religious scruples of many of the people. Solomon's encouragement and preference for these foreigners in the court also proved unpopular. *Solomon clung to these in love* (11:2). While many marriages had a political significance (such as the tie with Egypt through Pharaoh's daughter), apparently Solomon simply had a large appetite for women. He was intimate with all seven hundred wives in the harem.

Sadly, King Solomon disobeyed the Lord's command by marrying many foreign women. The law was specific: No marriage with women outside the faith, since a believer in Yahweh might be swayed from true worship. *The Lord had said to the people of Israel, "You shall not enter into marriage with them, neither shall they with you, for surely they will turn away your heart after their gods"* (11:2).

The wives continued to worship their own gods, and Solomon tolerated it. Ultimately, Solomon's many wives turned his heart away from God and led Solomon to worship their gods. *When Solomon was old his wives turned away his heart after other gods; and his heart was not wholly true to the Lord his God* (11:4).

Solomon went after Ashtoreth (11:5). Ashtoreth was the Canaanite fertility goddess. (Interestingly, "Ashtoreth" sounds similar to the Hebrew word for "shame." Perhaps the writer was indicating how shameful this particular activity of King Solomon was.) Solomon also went after *Milcom the abomination of the Ammonites* (11:5). Milcom was another fertility god, often demanding human sacrifice. The writer summed up Solomon's failing commitment to the Lord. *Solomon did what was evil in the sight of the Lord, and did not wholly follow the Lord* (11:6).

In addition to worship, Solomon built shrines where his wives could burn incense and offer sacrifices to their gods. *Solomon built a high place for Chemosh the abomination of Moab, and for Molech the abomination of the Ammonites, on the mountain east of Jerusalem* (11:7). Chemosh was the chief Moabite deity. Molech worship was condemned by Israel because children were burned alive to please this god. Most of these pagan shrines were built on a hill south of the Mount of Olives. It had for centuries been called the "hill of shame" because of the association with these sanctuaries where Solomon's wives *burned incense and sacrificed to their gods* (11:8).

The Lord was angry with Solomon because Solomon did not honor His commands. The Lord had twice warned Solomon, but Solomon refused to listen. *The Lord was angry with Solomon, because his heart had turned away from the Lord . . . who had appeared to him twice, and had commanded him concerning this thing, that he should not go after other gods; but he did not keep what the Lord commanded* (11:9, 10).

God punished Solomon by promising to take the kingdom away. *I will surely tear the kingdom from you and will give it to your servant* (11:11). However, the judgment was tempered with mercy. The promised judgment would not occur during Solomon's reign but during his son's. *I will tear it out of the hand of your son* (11:12). In addition, God promised to give one tribe to Solomon's son for the sake of David and Jerusalem.

Thus, for all his glory, Solomon effectively diluted Israel's faithfulness to God by supporting the worship of alien gods. This policy earned him the condemnation of God and the biblical writers.

SUGGESTIONS TO TEACHERS

Today's lesson is a case study of a person who starts well with God but who allows his loyalty to the Lord erode. The story of Solomon is intended to be more than the sad tale of another great king who began well but ended badly. Solomon's story should also act as a mirror for each of us. How easy it is to let our own loyalties to attractive "gods" in our culture crowd out the Lord in our lives!

1. DALLIANCES. Solomon's huge haram of wives, mistresses, and playmates was an attempt to fulfill every sexual urge. In some cases, alliances were sealed with foreign kings who, in turn, gave their daughters as wives. In any case, Solomon became a playboy. He might have had wisdom in government and commerce, but he showed stupidity in marriage and family life.

2. DISOBEDIENCE. Wanting to please his foreign wives, Solomon went along with their paganism. Some of these women imported disgusting worship practices, emphasizing fertility rituals. Having the palace swarming with heathen priests and priestesses undermined the place of the Lord in national life and in the personal lives of many Israelites. Worse, Solomon's lack of faithfulness to God signified a fundamental refusal to let the Lord remain at the center of the nation's life.

3. DISORDER. Disobedience brings disorder. God will not be mocked or fooled. For our own well-being, He calls us to live in trust and obedience before Him. Failure to remain loyal to the Lord means a rebellion against God's rule. Such rebellion is always doomed. In Solomon's situation, the refusal to obey brought restlessness and, eventually, rebellion in his land. Tragically, the final result was a fatal political division at Solomon's death, in which the ten northern tribes broke away under Jeroboam.

4. DECLINE. Instead of being a golden sunset, Solomon's final days were a dismal drizzle of intrigue and distrust, revolt and suffering. Solomon's choices were his own undoing. We humans choose our paths for ourselves.

TOPIC FOR ADULTS
TURNING AWAY FROM GOD

Wrong Influence. French ruler Charles IX was a loving, sensitive person when young. As a youth, he was deeply influenced by the Christian leader, Admiral Gaspard de Coligny. Admiral Coligny's sterling character and staunch faith was clearly reflected in young Charles. However, Charles' unscrupulous mother, Catherine de Médicis, resolved to control the young ruler. Through various intrigues, plots, and assassinations, the devious woman contrived to discredit Coligny and become the *de facto* ruler of France.

His mother's fanatic religiosity and hatred toward the Huguenots gradually affected Charles IX. The evil Catherine finally persuaded Charles to agree to exterminate all Protestants in France. The ghastly butchery known in history as the St. Bartholomew's Day massacre, August 24, 1572, took the lives of over fifty thousand Huguenot men, women and children.

Many years later, when King Charles IX was on his deathbed, he was so tormented by the memories of his terrible deed that he screamed: "Asleep or awake, I see the mangled forms of the Huguenots passing before me! They make hideous faces at me. They point to their open wounds and mock me." Charles's horrible visions appeared because he, like Solomon, allowed himself to be turned away from God by evil persons.

Self-Consumption. In the Beatles' cartoon movie "Yellow Submarine," there is a creature called the Vacuum Cleaner Monster. This contraption sucks up everything in its sight. Finally, it is the only thing left. Then the Vacuum Cleaner Monster in the cartoon sucks itself up, too.

This is an apt description of what happened to Solomon, or what happens to anyone who turns away from God. When self becomes supreme, it begins to devour everything, and finally manages even to consume one's very personality. The monster of self-will ends by sucking up itself. Only a life centered on the Lord endures.

Lost First Love. By the age of thirty-five, Thomas Alexander Erskine had achieved all the honors his native Scotland could bestow. His musical talent as a composer was so outstanding that the Edinburgh Music Society would unquestioningly perform any new music he wrote.

Erskine was born into an aristocratic family and given all the advantages a person could desire. He studied music at Mannheim, Germany, under Stamitz, becoming an accomplished violinist and a gifted composer. He returned in 1756 to Scotland and quickly won fame for his outstanding compositions. The leading Edinburgh music critic, Dr. Burney, was moved to comment that Thomas Erskine "possessed more musical science than any dilettante with whom I was ever acquainted" and "composed with extraordinary rapidity."

Acclaimed and fawned over by Edinburgh society, Erskine, once a devout Christian, seemed to fall away from the faith. He began to be recognized for accomplishments of a different sort—heavy drinking and coarse joviality. Turning from the Lord and immersing himself in social life, Erskine refused to change and refused also to move to another city where he would be challenged to create better music.

Without having to compose or play to earn a living, Erskine gradually lost his great love of music. His creative output slowed during the 1770s. Even when he wrote a new overture, he rarely bothered to get it published. As a result, many of his works are now lost. Erskine died at the age of 60, a bloated physical wreck, at a Belgian spa in 1781.

Questions for Students on the Next Lesson. 1. What was John the Baptist's message? 2. Why did the authorities dislike John the Baptist's preaching? 3. How did John the Baptist regard Jesus? 4. Why did Jesus insist on being baptized? 5. Why must we take guilt so seriously?

TOPIC FOR YOUTH
FALLING SHORT

Act Had Consequences. Daniel Allen, Jr., 46, was found dead in a shallow grave about a mile from his home. He had been shot in the head and his body set afire before being buried. Allen's fourteen-year-old daughter was charged with the murder.

Police were led to make the arrest by reading entries in the girl's diary, which revealed the girl's plot to kill her father. The entire plan was based on a movie the teenager had seen in which a boy murders his girlfriend. The young girl, however, did not seem to realize the terrible consequences of her plans. Although she, like Solomon, later regretted her actions, this girl had to live for the rest of her life with the consequences of her horrendous act.

Push Yields Abuse. A study published in the Journal of Studies on Alcohol revealed that there is a considerable amount of time spent depicting the consumption of alcohol on prime-time television. Two-thirds of the 195 episodes that were monitored contained references to alcohol. There were 8.1 alcohol acts per hour of prime-time television. The average viewer watching four hours of prime-time television each evening was exposed to 32 drinking acts per night or 11,826 drinking acts per year.

In addition, the under-twenty-one-year-old characters tended to deliver inappropriate messages about drinking. The tendency was to make the consumption of alcohol by underaged drinkers acceptable, attractive, problem-free, glamorous, and grown-up. Dr. Thomas Radecki concluded that it was clear that the TV advertising and programming depicting the use of alcohol was playing a major role in increasing the abuse of alcohol among teens.

We are strongly influenced by television. If so much of our viewing presents the wrong behavior, we'll need to work even harder to live as God has summoned us to live in Christ Jesus.

Consequential Influences. When Solomon disobeyed the Lord's commandment and worshiped the gods of his wives, was he really that much different than our leaders today? Perhaps not. Dr. Mary Ann Glendon, a Harvard Law School professor, states that political leaders often give up their ties to other people and traditions in order to obtain power and prestige. They tend to become far more liberal. Traditional morality comes to have little authority for them. The same can be true for leaders in education, the arts, and the entertainment industry.

In 1991, a report by Robert Lichter, Linda Lichter, and Stanley

Rothman, co-directors for the Washington-based Center for Media and Public Affairs, noted that on issues of sexual morality, abortion, and religion, people at the top of the television and movie industry were far more liberal than the rest of the country. For instance, a survey of 104 writers and executives in Hollywood found that only 49% believed adultery was wrong, while 85% of Americans believed adultery to be wrong.

Certainly, when Solomon turned from God, he abandoned the traditional morality. The potential for the country to go astray was very real because of the leader's influence. Solomon's sin cost him his kingdom.

Questions for Students on the Next Lesson. 1. What was the basic message of John the Baptist? 2. To whom does Isaiah 40:3 refer? 3. What is repentance? 4. What was the reaction of the religious officials and of the people of Jerusalem, Judea, and the region around the Jordan to John's message? 5. What did John mean when he described a baptism of the Holy Spirit and of fire?

DECEMBER 1994
JANUARY, FEBRUARY 1995

JESUS THE FULFILLMENT
(THE GOSPEL OF MATTHEW)

LESSON 1—DECEMBER 4

JOHN HERALDS JESUS' COMING

Background Scripture: Matthew 3:1-15
Devotional Reading: Isaiah 40:3-11

KING JAMES VERSION

MATTHEW 3:1 In those days came John the Baptist, preaching in the wilderness of Judaea,

2 And saying, Repent ye: for the kingdom of heaven is at hand.

3 For this is he that was spoken of by the prophet Esaias, saying, The voice of one crying in the wilderness, Prepare ye the way of the Lord, make his paths straight.

4 And the same John had his raiment of camel's hair, and a leathern girdle about his loins; and his meat was locusts and wild honey.

5 Then went out to him Jerusalem, and all Judaea, and all the region round about Jordan,

6 And were baptized of him in Jordan, confessing their sins.

7 But when he saw many of the Pharisees and Sadducees come to his baptism, he said unto them, O generation of vipers, who hath warned you to flee from the wrath to come?

8 Bring forth therefore fruits meet for repentance:

9 And think not to say within yourselves, We have Abraham to our father: for I say unto you, that God is able of these stones to raise up children unto Abraham.

10 And now also the axe is laid unto the root of the trees: therefore every tree which bringeth not forth good fruit is hewn down, and cast into the fire.

11 I indeed baptize you with water unto repentance: but he that cometh after me is mightier than I, whose shoes I am not worthy to bear: he shall baptize you with the Holy Ghost, and with fire:

12 Whose fan is in his hand, and he will

REVISED STANDARD VERSION

MATTHEW 3:1 In those days came John the Baptist, preaching in the wilderness of Judea, 2 "Repent, for the kingdom of heaven is at hand." 3 For this is he who was spoken of by the prophet Isaiah when he said, "The voice of one crying in the wilderness: Prepare the way of the Lord, make his paths straight." 4 Now John wore a garment of camel's hair, and a leather girdle around his waist; and his food was locusts and wild honey. 5 Then went out to him Jerusalem and all Judea and all the region about the Jordan, 6 and they were baptized by him in the river Jordan, confessing their sins.

7 But when he saw many of the Pharisees and Sadducees coming for baptism, he said to them, "You brood of vipers! Who warned you to flee from the wrath to come? 8 Bear fruit that befits repentance, 9 and do not presume to say to yourselves, 'We have Abraham as our father'; for I tell you, God is able from these stones to raise up children to Abraham. 10 Even now the axe is laid to the root of the trees; every tree therefore that does not bear good fruit is cut down and thrown into the fire.

11 "I baptize you with water for repentance, but he who is coming after me is mightier than I, whose sandals I am not worthy to carry; he will baptize you with the Holy Spirit and with fire. 12 His winnowing fork is in his hand, and he will clear his threshing floor and gather his wheat into the granary, but the chaff he will burn with unquenchable fire."

13 Then Jesus came from Galilee to the Jordan to John, to be baptized by him. 14 John would have prevented him, saying,

throughly purge his floor, and gather his wheat into the garner; but he will burn up the chaff with unquenchable fire.

13 Then cometh Jesus from Galilee to Jordan unto John, to be baptized of him.

14 But John forbad him, saying, I have need to be baptized of thee, and comest thou to me?

15 And Jesus answering said unto him, Suffer it to be so now: for thus it becometh us to fulfil all righteousness. Then he suffered him.

"I need to be baptized by you, and do you come to me?" 15 But Jesus answered him, "Let it be so now; for thus it is fitting for us to fulfil all righteousness." Then he consented.

KEY VERSE: *I baptize you with water for repentance, but he who is coming after me is mightier than I, whose sandals I am not worthy to carry; he will baptize you with the Holy Spirit and with fire. Matthew 3:11.*

HOME DAILY BIBLE READINGS

Nov.	28	M.	Malachi 3:1-7	*The Lord's Messenger*
Nov.	29	T.	Matthew 3:1-6	*John the Baptist Preaches Repentance*
Nov.	30	W.	Matthew 3:7-12	*One Mightier Than John Is Coming*
Dec.	1	T.	Matthew 3:13—4:1	*Jesus Convinces John to Baptize Him*
Dec.	2	F.	Matthew 4:12-17	*Jesus Lives in Galilee*
Dec.	3	S.	Matthew 4:18-25	*Jesus Calls Disciples and Ministers*
Dec.	4	S.	Acts 13:16-26	*God's Promise Fulfilled in Jesus*

BACKGROUND

Each Gospel writer had his own slant on the significance of Jesus. Like Mark, Luke, and John, Matthew wanted to emphasize the aspects of Jesus Christ's life that seemed most important to him. He was not merely writing a biography of Jesus, but was stating what the good news of God through Jesus meant. And Matthew's Jewishness shows through in his Gospel account. Since for him Jesus was the fulfillment of the Old Testament promises, Matthew arranged his material to show how Jesus lived out the prophesied messianic character and actions.

Matthew opened his report on "Jesus as the fulfillment" by setting the scene through presenting John the Baptist. Matthew wanted his readers to know that John the Baptist, the last of the Old Testament style of preacher-prophets, heralded Jesus as the embodiment of everything promised in the Hebrews' sacred writings.

What an impression John the Baptist made! His influence was so great, in fact, that a sect of followers persisted well into the first century, A.D. Paul himself encountered some of John's disciples in Ephesus about thirty years after John's death (see Acts 19:3, 4).

Although descended from a long line of priests, John chose the role of prophet and retreated into the desert to live a simple life. His message was an uncompromising call to repentance. Reflecting on the unfaithfulness of God's people, John demanded a radical break with sinful ways, symbolized by an act of baptism. This baptism of repentance was intended to indicate inward cleansing. John's harsh condemnation of the authorities for their failure to repent brought on the wrath of the temple leaders and, finally, Herod Antipas himself.

Most important, however, was John's assurance that a new era was about to dawn with the coming of the promised one. John proclaimed bluntly that the soon-to-come deliverer would baptize with the Spirit, in contrast to John's own practice of baptizing with water only. Yet when Jesus appeared, John was reluctant to baptize Him. However, Jesus convinced John to baptize Him in order to confirm that God's gracious, saving invitation to the whole human race remained intact.

NOTES ON THE PRINTED TEXT

In those days came John the Baptist, preaching in the wilderness of Judea (3:1). John the Baptist was a Jew who lived in the wilderness of Judea. This was a rough, harsh, barren, and hot region around the Dead Sea, filled with cliffs and ravines. Here the Jordan River emptied into the Dead Sea. Likely, John picked the location because it provided moving water, which was required for ritual cleansing. Here, on the eastern side of the Jordan River, John preached and baptized.

He preached repentance. *Repent, for the kingdom of heaven is at hand* (3:2). Repentance means returning to God through a change of heart. The Baptist called his listeners to change their minds and turn to God because His great kingdom was dawning and the Lord was coming. Matthew knew John's preaching was part of God's divine plan; it fulfilled the prophecy of Isaiah. John was the voice *crying in the wilderness: Prepare the way of the Lord, make his paths straight* (3:3).

Matthew added a description of John's unusual clothing and diet. He wore *a garment of camel's hair, and a leather girdle around his waist; and his food was locusts and wild honey* (3:4). John dressed like a traditional prophet. The kind of food John ate might indicate that he had taken a Nazirite vow of asceticism, though most likely John was simply eating traditional nomadic food. Although locusts, the insects, could be eaten, they were not particularly appetizing nor filling, and John would have had to expend the energy to catch them. The locusts mentioned here were more likely a part of the carob family, a vegetable pod high in glucose. The honey consisted not only of the golden syrup by itself but was likely mixed with farina or grain, then rolled and dried so that it was a leather-like sheet that could be torn and eaten in strips.

John's preaching attracted immense crowds. A steady stream of people came from *Jerusalem and all Judea and all the region about the Jordan* (3:5). His preaching also had effect; people confessed their sins and were baptized. Water baptism expressed personal repentance and functioned as an outward sign of inner cleansing.

John's preaching also attracted the attention of a small group of the community's religious leaders. Pharisees came (3:7). This group was dedicated to obediently keeping and promoting the law of Moses and the oral tradition that interpreted the law. Sadducees (3:7) also came. These were men of the wealthy priestly party, the important political leaders in Jerusalem. Although John did not refuse to baptize them, he warned them that they were not meeting God's demands. They needed true repentance; they must not presume that their descent from Abraham would bring salvation. *You brood of vipers! Who warned you to flee from the wrath to come? Bear fruit that befits repentance, and do not presume to say to yourselves, "We have Abraham as our father"; for I tell you, God is able from these stones to raise up children to Abraham* (3:7-9).

The coming judgment had already begun, John announced. *Even now the axe is laid to the root of the trees; every tree therefore that does not bear good fruit is cut down and thrown into the fire* (3:10). As a barren, unproductive tree was cut down and destroyed, so God would judge the religious leaders who did not truly repent and obediently follow God.

John proclaimed to all that a greater prophet was coming. *I baptize you with water for repentance, but he who is coming after me is mightier than I . . . he will baptize you with the Holy Spirit and with fire* (3:11). As influential and important as he was, John told his listeners that he himself was not the Messiah. The distinction between him and the coming one would be great. John was only a preparer, not even worthy to carry the Messiah's sandals.

Then Jesus came from Galilee . . . to John, to be baptized by him (3:13). Having made the long, 120-mile trip down the Jordan River Valley from Galilee, Jesus came to John to be baptized. *I need to be baptized by you, and do you come to me?* (3:14). John recognized Jesus as the Messiah and protested, saying that Jesus ought to baptize him instead.

Jesus insisted. *Let it be so now; for thus it is fitting for us to fulfill all righteousness* (3:15). Jesus knew that all people must prepare for God's kingdom. Representing the human race in His human nature, Jesus, the God-Man, submitted to baptism; though perfectly sinless, He would identify Himself with the very sinners He came to save. John consented and baptized Jesus in the Jordan River.

SUGGESTIONS TO TEACHERS

Have you ever been on one of those little narrow-gauge trains that wind through the Alps in Switzerland? As the railway climbs and circles, you get different views of the same magnificent scene. Passengers often find themselves looking at the same mountain several times—but from a new angle each time as the train emerges from another tunnel or rounds another curve. Such a trip offers a series of views of the same alpine scene, all from greater and greater heights.

Matthew's Gospel carries us from the announcement of Jesus' coming to greater and greater heights: we see Jesus as Lord and Savior, as victor over sin and death, and as the fulfillment of all that God has ever promised. Today's lesson is the start of that momentous biblical journey. It opens with John the Baptist shouting that God's great new era is at hand.

1. COMING. Ask class members to give thumbnail character sketches of John the Baptist. Make sure they understand that John prepared the way for the coming of the Messiah. Ask how Christians prepare for Christ's coming today. Do Christians need to "get ready" for Christ to be in

their lives or to offer Him to others? If so, how? The key, as the text from Matthew suggests, is personal *repentance*.

2. CONTRAST. Let the character study of John continue by contrasting his message with the attitudes of the religious leaders of the day. Point out that John lived simply; they, lavishly. John had a personal awareness of God; they, a hearsay understanding of the Lord's ways. If we seek to emulate John and the prophets, in the face of the outrageous commercialism of this season, what concrete steps might we take to move closer to the simple life?

3. CALL. Devote some lesson time to the call for repentance by this prophetic preacher. Get to the root of the word itself and discuss what it means "to change the mind." How can we actually turn away from greed and pure self-interest toward the Lord? You may wish to ask what comes to mind when we hear the word "repentance." What changes in life-style will likely follow genuine repentance?

4. CLAIM. John the Baptist insisted that he was not the promised deliverer. In fact, he stated that the one coming to inaugurate God's new realm would baptize with the Holy Spirit, whereas he himself could only baptize with water. John recognized and accepted his role of pointing toward the Messiah. Remind your class that this is the mission of every Christian today. Each person who knows the good news of salvation will want to point to the Christ who made that salvation possible.

5. CONFIRMATION. Some class members may be puzzled about why Jesus was baptized. After all, they may reason, Jesus was sinless and had no need to repent and be forgiven. Help students understand one of the primary meanings of Jesus' baptism—as a confirmation of Jesus' call to represent human beings in His future sacrificial work on the cross. Emphasize the meaning of the Scripture quotations "This is my beloved Son, with whom I am well pleased" (Matt. 3:17, taken from Psalm 2:7) and Isaiah 42:1 (part of the "Suffering Servant" songs). In other words, Jesus understood His divine mission as God's anointed, and He also understood that messiahship meant suffering on behalf of others.

TOPIC FOR ADULTS
PREPARE FOR A NEW LIFE

Prepared for the Coming. Many husbands arrive home late from work, but David Snow, of Cape Cod, probably holds the record. One day in 1775, Snow and his fifteen-year-old son, David, Jr., set out as usual from Truro to fish in Cape Cod Bay. At that time, British privateers sometimes prowled the coastline and snatched prisoners. A British ship swooped down on the Snows and carried them to Halifax, Nova Scotia. Not long after, the father and son were transferred to England and confined to the Old Mill prison near Plymouth. Mrs. Snow had no word about what had happened to her husband and son. But she refused to give up hope that they would come home.

In the Plymouth prison, David Snow eventually developed a clever escape plan. One evening, he and his accomplices broke out and raced the fifteen miles to Plymouth harbor. There, they could find only an old fishing boat, but they boarded it and launched into the English channel. They managed to capture a larger vessel when it approached, and they sailed to France, where they sold their prize for $40.

French officials sent them across the Atlantic; however, Snow and his son and the others landed in the colonies still far from home, somewhere in the Carolinas. The Revolutionary War was being fought primarily in the South at that time, and the two Snows had to plod north on foot.

Mrs. Snow still had no messages from her two loved ones, but she continued to expect them to return. By the time David Snow and his son reached Boston, seven years had elapsed since their capture. They booked passage to Provincetown, then started to walk home to Truro. They began meeting friends on the way, who had assumed they were dead. Nearing home, David Snow learned that he would find his wife sewing over at Isaac Small's. He entered the Smalls' house, and, according to tradition, Mrs. Snow looked up and said, "What took you so long?"

Mrs. Snow lived with expectancy and was prepared for a new life with her husband when he arrived. We are called to have the same outlook in respect to the Lord.

Ready for the Action. The coach was trying to prepare his football players to deal with various situations on the field. Outlining a hypothetical condition in a game, he would ask various team members to answer what play should be called. "Okay," barked the coach, "so it's fourth down. You're on the opponents' eight yard line. It's goal to go. What do you do?" Turning suddenly to a third-string tackle, he jabbed his finger at the scrub lineman, and demanded, "You! What would *you* do?"

After a pause, the boy answered, "Well, sir, I'd slide down the bench for a better view."

We can prepare for Christ's coming by preparing ourselves to serve Him and His people in the various situations that come our way. We don't have to sit on the bench and wait. The Scriptures give us the clear instructions we need.

Questions for Students on the Next Lesson. 1. Why was John the Baptist in prison? 2. Why did John send the message asking if Jesus were the promised Messiah? 3. What did Jesus answer when He heard John the Baptist's question? 4. What was Jesus' opinion of John the Baptist? 5. Why is John the Baptist compared to Elijah?

TOPIC FOR YOUTH
SPREADING THE NEWS

Rebuked Silently. A young man, one of thousands of college students, arrived at Daytona Beach, Florida, for spring break. As he walked along the beach path enjoying the sun, the fresh air, and the break from his studies, he failed to see a person wearing a clerical collar approaching from the opposite direction. The two collided. The young man quickly and discreetly folded his arms across the writing on his chest as he muttered an apology.

The minister, knowing full well what the boy was doing, said, "Ah, was it the University of Virginia?"

"No sir," replied the boy.

"Well then, drop your arms and let me read your sweatshirt," said the minister.

The boy sheepishly obliged and dropped his arms. The inscription on his sweatshirt read, "Help Stamp Out Virginity." The boy was ashamed. Something within him made him want to change his actions from that day forward. Though the minister didn't say another word, he had, like a modern-day John the Baptist, called the boy to repent.

Repented. During World War II, two chaplains were serving on an aircraft carrier. One of the chaplains was extremely upset about the terrible language and swearing that was common on the ship. He called together the crew and berated and rebuked them for their shabby language. The result of his speech was that the language and swearing only got worse.

The other chaplain spoke to the men one evening. "I really wish you guys would not talk about my Boss like that," he told them. The crew responded to his plea, listening to the leader who spoke with love toward them—and of love for his Lord. His love led them to change their behavior.

Oops! Did you ever try to keep a secret from your parents when you were younger? Little four-year-old Brad went with his father to shop for his mother's Christmas present. Brad's mother liked to collect ceramic Santa Clauses, so, after a long search, the two located a unique and expensive Santa. After purchasing it, they walked to the car as Brad's father patiently explained that Christmas was several weeks away. Brad must not say anything; the present was to be their secret.

The excitement and the secret were too much for Brad, though. How could a four year old keep something like that to himself? Running in the front door he excitedly announced to his mother (much to his father's chagrin): "We got you a Santa, Mom—Oops!" Brad, like many youth, wanted to be first to tell about an important event. He simply could not wait.

Perhaps John the Baptist would have understood Brad's feelings. For John, the coming of the Messiah was too exciting to keep to himself; that news had to be shared. Have you shared Christ's coming with the enthusiasm and excitement of a John or a Brad?

Questions for Students on the Next Lesson. 1. Why was John the Baptist imprisoned? 2. Why did John question Jesus from prison? 3. Are there signs that the Messiah is at work today? Give some examples. 4. Is it offensive to follow Jesus? Why? 5. Have there been others of John the Baptist's caliber who have effectively called people to repentance? Name some of them.

LESSON 2—DECEMBER 11

JESUS AFFIRMS JOHN'S MESSAGE

Background Scripture: Matthew 11:2-15
Devotional Reading: John 1:1-14

KING JAMES VERSION

MATTHEW 11:2 Now when John had heard in the prison the works of Christ, he sent two of his disciples,

3 And said unto him, Art thou he that should come, or do we look for another?

4 Jesus answered and said unto them, Go and shew John again those things which ye do hear and see:

5 The blind receive their sight, and the lame walk, the lepers are cleansed, and the deaf hear, the dead are raised up, and the poor have the gospel preached to them.

6 And blessed is he, whosoever shall not be offended in me.

7 And as they departed, Jesus began to say unto the multitudes concerning John, What went ye out into the wilderness to see? A reed shaken with the wind?

8 But what went ye out for to see? A man clothed in soft raiment? behold, they that wear soft clothing are in kings' houses.

9 But what went ye out for to see? A prophet? yea, I say unto you, and more than a prophet.

10 For this is he, of whom it is written, Behold, I send my messenger before thy face, which shall prepare thy way before thee.

11 Verily I say unto you, Among them that are born of women there hath not risen a greater than John the Baptist: notwithstanding he that is least in the kingdom of heaven is greater than he.

12 And from the days of John the Baptist until now the kingdom of heaven suffereth violence, and the violent take it by force.

13 For all the prophets and the law prophesied until John.

14 And if ye will receive it, this is Elias, which was for to come.

15 He that hath ears to hear, let him hear.

REVISED STANDARD VERSION

MATTHEW 11:2 Now when John heard in prison about the deeds of the Christ, he sent word by his disciples 3 and said to him, "Are you he who is to come, or shall we look for another?" 4 And Jesus answered them, "Go and tell John what you hear and see: 5 the blind receive their sight and the lame walk, lepers are cleansed and the deaf hear, and the dead are raised up, and the poor have good news preached to them. 6 And blessed is he who takes no offense at me."

7 As they went away, Jesus began to speak to the crowds concerning John: "What did you go out into the wilderness to behold? A reed shaken by the wind? 8 Why then did you go out? To see a man clothed in soft raiment? Behold, those who wear soft raiment are in kings' houses. 9 Why then did you go out? To see a prophet? Yes, I tell you, and more than a prophet. 10 This is he of whom it is written, 'Behold, I send my messenger before thy face, who shall prepare thy way before thee.' 11 Truly, I say to you, among those born of women there has risen no one greater than John the Baptist; yet he who is least in the kingdom of heaven is greater than he. 12 From the days of John the Baptist until now the kingdom of heaven has suffered violence, and men of violence take it by force. 13 For all the prophets and the law prophesied until John; 14 and if you are willing to accept it, he is Elijah who is to come. 15 He who has ears to hear, let him hear."

KEY VERSE: *Behold, I send my messenger before thy face, who shall prepare thy way before thee.* Matthew 11:10b.

HOME DAILY BIBLE READINGS

Dec.	5	M.	Matthew 9:35—10:4	*Jesus and His Disciples at Work*
Dec.	6	T.	Matthew 10:5-15	*Jesus Sends Out Twelve Disciples*
Dec.	7	W.	Matthew 10:37—11:1	*Being Disciples of Jesus*

Dec.	8	T.	Matthew 11:2-6	Jesus' Deeds Answer John's Inquiry
Dec.	9	F.	Matthew 11:7-15	Jesus' Affirmation of John
Dec.	10	S.	Matthew 11:16-24	Jesus' Rebuke of the Unrepentant
Dec.	11	S.	Matthew 11:25-30	Jesus' Invitation to Come to Him

BACKGROUND

John the Baptist's blunt words won him a wide audience among the common people, but his preaching did not endear him to the establishment, the group of religious and political leaders. When Herod Antipas, Rome's puppet king in the region, entered into a scandalous relationship with his married sister-in-law (his brother Philip's wife), John denounced Herod. As a result, Herod captured John and dropped him into a dungeon deep in the grim fortress-castle of Machaerus.

Machaerus sat atop a steep, towering rock formation, soaring thirty-six hundred feet above the Dead Sea in one of the bleakest parts of the earth. The huge fortifications were virtually impregnable and escape-proof. Herod's palace within Machaerus was later the scene of a night of sinful indulgence that ended in Herod's agreeing to have John the Baptist beheaded.

John languished helplessly in his cell, occasionally hearing rumors of Jesus' ministry. Finally, he was able to smuggle out a message to some followers asking whether or not Jesus was really the long-expected Messiah. John obviously was having second thoughts about Jesus. After weeks and weeks in a dismal dungeon, he was questioning whether Jesus or anyone could ever deliver him. If Jesus were actually the promised messianic deliverer, why hadn't things taken place the way John had thought they should? Why weren't the wicked people destroyed? Where was the great day of judgment and the clearing of the righteous? In other words, why wasn't Jesus acting the way a Messiah ought to act?

Jesus had created a sensation by His words and works in the Jewish towns of Galilee. People were crowding to hear Him preach and to witness His miraculous cures. Jesus had gathered a core of followers who were whispering that He truly was the anointed Deliverer.

When John's disciples asked Jesus about being the Messiah, Jesus told them to report to John what they had personally heard and seen: that the signs of new life He gave to the hurting and hopeless were all the evidence anyone needed to realize that He was beginning God's rule in a wondrous new way.

Jesus deliberately contrasted what John and his followers expected of a messiah and what God's true Messiah would be. Jesus stated that He came not to destroy the wicked then and there, as John expected, but to restore, to heal, to save. The great power of God's coming reign was already at work.

NOTES ON THE PRINTED TEXT

John heard in prison about the deeds of the Christ (11:2). Herod Antipas (grandson of Herod the Great) had John the Baptist shut up in the forbidding mountain fortress of Machaerus, which was located east of the Dead

Sea. John had strongly spoken against the "marriage" of Herod to Herodias, the wife of Herod's half brother Philip and granddaughter of his own father, Herod the Great. This marriage had been arranged without the benefit of a divorce from Herodias's husband, Philip. Furthermore, such a marriage was contrary to Jewish law, which forbade marriage to a brother's wife if the brother was still living.

While in prison, through his loyal disciples, John heard about the miracles of Jesus. *Are you he who is to come, or shall we look for another?* (11:3). Perhaps John was considering whether Jesus was a political Messiah about to liberate Israel. Maybe he wondered if Jesus was going to free him from prison, since Isaiah had prophesied that the Messiah would free the prisoners, especially those who were imprisoned for their obedience to God. Whatever the motivation, John sent his trusted disciples to ask Jesus if He truly was the promised Messiah.

Jesus did not directly answer John. He simply called attention to His preaching and to His works. *Go and tell John what you hear and see* (11:4). Jesus then further built His response on Isaiah's prophecies. *The blind receive their sight and the lame walk, lepers are cleansed and the deaf hear, and the dead are raised up, and the poor have good news preached to them* (11:5). Jesus reminded John that the Messiah would heal sickness and preach the story of God's love to all the lowly of the world. If John understood these signs of God's work, then he would have the answer to his original question. *Blessed is he who takes no offense at me* (11:6).

As the messengers were departing, Jesus spoke of John and his mission. *What did you go out into the wilderness to behold? A reed shaken by the wind?* (11:7). Jesus' second question would summon an obvious "No!" for an answer. The crowds did not make that difficult journey down to the banks of the Jordan River to stand and idly stare at some cane grass and cattails. They went to see a courageous and powerful man. *Why then did you go out? To see a man clothed in soft raiment? Behold, those who wear soft raiment are in kings' houses* (11:8). Again, the second question anticipated a negative answer. The crowds did not journey into the wilderness to see a frail man in luxurious clothing. John was no soft aristocrat who worried about his own comfort, Jesus affirmed. *Why then did you go out? To see a prophet?* (11:9). Pressing His audience, Jesus asked a third time about John. This time, though, Jesus answered His own question. *Yes, I tell you, and more than a prophet* (11:9). John was a prophet, but he was also more than one of the ordinary prophets who spoke for God. John was the forerunner of the Messiah. God had sent John to prepare the way as the prophet Malachi had prophesied. *Behold, I send my messenger before thy face, who shall prepare thy way before thee* (11:10).

Jesus declared that no greater person had appeared. *Among those born of women there has risen no one greater than John the Baptist* (11:11). However, as great as John was, the least disciple who committed himself or herself to Jesus was greater than John, Jesus declared. *Yet he who is least in the kingdom of heaven is greater than he* (11:11).

From the days of John the Baptist until now the kingdom of heaven has suffered violence, and men of violence take it by force (11:12). From John's time onward, human beings have violently tried to grab or seize the

Kingdom and keep individuals from accepting God's rule. (Another interpretation is that with John's arrival, people were storming their way afresh into the kingdom Christ was bringing.) John's coming brought an end to the predictions of the Kingdom by the prophets. Now their prophecies had been fulfilled in Jesus Himself. *For all the prophets and the law prophesied until John* (11:13).

Jesus told the people that John's message was like that of the prophet Elijah. The people believed that Elijah would return to announce the Messiah's coming, and Jesus announced that John himself had fulfilled Elijah's function. *If you are willing to accept it, he is Elijah who is to come* (11:14). It was a time of choice and opportunity. Those who were alert must act. *He who has ears to hear, let him hear* (11:15).

SUGGESTIONS TO TEACHERS

The stores and malls seem to be the primary focus of Christmas preparation these days. "Only thirteen shopping days left," the newspapers remind us, reinforcing the idea that getting ready for December 25th means a lot of gift buying.

Last week, we heard that John the Baptist called to prepare the way for Christ's coming by repenting. What a contrast to our way of preparing! This week, our lesson continues with John the Baptist and his probing question about Jesus' identity.

1. ASKING. John the Baptist asks the key question in life when he inquires of Jesus, "Are you he who is to come, or shall we look for another?" Ultimately, every person must face up to that question. Is Jesus the one? Or is He merely another prophet, teacher, or guru claiming a place in the spotlight? As we find ourselves caught up in the trappings of a highly secularized holiday, we need to ask John's question again and again. Your class may find it helpful to discuss the doubts or reservations some may have about Jesus' claims. How could such doubters be helped to see Jesus more clearly in His true identity?

2. ANSWERING. Note that Jesus did not answer John by launching into a theological discourse. Instead, He told John's followers to report what they personally had seen or heard. The blind could see; cripples walked; lepers were cleansed; the deaf heard again; the dead came to life; poor people knew good news. Here is the best method of answering critics and winning others to Christ: Tell what you personally have experienced from the Lord. The best evangelism technique is simply sharing what you have seen and heard as good news.

Encourage your group members to recall what they have seen and heard of Jesus in their spiritual journeys so far. Think of the various kinds of healing that Jesus has made possible in their lives and in the lives of persons they know. Blindness can also mean more than losing physical eyesight; being crippled can be understood in ways other than not being able to use one's legs.

3. AFFIRMING. Jesus does not put down John for his question, but instead affirms John's greatness. He acknowledges that John the Baptist truly is the God-sent messenger who prepares the way for the coming of God's Anointed One. You may suggest to your group members that each

person present is intended to be a God-sent messenger also, preparing the way for the full manifestation of Christ's rule.

4. ANNOUNCING. Jesus makes it clear that He stands above John the Baptist. He uses the code words comparing John to Elijah to indicate that the Messiah truly has come. "He who has ears to hear, let him hear" is Jesus' way of saying that any person alert to the Spirit, to Scripture, and to Jesus' own words and works will realize that Jesus is the Messiah. God's new era has broken into human history.

TOPIC FOR ADULTS
HOLD ON TO YOUR FAITH

Sent as Road Builders. In the summer of 1949, three seminary classmates and I (William P. Barker) drove up the Alcan Highway to Alaska in an old '36 Plymouth. The Alcan then was a tortuous, fifteen-hundred-mile track of mud, sand, and gravel through desolate wilderness. Occasionally we would see places where the road set out through the tundra into such hopeless swamps that the section had to be abandoned and new routes found. Washouts collapsed bridges, and sharp stones made six-ply tires absolutely essential. Heavy dust and rough washboard sections (where soil was pushed over logs to form a road base) made the trip arduous and long.

Working in Alaska that summer, I met a couple of the grizzled workmen who had helped build the highway. They described how it was built as a lifeline to Alaska during World War II and placed on the eastern side of the Rockies instead of the easier and more direct western slope because of fear of a Japanese invasion. These old-timers recounted instances of having big pieces of equipment swallowed in the soft tundra, or mile-long sections carried away by raging torrents after a rain. Road building, they testified, was neither fun nor easy.

Why did they do it? These old highway crew members, not given to glory or speeches, offered no grandiose or heroic reasons. In their rough language, they made it clear that it was a case of following orders and of being loyal citizens of the realm. A 265-pound diesel caterpillar operator named "Tiny" put it well: "We belonged to the nation and we got sent!"

We belong to Christ. And we are sent! In the tradition of John the Baptist, we are sent to build the road for Christ's rule everywhere in the world. Prepare for His coming. Hold on to your faith and open the way for Him.

Expecting the Messiah. Israeli Jews tell the legendary story of a Russian Jew who asked his rabbi for a job. The rabbi tells the man to stand at the village gate each day and wait to greet the Messiah when He arrives. The rabbi says that he will pay the man one ruble a month for carrying out this task—for as long as the Messiah tarries. When the man protests that the pay is too low, the old rabbi smiles and replies, "Of course the pay is low. But the job security is excellent."

Like the old rabbi, many Christians today do not really expect God to visit their lives. John the Baptist began to have such thoughts about Jesus, asking whether he should wait for Jesus to show that He truly was the Messiah, or should he look for another. In any case, the waiting seemed almost futile.

This sense of pointlessness in looking for God to involve Himself pervades the lives of many. But hold on to your faith. God has acted in the person of Jesus. Look at Jesus' acts and teaching again, and take Him at His word.

Undimmed Hope. Several years ago, a fire swept through a candle factory in New York City, completely destroying the huge Candle of Peace. This symbolic candle, sixteen feet high, with a wick the size of a rope, weighing more than 2,200 pounds and costing more than $25,000, was the gift of the Ajello family to the United Nations. They presented it with the request that it should be lighted for one day each year, on the birthday of the United Nations. It was designed and built to serve in this way for two thousand years. To add to its significance, they had the flags of all the nations painted in fadeless oils upon its surface. In a few moments of time, this symbol of humankind's organization for peace lay in a molten, shapeless mass.

How often elaborate preparations for peace have melted into nothingness in a moment of time! Our faith, however, need not be extinguished. God comes through Jesus Christ in spite of the ashes and ruins of our efforts to effect a new beginning.

Questions for Students on the Next Lesson. 1. How did Joseph first react when he learned that Mary was expecting a child? 2. What could Joseph have done, if he so chose, when he first heard of Mary's pregnancy? 3. What does the name "Jesus" mean? 4. What does "Emmanuel" mean? 5. What is the significance of Jesus' being born to a virgin?

TOPIC FOR YOUTH
BELIEVING THE NEWS

No Appearance. On September 1, 1992, over six thousand people of all ages and from many states waited expectantly inside and outside St. Joseph's Church in Cold Spring, Kentucky. They believed a prediction that the biblical Mary would come to visit the church at midnight!

At exactly 12:00 a.m., the anticipation reached a fever pitch. The Rev. Leroy Smith urged the fifteen hundred people jammed into the church to welcome the mother of Jesus into their midst. Although a few claimed that they did see Mary in the pine trees, most said they saw nothing and went home. The excitement had started two months earlier when Smith caused a sensation by announcing that an unidentified mystic told him the church would receive a visitation.

Like Smith and the six thousand hopefuls, many of us want detailed predictions of the future. However, every time someone tries to pinpoint a date for the miraculous, there is disillusionment and disappointment.

Never Alone. Suicide is a leading cause of death among teenagers. Studies have repeatedly shown that adolescents who try to take their own lives suffer from an overwhelming sense of "I am alone." Discouragement gives way to feelings of hopelessness and total isolation. That includes isolation from parents, other loved ones, friends, and even God.

John the Baptist's message of the coming of the Messiah, Jesus, means that we need never feel alone. Through Jesus Christ, we are loved and strengthened by the Creator, who can become our loving Father.

What Kind of Integrity? The electronic church was a billion-dollar industry at its zenith in the 1980s. The eight best-known television programs received approximately 500 million dollars alone. To buy time on the commercial stations, religious producers spent at least 600 million dollars a year.

Then, in the mid to late 1980s, came some shocking revelations. Jim Bakker, star of the PTL Club, was implicated in a scandal. If that was not bad enough, he was eventually convicted of tax fraud by the United States government. Jimmy Swaggart, another giant in the religious broadcasting industry, was discovered to have had several affairs with prostitutes. The scandals and revelations damaged not only these men's ministries, but also those of other televangelists and other ministers. Some people, youth included, questioned the sincerity and integrity of religious leaders and crusaders in general.

Interestingly, no one questioned John's integrity. Everyone accepted him as a pointer sent by God to prepare the way for the real power, Jesus Christ. Yet as great as John unquestionably was, he willingly stepped aside, pointing everyone to Jesus. He humbly claimed he was not worthy to carry Jesus' sandals. Here was a man of impeccable integrity that was squeaky clean.

Questions for Students on the Next Lesson. 1. What does betrothal mean? 2. What kind of man was Joseph? 3. How did God communicate with Joseph? Does God communicate like this today? 4. What was God's message to Joseph? 5. What does the name "Jesus" mean?

LESSON 3—DECEMBER 18

JESUS IS BORN

Background Scripture: Matthew 1:18-25
Devotional Reading: Isaiah 9:2-7

KING JAMES VERSION

MATTHEW 1:18 Now the birth of Jesus Christ was on this wise: When as his mother Mary was espoused to Joseph, before they came together, she was found with child of the Holy Ghost.

19 Then Joseph her husband, being a just man, and not willing to make her a publick example, was minded to put her away privily.

20 But while he thought on these things, behold, the angel of the Lord appeared unto him in a dream, saying, Joseph, thou son of David, fear not to take unto thee Mary thy wife: for that which is conceived in her is of the Holy Ghost.

21 And she shall bring forth a son, and thou shalt call his name JESUS: for he shall save his people from their sins.

22 Now all this was done, that it might be fulfilled which was spoken of the Lord by the prophet, saying,

23 Behold, a virgin shall be with child, and shall bring forth a son, and they shall call his name Emmanuel, which being interpreted is, God with us.

24 Then Joseph being raised from sleep did as the angel of the Lord had bidden him, and took unto him his wife:

25 And knew her not till she had brought forth her firstborn son: and he called his name JESUS.

REVISED STANDARD VERSION

MATTHEW 1:18 Now the birth of Jesus Christ took place in this way. When his mother Mary had been betrothed to Joseph, before they came together she was found to be with child of the Holy Spirit; 19 and her husband Joseph, being a just man and unwilling to put her to shame, resolved to divorce her quietly. 20 But as he considered this, behold, an angel of the Lord appeared to him in a dream, saying, "Joseph, son of David, do not fear to take Mary your wife, for that which is conceived in her is of the Holy Spirit; 21 she will bear a son, and you shall call his name Jesus, for he will save his people from their sins." 22 All this took place to fulfil what the Lord had spoken by the prophet: 23 "Behold, a virgin shall conceive and bear a son, and his name shall be called Emmanuel" (which means, God with us). 24 When Joseph woke from sleep, he did as the angel of the Lord commanded him; he took his wife, 25 but knew her not until she had borne a son; and he called his name Jesus.

KEY VERSE: Behold, a virgin shall conceive and bear a son, and his name shall be called Emmanuel. Matthew 1:23a.

HOME DAILY BIBLE READINGS

Dec.	12	M.	Isaiah 9:2-7	*From Darkness to Light*
Dec.	13	T.	Isaiah 52:1-10	*The Salvation of God Is Coming*
Dec.	14	W.	Matthew 1:18-25	*The Angel's Message about Jesus*
Dec.	15	T.	Luke 2:1-7	*The Birth of Jesus*
Dec.	16	F.	Luke 2:8–21	*Praise from Angels and Shepherds*
Dec.	17	S.	Luke 2:22-35	*Jesus' Presentation in the Temple*
Dec.	18	S.	Luke 2:36-40	*Anna Gives Thanks for Jesus*

BACKGROUND

Naturally, Matthew wrote from a Jewish slant. He probably also had Jewish readers in mind. Repeatedly, this Gospel writer took pains to show that Jesus was the fulfillment of everything promised in the Hebrew Scriptures. In fact, Matthew opened his Gospel account by tracing Jesus' genealogy back to the father of the faith, Abraham. Matthew also made sure that his readers realized that Jesus' family tree included the great hero-king, David.

Matthew's thesis was that Jesus fulfilled the writings of the prophets. More than any other Gospel writer, Matthew quotes proof texts from the Old Testament, as in his reference to Isaiah 7:14 about a virgin conceiving and the quotation from Micah 5:2 about the birthplace in Bethlehem (see Matt. 2:6).

Although Matthew was convinced of the miraculous virgin birth, he related the Christmas story from Joseph's point of view. (By contrast, Luke's version flowed from Mary's viewpoint.) Matthew brought out the disappointment and anguish that Joseph first felt upon learning that his betrothed was pregnant. (Betrothal in the Jewish community was as legally binding as marriage. Although the betrothed couple did not sleep together, betrothal could be dissolved only only by formal divorce procedures.) Matthew indicated what an honorable man Joseph was in trying to spare Mary further shame or hurt before the angel disclosed the truth in a dream. In those times, Joseph could even have urged that Mary be stoned to death for adultery.

Joseph showed his piety and faithfulness to God when he awoke from the dream and obeyed the instructions of the angel to marry Mary. What a great act of trust in God: marrying a girl who was pregnant with a child that he had not conceived!

Matthew knew that the very name "Jesus" carried immense significance, for it is the Greek form of Joshua, meaning "Yahweh is salvation." Matthew's report of the angel's message that Jesus "will save his people from their sins" alluded to Psalm 130:8: "He alone will set Israel free from all their sins." Countless people from the time of that wondrous birth have discovered the truth of Jesus' saving, freeing love.

NOTES ON THE PRINTED TEXT

When his mother Mary had been betrothed to Joseph, before they came together she was found to be with child of the Holy Spirit (1:18). In New Testament times, betrothal was the first step in marriage, a permanent contract between the man and the woman, considered a legally binding obligation. Betrothal could only be broken by divorce papers and a payment of a fine. If it was a woman's first marriage, she was considered to be under the jurisdiction of the intended husband for the one year of betrothal. The couple did not actually live together and normally refrained from sexual relations. It was assumed that the two would remain faithful to one another, and infidelity during this period was considered adultery. The wronged partner could demand the penalty of death by stoning.

During this period of betrothal, Mary was found to be pregnant. Since Joseph and Mary had not had sexual relations, Joseph believed Mary had violated their marriage contract by having a sexual relationship with another man. Angry and hurt, Joseph weighed his options. He could have Mary executed as an example to other girls in the village. His case was airtight (see Deuteronomy 22:23, 24).

Because Joseph was a sensitive man, he decided to end the betrothal without publicly shaming or disgracing Mary. He would follow the less strict judicial option. *Joseph, being a just man and unwilling to put her to shame, resolved to divorce her quietly* (1:19). The procedure would require only two witnesses and could be done privately.

But as he considered this . . . an angel of the Lord appeared to him in a dream (1:20). Most people in the ancient world believed that God communicated with humans through dreams. In this case, God did interrupt Joseph's sleep with a divine announcement: *Joseph, son of David, do not fear to take Mary your wife, for that which is conceived in her is of the Holy Spirit; she will bear a son, and you shall call his name Jesus, for he will save his people from their sins* (1:20, 21). The angel told Joseph not to divorce Mary but to accept her as his wife and marry her. The child she was carrying was holy and set aside for God's purpose—to provide salvation for humankind. The name "Jesus" indicated the child's purpose of delivering His people from sin, in fulfillment of Isaiah's prophecy (see Isaiah 7:14). *Behold, a virgin shall conceive and bear a son, and his name shall be called Emmanuel (which means, God with us)* (1:23). The child would be the fulfillment of all the hopes of God's people.

When Joseph awoke, he obediently followed God's command. *When Joseph awoke from sleep, he did as the angel of the Lord commanded him; he took his wife* (1:24). Joseph did not divorce Mary, rather he accepted her as his wife.

Throughout the early months of marriage, Joseph had no sexual relations with Mary until the child had been born. In obedience to God's order, the child was named Jesus. *[He] knew her not until she had borne a son; and he called his name Jesus* (1:25).

SUGGESTIONS TO TEACHERS

As teacher, you may feel that because everyone has heard the Christmas story so many times you'll find it difficult to put together an entire lesson on the birth of Jesus. It's not that you think that Christ's coming isn't special; rather, you may wonder: "What can I say that has not already been said many times before?"

Today, however, look at the glorious story as reported by Matthew. Pick out the unique emphases that Matthew has put into his account. Then you'll discover that this lesson can bring refreshingly interesting and helpful insights to your students.

1. ILLUSTRIOUS ANCESTRY. Matthew traces Jesus' lineage back through David to Abraham. This list conveys much more than Jesus' family tree. Matthew emphasized through the genealogy that Jesus summed up and fulfilled all that had gone before, all that Hebrew history had promised.

Look closely at some of the names. Probably you have not heard of many of them. Who were Azor and Zadok, to pick out just two? These obscure personalities would be completely forgotten had it not been for Jesus. Likewise for us, we may think we are insignificant. Who will remember us in a few generations? In the light of Jesus, however, we have a place. Because of Jesus, we may be confident that we will always be remembered by God.

2. UNEXPECTED INTERRUPTION. Matthew told about the birth of Jesus from Joseph's point of view, so look at the story specifically through Joseph's eyes. Encourage your students to let their imaginations go for a while in reflecting on Joseph. How must he have felt when he heard Mary was going to have a baby? Help students appreciate how deep was Joseph's sense of fairness (before the angel's announcement) and how profound was his sense of trust in God's message (after the angel's words to him). Here is true faith.

Point out that Joseph was not one of the elite in his community, but a village carpenter. God uses ordinary people to serve Him for extraordinary purposes.

3. ANGELIC ANNOUNCEMENT. Christmas should also be a time simply to wonder. The beautiful report of the virgin birth is more than a doctrine to be defended. Jesus' miraculous birth through the intervention of the Holy Spirit is a reason to stand in awe of God's wondrous ways.

4. INSTANT OBEDIENCE. Faith is more than feelings; it is doing, acting on behalf of God. Joseph acted. He obeyed the instructions of the Lord that came to him through the dream. Sometimes the Lord's messages can get through to us only when all our barriers are down in the midst of sleep. Without delving into unnecessary psychological discussions about dreams, remind your group members that the key theme is Joseph's obedience in taking Mary as his wife. Talk with your students about the role of obedience in the Christian life today. When is it hardest? How do we go about discerning what God wants us to do?

TOPIC FOR ADULTS
JESUS IS BORN

Major Production? A few years ago, a Hollywood director was making a film attempting to cover the story of the Bible. In his stage directions, he stated: "Enter God. Begin with an earthquake and work up to a climax."

That may be the way of the movie moguls, but it is not the way of God in the Scriptures. Quietly, gently, unexpectedly, God presents Himself in human form through the birth of a baby to a peasant girl in Bethlehem. However, this wondrous event, the coming of Jesus the Christ, is the high point of God's working in human history. No earthquakes. No dramatic special effects. Only the miracle of a newborn, held by a loving mother in a stable cave, in an obscure provincial town. God came quietly among us in the person of that child.

Joseph's Mousetrap. In his version of the birth of Jesus, Matthew provides wonderful insights into Joseph's character. Although the Gospel writer doesn't offer details of Joseph's life beyond this, we can be sure that Joseph had a profound influence on Jesus as a child.

Interestingly, some medieval artists seemed to see Joseph in a particularly sympathetic light. The magnificent Merode Altarpiece, for example, now in the Cloisters in New York, is a folding painting in which the right wing of the three-section masterpiece features Joseph. In this scene, Joseph is depicted at work in his carpentry shop making a mousetrap.

A mousetrap? Art historians and medieval scholars remind us that the mouse was regarded as a symbol of evil. Going back to St. Augustine's saying, "The Cross of the Lord was the devil's mousetrap, the bait by which he was caught by the Lord's death," the artist of this triptych no doubt used the metaphor of the mousetrap to convey the meaning of Christ's death on the cross. The creator of this work of art also saw Joseph as a man who must have understood that Mary's son would pay an awful price one day to bring the powers of evil to bay. Whether Joseph fully comprehended it or not, Jesus was God's chosen instrument to capture and conquer the devilish forces loose in the world.

From Suicide to the Savior. Everyone in the little country church noticed Mike. Who wouldn't? The thirty-six year old biker complete with tattoos certainly looked out of place.

Mike, an ex-con, was an alcoholic who also used drugs regularly. When Mike lost his job (because of his drunkenness), he became so discouraged he decided to commit suicide. However, God crossed his path with a pastor who would not give up on Mike. Mike agreed to go with this pastor to a citywide Christian concert. Hearing the Gospel through the music, Mike jumped from his seat and virtually ran down the aisle when the invitation was given.

Meeting Jesus opened up a new life for Mike. He threw away his pornographic magazines and began reading the Bible. He even decided to sell his beloved motorcycle and use the money to help others meet his Savior.

Questions for Students on the Next Lesson. 1. Exactly who were the wise men? 2. Why was Herod troubled at the report of a newborn king? 3. How did Mary, Joseph, and Jesus escape Herod's horrible decree of death of male babies in Bethlehem? 4. In what ways have you found your life to be a journey in search of meaning in life? 5. What are the best gifts you can give to those you love? To the Lord?

TOPIC FOR YOUTH
EXPERIENCING THE NEWS

Living Up to His Name. Twenty-two-year-old Daniel F. Boone, a fifth-generation descendant of the legendary frontiersman, took his name very seriously. The young man was entering basic training for the army and said he considered it an honor to be named Daniel Boone. He also felt that he built up his own name by living under another's.

Good point! Names can confer personhood. Names tell you who you are and what you stand for as a person. That is why such care goes into choosing a name for a child.

God chose the name for Joseph's child, and the name "Jesus" reminded everyone that God was acting to save His people. The one who owned that name lived up to it in every way.

Parents-to-Be. Each year, one in ten teenage girls becomes pregnant. Of girls currently fourteen years old, four in ten will be pregnant by age twenty. While the number of abortions increases among unmarried teens, there are still three births for every five abortions.

This puts an enormous economic burden on society and creates health problems for both the mother and the child. Meanwhile, the social stigma against giving birth out of wedlock has declined. Girls are no longer asked to leave high schools when they become pregnant. In fact, social workers note that a strange, perverse twist has been thrown into this challenging situation: Some unwed teens now consider having a baby a status symbol!

Joseph and Mary felt very differently. For Joseph, Mary's pregnancy was cause for hurt and worry; Mary was troubled. Neither saw the impending birth as a status symbol at all. God, however, reassured both that He was with them. This was not a case of immorality, but a special case of divine intervention.

Having experienced His news, they obeyed His command. The two became parents to the infant Jesus. Both would grow and mature, experiencing God's power in their child.

The Greatest Miracle. Over one thousand years ago, tribespeople gathered at the Pyramid of the Sun in Teotihuacán, Mexico, to watch an eclipse. To the ancients, the phenomenon that turned the daytime into night was a great, mysterious miracle.

On July 11, 1991, millions of people gathered along a 9,320-mile-long path, which stretched from the western Pacific to Brazil, gasping and cheering as they watched the moon's shadow turn daytime into nighttime once again. Although they had a scientific explanation for what was happening, the event was no less spectacular. It was an amazing event.

Whether it is an eclipse or the birth of a child, wonders continue to occur all around us. The great miracle of history, however, remains the Incarnation—God's coming to earth, as one of us, to save us from our sins.

Questions for Students on the Next Lesson. 1. From where did the wise men come? 2. Why did they go to Jerusalem? 3. Why was Herod upset with the wise men's announcement? 4. What plans did Herod make when he heard of the birth of a new king? 5. What kinds of gifts did the Magi offer, and what is the significance of those gifts?

LESSON 4—DECEMBER 25

THE WISE MEN WORSHIP JESUS

Background Scripture: Matthew 2
Devotional Reading: Isaiah 11:1-9

KING JAMES VERSION

MATTHEW 2:1 Now when Jesus was born in Bethlehem of Judaea in the days of Herod the king, behold, there came wise men from the east to Jerusalem,

2 Saying, Where is he that is born King of the Jews? for we have seen his star in the east, and are come to worship him.

3 When Herod the king had heard these things, he was troubled, and all Jerusalem with him.

4 And when he had gathered all the chief priests and scribes of the people together, he demanded of them where Christ should be born.

5 And they said unto him, In Bethlehem of Judaea: for thus it is written by the prophet,

6 And thou Bethlehem, in the land of Juda, art not the least among the princes of Juda: for out of thee shall come a Governor, that shall rule my people Israel.

7 Then Herod, when he had privily called the wise men, enquired of them diligently what time the star appeared.

8 And he sent them to Bethlehem, and said, Go and search diligently for the young child; and when ye have found him, bring me word again, that I may come and worship him also.

9 When they had heard the king, they departed; and, lo, the star, which they saw in the east, went before them, till it came and stood over where the young child was.

10 When they saw the star, they rejoiced with exceeding great joy.

11 And when they were come into the house, they saw the young child with Mary his mother, and fell down, and worshipped him: and when they had opened their treasures, they presented unto him gifts; gold, and frankincense, and myrrh.

12 And being warned of God in a dream that they should not return to Herod, they departed into their own country another way.

REVISED STANDARD VERSION

MATTHEW 2:1 Now when Jesus was born in Bethlehem of Judea in the days of Herod the king, behold, wise men from the East came to Jerusalem, saying, 2 "Where is he who has been born king of the Jews? For we have seen his star in the East, and have come to worship him." 3 When Herod the king heard this, he was troubled, and all Jerusalem with him; 4 and assembling all the chief priests and scribes of the people, he inquired of them where the Christ was to be born. 5 They told him, "In Bethlehem of Judea; for so it is written by the prophet: 6 'And you, O Bethlehem, in the land of Judah, are by no means least among the rulers of Judah; for from you shall come a ruler who will govern my people Israel.' "

7 Then Herod summoned the wise men secretly and ascertained from them what time the star appeared; 8 and he sent them to Bethlehem, saying, "Go and search diligently for the child, and when you have found him bring me word, that I too may come and worship him." 9 When they had heard the king they went their way; and lo, the star which they had seen in the East went before them, till it came to rest over the place where the child was. 10 When they saw the star, they rejoiced exceedingly with great joy; 11 and going into the house they saw the child with Mary his mother, and they fell down and worshiped him. Then, opening their treasures, they offered him gifts, gold and frankincense and myrrh.

12 And being warned in a dream not to return to Herod, they departed to their own country by another way.

KEY VERSE: *Going into the house they saw the child with Mary his mother, and they fell down and worshiped him. Then, opening their treasures, they offered him gifts, gold and frankincense and myrrh.* Matthew 2:11.

HOME DAILY BIBLE READINGS

Dec.	19	M.	Isaiah 11:1-9	*The Rule of the Messiah*
Dec.	20	T.	Zechariah 9:9-13	*The Day of Deliverance*
Dec.	21	W.	Micah 5:1-5a	*The Deliverer to Come from Bethlehem*
Dec.	22	T.	Matthew 2:1-6	*The Wise Men Directed to Bethlehem*
Dec.	23	F.	Matthew 2:7-12	*The Wise Men Worship Jesus*
Dec.	24	S.	Matthew 2:13-18	*Escape to Egypt*
Dec.	25	S.	Matthew 2:19-23	*Return from Egypt*

BACKGROUND

The original "Star Trek" took place approximately two thousand years ago when a group of wise men, known as Magi, traveled from the East to Bethlehem. Roughly the equivalent of astrophysicists in our society, greatly respected for their knowledge in the ancient world, these Magi, similar to research scientists, kept careful records of their studies of the night skies. One band of Magi became so impressed upon observing an unusual occurrence in the heavens that they concluded that a momentous event was about to take place. When the intense light of a new star continued, they decided to leave their homes in what is perhaps today's Iran and head in the direction of the star. Tradition says there were three Magi. Scripture, however, does not mention the number of men or their names.

It is interesting that Matthew, the writer who took such pains to relate the coming of Jesus to its prophecies, should be the one to include the story of the visit of these mysterious strangers to the manger. Luke tells about shepherds, but Matthew tells that a group of outsiders to the community of faith were the only ones who noticed the birth of Jesus and the only ones who came and worshiped Him. Matthew in his own way wanted to point out that the Messiah's birth was significant not only for Israel but for the whole world. At the beginning of his story of Jesus, Matthew inserted the account of the non-Jewish visitors to the manger; at the close of his story, Matthew reported the account of the non-Jewish Roman centurion at the cross stating "Truly this was the Son of God!"

The visit of the Magi to Jerusalem created a stir. Their questions about a royal birth quickly brought them to King Herod's attention. Herod convened his own wise men, the chief priests and scribes, and learned that Micah the prophet had indicated the Messiah would be born in Bethlehem, less than seven miles to the south.

The wily, deceitful Herod sent the Magi on to Bethlehem with instructions to report back to him so that he, too, would be able to go and worship the newborn Messiah. The powerful king was so threatened by the possibility of any rival, however, that he made secret plans to kill off all male babies in the Bethlehem area.

NOTES ON THE PRINTED TEXT

Matthew began his Gospel by placing Jesus historically. *Jesus was born in Bethlehem of Judea in the days of Herod the king* (2:1). Jesus was born in a small town in southern Judea, Bethlehem, which is Hebrew for

"House of Bread." Jesus was born in roughly 4 B.C. while the cruel king, Herod the Great, still ruled.

Wise men from the East came to Jerusalem (2:1). These wise men, the learned scholars of their time, were astronomers of a priestly class who studied the stars with great religious interest. They likely came from such modern cities as Ramadan, Ahwaz, or Basra, traveling west through Baghdad, Palmyra, and Damascus in order to reach Jerusalem.

Where is he who has been born king of the Jews? For we have seen his star in the East, and have come to worship him (2:2). When the wise men arrived in Jerusalem, they sought an audience with the king and his advisers. They needed more detailed information found only in the ancient writings of which they had at least some knowledge. Being of high social rank, they received an audience and were able to ask where the king of the Jews was to be born. The star they had seen and followed was no doubt a herald of a new king's birth.

As professional stargazers, the wise men noticed extraordinary sights. What was the Christmas star that guided them? Was it a comet or a fireball or a meteor? Was it a nova or was it a planetary conjunction? Between 7 B.C. and 1 B.C., all of these astronomical effects occurred. There still is no absolute identification of the star of Bethlehem, though some scholars point to the conjunction of the planets Venus and Jupiter, which occurred in August of 3 B.C and again in March of 2 B.C. Nevertheless, its supernatural function is indicated in Matthew 2:9, 10.

[Herod] was troubled, and all Jerusalem with him (2:3). Herod and his court were unaware of a new king's birth. Weakening under old age, illness, and his ever-present paranoia about a rival to his throne, Herod was uneasy. He, too, needed more information.

He assembled the chief priests and scribes and quizzed them on where the Hebrews' Messiah was to be born. The members of the Sanhedrin, all biblical experts, replied by using a Scripture text stating the Messiah was to be born in Bethlehem, as foretold by the prophet Micah. Herod now knew the place of the new king's birth.

Then Herod summoned the wise men secretly and ascertained from them what time the star appeared (2:7). Herod was rapidly gathering the necessary information, but he needed to know the child's approximate age. *Go and search diligently for the child, and when you have found him bring me word, that I too may come and worship him* (2:8). Herod wanted the visitors to find the child for him. He had a plan. Hiding his real motive, he pretended to be interested in worshiping Israel's new king.

Undoubtedly, Herod's agents followed the wise men and alerted the garrison at Herod's desert fortress, Herodium, just four miles southeast of Bethlehem. Once the child was located, soldiers would eliminate the potential rival to Herod's throne. Murder was an extension of Herod's politics; he had already executed four family members suspected of plotting to take his throne. A few more murders would not matter.

They went their way; and . . . the star . . . went before them, till it came to rest over the place where the child was (2:9). If the star was a planetary conjunction, it would have appeared before the wise men in the southwestern sky. Led by the star, the wise men traveled to Bethlehem, and there they discovered the child with his family.

They offered him gifts, gold and frankincense and myrrh (2:11). The wise men offered expensive and costly gifts appropriate for a king, symbolizing their submission and allegiance. Frankincense and myrrh both come from southern Arabia. In 1992 archaeologists excavating in Oman unearthed the lost city of Ubar, the ancient hub of the frankincense trade. The city lay close to the waters near the Qara mountains, where the trees that are the major source of this aromatic resin still grow.

SUGGESTIONS TO TEACHERS

The traditional Christmas pageant! Three kids wearing bathrobes, cotton beards, and cardboard crowns carry cookie tins of "gold, frankincense, and myrrh" down the aisle. Shepherd boys, embarrassed to be clad in dresslike costumes, kneel before an apple box manger. The scene in the Bethlehem stable has been reduced to a cute tableau for parents of young children.

Your big task for today will be to inject the true biblical story into fond pageant memories. By concentrating exclusively on Matthew's account, you will quickly discover that the wise men and Herod are the principal supporting characters in Matthew's version of the Christmas story. And you also recognize that Matthew's story has a different feeling than the typical Christmas pageant. Matthew takes us into the world of the intellectuals, the wise men from the East, and into the world of ruthless power politics carried out by Herod and his henchmen.

1. WEARY SEARCHERS. Focus for a time on the wise men. Ponder what motivated these men to make such a long, tiring journey from their homeland. Consider the fact that they found the object of their quest when they found the infant Jesus. Wise men and women of every age have come to realize that the search for wisdom starts with pondering God's activity in the world. And the search inevitably leads to an encounter with Jesus Christ.

2. WARY SADIST. Bring Herod into the story. This cruel, devious tyrant felt so threatened by Jesus that he ordered the slaughter of any possible rivals, including male babies born in Bethlehem at the time of the wise men's arrival in Jerusalem. Herod shows that one cannot forever be neutral about Jesus Christ. Ultimately, a person will decide either to worship Him, or to fight against Him.

3. WORSHIPFUL SCENE. The journey's end for the Magi and the fulfillment of their quest was finding Jesus. Their response: worship and giving gifts that represented sacrifice. The final response of the wise men was to return home with the good news of the Christ's birth.

Here is the true significance of Christmas: finding that Jesus is the end of our search for meaning in life. Our response, like that of the wise men, must include worship, personal sacrifice, and witnessing to the Good News. Discuss each of these aspects of Christian commitment with your class members.

4. WONDROUS SOJOURN. Joseph, Mary, and the infant Jesus make their way to Egypt, then to Nazareth, escaping the horrid massacre decreed by the treacherous Herod. We need to remember that there are voices of grief and anguish as well as the songs of angels in the Christmas

story. Evil is present in the world, and Christ's coming demands that we not retreat into pleasant cocoons of personal comfort and security in order to shield ourselves. We are called to stand with our Savior in the conflict that led Him to the cross.

TOPIC FOR ADULTS
GOD'S GREAT GIFT

Thanks to Jesus. Beatrice Stevenson describes a Christmas she spent with her husband, Dr. Theodore Stevenson, in the mission hospital in western India. Dr. Stevenson was a visiting surgeon at the Miraj Medical Center. Far from home and her children, Mrs. Stevenson became a patient herself in the Miraj hospital. The hot, dirty, smelly city made her depressed and homesick, and she felt she could never celebrate Christmas in such an alien place. The Christmas Eve festivities at the mission hospital, however, made that Christmas one of the most memorable Beatrice had ever experienced.

The Christian staff presented a lovely pageant, complete with live animals and even a real baby borrowed from an Indian mother in the maternity ward. The crowd of townspeople followed the proceedings with interest. After the usual cast of characters had gathered around the manger, and the choir sang a carol, a young woman wearing a white sari and a nurse's cap stepped on to the stage and knelt before the manger. The nurse told the audience how she enjoyed serving the Lord as a Christian nurse. She was followed by an Indian workman carrying a hoe, one of the maintenance staff, who mounted the platform. This man knelt before the manger, then announced to the startled audience that he had once had leprosy and had been doomed to a life of begging. He continued, telling how the caring Christian medical staff had treated his disease and performed surgery on his once-useless hands.

Finally, a third person stepped up. Everyone recognized that it was a surgeon, Dr. Chopade, wearing operating room attire. The surgeon bowed low before the manger, and then, rising to his feet, the man quietly stated that no one present knew that he had been born an "untouchable"—a member of the lowest social and religious caste of that Hindu culture. A murmur of disapproval rumbled through the audience; untouchables were not supposed to become surgeons!

Dr. Chopade then described his wretched boyhood, in which he and his family were segregated from the rest of the village. His widowed mother cleaned latrines to support the family, and young Chopade searched the garbage heaps for food. He told how he was prohibited from attending the village school or even using the village well. Some angry voices in the audience shouted that he had only experienced what he deserved as an untouchable.

The surgeon quietly continued, telling about his eventual encounter with a kind mission doctor, who had inspired Chopade to become a doctor himself. Dr. Chopade's journey into medicine demanded years of tremendous toil and study, but with the help of missionaries he finally graduated from college and medical school. He told in simple language that he felt he wanted to serve the Lord and His people, and he became a Christian and a surgeon at Miraj. Gazing out on the now silent audience, Dr. Chopade stood immobile for a time. Then, putting his palms together in the traditional Indian greeting, this noted Indian surgeon from the untouchables turned again to the manger. Bowing his head, he murmured, "Thank you, thank you, Lord Jesus."—adapted from Beatrice S. Stevenson, "Christmas Eve at Miraj," in *Presbyterian Survey,* December, 1992.

Legend of the Wise Men. An old story relates that Marco Polo, in his travels through ancient Persia, had found the village where the wise men had lived. He reported that the villagers told him that there were three Magi named Caspar, Melchior, and Balthasar. The legend stated that Caspar was young and beardless, Melchior was elderly, with a long beard and white hair, and Balthasar was a swarthy, middle-aged man. Marco Polo's story claimed that the Magi brought different kinds of gifts to be able to offer whatever tribute would be most suitable for the one they were seeking. They carried gold in case the new one should be royalty, a king. They also brought frankincense in the event that the one they sought had an aura of divinity. Finally, they included myrrh in their chest if they found him to be a physician.

The legend related that when these three finally arrived in Bethlehem they entered one at a time into the small, crowded cave where Mary had brought forth her baby. First, Melchior, the old man, went in to visit the child. Next, Balthasar crouched and entered the stable. Then the youngest, Caspar, made his visit. Afterward, the three wise men compared notes. They agreed that all three of their gifts should be left because the baby Jesus, they realized, was a king, was possessed with divinity, and also was the one who would bring healing.

Pious legend, yes. But the point is true: Jesus fulfills every person's quest. At the manger, God met every human's needs. The search is over once a person has knelt before Christ.

Questions for Students on the Next Lesson. 1. Why were the two demoniacs forced to live where they did? 2. How did the local people react when Jesus healed the two demoniacs? 3. Why did Jesus shock the authorities when He assured the paralytic that his sins were forgiven? 4. What accusation did these authorities bring against Jesus? 5. How is the Christian Gospel able to deal with guilt?

TOPIC FOR YOUTH
DELIGHTING IN THE NEWS

Pilgrims. Lourdes is the largest of France's 937 pilgrimage shrines. The magnificent cathedral was erected at the spot where a young peasant girl, Bernadette, reputedly saw the virgin Mary in 1858. Lourdes draws an average of 5.5 million visitors each year, having a particular attraction for the ill and the aged. However, Lois Bondu, spokesman for the site, says that 10 percent of the pilgrims today are twenty-five years old or younger and the percentage is growing.

Obviously a strong conviction and expectation attracts more than five million people a year. Centuries before, the Magi found a magnetic attraction in a star that sent them to Bethlehem and the Savior.

Hugged a Queen. In May, 1991, sixty-seven-year-old Alice Frazier was surprised to find that a foreign dignitary had visited her public housing project. Before her stood Elizabeth II, Queen of England. Without a thought, Alice gave the queen the only thing she could, a big hug!

While the world gasped at the breach of etiquette (no one is supposed to touch the queen), it was a beautiful, spontaneous expression of friendliness and love. And Queen Elizabeth accepted it as such.

What a wonderful response! Have you welcomed the King of Kings, your Sovereign Lord, into your life with equal love and enthusiasm?

A Child Led Them. The White House Rose Garden was full of politicians, dignitaries, President and Mrs. Bush, and members of the two-time Stanley Cup hockey champions, the Pittsburgh Penguins. The president had summoned the team to the White House to recognize the team's championship victory. However, a little four-year-old girl, Ashley Barrasso, daughter of goalie Tom and Megan Barrasso, stole the show and became the center of attention.

Ashley had cancer, and Mr. Bush spoke of the team's support for the foundation that was battling childhood cancer. The president's daughter, Robin Bush, had died of leukemia at about the same age as Ashley was then. Later, the president led Ashley off for a private tour of the White House and a chance to play with his dog, Millie.

Long ago, another child occupied center stage. In the midst of family, friends, and foreign dignitaries, this infant lay in a manger. Expensive gifts were presented. However, the child Jesus was the focus of everyone's attention. That child grew and continues to occupy our attention. Delight in that child's birth, for He provides your life today.

Questions for Students on the Next Lesson. 1. How did people in the ancient world respond to those who were demon-possessed? 2. How did Jesus treat the demon-possessed? 3. What was the response of the villagers to Jesus' healing actions? Why? 4. Is your church involved in a mission of healing and empowerment? Explain.

LESSON 5—JANUARY 1

DELIVERANCE AND FORGIVENESS

Background Scripture: Matthew 8:1—9:8
Devotional Reading: Luke 4:16-21

KING JAMES VERSION

MATTHEW 8:28 And when he was come to the other side into the country of the Gergesenes, there met him two possessed with devils, coming out of the tombs, exceeding fierce, so that no man might pass by that way.

29 And, behold, they cried out, saying, What have we to do with thee, Jesus, thou Son of God? art thou come hither to torment us before the time?

30 And there was a good way off from them an herd of many swine feeding.

31 So the devils besought him, saying, If thou cast us out, suffer us to go away into the herd of swine.

32 And he said unto them, Go. And when they were come out, they went into the herd of swine: and, behold, the whole herd of swine ran violently down a steep place into the sea, and perished in the waters.

33 And they that kept them fled, and went their ways into the city, and told every thing, and what was befallen to the possessed of the devils.

34 And, behold, the whole city came out to meet Jesus: and when they saw him, they besought him that he would depart out of their coasts.

9:1 And he entered into a ship, and passed over, and came into his own city.

2 And, behold, they brought to him a man sick of the palsy, lying on a bed: and Jesus seeing their faith said unto the sick of the palsy; Son, be of good cheer; thy sins be forgiven thee.

3 And, behold, certain of the scribes said within themselves, This man blasphemeth.

4 And Jesus knowing their thoughts said, Wherefore think ye evil in your hearts?

5 For whether is easier, to say, Thy sins be forgiven thee; or to say, Arise, and walk?

6 But that ye may know that the Son of man hath power on earth to forgive sins, (then saith he to the sick of the palsy,) Arise, take up thy bed, and go unto thine house.

7 And he arose, and departed to his house.

8 But when the multitudes saw it, they marvelled, and glorified God, which had given such power unto men.

REVISED STANDARD VERSION

MATTHEW 8:28 And when he came to the other side, to the country of the Gadarenes, two demoniacs met him, coming out of the tombs, so fierce that no one could pass that way. 29 And behold, they cried out, "What have you to do with us, O Son of God? Have you come here to torment us before the time?" 30 Now a herd of many swine was feeding at some distance from them. 31 And the demons begged him, "If you cast us out, send us away into the herd of swine." 32 And he said to them, "Go." So they came out and went into the swine; and behold, the whole herd rushed down the steep bank into the sea, and perished in the waters. 33 The herdsmen fled, and going into the city they told everything, and what had happened to the demoniacs. 34 And behold, all the city came out to meet Jesus; and when they saw him, they begged him to leave their neighborhood.

9:1 And getting into a boat he crossed over and came to his own city. 2 And behold, they brought to him a paralytic, lying on his bed; and when Jesus saw their faith he said to the paralytic, "Take heart, my son; your sins are forgiven." 3 And behold, some of the scribes said to themselves, "This man is blaspheming." 4 But Jesus, knowing their thoughts, said, "Why do you think evil in your hearts? 5 For which is easier, to say, 'Your sins are forgiven,' or to say, 'Rise and walk'? 6 But that you may know that the Son of man has authority on earth to forgive sins"—he then said to the paralytic—"Rise, take up your bed and go home." 7 And he rose and went home. 8 When the crowds saw it, they were afraid, and they glorified God, who had given such authority to men.

KEY VERSE: [Jesus] said to the paralytic, "Take heart, my son; your sins are forgiven." Matthew 9:2b.

HOME DAILY BIBLE READINGS

Dec.	26	M.	Matthew 5:1-12	*Teachings on the Mountain*
Dec.	27	T.	Matthew 7:1-5	*Do Not Judge Others*
Dec.	28	W.	Matthew 7:24-29	*Hearers and Doers of Jesus' Words*
Dec.	29	T.	Matthew 8:1-13	*Healing a Leper and a Centurion's Servant*
Dec.	30	F.	Matthew 8:14-22	*Healing and Fulfillment of Prophecy*
Dec.	31	S.	Matthew 8:23-34	*Restoring Two Demoniacs*
Jan.	1	S.	Matthew 9:1-8	*Forgiving and Healing a Paralytic*

BACKGROUND

Matthew had been a tax collector. As the author of the Gospel account by his name, he apparently brought his bookkeeping organizational skills and his tidy accountant mind to bear as he prepared an orderly report of how Jesus revealed the Kingdom. Earlier in his Gospel writing, Matthew collected Jesus' teachings. Chapters 5, 6, and 7 contain what we call the Sermon on the Mount, and give us a summary of Jesus' instructions.

The material in today's lesson is Matthew's careful and systematic list of examples of Jesus' acts. Like the teachings in the earlier chapters, the deeds reported in these chapters illustrate Matthew's claim that God's kingdom had broken through into human history.

Jesus' miraculous healings in Galilee gave Him fame among the common people. The religious authorities, however, were uneasy. Who was this young rabbi creating such a reputation? Their uneasiness quickly hardened to suspicion, then to hostility, when they heard that Jesus had assured people their sins were forgiven. The scribes, the legalistic interpreters of the religious code, huffed that only God could grant forgiveness. Who was this Jesus to claim the authority that was reserved only for the Almighty?

To those whom Jesus healed, both deliverance and forgiveness had indeed been granted. The lepers who had been outcasts, the emotionally disturbed, the hopelessly ill—these folks knew that they had been given new life, physically and spiritually. They clearly recognized the extraordinary authority of the rabbi who showed them such compassion.

NOTES ON THE PRINTED TEXT

At Kursi, on the eastern shore of the Sea of Galilee, a cupola with mosaics and a picture of a cross was discovered. It likely marked the site where Jesus cured the demoniacs. In all probability, it was abandoned after a disastrous earthquake in A.D. 746–747, when the monastery was destroyed. Soil gradually covered the place, and it disappeared. Ironically, it was discovered more than a thousand years later by a bulldozer. Today, we remove the layers of familiarity that have covered this story and rediscover what happened in the land of Gadara.

After crossing the Sea of Galilee, Jesus and the disciples landed on the eastern shore of the lake in the vicinity of the Gadarenes, a Gentile region. There Jesus and the disciples were met by two demoniacs. These frightening individuals roamed the area naked, had tremendous strength, were deranged, and lived in the small antechambers of the cut rock tombs.

What have you to do with us, O Son of God? Have you come here to torment us before the time? (8:29). The demons were afraid, recognizing Jesus and His authority over them. They knew Him to be their master and understood that God had come. Their judgment and destruction would take place as a result.

Now a herd of many swine was feeding at some distance from them (8:30). For the Jews, pigs were unclean. The presence of so many pigs, some two thousand, indicated that Jesus was in a largely Gentile area. *If you cast us out, send us away into the herd of swine* (8:31). The demons begged Jesus to send them into the herd of pigs. Perhaps the demons did not want to be homeless. Perhaps the entry into the pig herd would confirm their departure from the two men. Whatever the reason, Jesus did order them to enter the pigs.

Many people in the ancient world believed that exorcised demons demonstrated their rage by initiating some terrible deed that would be visible to others. The whole pig herd stampeded uncontrollably down the steep hill and fell off the steep cliff. Every animal was killed. The shocked pig herders, responsible for the animals, rushed to the city to explain to the owners what had happened to the pigs and the demoniacs.

All the city came out to meet Jesus; and . . . they begged him to leave their neighborhood (8:34). People in the city were upset due to the huge financial loss Jesus had caused. He was viewed as a troublemaker, a man with mysterious power. Jesus made them uneasy so they asked Him to leave their district.

Jesus got back into the boat, recrossed the Sea of Galilee, and landed at Capernaum. A man whose legs were paralyzed was put on a makeshift stretcher by his friends and brought to Jesus.

Jesus looked at the man and the men who had carried the cot. He sensed their faith. He also knew that the sick needed compassion, understanding, and forgiveness. *Take heart, my son; your sins are forgiven* (9:2).

This man is blaspheming (9:3). The scribes were furious, believing that Jesus had taken God's position. Only God could forgive sins. To them, Jesus did not have that authority; He should be stoned to death.

Why do you think evil in your hearts? (9:4). Jesus knew what the scribes were thinking in their hearts, though their hostility must have been plainly evident on their faces and in their eyes as well. So Jesus proposed a test. *Which is easier, to say, "Your sins are forgiven," or to say, "Rise and walk"?* (9:5). He argued that it would be easy to say that the man's sins were forgiven. There simply was no way to prove or disprove such a statement. To command the man to walk, however, opened up the possibility of failure. This could be tested; this raised the possibility of discrediting Jesus.

To demonstrate His authority to forgive sins, Jesus commanded the paralytic, *Rise, take up your bed and go home* (9:6). Jesus forgave and healed the man. The man rose and departed for his home as he had been ordered. The crowds of onlookers were *afraid* (9:8). They immediately sensed Jesus' divine power and authority. *They glorified God, who had given such authority to men* (9:8).

SUGGESTIONS TO TEACHERS

People make resolutions on New Year's Day. But have you ever considered that God has also made a resolution? His resolution has been spelled out through Jesus: God has resolved to bring you and everyone who will accept Him, deliverance and forgiveness.

Today's lesson proclaims that resolution by God in the form of Jesus' acts of mercy and healing as recounted by Matthew. The events from Matthew provide so much illustrative material that you will have plenty to discuss.

1. CLEANSING. Turn first to the leper. Point out to your students what any skin disorder, especially leprosy, meant in the time of Jesus. Lepers were shunned just as AIDS victims often are today. Jesus, however, deliberately reached out (and literally touched) this unfortunate man. Remind your group members that Jesus was willing to risk touching the untouchables. (Actually leprosy is not that contagious, except from prolonged contact. But people in the first century thought anyone who even got close to a leper was automatically made unclean. Strict rules and elaborate cleaning procedures were decreed for all Jews).

2. COMPASSION. Move on to the healing of the centurion's servant. Remember that a centurion was a member of the hated Roman occupation army. Self-respecting, patriotic Jews scorned associating with such Romans. So Matthew picked an example of a second person to show Jesus' caring. In fact, the centurion was lauded by Jesus as a model of confident trust.

3. CONCERN. A third "case study" of Jesus' resolve to bring deliverance and mercy to someone on the fringe of society is the episode of healing a woman, in this case Peter's mother-in-law. Remember that women were definitely second-class persons in the eyes of that society. Furthermore, illness was usually interpreted as punishment for sin. Jesus' healings signified forgiveness. He broke societal taboos in order to bring women a sense of worth before God.

4. COST. Be sure to bring in the account of the would-be follower, the man who recklessly announced that he would follow Jesus some time in the future. The statement about first burying his father meant that the man intended to hold off becoming a disciple for as long as his father was alive (not that his father had already died and the funeral was about to take place). Jesus called the man's bluff! Jesus sees through our dodges and hedging. Discipleship costs.

5. CALM. The scene switches to the Sea of Galilee. Jesus' fishermen-disciples feared for their lives when a severe squall suddenly swept upon them as they crossed the lake at night. Matthew would have us remember that these men were seasoned seamen. The storm must have been severe, and so the disciples' terror extreme. Jesus' presence, however, brought calm and confidence. In the storms of life, Jesus continues to instill reassurance and a sense of calmness when we call on Him.

6. COMPETENCE. Matthew offered another example of Jesus' remarkable ability to bring deliverance and forgiveness in the face of terror. Look at the account of the demoniacs. Here were two men so spiritually and emotionally disturbed that they had been exiled to a graveyard where others wouldn't be threatened by them. Hopelessly shunned, driven from society to the most hideous and polluted place imaginable, these two possessed by demons were blessed with new life by Jesus. Our Deliverer is competent to handle any situation.

7. CARING. Finally, Matthew offered the account of Jesus healing a paralytic. Be sure to bring out the fact that Jesus assumed He had the authority and power to bestow forgiveness on the helpless man. The good news for us is that we know we need not be paralyzed with guilt. Through Jesus, God brings deliverance and forgiveness to us as we put our faith in Him.

TOPIC FOR ADULTS
DELIVERANCE AND FORGIVENESS

Editing Job. A daughter gave her elderly father a videocasette recorder as a Christmas gift. The old man didn't know how to operate the machine but was grateful for the gift. He decided to record a favorite program on television at Christmas. Unfortunately, he pressed the "pause" button on the remote control device at the wrong times and was unaware of his mistake until he decided to play back the tape. To his dismay, he discovered that he had carefully edited out the Christmas program and taped all the commercials and station breaks!

Sometimes we edit out parts of the story of Jesus, intending to remember only the parts we think we like. We may want to keep the story of the manger with the baby Jesus surrounded by shepherds and wise men, but we may wish to skip lightly over the less pleasant parts of his ministry: the opposition, the angry crowds, the crucifixion. Yet we dare not mentally press the "pause" button on Jesus after the Christmas holiday. We must turn to Him daily as the risen Lord.

What Have You Heard? Church bulletins sometimes carry unintentional misprints, and some of these errors are quite amusing. Consider, for instance, the Sunday morning in a West Coast congregation during which the worshippers read in the bulletin: "The Choir will sing "I Heard the Bills on Christmas Day." More than a few attending that day felt that the typo in the bulletin was closer to the truth than anyone wanted to admit.

Now that the holiday is past, many folks may feel they've heard only about the bills on Christmas. Jesus seems to have been forgotten. The commercialism of the season can wipe out any significant awareness of the meaning of Christ's wondrous birth and the significance of His life.

Focus on His caring for the sick in mind, body, and spirit, as demonstrated in today's Scripture. Discover that Christ's coming enables you to hear the voice of God above the din of the sales registers.

Future Tense. Language experts and translators continue to work with many African dialects that have never been put into writing. Sometimes these workers discover strange linguistic phenomena. In the Masai language, for example, there is no future tense. To convey a sense of the future, the speaker must employ a series of adverbs and use a complicated sentence structure. Even then, the meaning will not always be clear that you are trying to refer to something that is yet to come.

Missionary translators working with the Masai tribe have finally introduced the notion that God brings a future. The Rev. Vincent Donovan, who served as a missionary translator among the Masai for years, states that evangelizing the Masai requires putting a future tense in their language—and also in their lives.

Jesus brought a future to those He healed. He continues to bring new beginnings to all who respond to Him in faith. With Jesus Christ, there is always a future!

Questions for Students on the Next Lesson. 1. Who were the Pharisees? 2. Why were they so critical of Jesus? 3. Why didn't Jesus wait until the sabbath was over before He healed the man with the withered hand? 4. What does the phrase "Son of David" mean? 5. Do rules and institutions sometimes seem more important than people in our society?

TOPIC FOR YOUTH
HELP FOR PEOPLE IN NEED

Cash Rash. A bank teller developed a strange skin rash on her fingers. Initially, she ignored the rash, but the itching and unsightly redness continued to bother her. Finally, she consulted a dermatologist and was surprised to discover that she was allergic to money! Actually, it was the chemicals within the ink. The constant contact with the money was producing her rash.

The love of money and possessions can poison each of us by making us greedy. The feel of money in our hands can cause us to have no feelings of compassion in our heart.

The owners of the pigs in Matthew 8 saw only their economic losses. Perhaps money had poisoned them in some way. They failed to appreciate that two men were restored to health by one with healing and compassion in His hands. Do not let the same happen to you!

"I Am Number One." A survey of 200,000 students found that most went to college with the hope that the education and the degree they received would enable them to earn more money. The survey, done by the American Council of Education, found that twenty years ago only 39 percent of students considered affluence as a main goal. Today, 75 percent claim that as a goal.

Sometimes we place too high a value on possessions. The people around Jesus were like that. Jesus tried to teach them that people were more important; however, they forced Him to leave, favoring their possessions. Hopefully, we will not make the same mistake.

Opportunity Stood in the Door. People who move on and off of the subway trains in London's tube must act quickly and deliberately. Recently, a mother and her three small children were visiting London. The two older girls, ages seven and nine, rushed down the subway platform ahead of their mother and jumped into the subway as the doors opened. The two did not realize they had entered the wrong train. They also did not hear their frantic mother calling to them to get back off of the subway car.

The doors closed. The poor mother pounded on the subway door yelling, "Wait!" No one apparently heard, and the train moved forward.

The two children looked terrified. Mother was outside and rapidly vanishing as the train increased its speed. Alone and in a strange city, the girls began to cry.

Two teenage girls asked the two little girls to sit with them. They told the little girls not to worry; they would all get off at the next stop and catch the next train going in the opposite direction, back to where Mom would be waiting. Simply having someone who cared about them cleared the tears in the girls' eyes and comforted them.

Questions for Students on the Next Lesson. 1. What rules were in effect for the sabbath? 2. How does Jesus respond to the rules in regard to human need? 3. What was the response of the Pharisees? 4. How did Jesus interpret His mission? 5. Have you ever been curious about the enterprise of "faith healing"? Is it authentic?

LESSON 6—JANUARY 8

JESUS, THE SON OF DAVID

Background Scripture: Matthew 12
Devotional Reading: Isaiah 42:1-9

KING JAMES VERSION

MATTHEW 12:9 And when he was departed thence, he went into their synagogue:

10 And, behold, there was a man which had his hand withered. And they asked him, saying, Is it lawful to heal on the sabbath days? that they might accuse him.

11 And he said unto them, What man shall there be among you, that shall have one sheep, and if it fall into a pit on the sabbath day, will he not lay hold on it, and lift it out?

12 How much then is a man better than a sheep? Wherefore it is lawful to do well on the sabbath days.

13 Then saith he to the man, Stretch forth thine hand. And he stretched it forth; and it was restored whole, like as the other.

14 Then the Pharisees went out, and held a council against him, how they might destroy him.

15 But when Jesus knew it, he withdrew himself from thence: and great multitudes followed him, and he healed them all;

16 And charged them that they should not make him known:

17 That it might be fulfilled which was spoken by Esaias the prophet, saying,

18 Behold my servant, whom I have chosen; my beloved, in whom my soul is well pleased: I will put my spirit upon him, and he shall shew judgment to the Gentiles.

19 He shall not strive, nor cry; neither shall any man hear his voice in the streets.

20 A bruised reed shall he not break, and smoking flax shall he not quench, till he send forth judgment unto victory.

21 And in his name shall the Gentiles trust.

22 Then was brought unto him one possessed with a devil, blind, and dumb: and he healed him, insomuch that the blind and dumb both spake and saw.

23 And all the people were amazed, and said, Is not this the son of David?

REVISED STANDARD VERSION

MATTHEW 12:9 And he went on from there, and entered their synagogue. 10 And behold, there was a man with a withered hand. And they asked him, "Is it lawful to heal on the sabbath?" so that they might accuse him. 11 He said to them, "What man of you, if he has one sheep and it falls into a pit on the sabbath, will not lay hold of it and lift it out? 12 Of how much more value is a man than a sheep! So it is lawful to do good on the sabbath." 13 Then he said to the man, "Stretch out your hand." And the man stretched it out, and it was restored, whole like the other. 14 But the Pharisees went out and took counsel against him, how to destroy him.

15 Jesus, aware of this, withdrew from there. And many followed him, and he healed them all, 16 and ordered them not to make him known. 17 This was to fulfil what was spoken by the prophet Isaiah:

18 "Behold, my servant whom I have chosen, my beloved with whom my soul is well pleased. I will put my Spirit upon him, and he shall proclaim justice to the Gentiles.

19 He will not wrangle or cry aloud, nor will any one hear his voice in the streets; 20 he will not break a bruised reed or quench a smoldering wick, till he brings justice to victory; 21 and in his name will the Gentiles hope."

22 Then a blind and dumb demoniac was brought to him, and he healed him, so that the dumb man spoke and saw. 23 And all the people were amazed, and said, "Can this be the Son of David?"

KEY VERSE: *It is lawful to do good on the sabbath.* Matthew 12:12.

HOME DAILY BIBLE READINGS

Jan.	2	M.	Isaiah 42:1-9	The Lord's Servant Shall Bring Forth Justice
Jan.	3	T.	Matthew 12:1-8	Lord of the Sabbath
Jan.	4	W.	Matthew 12:9-14	Healing on the Sabbath
Jan.	5	T.	Matthew 12:15-21	The Mission of God's Chosen Servant
Jan.	6	F.	Matthew 12:22-37	Jesus' Power Comes from God
Jan.	7	S.	Matthew 12:38-42	Request for a Sign
Jan.	8	S.	Matthew 12:43-50	Jesus' True Family

BACKGROUND

Matthew, writing from his Jewish perspective, wanted to make it clear that Jesus fulfilled everything promised in the prophets and embodied everything decreed in the law. Matthew also carefully presented evidence to back Jesus' claim to authority in all matters of faith and practice.

Needless to say, these claims to be the final authority did not sit well with those who thought they themselves had the authority to decide such matters—the scribes, Pharisees, and the temple leaders. After all, they reasoned, they either had inherited or had earned the right to interpret the rules. Who was this upstart rabbi from Galilee to tell them how to relate to God?

Take the matter of observing the sacred sabbath. The fourth commandment decreed that the seventh day was to be honored as God's. By Jesus' day, however, an enormous cluster of rules and interpretations had been added to the commandment. What had been intended as a time each week to celebrate the Creator's goodness had been turned into a thicket of burdensome regulations. For example, since work was not permitted on the sabbath, the religious authorities laid down a complicated set of thirty-nine prohibited activities, including reaping grain and preparing meals.

Jesus and His disciples were suspected of being lax in observing the requirements of the law. The authorities and their sympathizers were watching Jesus, hoping to pounce when they found Him breaking the religious rules, thereby discrediting Him. When they saw Jesus and His followers satisfying their hunger by taking some grain, rubbing it in their hands to remove the husks, and eating it on the sabbath, they proudly accused Jesus of a serious breach of the religious laws. According to these critics, Jesus' party was guilty of a) reaping or plucking grain; b) threshing; c) preparing a meal—all serious infractions of the accepted sacred rules for keeping the sabbath.

The legalistic attitude of Jesus' critics comes through clearly. Likewise, Matthew 12 discloses the growing intensity of the opposition to Jesus.

NOTES ON THE PRINTED TEXT

And he went on from there, and entered their synagogue (12:9). Jesus left the grainfield and entered the neighboring town's synagogue. But He did not leave the controversy; the Pharisees continued to look for a way to accuse Him.

Is it lawful to heal on the sabbath? (12:10). The presence of a man with a withered hand in the synagogue was an attempt to trap Jesus with a difficult question. Jesus could have offered the accepted legalistic answer: It was indeed legal to heal in a life-threatening situation where death could result. However, a disfigured hand was not a true emergency. If Jesus stated that it was permissible to heal, then He would contradict their strict sabbath rules. If Jesus said it was not legal to heal, then He would appear to be terribly callous and guilty of a lack of compassion. He would lose credibility with the people.

What man of you, if he has one sheep and it falls into a pit on the sabbath, will not lay hold of it and lift it out? (12:11). Jesus replied by citing the law of Moses directly. Rescuing an animal that had fallen into a pit or was in danger of dying or had suffered an accident was permitted on the sabbath. This was considered the humane thing to do rather than let the animal suffer. Jesus took that principle one step further. If the rescue of an animal was lawful, then healing a person was also lawful. Was helping a person not of greater priority than helping an animal? *Of how much more value is a man than a sheep! So it is lawful to do good on the sabbath* (12:12).

Jesus then healed the man's withered hand, commanding, *Stretch out your hand* (12:13). The man did as he was told, and the atrophied hand was restored. In spite of this marvelous miracle, the Pharisees were furious. Sacred religious tradition had been ignored, and their plot had failed. Their standing in the community would suffer. *The Pharisees went out and took counsel against him, how to destroy him* (12:14).

Aware of their intentions, Jesus withdrew. However, *many followed him* (12:15). Jesus' attempts to find peace and quiet failed, but He responded by healing all those sick people that came to Him for help.

Jesus wanted a minimum of public attention at this time in His ministry, fulfilling Isaiah's prophecy of a silent, suffering servant. In addition to avoiding arguments whenever possible, the servant would have God's Spirit upon Him, enabling Him to proclaim justice. God's beloved one would accomplish the works of righteousness and justice for all people, Jew and Gentile alike. The servant would not draw attention to His works. *He will not wrangle or cry aloud, nor will any one hear his voice in the streets* (12:19). The servant would show God's compassion for all broken or damaged lives and God's gentle love and interest in the weak and the powerless. *He will not break a bruised reed or quench a smoldering wick* (12:20). He would patiently work until victory was achieved for all righteous people, Jew and Gentile, *till he brings justice to victory* (12:20).

Another demon-possessed man was brought before Jesus. The demon had made the man blind and unable to speak, so when Jesus cured the man the onlookers were amazed. Literally, they were beside themselves, cautiously wondering aloud if Jesus was the Messiah. *Can this be the Son of David?* (12:23). In their minds they rightly understood that only God's anointed one could possess the power that Jesus demonstrated.

SUGGESTIONS TO TEACHERS

"I don't trust any leader. Not anymore." The young attorney at a party spoke bitterly of her disillusionment with leaders. She recited her surprise when she learned of the deceit and scandal by national leaders: Johnson's escalation of involvement in Vietnam, Nixon's Watergate, Reagan's Iran-Contra disaster, the House check-bouncing scandal. She recounted the greed by leaders on Wall Street and in the Savings and Loans scandal. The young lawyer pointed to the way leaders in the military had degraded women in such episodes as the Tailhook parties. She didn't spare leaders in the church, either, reminding her listeners of the dismal list of priests and ministers being found guilty of scandalous sexual behavior.

Politics aside, some students in your class may agree with this attorney. Polls continue to report that a gulf continues to exist between the public and its leadership. The trust level is low.

How may we regard Jesus as a leader? Today's lesson offers a closer look at Jesus' leadership.

1. COUNTERS WITH CHALLENGES. Start your lesson by examining the scene in which the Pharisees accused Jesus and His disciples of breaking the sabbath by picking some grain kernels (Matt.12:1-8). In the exchange, Jesus showed that He knew the Bible better than His accusers. He related episodes from the Scriptures as precedents for His actions and silenced the Pharisees. Jesus' intelligence was obvious. Likewise, Jesus showed that He had great authority: "Something greater than the temple is here" (12:6).

2. CHALLENGES WITH COMPASSION. Move on to the scene in the synagogue in which Jesus heals the man with the withered hand. Jesus recognized that this unfortunate man could not work because of his handicap, and consequently lacked money and dignity. Jesus faced the indignant legalists who accused Him of violating the sabbath by the act of healing. He pointed out that they had more sensitivity for the suffering of an animal than for a human being. Once again, by throwing their own rules back at them, Jesus displayed superior leadership by being one who served.

3. CAUTIONS WITH QUOTATIONS. The opposition to Jesus intensified. At the same time, many followers wanted to proclaim Him Messiah. Jesus realized that many would assume that His messiahship would be purely political. Jesus' model of messiahship, however, was the Suffering Servant from Isaiah. Jesus came to conquer through serving and suffering. Discuss the meaning of the two kinds of leadership presented here, namely the dictator-type versus the servant kind.

4. CONDEMNS WITH CLEANSING. Look next at the report of Jesus healing the man who was blind and also unable to speak. When Jesus brought this unfortunate man wholeness, the Pharisees accused Him of being in league with forces of evil. Jesus refuted these accusers and denounced them for *their* blasphemy. This introduces the saying about the impossibility of forgiving one speaking against the Holy Spirit. Discuss the meaning of Jesus' words in Matthew 12:31-37.

5. CONFOUNDS WITH CLAIMS. For those demanding a "sign" of His messiahship, Jesus answered with the reference to Jonah's return from the belly of the fish, thereby claiming that His resurrection would be a sign everyone would eventually see. Discuss the fact that Christ's resurrection is the great and final "sign" to all people. We need no additional "signs." Easter says it all!

6. CLARIFIES WITH INCLUSIVENESS. Finally, work in that report of Jesus' family from Nazareth nervously wanting Jesus to come home and avoid the notoriety surrounding His words and actions. Jesus' reply clarified who truly belongs to His family (Matt. 12:49, 50).

TOPIC FOR ADULTS
A LEADER WHO SERVES

Leader Who Serves. Dr. Anatoli Bereslov was a professor of neurology in the medical school in Moscow. Dr. Bereslov is also a Christian. Although he could have remained at his secure post as a tenured faculty member and avoided unpleasant or difficult involvement with patients, this committed, compassionate physician chose to accept the post of director of Moscow's first cerebral palsy rehabilitation center when it opened in 1991. In Russia's crumbling national health system, Dr. Bereslov is unusual because of his humble attitude and his true concern for his patients. He takes time with each one personally and inspires everyone in the rehabilitation center to acts of courage. His example as a leader who serves is making the staff and patients aware of an alternative to a cold health service run by an impersonal bureaucracy.

Dr. Bereslov, now recognized as a leader also in his profession, quietly says, "When I first came here, I decided I was not going to work for the sick. I was going to serve them, just as I serve God. I take their problems on as my personal pain."

Difficult Leadership Role. Being a parent is one of the toughest servant-leader roles. Yet a mother or father of growing children is called to emulate the servant-leader of Nazareth.

A little boy was born to a frontier family, the McGuffeys, in Claysville, Pennsylvania, in 1800. The family moved to a farm near Youngstown, Ohio, when the boy was small. Mrs. McGuffey was concerned that her son receive an education, and she prayed fervently for a teacher.

One day, Thomas Hughes, the head of a small academy in Greensville (now Darlington, Pennsylvania) overheard Mrs. McGuffey praying aloud in her yard. Hughes was so moved that he offered to assist the family by enrolling the youngster in his school. Young William McGuffey received his early education from Hughes, and later at Washington (Pennsylvania) College.

William never forgot his mother's example as a leader and servant. He became a minister and educator, eventually developing a set of textbooks to help little ones learn to read. His series of McGuffey's Eclectic Readers, emphasizing faith and learning, taught millions of children who used them as their school textbooks. Several generations of school children were taught to be leaders who serve because of William McGuffey, who, in turn, had been taught by his mother. Parents are leaders who serve!

Fulfilled Dream. Acharn Matthew, a minister of the Mar Thoma Church in southern India, tells of another minister who had a dream about Jesus. In the dream, this minister was told that Jesus would visit his church at nine o'clock that morning. The minister hurried to the church to meet the Lord. On the way, however, he encountered a leper, who asked to be taken to the church. Time was running out. In only a few minutes it would be nine o'clock, the hour in which Jesus was to come. Nevertheless, the minister reached down and picked up the dirty, loathsome-looking outcast.

Panting with exertion, the minister staggered into the church with only a few minutes to spare. The minute hand read 8:58. The minister waited. 8:59 came. Finally, the clock struck 9:00. . . . But nothing happened. The minister waited another minute, and still another. With a tone of disappointment mixed with bitterness, the minister said in a kind of prayer, "Lord, you have deceived me." But his words were cut off by a voice that said, "My son, you had the privilege of carrying me."

Questions for Students on the Next Lesson. 1. Why was Jesus in the country of the Syrophoenicians? 2. What is surprising about Jesus' conversing with a woman from this area? 3. Why did respectable Jews look down on Canaanites with contempt? 4. How did Jesus respond to the Canaanite woman's plea? 5. What part does faith play in healing?

TOPIC FOR YOUTH
RISKS THAT PRODUCE RESULTS

Profile in Courage. Joe Kennedy, eldest son of the late Senator Robert Kennedy and the nephew of former President John Kennedy, was on vacation near Kailua-Kona, Hawaii. The crew of the charter fishing boat heard a distress call when they were three miles off the west side of the Hawaiian Island. A woman claimed her boat had been overturned by a huge 485-pound marlin, and the boat was sinking. In her fright and confusion, she gave four different locations.

Fortunately, Kennedy's boat headed in the right direction. They found a man and a woman clinging to an overturned fishing boat. Kennedy and two others jumped into the shark-filled waters and swam to the boat. Kennedy and another fellow grabbed the terrified woman, Mildred Akaka, and swam back to their boat, while the third helped Mildred's friend make his way to safety.

Kennedy was willing to risk his life without thinking of the consequences. Jesus did the same; without concern for the consequences, He healed the hurting. He put a higher priority on people than on keeping the petty laws of people who could hurt Him.

Accepting the Hazards of Helping. Ed and Joy had no children of their own and they desperately wanted a family. After years of trying everything medical specialists could suggest and still not being able to have a baby, they finally decided to adopt. To their disappointment, no babies or small children were available for adoption. Ed and Joy were put on a list, but they were cautioned not to have high hopes.

Two years passed. Still no call from the agencies. Then one morning, a social worker from the county Children and Youth Services telephoned and asked to meet with them. The woman caseworker asked Ed and Joy if they would consider making a home for two boys, Timmy and Joey, ages four and six. She related the facts: The two boys' biological mother was in prison for passing bad checks and had a long police record as an alcohol and drug abuser. The mother had neglected Timmy and Joey almost completely from the time they were born. Both youngsters had been physically abused. Neither was toilet trained. They could barely speak. The two fought each other and others almost constantly. Both yelled and vied for attention. They had been sent to two foster homes, but the foster parents had sent them back, wearily saying they couldn't cope with such hostile, uncooperative boys.

Pausing after her long account of the difficulties in handling Timmy and Joey, the county agency worker asked, "Would you accept the risk of taking these two into your home?"

Ed and Joy looked at each other. Finally Ed said, "Well, we're Christians, and would you mind if we prayed about this, and talked it over with our minister?" The social worker agreed and asked them to call her as soon as they made a decision.

That evening, Ed and Joy talked far past midnight. They kept remembering the report about Timmy and Joey having such extreme behavioral problems. They wondered if they had the wisdom or the stamina to cope with such disturbed children. Later, they reminded each other that they had said they would pray about the matter. Taking each other by the hands, Ed and Joy asked the Lord to guide them. Raising their heads, they looked at each other and agreed to take the risk of trying to make a home for Timmy and Joey.

It was not easy. But Ed and Joy accepted the risk. With patience and caring, in spite of many setbacks and problems, they gave themselves to being parents for the two scarred and scared little boys. This Christian couple is seeing that their risk-taking has produced astonishing results. Both Timmy and Joey are now developing into youngsters who are stable, trusting, and loving.

Active Compassion. On August 12, 1978, Darryl Stingley, a wide receiver for the New England Patriots, lined up on the right side of the twenty-four-yard line. It was an exhibition game against the Raiders in Oakland. He ran eight yards and slanted toward the middle to catch a high pass from the Patriots' quarterback, Steve Grogan. Darryl leaped for the ball but missed it. Jack Tatum of the Oakland Raiders crashed into him, and Darryl collapsed to the turf. He did not move even when carried off the field on a stretcher. When the game ended, everyone heard the hospital's report: Darryl was paralyzed from a broken neck.

Raiders' coach John Madden went to Eden Valley Hospital in Castro Valley, to the operating room where Darryl was to be fitted for a "halo," a steel ring attached to an eighty-pound weight that would immobilize Darryl's head.

Madden demanded to see Darryl, but Dr. Don Fink said that would be impossible because Madden lacked the proper sterile clothing for the operating room. However, Madden insisted, and, appropriately clothed, he entered the operating room and was able to offer his support and care to a frightened Stingley.

Madden never wanted to be recognized for what he had done. His belief was that Darryl was a person, a human being, not a "body" to be used in the game of football. His realization that few people in professional football really cared about the players finally led him to retire from coaching. Fortunately, Jesus is our leader who always cares.

Questions for Students on the Next Lesson. 1. Do you believe that some people are outside God's interest? Why, or why not? 2. How can we help people realize that God cares about them? 3. What attitude should we have when we look at others? 4. Do you see any miracles today? 5. How can a Christian be involved in the healing of the sick?

LESSON 7—JANUARY 15

A FOREIGNER'S FAITH

Background Scripture: Matthew 15:1-31
Devotional Reading: Isaiah 35:5-10

KING JAMES VERSION

MATTHEW 15:21 Then Jesus went thence, and departed into the coasts of Tyre and Sidon.

22 And, behold, a woman of Canaan came out of the same coasts, and cried unto him, saying, Have mercy on me, O Lord, thou son of David; my daughter is grievously vexed with a devil.

23 But he answered her not a word. And his disciples came and besought him, saying, Send her away; for she crieth after us.

24 But he answered and said, I am not sent but unto the lost sheep of the house of Israel.

25 Then came she and worshipped him, saying, Lord, help me.

26 But he answered and said, It is not meet to take the children's bread, and to cast it to dogs.

27 And she said, Truth, Lord: yet the dogs eat of the crumbs which fall from their masters' table.

28 Then Jesus answered and said unto her, O woman, great is thy faith: be it unto thee even as thou wilt. And her daughter was made whole from that very hour.

29 And Jesus departed from thence, and came nigh unto the sea of Galilee; and went up into a mountain, and sat down there.

30 And great multitudes came unto him, having with them those that were lame, blind, dumb, maimed, and many others, and cast them down at Jesus' feet; and he healed them:

31 Insomuch that the multitude wondered, when they saw the dumb to speak, the maimed to be whole, the lame to walk, and the blind to see: and they glorified the God of Israel.

REVISED STANDARD VERSION

MATTHEW 15:21 And Jesus went away from there and withdrew to the district of Tyre and Sidon. 22 And behold, a Canaanite woman from that region came out and cried, "Have mercy on me, O Lord, Son of David; my daughter is severely possessed by a demon." 23 But he did not answer her a word. And his disciples came and begged him, saying, "Send her away, for she is crying after us." 24 He answered, "I was sent only to the lost sheep of the house of Israel." 25 But she came and knelt before him, saying, "Lord, help me." 26 And he answered, "It is not fair to take the children's bread and throw it to the dogs." 27 She said, "Yes, Lord, yet even the dogs eat the crumbs that fall from their masters' table." 28 Then Jesus answered her, "O woman, great is your faith! Be it done for you as you desire." And her daughter was healed instantly.

29 And Jesus went on from there and passed along the Sea of Galilee. And he went up on the mountain, and sat down there. 30 And great crowds came to him, bringing with them the lame, the maimed, the blind, the dumb, and many others, and they put them at his feet, and he healed them, 31 so that the throng wondered, when they saw the dumb speaking, the maimed whole, the lame walking, and the blind seeing; and they glorified the God of Israel.

KEY VERSE: *O woman, great is your faith!* Matthew 15:28b.

HOME DAILY BIBLE READINGS

Jan.	9	M.	Isaiah 35:3-7	*Help Promised for God's People*
Jan.	10	T.	I Peter 2:4-10	*Gentile Believers are the People of God*
Jan.	11	W.	Matthew 15:1-9	*Tradition: Good or Bad?*

BACKGROUND

Matthew, once a tax collector, must have known how to do double-entry bookkeeping, carefully showing the plus and minus sides of the ledger's accounts. Carrying those habits into his Gospel writing, Matthew outlined the contrast between the unbelief of the religious officials of Israel and the humble faith of a foreign woman. In chapter 15, Matthew deliberately demonstrated the stubborn refusal of the super-pious scribes and Pharisees to accept Jesus' authority, then followed with the persistent plea of a Canaanite woman who recognized Jesus' authority.

The scribes and Pharisees had been sent up from Jerusalem to keep an eye on the followers of the controversial rabbi named Jesus. The temple authorities suspected that neither the outspoken Jesus nor His disciples were strictly adhering to the Mosaic law. They quickly pounced on Jesus' companions who did not practice the elaborate ceremonial hand washing before eating.

Jesus counterattacked. Using a technique all rabbis used when arguing points of the law, Jesus asked a probing question in which His adversaries had to recognize that their insistence on tradition must take second place to "the commandment of God." Jesus beat them at their own game, to their embarrassment and annoyance. His concluding comments to them stung: "You hypocrites!" This was followed by a quotation from Isaiah 29:13 describing those honoring God in words but not in their hearts.

Jesus felt it necessary to retreat temporarily to safer territories, where He met with a foreign woman and compared her faith with the lack of faith shown by the scribes and Pharisees. The Gospel writer calls her a "Canaanite woman," using a term that conveyed the deep enmity and contempt many Jews had felt toward inhabitants of Canaan from the time of Joshua. Mark had declined to call the woman a "Canaanite," but used a less harsh description, referring to her as a "Greek, a Syrophoenician" (Mark 7:26). Matthew, however, lets all the ancient meaning of the word "Canaanite" sink in to make his point: this woman was a model of trust from whom the religious leaders of Israel could learn.

NOTES ON THE PRINTED TEXT

Jesus went away from there and withdrew to the district of Tyre and Sidon (15:21). Jesus departed from the Galilean hill country and traveled northwest for roughly thirty to fifty miles to the coastal area of Phoenicia. This was Gentile territory and the location of two large cities. Tyre was dubbed the "metropolis of Phoenicia." It had fine, wide streets, some paved with mosaics and bordered with columned porticoes of green and white marble. Large multistoried buildings and a huge stadium attested to the city's importance. Slightly to the north was another large city, Sidon.

Have mercy on me, O Lord, Son of David; my daughter is severely possessed by a demon (15:22). A Canaanite woman met Jesus and begged Him to help her daughter. The girl was possessed by a demon. (A bowl in the Hebrew University library of Israel records an incantation that persuades demons not to harm a child. Worry that demons would possess children was obviously quite a concern during Jesus' time.) The woman was insistent. The Greek verb indicates that she repeatedly called on Jesus to help her daughter. She had heard of Jesus' power and knew He could help.

Jesus was strangely silent. *He did not answer her a word* (15:23). The disciples, though, were upset and vocal because this woman had become a nuisance to them, and her repeated pleas were bothersome. They begged Jesus to send her home. *Send her away, for she is crying after us* (15:23). Then Jesus pointed out to the woman that His mission was only to God's people of Israel. His mission was not to the Gentiles. *I was sent only to the lost sheep of the house of Israel* (15:24). The woman continued to ask for help. Finally, she knelt before Jesus and implored, *Lord, help me* (15:25). She was still confident that Jesus would help.

It is not fair to take the children's bread and throw it to the dogs (15:26). Jesus made it clear that His mission was to His own people. Although the Gentiles were referred to as "dogs," Jesus spoke of the household pet, not the garbage-scavenging mongrel of the streets. Was He smiling or speaking with witty irony? Probably. Jesus referred to a common family practice in His response: Children were fed first, then the family pup. No one would have taken the children's food and fed the dog first. Jesus wanted the woman to know that God's chosen people must come first.

Yes, Lord, yet even the dogs eat the crumbs that fall from their masters' table (15:27). The woman understood Jesus' statement and cleverly pointed out that even the family pet's needs were adequately met. She hoped that Jesus' word was not yet final and that He could still help without losing the real focus of His mission.

O woman, great is your faith! Be it done for you as you desire (15:28). Jesus saw her faith. He sensed the deep love and commitment to her daughter that compelled her to be so persistent. He praised her for both her trust and love and assured her that He would help her daughter. Matthew added that the girl was healed instantly.

Returning to the area of the eastern shore of the Sea of Galilee, Jesus went into the hill country, still in Gentile territory. His fame had apparently preceded Him because great crowds came to Him bringing their sick friends who needed healing. Jesus healed those who were lame, maimed, blind, and dumb. When Jesus healed them, they glorified Israel's God. *They glorified the God of Israel* (15:31).

SUGGESTIONS TO TEACHERS

"He can talk the talk, but can he walk the walk?" Members of the African-American community have used this vivid expression to ask whether those professing sympathy with their plight are prepared to offer more than lip service to the cause of civil rights. Today's lesson depicts a foreign woman with a pagan background who could "walk the walk" of faith, as contrasted to some religious leaders who could only "talk the talk." The fifteenth chapter of Matthew makes this lesson especially interesting to teach.

1. TRANSGRESSION OF TRADITIONALISM. Have the class look hard at the scribes and Pharisees who accost Jesus. Note that their motives were those of decent, law-abiding people who wanted to uphold what they believed was sacred. They also had deep misgivings about anyone who failed to observe the traditional ways. In many ways, these scribes and Pharisees sound like the respectable church people in nearly every community. But their fault was that they put tradition ahead of God. In effect, the scribes and Pharisees insisted on worshiping their traditions.

Not that all traditions are bad. But Jesus criticizes these traditionalists for misplaced loyalties. Ask the class to indicate some of the important traditions held dear in our culture and in our churches. Are these allowed to come before Christ?

2. TEMPER OF TAINT. Jesus' words about what defiles a person should be given careful consideration. Not external mannerisms but an inner disposition is what truly defiles. Slavery to tradition, in fact, leads to a fake religion of outward practices only. Jesus insists that the thought behind the act is more important and calls for a conversion of the heart.

3. TESTIMONY OF TRUTHFULNESS. Devote plenty of time to the exchange between Jesus and the Canaanite woman. Her conversation revealed her sincerity and integrity. Make sure your class understands that this person was an extremely unlikely prospect for conversation with a Jewish man because she was 1) a woman, and 2) a Canaanite woman. Bring out the significance of Jesus' breaking all the taboos by associating with this foreign female.

4. TRIUMPH OF TRUST. The Canaanite woman's trust in Jesus succeeded in gaining healing for her little girl. In contrast to the unbelief of the pious Jerusalem religious leaders, the faith of this outsider is held up as an example of truly "walking the walk" with the Master.

TOPIC FOR ADULTS
PERSISTENT FAITH

Willing to Fly. A sign on the wall of a local business reads: "According to the theory of aerodynamics, and as can readily be proven by wind tunnel experiments, the bumblebee is unable to fly. Why? Because the size of its wings in relation to the size of its body makes flying impossible.

"But the bumblebee, being unacquainted with these scientific truths goes ahead and flies anyway and gathers a little honey every day."

A problem we have in the church today is that we are too practiced. We spend so much time and energy on finding ways and reasons why something can't be done, rather than trusting by faith and the help of God's Holy Spirit to direct our efforts.

Perhaps we should unacquaint ourselves with practical truths and reacquaint ourselves with the Ultimate Truth, because churches that grow are willing to trust God to risk to do it. People who grow as Christians are willing to trust God to risk too.

As the people of God, beginning in this coming church year, let's try to be a riskier people, a more adventurous people, taking on the work God has given us to do without asking whether it can be done, but just doing it. It's an impractical idea, but who ever said the church of Jesus Christ is supposed to be practical?—Kenneth C. Roscoe.

Faith in Grandpas. A small boy approached a white-haired gentleman in a store and asked shyly, "Are you a grandpa?"

"Yes," replied the elder with a kind smile.

"Good," said the little boy. "My grandpa isn't here, and I want a candy bar, please."

Cost of Traditionalism. The Pharisees in our lesson today were so caught up in their religious traditions that they failed to care for suffering persons. Traditionalism can kill the nerve of compassion. In fact, traditionalism can even kill, period.

A tragic bus accident occurred in India a couple of years ago. It seems that the bus was packed with people when it swerved off the road and plunged into a deep ravine. The wreck was quickly engulfed in flames. Seventy-eight people died. However, not all these seventy-eight needed to die. A rescuer hurried with a rope, fastened it to a tree, and lowered the end to a group of passengers crawling from the smashed, fiery wreckage. Eleven pulled themselves up the steep, slippery slope to safety, using the rope. However, the other passengers refused to handle the rope because the eleven who had hauled themselves up were members of the untouchable caste. The seventy-eight others, bound by the tradition of the caste system in their religion, could not bring themselves to use the rope that had been touched by the despised members of the lowest caste. The seventy-eight, refusing to have anything to do with the rope, perished needlessly.

Questions for Students on the Next Lesson. 1. Why did Jesus take Peter, James, and John up the mountain? 2. What does the word "Transfiguration" mean? 3. What was the significance of the appearance of Moses and Elijah to the disciples? 4. What did the words of the Voice signify? 5. What was Peter's suggestion after the experience on the mountain, and why did Jesus turn it down?

TOPIC FOR YOUTH
FAITH THAT IS REWARDED

Healing Touch. A gentleman called "a divine healer" was led into a pediatric unit in a large university medical complex. The doctors were skeptical. Their sophisticated techniques were having little impact on a paralyzed little girl.

The "healer" laid his hands on the little girl's head after "anointing" the child. He said a prayer and promised that the little girl would be freed from her paralysis.

Over the next two weeks, the little girl grew visibly better. The doctors were encouraged. Finally, they felt she was strong enough to begin rehabilitation. Today, the little girl is an enthusiastic teenage cheerleader.

Healing is a controversial issue within many churches. It can cause disagreement. Often it conjures up a discussion of charismatic personalities on television. However, God can heal—spiritually, emotionally, and physically. Surrender yourself to whatever may be God's best for you.

Persistence. "Mom, there's a snake at your feet!" yelled Johnny. Poor Mom had had her share of those alarming statements over the last twelve years. She had fallen for many of them only to watch the boy double over in laughter. She had ignored others and seen the look of disappointment in his face. Sitting in the hotel lobby in Bangkok, Thailand, she decided she was not about to look silly and gullible again.

Johnny again called, "Mom! There's a snake by the leg of the sofa, next to your feet!" Obviously Mom's lack of interest was not going to dampen John's enthusiasm.

"But Mom, there really is a snake there," he pleaded. Perhaps it was the note of urgency. Perhaps it was his persistence. Finally, Johnny's mother looked. There really was a snake! Hotel officials rushed in and immediately killed the snake. It proved to be a "three stepper." Bitten by this snake, a victim can only stumble three steps before the lethal venom affects his nervous system.

Johnny's persistence saved his mother. The woman before Jesus was equally persistent and saved her daughter.

The Effects of Anger. Paul Tournier related a story about a doctor friend. This doctor had been treating a young woman for several months for anemia, and he was having little success. Finally he referred the girl to a specialist whom he hoped would admit the girl to a medical institution or sanitarium.

One week later his patient had returned. The specialist had approved the request but said that the blood analysis he had done did not agree with the doctor's analysis. The doctor had another blood analysis done from a brand-new blood sample. Sure enough, the blood chemistry had changed! Nothing the doctor could recall could have contaminated the blood or caused it to change. He asked his patient if anything out of the ordinary had happened in her life over the last few weeks.

The woman answered that she had forgiven and made peace with a friend with whom she had had a terrible fight. Forgiveness and the end of anger brought healing.

How much do our emotional states influence our health? Obviously anger, resentment, or guilt can make us ill. Complete healing requires a change of heart, and the wholeness we receive through Jesus involves the deepest part of our souls.

Questions for Students on the Next Lesson. 1. Why did Jesus take only Peter, James, and John up the mountain? 2. Why were Moses and Elijah present with Jesus? 3. Why did Peter want to build three booths? 4. What was the significance of the cloud? 5. Why did Jesus command the disciples to tell no one about the event?

LESSON 8—JANUARY 22

JESUS IS TRANSFIGURED

Background Scripture: Matthew 17:1-23
Devotional Reading: II Peter 1:16-21

KING JAMES VERSION

MATTHEW 17:1 And after six days Jesus taketh Peter, James, and John his brother, and bringeth them up into an high mountain apart,

2 And was transfigured before them: and his face did shine as the sun, and his raiment was white as the light.

3 And, behold, there appeared unto them Moses and Elias talking with him.

4 Then answered Peter, and said unto Jesus, Lord, it is good for us to be here: if thou wilt, let us make here three tabernacles; one for thee, and one for Moses, and one for Elias.

5 While he yet spake, behold, a bright cloud overshadowed them: and behold a voice out of the cloud, which said, This is my beloved Son, in whom I am well pleased; hear ye him.

6 And when the disciples heard it, they fell on their face, and were sore afraid.

7 And Jesus came and touched them, and said, Arise, and be not afraid.

8 And when they had lifted up their eyes, they saw no man, save Jesus only.

9 And as they came down from the mountain, Jesus charged them, saying, Tell the vision to no man, until the Son of man be risen again from the dead.

10 And his disciples asked him, saying, Why then say the scribes that Elias must first come?

11 And Jesus answered and said unto them, Elias truly shall first come, and restore all things.

12 But I say unto you, That Elias is come already, and they knew him not, but have done unto him whatsoever they listed. Likewise shall also the Son of man suffer of them.

13 Then the disciples understood that he spake unto them of John the Baptist.

REVISED STANDARD VERSION

MATTHEW 17:1 And after six days Jesus took with him Peter and James and John his brother, and led them up a high mountain apart. 2 And he was transfigured before them, and his face shone like the sun, and his garments became white as light. 3 And behold, there appeared to them Moses and Elijah, talking with him. 4 And Peter said to Jesus, "Lord, it is well that we are here; if you wish, I will make three booths here, one for you and one for Moses and one for Elijah." 5 He was still speaking, when lo, a bright cloud overshadowed them, and a voice from the cloud said, "This is my beloved Son, with whom I am well pleased; listen to him." 6 When the disciples heard this, they fell on their faces, and were filled with awe. 7 But Jesus came and touched them, saying, "Rise, and have no fear." 8 And when they lifted up their eyes, they saw no one but Jesus only.

9 And as they were coming down the mountain, Jesus commanded them, "Tell no one the vision, until the Son of man is raised from the dead." 10 And the disciples asked him, "Then why do the scribes say that first Elijah must come?" 11 He replied, "Elijah does come, and he is to restore all things; 12 but I tell you that Elijah has already come, and they did not know him, but did to him whatever they pleased. So also the Son of man will suffer at their hands." 13 Then the disciples understood that he was speaking to them of John the Baptist.

KEY VERSE: This is my beloved Son, with whom I am well pleased; listen to him. Matthew 17:5b.

HOME DAILY BIBLE READINGS

BACKGROUND

Jesus clearly spoke of the suffering He would have to face, but His disciples seemed unable to understand. They persisted in thinking that Jesus' messiahship would mean a triumphant takeover of the country in which He would rule in splendor and they would be rewarded gloriously for supporting His cause. Jesus repeatedly stated that His ministry would lead to a sacrificial death, but even after the teaching in the area of Caesarea Philippi (see Matt. 16) the disciples didn't seem to grasp the meaning or the message of their master.

Jesus finally took the inner circle—Peter, James, and John—away for a private retreat up the slope of Mount Hermon, the great snow-covered peak that rose up beyond Caesarea Philippi. During their time in this secluded area, Jesus' identity and purpose was dramatically transformed for this trio. Jesus was transfigured in their thinking from being the rabbi-messiah they thought they knew into a cosmic figure, divinely appointed. The vision on the height of Mount Hermon gave Peter, James, and John much-needed insight into Jesus' destiny.

The details of this event are rich in symbolism. The mention of the two key figures in Jewish thinking, Moses and Elijah, signify that Jesus fulfills everything promised about Him in the Hebrew Scriptures. Moses, the representative of the Jewish law who, according to tradition, had not died but had been taken up into heaven, and Elijah, the representative of the prophets who also according to tradition had been translated into heaven, confirm Jesus' messiahship. Furthermore, Elijah was believed to be the forerunner who would prepare the way for the Messiah's coming, while Moses' appearance was thought to acknowledge Jesus as the new lawgiver, the giver of the Gospel. The experience on Mount Hermon, in other words, was a second Mount Sinai. God was indeed ushering in the Kingdom through His chosen one, Jesus.

NOTES ON THE PRINTED TEXT

After six days Jesus took with him Peter and James and John his brother, and led them up a high mountain apart (17:1). More than six days after the events at Caesarea Philippi, Jesus took His three favorite disciples on a brief retreat. Perhaps Jesus needed some rest; maybe He wanted to spend some extra time with His three closest friends or offer them a special lesson that would deepen their understanding of Him and His mission. They hiked up one of the high mountains, perhaps nearby snow-covered Mount Hermon.

He was transfigured before them, and his face shown like the sun, and his garments became white as light (17:2). On the mountain, Peter, James, and John experienced something indescribable and inexplicable. Jesus was "transfigured," or transformed. Our word "metamorphosis" comes from the Greek word used here. Jesus was changed. Matthew tells us that Jesus' appearance and His clothes radiated like the sun with a brilliant, white light. The light indicated God's presence, that God was gloriously and mysteriously acting on the mountain, pointing to Jesus' messiahship.

There appeared to them Moses and Elijah, talking with him (17:3). The three disciples saw two of the "greats" of their faith conversing with Jesus. Moses was the great lawgiver, and Elijah was regarded as the forerunner of the Messiah and the greatest of the prophets. Popular belief held that both never really died. The two heavenly visitors conversed with Jesus, who would shortly join them in heaven. Their presence also suggested that both the Law and the prophets were confirming Jesus' statement that the Messiah must shortly die in a new exodus as He had earlier indicated. Yet, to the disciples' way of thinking, a suffering Messiah was impossible.

Lord, it is well that we are here. . . . I will make three booths here (17:4). Impulsive and practical, Peter suddenly overcame his shock. Rather than simply watch, he realized that the three disciples must serve the heavenly visitors. The least that they could do was provide shelter for each of them for the night.

This is my beloved Son, with whom I am well pleased; listen to him (17:5). However, before the three could act and gather the necessary building materials, a bright cloud covered them. From within the cloud, the disciples heard God's voice confirming Jesus' divine sonship.

Peter, James, and John were overwhelmed. Realizing they were in God's presence and hearing His voice, they collapsed facedown on the ground and closed their eyes. As they listened to God's voice, a mixture of awe, panic, and fear filled them until they felt Jesus' touch. Jesus stood alone beside them, reassuring them and ordering them to get up and not to be afraid. *Rise, and have no fear* (17:7).

Tell no one the vision, until the Son of man is raised from the dead (17:9). Having had confirmed that Jesus was the long-awaited Messiah, they were commanded not to tell anyone what they had seen until after He was raised from the dead.

Then why do the scribes say that first Elijah must come? (17:10). The disciples offered the traditional viewpoint. Before the Messiah came, Elijah must first appear. Based on certain prophecies in Malachi, Elijah was believed to be the forerunner, and he had not yet come and judged.

Jesus affirmed that the Elijah tradition was true. *Elijah does come, and he is to restore all things* (17:11). However, Jesus continued, *Elijah has already come, and they did not know him, but did to him whatever they pleased* (17:12). The scribes failed to see that Elijah had already come. He had come but was not recognized. Therefore, the people were unprepared for the Messiah. As the leaders in their ignorance did to John, so they will do to Jesus. *So also the Son of man will suffer at their hands* (17:12).

An understanding of God's plan dawned on the disciples. Now they could see John's relationship to Jesus. *Then the disciples understood that he was speaking to them of John the Baptist* (17:13).

SUGGESTIONS TO TEACHERS

The wall of the narthex of the Unitarian-Universalist building in Rockford, Illinois, is dominated by a circular art glass window that symbolically embraces Islam, Hinduism, Judaism, Taoism, Buddhism, and Christianity. After hearing a visitor describing the window, a woman commented, "Well, I wish all the churches had that attitude. If they could only get away from all the fuss and attention centered on Christ."

This woman's remark reflects the feeling of some people who fail to see anything unique about Jesus, and who are inclined to downplay His authority. The woman making the remark about disliking the "fuss and attention centered on Christ"—and all of us, for that matter—need to ascend Mount Hermon to experience a personal awareness of the meaning of the transfiguration.

Your task this Sunday will be to try to impart the impact of the vision that gripped Peter, James, and John. Through the account of this revelation of Jesus' identity, help your class members comprehend more deeply the supremacy of Jesus over all other claims to religious truth.

1. SHAKING OF ASSUMPTIONS. Do your class members understand what Peter, James, and John and the other followers had been thinking of Jesus before the transfiguration? What had been their assumptions about their rabbi? Was He a conquering hero? An exceptionally able teacher? The transfiguration shook those assumptions and gave these disciples a new perspective. Invite your class members to share any personal experiences when their previous assumptions about the Lord were shaken.

2. SUPREMACY OF JESUS. The heavenly announcement disclosed Jesus' uniqueness. The astounding claim is that Jesus stands supreme above all others. It took a revelation from God to get this across to the disciples because they hadn't been able to figure it out on their own. Nor had they understood when Jesus had tried to tell them.

God continues to grant greater appreciation of Jesus to those trying to follow Him faithfully. Here is the place of prayer and worship in the life of your class members. God reintroduces Jesus as His beloved Son to those who obey.

3. SACREDNESS OF JESUS. Explore with your group members the meaning of the words "This is my beloved Son, with whom I am well pleased; listen to him" (17:5). Bring out the meaning of the term "Son" in this verse so that your students understand better the sacred standing belonging to Jesus. Likewise, discuss what it means to "listen to him." To listen means to obey.

4. STUBBORNNESS OF THE DISCIPLES. Jesus would not permit the three followers to remain on the mountain but led them back down to a world of hurting people. They immediately encountered the desperate father of an epileptic son begging for help. The other followers of Jesus hadn't been able to bring healing because of their "little faith" (17:20). Talk with your students about what faith means. Share examples from personal experience in which faith prevailed. Key in on Jesus' words about trust.

TOPIC FOR ADULTS
CHALLENGED TO HEAR

Seeing in a New Light. Have you ever had the experience of thinking that you know someone, then, in a sudden flash of insight, you discover that you are seeing that person in a new light? I have had that experience many times.

I recall one such experience in regard to my father when I was a boy. I had looked on my father for many years, but I had not really *seen* him until one day when I was about sixteen. I was at the obnoxious stage when a boy assumes he has near-perfect insights, infallible judgment, and far more knowledge than his father.

My father was a minister, and my opinion of him at that time was that he was an honest, sincere person who meant well, but who was hopelessly lacking in intellectual and oratorical abilities. I even felt a bit embarrassed to admit my father was a minister since I could not see that he or any minister really commanded any respect except among a few elderly ladies of the quilting group. I was certain that I knew all about my father.

One afternoon the doorbell rang. I answered it and was startled to find a portly, well-dressed man at the door. When he gave his name, I was more surprised. It was T. K. Phillips.

T. K. Phillips? The richest man in town? The guy who owned half the county, and whose real estate business and signs were a byword? What was he doing at our front door?

"When may I speak with your father?" Mr. Phillips inquired.

"I think he's making calls now. Would you like to stop by later?" I replied.

"Thank you, but I'd like to wait for him, if you don't mind. May I come in?"

I was dumbfounded. Mr. T. K. Phillips waiting to see my father? I couldn't understand why this man of such means and importance wanted to wait to see my father. T. K. Phillips was the type of man who summoned people to see him and made people wait until he was ready to have them come into his presence. Here he was, humbly preparing to sit for as long as necessary to have an interview with my father. From the worried look on his face, I sensed that he seemed to have a lot on his mind. But why come and ask to talk to my father?

Much later that evening, I asked bluntly, "Hey, Dad, what did old T. K. want with you? Why, he's not even a member of our church." My tone carried a slight note of contempt. I could not imagine a tycoon who could pick up a telephone and get through to almost anyone in the country wanting to bother talking with my father.

Father quietly and reluctantly told me what had happened. T. K. had come from his doctor's office, where he'd been told that he had cancer. He was so depressed that he was considering suicide. But he felt the one person who would understand and could help him was my father. No boasting by my father. Merely a matter-of-fact response to my question.

But in that moment I saw my father in a new light. I saw him as not merely a busy pastor and ordinary preacher, but as a trusted, beloved counselor to the richest, most influential person in the community as well as to the poorest, most insignificant widow in his congregation. I had looked at my father but had not really seen him until then.

Peter, James, and John had looked at Jesus countless times, but they had not really seen Him until one day on a mountain with Him. They thought that they knew Jesus. They had traveled with Him. They had listened to His words. But that day on the mountain, they *saw* Jesus. They understood him in a deeper and different way.—William P. Barker

Looking at or Seeing? We are inclined to take for granted that we know all about Jesus, but the truth for most of us is that we have not really seen Him for all He is. We need on occasion to do more than look on Him.

Knowing *about* someone and *knowing* someone are not the same. For instance, a man who had done blood research on the blood type of George Washington at the University of Wisconsin medical facility reports that the father of our country had type B blood. This learned doctor, working with a lock of Washington's hair in the laboratory and carrying out astonishing feats of analysis, discovered a lot about the national hero's physical condition. But he really doesn't know who the first president of our republic truly was.

By contrast, a young African-American woman, working as a National Park Service guide at Independence Hall in Philadelphia, really knows Washington. Her comments indicate that she knows more than facts about George Washington. This woman has not merely looked at Washington; she has "seen" him. She knows him! She has reflected on the man and his work so deeply that Washington means more to her than he does to the research scientist in Madison, Wisconsin.

What about you? Have you merely looked at Jesus, or have you seen Jesus for who He is and what He claims to be?

Questions for Students on the Next Lesson. 1. Why did Jesus have the disciples get a donkey and a colt for His entrance to Jerusalem? 2. What is Zechariah's prophecy about the entrance of the Messiah? 3. Why were the authorities so upset by Jesus' actions in the temple? 4. How do you think Jesus would be received if He were to enter your town or city? 5. What does "Hosanna" mean?

TOPIC FOR YOUTH
MOMENTS THAT HAVE MEANING

No Withdrawal. In the third and fourth centuries A.D., many Christians were offended by the immorality around them. Some wanted to flee and find a place where they could worship and approach God individually.

Anthony, the founder of Christian monasticism, was born in Koma in central Egypt. He prayed constantly, fasted, practiced self-denial, and tried to be absolutely alone. Pachomius, another Egyptian, organized a group of people who wanted to withdraw from the corrupt society around them. Athanasius introduced monasticism to the west, influencing such great church leaders as Jerome, Ambrose, Augustine, and Benedict.

Peter, James, and John wanted to build three booths and stay locked up in their little monasteries on the hill. There they could study, pray, worship, and hold all of the treasures of their culture. They could look at the terrible conditions around them but shut the door and keep them out. For them, the religious experience was an escape.

God reminded them on that mountain that Jesus was Lord and that they had to go and tell others. They were not to keep their faith walled up in a church. Their faith meant coming back down from the mountain, the place of quiet and refuge, to reenter the world of people, problems, and temptations.

Your faith is not an escape. It must be visible and of practical value to others.

Remembrance. Shunned by youth in the 1960s, the senior prom returned to fashion during the 1980s. Today's proms, though, are a far cry from the fancy dance in the school's gym.

A strict code of etiquette governs the prom. It must be held in a fancy ballroom. Tuxedos are a must for the boys, and gowns for the girls. A limousine ride is now a necessity. The most popular party favor is a memory book emblazoned with the school's emblem or crest. This enables the prom-goer to remember the special evening; high school's last, gaudy fling of youth. It reminds students of what life was like when they were young and carefree.

The three disciples wanted a similar way of remembering the moment by constructing the booths. God had a different idea. Far from memorializing the moment, God sent the disciples out to share the faith that had been strengthened by the moment on the mountain.

Experiential. Near Washington's National Mall, four hundred yards from the Washington Monument, is the United States Holocaust Memorial. It is the biggest Holocaust Museum outside of Israel. The five-story building of brick and granite matches the neighboring buildings. Only the towers, which duplicate the towers at Auschwitz death camp, suggest what is inside.

The museum includes an actual boxcar used to transport Jews to the Treblinka death camp, a Gypsy caravan whose occupants were all killed, and a tree trunk with bullets embedded in it where Polish journalists and intellectuals were shot. Inside the Hall of Witnesses, the windows are boarded up, and the ceiling trusses are twisted as they were in death camps.

Each visitor is issued an ID upon entering. On the ID card, the visitor reads a short biography of an individual and learns that person's story. The horror of the Holocaust becomes vivid as the visitor passes through the museum. Along the way, the visitor also discovers the fate of the person whose story is on the ID card.

The idea was to make the museum experiential. The more a visitor viewed and actually experienced the Holocaust, the more he or she would understand it.

The transfiguration was an experiential event for the three disciples. Jesus could have merely told them He was God's Son. But the disciples understood much more through experiencing His awesome preeminence.

Questions for Students on the Next Lesson. 1. Why did Jesus go to Jerusalem? 2. How do you explain the fleeting loyalty of the crowd? 3. Why were the religious leaders angry? 4. What prophecies existed about Israel's coming king? 5. How can we proclaim Jesus as the Messiah in our daily lives?

LESSON 9—JANUARY 29

THE PEOPLE PROCLAIM JESUS THE SON OF DAVID

Background Scripture: Matthew 20:17—21:17
Devotional Reading: Matthew 20:17-28

KING JAMES VERSION

MATTHEW 21:1 And when they drew nigh unto Jerusalem, and were come to Bethphage, unto the mount of Olives, then sent Jesus two disciples,

2 Saying unto them, Go into the village over against you, and straightway ye shall find an ass tied, and a colt with her: loose them, and bring them unto me.

3 And if any man say ought unto you, ye shall say, The Lord hath need of them, and straightway he will send them.

4 All this was done, that it might be fulfilled which was spoken by the prophet, saying,

5 Tell ye the daughter of Sion, Behold, thy King cometh unto thee, meek, and sitting upon an ass, and a colt the foal of an ass.

6 And the disciples went, and did as Jesus commanded them,

7 And brought the ass, and the colt, and put on them their clothes, and they set him thereon.

8 And a very great multitude spread their garments in the way; others cut down branches from the trees, and strawed them in the way.

9 And the multitudes that went before, and that followed, cried, saying, Hosanna to the son of David: Blessed is he that cometh in the name of the Lord; Hosanna in the highest.

10 And when he was come into Jerusalem, all the city was moved, saying, Who is this?

11 And the multitude said, This is Jesus the prophet of Nazareth of Galilee. . . .

14 And the blind and the lame came to him in the temple; and he healed them.

15 And when the chief priests and scribes saw the wonderful things that he did, and the children crying in the temple, and saying, Hosanna to the son of David; they were sore displeased,

16 And said unto him, Hearest thou what these say? And Jesus saith unto them, Yea; have ye never read, Out of the mouth of babes and sucklings thou hast perfected praise?

REVISED STANDARD VERSION

MATTHEW 21:1 And when they drew near to Jerusalem and came to Bethphage, to the Mount of Olives, then Jesus sent two disciples, 2 saying to them, "Go into the village opposite you, and immediately you will find an ass tied, and a colt with her; untie them and bring them to me. 3 If any one says anything to you, you shall say, 'The Lord has need of them,' and he will send them immediately." 4 This took place to fulfil what was spoken by the prophet, saying, 5 "Tell the daughter of Zion, Behold, your king is coming to you, humble, and mounted on an ass, and on a colt, the foal of an ass." 6 The disciples went and did as Jesus had directed them; 7 they brought the ass and the colt, and put their garments on them, and he sat thereon. 8 Most of the crowd spread their garments on the road, and others cut branches from the trees and spread them on the road. 9 And the crowds that went before him and that followed him shouted, "Hosanna to the Son of David! Blessed is he who comes in the name of the Lord! Hosanna in the highest!" 10 And when he entered Jerusalem, all the city was stirred, saying, "Who is this?" 11 And the crowds said, "This is the prophet Jesus from Nazareth of Galilee.". . .

14 And the blind and the lame came to him in the temple, and he healed them. 15 But when the chief priests and the scribes saw the wonderful things that he did, and the children crying out in the temple, "Hosanna to the Son of David!" they were indignant; 16 and they said to him, "Do you hear what these are saying?" And Jesus said to them, "Yes; have you never read, 'Out of the mouth of babes and sucklings thou has brought perfect praise'?"

KEY VERSE: Hosanna to the Son of David! Blessed is he who comes in the name of the Lord! Hosanna in the highest! Matthew 21:9b.

HOME DAILY BIBLE READINGS

Jan.	*23*	*M.*	Psalm 118:19-29	*Thanksgiving for God's Salvation*
Jan.	*24*	*T.*	Matthew 20:17-28	*Followers of Jesus Must Serve Others*
Jan.	*25*	*W.*	Matthew 20:29-34	*Jesus Heals Two Blind Men*
Jan.	*26*	*T.*	Matthew 21:1-5	*Jesus Approaches Jerusalem*
Jan.	*27*	*F.*	Matthew 21:6-11	*The Crowds Welcome Jesus*
Jan.	*28*	*S.*	Matthew 21:12-17	*Jesus Cleanses the Temple and Heals*
Jan.	*29*	*S.*	Matthew 21:23-32	*Jesus' Authority Questioned*

BACKGROUND

We might title this lesson "Jesus Goes Public, or "Jesus Challenges the Leaders to a Showdown." Up to this point, Jesus had commanded people not to talk openly about His identity as Messiah. And with good reason. "Messiah" was a loaded word. To most, it meant a political ruler and military hero. But Jesus was not about to issue a call to armed revolt or to institute a civil government.

In addition, Jesus knew how determined His opposition was. More than any follower, Jesus realized that the religious authorities intended to silence Him at all costs. His march into Jerusalem would be the one final chance for the temple hierarchy to recognize who He was.

Jesus carefully arranged for His triumphal entry into the holy city. Every detail was loaded with symbolic meaning. The donkey, for instance, signified the fulfillment of Zechariah's prophecy of the promised King arriving to institute *Shalom* (Zech. 9:9, 10) and announce His royalty.

Jerusalem's streets and surrounding area teemed with religious pilgrims. It was Passover time. Every devout Jew wanted to celebrate the great feast in the holy city if possible, and throngs poured into Jerusalem from all parts of the Mediterranean world.

It was also a tense time for the Roman authorities. Judea as an occupied country seethed with revolt. Rumors of plots and uprisings made Pilate, the military governor, very uneasy, especially during Passover season when the city filled with excitable crowds. His anxieties were shared by the temple leaders. Like their Roman overlords, the priestly authorities dreaded a possible popular uprising. Reports of Jesus' words and great following, of course, had reached their ears.

When Jesus' entry stirred a jubilant demonstration, both the Roman army and the religious hierarchy felt uneasy. But when Jesus challenged the priestly party by daring to prevent business in the temple, the authorities moved to arrest Jesus. Jesus knew that He would be forced to make the supreme sacrifice.

NOTES ON THE PRINTED TEXT

Go into the village opposite you, and immediately you will find an ass tied, and a colt with her; untie them and bring them to me (21:2). The road from Jericho to Jerusalem was a long, steep climb. It passed through Bethphage [BETH-fah-jee], a village situated on a ridge on the Mount of

Olives, directly across the Kidron Valley from Jerusalem. In the nearby village of Bethany, the disciples were told that they would find a donkey and a colt (a young immature donkey that had not yet been separated from its mother). If the owner of the two animals objected, Jesus instructed the two disciples to respond, *The Lord has need of them* (21:3).

The animals fulfilled prophecy by Zechariah that had emphasized the rider's kingship and humility. Jesus wanted to demonstrate that He was the Messiah; however, He did not come as the military and political leader the people expected but as the suffering servant described by Isaiah. *Tell the daughter of Zion, Behold, your king is coming to you, humble, and mounted on an ass, and on a colt, the foal of an ass* (21:5).

The disciples did as they had been instructed. They brought the two animals and *put their garments on them* (21:7). They padded the backs of the animals with their cloaks, thus making a crude saddle. Upon this, Jesus sat.

The crowds perceived that Jesus was making a claim to be the Messiah, the new king of Israel. Thrilled with expectation, they treated Him as a triumphant king. As a sign of homage and tribute to Him, they spread their cloaks and cut branches on the road. *Most of the crowd spread their garments on the road, and others cut branches from the trees and spread them on the road* (21:8).

Hosanna to the Son of David! Blessed is he who comes in the name of the Lord! (21:9). The crowds shouted out, welcoming Jesus as the promised Son of David, their deliverer. Their cry, "Hosanna," literally meant "Save now! Help!" It was both a cry for help and an invocation of blessing. He deserved their praise for He was the long-expected Messiah, God's Servant and Savior.

He entered Jerusalem (21:10). The path down the hillside became a green highway of cut palm leaves and people's cloaks. Jesus approached the eastern wall and its double gate, called *Shushan*, and entered Jerusalem.

Amid the jubilant shouts of the pilgrims (the noise of the crowd was described in Greek by Matthew as being like that of an earthquake), some residents of Jerusalem asked, *Who is this?* (21:10). The crowds of Galilean pilgrims responded, *This is the prophet Jesus from Nazareth of Galilee* (21:11). Perhaps some believed Jesus to be a prophet like Moses.

Entering the temple. Jesus stood in the huge Court of the Gentiles. He healed some sick and crippled people. The children shouted in the temple area *Hosanna to the Son of David!* (21:15). They were echoing their parents' words that Jesus was the Messiah. To the religious leaders, all of this behavior was shocking, and the children's statement about Jesus' being the Messiah was scandalous. Furious, the authorities challenged Jesus. *Do you hear what these are saying?* (21:16). To their way of thinking, Jesus should have stopped the children's shouts. How could He let them utter such blatant lies?

Yes (21:16), Jesus responded. He then reminded the angry leaders that the response of the children was the fulfillment of prophecy. God had prepared for Christ this perfect praise, which was sung by children. *Out of the mouth of babes and sucklings thou hast brought perfect praise* (21:16).

SUGGESTIONS TO TEACHERS

Today's Scripture covers the entry of Jesus into Jerusalem. It is usually associated with Palm Sunday. Perhaps it is good to study this passage at a time when we are not caught up with the rush and tradition of the Easter season.

1. SACRED MISSION. The key to understanding Jesus' entry into Jerusalem can be found in Matthew 20:17-19. Jesus announced in unmistakable terms that He would be condemned, crucified, and raised. He courageously took His claim to the highest authorities of His nation and religion but knew that that claim would be rejected. Help your class members see that Jesus was no innocuous teacher, merely offering nice platitudes on "love." Rather, Jesus was the God-sent Messiah who was aware that His calling would cost Him dearly; yet He persevered.

2. SELFISH MISUNDERSTANDING. Pause in the scriptural narrative to observe the request of the mother of James and John for special honors for her sons. Here is Jesus' wonderful teaching on greatness. Remind your students that our society advocates seeking preferential treatment, and assumes that greatness means acquiring power. Emphasize Jesus' words about being a "servant" and, most of all, His words about His own servanthood. True greatness comes from living a life of sacrifice for others, even as our Lord Himself did.

3. SAVIOR'S MERCY. Take a few moments to reflect on the episode mentioned in Matthew 21:19-34. Jesus was hurrying to Jerusalem with a lot on His mind. Time was running out for Him, yet He paused to heal two blind men. Note the words describing Jesus' compassion. Also call attention to the way Jesus noticed and cared for two roadside beggars whom others regarded as loudmouthed nuisances. Jesus cares for the most unattractive imaginable.

4. SPECIAL MARCH. The parade down the Mount of Olives that first Palm Sunday was planned with great attention to detail by Jesus. Through the symbolic aspects of His procession into Jerusalem, He disclosed His identity as the Messiah. The bystanders recognized that claim and cheered. Here was the long-expected Son of David.

5. SUPERIOR MESSIAHSHIP. Have students examine the various details of the temple cleansing. The Court of the Gentiles was the outer area where any non-Jew could pray but which had been turned into a market area for buying sacrificial animals and converting money to sacred temple coinage.

Jesus' concern for outsiders was apparent in this incident. He secured the Court as a place where everyone could be welcomed to worship. This act also deliberately proclaimed to the temple hierarchy, all its priests and scribes and everyone associated with the nation's religion, that Jesus intentionally placed His authority above theirs. Jesus presented His claim as the Messiah, the Savior, in terms no one could misinterpret or ignore.

TOPIC FOR ADULTS
WELCOME THE SAVIOR

The Jerusalem Syndrome. Mental health staff workers in Jerusalem have been having problems with some visitors to the Holy Land during the past few years. Psychiatrists call these cases the "Jerusalem Syndrome." About one hundred tourists each year require treatment for their bizarre behavior after arriving in the city. A study of eighty-nine such patients in 1991 revealed that a third of them thought they were the Messiah, and the next largest group claimed to be God. Most of them were found to be acting peculiarly, such as the thirty-three-year-old American school teacher who raced naked through the Arab quarter of the Old City with a sword, shouting that God had anointed him as the Messiah. A forty-one-year-old German visitor walked into the hotel's kitchen insisting that He was Jesus, then filed a complaint when the cook appeared skeptical.

Significantly, no one can dismiss Jesus as being deluded or behaving as a victim of the "Jerusalem Syndrome." Nor may you dismiss Him as a harmless eccentric or misguided fool. You dare not write Him off as a pathetic case of messianic delusion. Jesus was the most sane, stable, mature personality ever to live. His claims still stand and He maintains that He is the ruler of your life. Jesus does not care about your patronage; He demands your allegiance. He is not interested in accolades; He insists on obedience. As He went public with His claims, He calls you to go public with your faith in Him.

Kingdom of Self-interest. Simone Weil, the French woman who died tragically young in the middle of World War II, described occupied Paris shortly after the fall of France in 1940. She told of observing Parisians standing in long lines in freezing rain for hours just to buy one egg for themselves. Weil commented that these same people would not do a thing for their country only a few weeks earlier. She stated that the kingdom of self-interest claimed the allegiance of her fellow citizens.

The kingdom of self-interest or the Kingdom of Jesus? Which is it for us?

Waving at the King. In 1950, while under house arrest, King Tribhuvan escaped and overthrew the usurpers in Katmandu, Nepal. Upon his death, his grandson, King Birendra Bir Shah Dev, began his rule. Like his grandfather, he was regarded as a deity.

However, King Tribhuvan lived on. Once a year, the old monarch's life-sized cutout photograph was put on parade. Riding in an open carriage, the smiling picture with raised right arm passed through the streets for the people to salute.

You may approach Palm Sunday in much the same manner. You may come to watch the parade and wave at Jesus. If so, for you Jesus comes off as a life-sized cutout on parade. You take your palm leaves, glance in Jesus' direction, then go on.

The lesson of this day emphasizes His kingship. The Messiah is coming! You are meant to hail a living, present king.

Questions for Students on the Next Lesson. 1. What is the feast of Passover? 2. How did Jesus treat Judas at the Last Supper? 3. What exactly is meant by the "blood of the covenant"? 4. Why do we always refer to "the cup of the new covenant" when we celebrate the Lord's Supper? 5. What does Communion mean to you, personally?

TOPIC FOR YOUTH
CELEBRATIONS THAT COUNT

Hero to Heel to Hero. Terry Bradshaw, former quarterback of the four-time Super Bowl Champion Pittsburgh Steelers, often spoke of being a hero one day and a heel the next day. On one day, the quarterback might be highly favored with the fans, the man of the hour. The next week, he could swiftly fall out of favor.

Bradshaw described the girl who ran the cash register at the parking garage where he kept his car. Sometimes she would greet him with a big smile and a cheery greeting. If the game had not gone well that week or the Steelers had lost, she greeted him with a sneer.

On another occasion, Terry was pulling out of a local gas station when two teenagers stopped him and excitedly knocked on his car window. He rolled down the window, thinking that the two wanted his autograph. Without warning, they spit in his face!

Jesus would have understood. The crowd had the ability to change its mind quickly. One day He was a hero with the crowd's acclaim of "Hosanna!" Another day, some of the same crowd treated Him as a heel by their cries of "Crucify Him! Crucify Him!" Few realized that the true Savior was before them.

Parade Feelings. Parades have a way of stirring up our emotions. On November 22, 1963, a motorcade drove through the streets of Dallas, Texas. President John F. Kennedy sat in an open car with his wife and waved at the cheering crowds. Many children, caught up in the moment, waved back. At 12:30 p.m., Kennedy was shot in the head by assassin Lee Oswald.

Three days later, grim-faced people silently lined a street. Over one million persons lined the route that the flag-draped, horse-drawn caisson traveled as it moved to St. Matthew's Cathedral. Many of the mourners cried. One little girl held her mother's hand and kept cupping and uncupping it because her mother had told her that she could not wave.

Even under those dignified and somber circumstances her little heart was moved. She simply had to express herself. Slowly the little hand rose and waved one final farewell to the president of the United States. The youngster had to celebrate the life of her president.

Like this little girl, our hearts should be moved to celebrate the life of our King.

Celebrating Jesus Each Day. Welcoming Jesus as Messiah means more than singing Hallelujahs at a Palm Sunday service. It means welcoming Him into your daily world. One college sophomore found this was the litmus test of her faith.

She attended a party with others from the university. Her date and most of the others present indulged in heavy drinking. Then various couples began to drift off to bedrooms. The young woman admits that she has had many doubts about her beliefs, but she states that somehow she senses that she belongs to Christ. This sophomore realizes that if she is a Christian, then Christ must really be a presence in her world. That night at the party, she showed that Jesus Christ had been welcomed to her world. She left the party.

Questions for Students on the Next Lesson. 1. How did Jesus deal with betrayal? How do you deal with it? 2. What meal was Jesus observing? What is its significance? 3. What does the bread symbolize at the Lord's Supper? 4. What does the cup symbolize at Communion? 5. What does Communion mean to you, personally?

LESSON 10—FEBRUARY 5

JESUS INSTITUTES THE LORD'S SUPPER

Background Scripture: Matthew 26:17-35
Devotional Reading: John 6:30-40

KING JAMES VERSION

MATTHEW 26:20 Now when the even was come, he sat down with the twelve.

21 And as they did eat, he said, Verily I say unto you, that one of you shall betray me.

22 And they were exceeding sorrowful, and began every one of them to say unto him, Lord, is it I?

23 And he answered and said, He that dippeth his hand with me in the dish, the same shall betray me.

24 The Son of man goeth as it is written of him: but woe unto that man by whom the Son of man is betrayed! it had been good for that man if he had not been born.

25 Then Judas, which betrayed him, answered and said, Master, is it I? He said unto him, Thou hast said.

26 And as they were eating, Jesus took bread, and blessed it, and brake it, and gave it to the disciples, and said, Take, eat; this is my body.

27 And he took the cup, and gave thanks, and gave it to them, saying, Drink ye all of it;

28 For this is my blood of the new testament, which is shed for many for the remission of sins.

29 But I say unto you, I will not drink henceforth of this fruit of the vine, until that day when I drink it new with you in my Father's kingdom.

30 And when they had sung an hymn, they went out into the mount of Olives.

REVISED STANDARD VERSION

MATTHEW 26:20 When it was evening, he sat at table with the twelve disciples; 21 and as they were eating, he said, "Truly, I say to you, one of you will betray me." 22 And they were very sorrowful, and began to say to him one after another, "Is it I, Lord?" 23 He answered, "He who has dipped his hand in the dish with me, will betray me. 24 The Son of man goes as it is written of him, but woe to that man by whom the Son of man is betrayed! It would have been better for that man if he had not been born." 25 Judas, who betrayed him, said, "Is it I, Master?" He said to him, "You have said so."

26 Now as they were eating, Jesus took bread, and blessed, and broke it, and gave it to the disciples and said, "Take, eat; this is my body." 27 And he took a cup, and when he had given thanks he gave it to them, saying, "Drink of it, all of you; 28 for this is my blood of the covenant, which is poured out for many for the forgiveness of sins. 29 I tell you I shall not drink again of this fruit of the vine until that day when I drink it new with you in my Father's kingdom."

30 And when they had sung a hymn, they went out to the Mount of Olives.

KEY VERSE: *This is my blood of the covenant, which is poured out for many for the forgiveness of sins. Matthew 26:28.*

HOME DAILY BIBLE READINGS

Jan.	30	M.	John 6:30-40	*Jesus Is the Bread of Life*
Jan.	31	T.	Matthew 22:34-40	*The Great Commandment*
Feb.	1	W.	Matthew 26:6-13	*A Woman Anoints Jesus*
Feb.	2	T.	Matthew 26:14-25	*Judas Will Betray Jesus*
Feb.	3	F.	Matthew 26:26-30	*Jesus' Last Supper with His Disciples*
Feb.	4	S.	Matthew 26:31-35	*The Disciples Promise to Remain Loyal*
Feb.	5	S.	I Corinthians 11:23-29	*In Remembrance of Jesus*

BACKGROUND

The crowds of Galilean pilgrims in the streets of Jerusalem that Passover season might have been stirred by Jesus, but the Jewish leaders resented the challenge He posed. When Jesus boldly threw out the money-changers and livestock from the temple, those leaders realized that He was asserting His authority even over the sacred temple. They could not let such a controversial intrusion go unpunished. The lines were drawn. Their hostility hardened. The chief priests and the lesser religious authorities determined to silence Jesus.

At first they tried to show Him up as a fool in public. But instead of discrediting Jesus before His audience, their spokesmen retreated before His superior skills and knowledge as a rabbi. Their trick questions not only failed to trap Jesus but were turned by Him to His advantage. Worse in their eyes, Jesus went on the offensive by presenting a series of parables that pointedly challenged the leaders to accept His authority as the God-sent Deliverer. Infuriated that He had bested them in all their debates and had attacked them for failing to accept His claim, they plotted to have Him killed.

Jesus' days were numbered, and He knew it. He also realized that His disciples were flawed and forgetful. The time of Passover commemorating God's great act of deliverance in Moses' day, He was aware, would be the last time during His earthly ministry when He would sit at table with those followers. Jesus also realized that Judas was no longer the loyal follower he once was, and had, in fact, negotiated with the temple authorities to assist them in eliminating Jesus. Nevertheless, Jesus welcomed all members of the twelve to the sacred and intimate meal with Him. During this moving part of the beautiful Passover celebration—a supper together, with the traditional ceremonies recalling God's earlier deliverance of His people—Jesus inaugurated the sacred institution whereby all His followers from that day still find Him and His new covenant presented to them. Jesus gave those disciples bread and wine, through which He promised He would always reintroduce Himself as loving Lord.

NOTES ON THE PRINTED TEXT

Oxford University carefully preserves a second-century A.D. papyrus that contains fragments of Matthew 26. It shows the importance that the early Christians associated with the institution of the Lord's Supper.

Truly, I say to you, one of you will betray me (26:21). On Thursday evening, Jesus and the disciples gathered in an upper room to celebrate the Passover. The meal was eaten after sunset and in a reclining posture, not in the daylight sitting on chairs as da Vinci's "Last Supper" painting depicts. The atmosphere was no doubt tense and troubled when Jesus made a chilling declaration. One of the twelve that had been with Him for three years was a traitor. *Is it I, Lord?* (26:22), Jesus was asked. The Greek form of the question expected a negative answer.

He who has dipped his hand in the dish with me, will betray me (26:23). Jesus did not specify an individual. It was obviously someone within the group that shared the common bowl set before Him. The meal was to be shared among family and friends, but the communal nature of the meal had been shattered by deceit and betrayal.

Jesus understood that His death was part of God's plan, predicted by the Scriptures. However, God's plan provided for choices. Judas had the freedom to choose, and he had deliberately acted to betray Jesus. Judas was therefore responsible for his actions and would be judged accordingly. *The Son of man goes as it is written of him, but woe to that man by whom the Son of man is betrayed! It would have been better for that man if he had not been born* (26:24).

Quietly and cautiously, Judas asked, *Is it I, Master?* (26:25). The older texts have Judas addressing Jesus as Master, or Rabbi (Teacher). The other disciples referred to Jesus as Lord. Clearly, Judas's loyalty had faded.

Jesus solemnly replied, *You have said so* (26:25), meaning "Yes," although the response could also be interpreted, "You have said it, not I."

Throughout the meal, Jesus presided like the father of a Jewish family at the Passover. However, prior to the last cup of the Passover meal (there were four), Jesus altered the liturgy. Normally there were statements regarding the meaning of the bread and the lamb, but following the traditional thanksgiving to God for providing the bread, Jesus reinterpreted the meaning of the bread, *Take, eat; this is my body* (26:26). As the bread was broken, so, too, would Jesus' body be broken. As salvation was provided by God and recalled through the Passover meal, so, too, would the disciples participate in God's plan of salvation by eating the bread.

If the thought of His sacrificial death was not entirely evident, it became more so when Jesus took a cup in His hand (perhaps this was the fourth and final cup of the Passover meal). Once again He offered a traditional prayer of thanksgiving. *Drink of it, all of you; for this is my blood of the covenant, which is poured out for many for the forgiveness of sins* (26:27, 28). The wine symbolized His blood. His death was an atonement for sins which would establish a new covenant for the deliverance of many.

Jesus said that He would next drink the cup with His disciples in the kingdom of His Father. *I tell you I shall not drink again of this fruit of the vine until that day when I drink it new with you in my Father's kingdom* (26:29). Jesus saw His coming death not as a defeat but as part of God's plan for human salvation. Beyond His death lay life. He employed the Jewish idea of a heavenly banquet. Later, when God's kingdom was established, He would be reunited with His disciples.

The meal ended in the traditional Jewish manner. The group sang a hymn, perhaps one of the Psalms of Praise (see Pss. 113—118), and went out. *And when they had sung a hymn, they went out to the Mount of Olives* (26:30).

SUGGESTIONS TO TEACHERS

What name does your church give to the sacred occasion when members receive a piece of bread and sip from a cup? The Lord's Supper? Holy Communion? The Eucharist? Regardless of the title, you and your class hold this special event as paramount in the worship of your congregation. Whether you celebrate it weekly, monthly, or quarterly, and whether the cup contains wine or juice, you and the class realize that this act of worship takes place because of Jesus' specific instructions to His disciples.

True, we cannot dissect the profound meaning of the communion of sharing bread and cup. And the mystery of the presence of Jesus Christ could never be "explained" to an outsider. But this does not mean your class will not benefit from reexamining the story of the upper room and the institution of the sacred meal.

1. PASSOVER PREPARATION. Preparation was necessary. Jesus instructed some followers to get the room and the meal ready for the Passover celebration. So for us, careful preparation is required—not merely of the bread and cup, but of ourselves. Earlier generations had a "Preparatory Service" on a Thursday evening prior to celebrating the Lord's Supper on a Sunday in some Protestant traditions. Discuss what we should do to get ready for the Lord's Supper. The ordinance will have meaning for those who prepare to receive it.

2. PAINFUL PREDICTION. Some in your class will be inclined to focus exclusively on the case of Judas. While it may be interesting to devote all the lesson to examining the betrayer's motives, your lesson should be more than an occasion to "psychologize." Keep the spotlight on Jesus, not Judas. Remark about how Jesus welcomed Judas to the sacred meal and even seated him at a place near Him. Some commentators think that Jesus was demonstrating His love for Judas even though He knew the plot Judas was hatching.

3. PERMANENT PACT. Help your class comprehend the meaning of Jesus' words about the "new covenant." The broken bread, representing His broken body on the cross, and the poured out wine, signifying His shed blood on the cross, usher in that new covenant. And God's sacred promise through those elements of bread and wine is that through the sacrificial death of Jesus Christ He forgives us! That promise of mercy is communicated each time believers participate in the Lord's Supper.

4. PRIDEFUL PROMISE. As time permits, move on to Peter's proud speech after Jesus' warnings of difficult times to come after His arrest and death. In spite of Jesus' stern warning and a solemn assurance of the Resurrection, Peter glibly assumes that he can handle everything and will remain steadfast in the faith. Discipleship means more than a shallow pledge to stay with Jesus. True discipleship calls for a recognition of one's weaknesses and one's inclination to fall away. This is why Christians continuously require memorials of the new covenant.

TOPIC FOR ADULTS
CELEBRATING THE COVENANT

No Picnic. Fearing an attack and a blockade of Alaskan seaports followed by an all-out invasion after Pearl Harbor, American and Canadian authorities determined to safeguard Alaska by building a highway through northern British Columbia to Alaska. The construction project, however difficult and expensive, became a top priority. Survey crews flagged a route through the wilderness, and in June, 1942, the work began. Tight stands of spruce and seemingly bottomless bogs, violent storms, and extreme temperatures constantly slowed progress. When the Japanese bombed Dutch Harbor, Alaska, and invaded the Aleutian

Islands of Kiska and Attu, everyone knew the highway needed to be completed with all haste. The growing work force was a mixture of military personnel and civilians. A famous advertisement cautioned would-be civilian workers what they could expect:

> "NO PICNIC. Men hired for this job will be required to work and live under the most extreme conditions imaginable. Temperatures will range from ninety degrees above zero to seventy degrees below zero. Men will have to fight swamps, rivers, ice, and cold. Mosquitoes, flies, and gnats will not only be annoying but will cause bodily harm. If you are not prepared to work under these and similar conditions, DO NOT APPLY."

This type of "No Picnic" sign should be flashed before each of us whenever we take the bread and cup at Christ's table. When we partake of the Lord's Supper, we are enlisting for Christ's service, and that entails sacrifice.

The Face. There is a story about Leonardo da Vinci and his first painting of the Last Supper. He put such wealth of art into two cups that a friend, when he saw the painting, exclaimed in wonder at the beauty of the cups. Whereupon the artist wiped them with his brush, crying: "That is not what I want you to see. It is the face!"

Some worshipers become so focused on the beauty of their emotions that they overlook the presence of Christ in the Lord's Supper. It is not our feelings that are important; it is the risen Lord. Still other worshipers at Communion become overly concerned about the externals—whether the contents of the cup are fermented or unfermented, whether the bread is a wafer or a loaf or a diced slice; whether at the altar rail or in the pew; whether kneeling or sitting or standing. These are not what we are to see or to consider so crucial. It's Jesus!

Oath of Allegiance. The word "sacrament" comes from the Latin word *sacramentum,* which originally referred to the oath of allegiance to the emperor taken by a Roman soldier. Whenever we receive the Lord's Supper, we are repeating an oath of allegiance to Jesus Christ, our Emperor. Beginning at the upper room on the night of Jesus' betrayal and arrest, the new covenant was instituted by the Lord. Accepting the bread and cup of that solemn promise of God means reiterating our undying commitment to serve Jesus.

Questions for Students on the Next Lesson. 1. What did Peter do after Jesus' arrest? 2. What charges did the high priest and his cohorts make against Jesus? 3. How did Jesus react to their charges? 4. How did Jesus respond to the violent abuse He experienced? 5. How have you felt when you were rejected or misunderstood?

TOPIC FOR YOUTH
AT THE LORD'S TABLE

Betrayal? How is it possible that pockets of starvation exist in America, the land of plenty, if 100 million Christians have heard Jesus say, "I was hungry and you fed me." How can 2.4 million children be abused if 100 million Christians have heard Jesus say, "You welcomed me"?

How can 7 million children (one in every four) be latchkey children if 100 million Christians have heard Jesus say, "You came to me"? How can 1.3 million juveniles be disposed of and left alone in detention institutions in Ohio, Pennsylvania, and West Virginia if 100 million Christians have heard Jesus say, "I was in prison and you visited me"?

Is this not a form of betrayal too?

No Tests for Commitment. When you were born, your blood was tested. As you grow, your IQ is tested. You receive a TB test, eye test, speech test, hearing test, and personality tests. You will take a driving test, aptitude tests, and perhaps college board tests. All these tests confirm or verify things about you and what is within you.

However, can character be tested? Can an individual's reliability be tested? Can a person's loyalty be tested? Judas had great potential. He was a man of ability and resourcefulness. He handled people well, was trusted, and had a keen business mind. He had contacts in the right places and was highly motivated, ambitious, and responsible.

Yet, he betrayed Jesus. Of all the disciples (most of whom lacked an education), it was Judas who proved to be the traitor.

Betrayal Is Not Rewarded. As students studying the Revolutionary War, you've probably discovered the name of Benedict Arnold, a name that is not spoken with much respect. Here was an American army officer who fought with Ethan Allen at Fort Ticonderoga in 1775. This man was the brigadier general who halted the British advance from Canada down Lake Champlain in 1776. In 1777, as a major general, he repulsed the British forces in the Mohawk Valley and later aided at Burgoyne's surrender.

Yet, after a court martial and a reprimand for certain irregularities, he began some treasonous correspondence with the British in 1779. In 1780, He planned to surrender to the British West Point, a key American defensive position that he commanded. However, the plot was discovered when Americans captured a Major Andre on September 23, 1780. Arnold fled to the British lines, where he commanded forces that raided Virginia in 1780 and Connecticut in 1781. After the war, he fled to England, where he died in poverty and disgrace.

Judas' biography reads much the same. Betrayal is seldom rewarded. On the other hand, commitment often is rewarded.

Jesus showed real commitment to us on the cross, an act He explained at the Last Supper.

Questions for Students on the Next Lesson. 1. Who was Caiaphas? 2. Why did he want to kill Jesus? 3. What is blasphemy? Was this charge legitimate? 4. How would you describe Jesus' defense? 5. Have you ever been a victim of injustice or a scapegoat? If so, when? How did you feel?

LESSON 11—FEBRUARY 12

JESUS IS REJECTED

Background Scripture: Matthew 26:36-68
Devotional Reading: Isaiah 53:1-12

KING JAMES VERSION

MATTHEW 26:57 And they that had laid hold on Jesus led him away to Caiaphas the high priest, where the scribes and the elders were assembled.

58 But Peter followed him afar off unto the high priest's palace, and went in, and sat with the servants, to see the end.

59 Now the chief priests, and elders, and all the council, sought false witness against Jesus, to put him to death;

60 But found none: yea, though many false witnesses came, yet found they none. At the last came two false witnesses,

61 And said, This fellow said, I am able to destroy the temple of God, and to build it in three days.

62 And the high priest arose, and said unto him, Answerest thou nothing? what is it which these witness against thee?

63 But Jesus held his peace. And the high priest answered and said unto him, I adjure thee by the living God, that thou tell us whether thou be the Christ, the Son of God.

64 Jesus saith unto him, Thou hast said: nevertheless I say unto you, Hereafter shall ye see the Son of man sitting on the right hand of power, and coming in the clouds of heaven.

65 Then the high priest rent his clothes, saying, He hath spoken blasphemy; what further need have we of witnesses? behold, now ye have heard his blasphemy.

66 What think ye? They answered and said, He is guilty of death.

67 Then did they spit in his face, and buffeted him; and others smote him with the palms of their hands,

68 Saying, Prophesy unto us, thou Christ, Who is he that smote thee?

REVISED STANDARD VERSION

MATTHEW 26:57 Then those who had seized Jesus led him to Caiaphas the high priest, where the scribes and the elders had gathered. 58 But Peter followed him at a distance, as far as the courtyard of the high priest, and going inside he sat with the guards to see the end. 59 Now the chief priests and the whole council sought false testimony against Jesus that they might put him to death, 60 but they found none, though many false witnesses came forward. At last two came forward 61 and said, "This fellow said, 'I am able to destroy the temple of God, and to build it in three days.' " 62 And the high priest stood up and said, "Have you no answer to make? What is it that these men testify against you?" 63 But Jesus was silent. And the high priest said to him, "I adjure you by the living God, tell us if you are the Christ, the Son of God." 64 Jesus said to him, "You have said so. But I tell you, hereafter you will see the Son of man seated at the right hand of Power, and coming on the clouds of heaven." 65 Then the high priest tore his robes, and said, "He has uttered blasphemy. Why do we still need witnesses? You have now heard his blasphemy. 66 What is your judgment?" They answered, "He deserves death." 67 Then they spat in his face, and struck him; and some slapped him, 68 saying, "Prophesy to us, you Christ! Who is it that struck you?"

KEY VERSE: *Then the high priest tore his robes, and said, "He has uttered blasphemy. Why do we still need witnesses? You have now heard his blasphemy. What is your judgment?" They answered, "He deserves death."* Matthew 26:65, 66.

HOME DAILY BIBLE READINGS

BACKGROUND

The word *Gethsemane* means "oil press." The place was an olive grove in which a set of heavy circular stones was used to press out the oil from the olive crop. On the night before Jesus' death, Gethsemane was also the scene where rejection and loneliness pressed in on Him in a way no other human has experienced.

After the meal in the upper room, Jesus and the eleven disciples remaining with Him walked from the city across the deep valley to the slope of the Mount of Olives, where Gethsemane lay. Jesus and His party had probably been staying each night under the olive trees. Jerusalem was packed with Passover pilgrims, and many visitors wrapped themselves in their heavy outer garments at night and slept in the groves surrounding the city.

Judas had left the upper room knowing he could lead hired thugs sent by the temple leaders to the place where Jesus stayed at night. The authorities knew that they did not dare arrest Jesus in the city during daylight for fear of stirring a violent protest. Their challenge was to find Jesus amidst the thousands of other pilgrims in the darkness. Judas solved that difficulty by agreeing to lead a party to seize Him.

Meanwhile, Jesus wanted the support and companionship of trusted friends. The agony of realizing that He would soon be arrested, tortured, and executed pressed on Him. He asked the three closest, the trio who had been on the Mount of Transfiguration with Him, to sit with Him. Then He prayed, asking that the cup of suffering might not have to be given Him, but finally surrendering to the will of the Father. To His dismay, however, Jesus noticed that those three friends had failed Him and had fallen asleep. Three times Jesus asked Peter, James, and John to watch with Him and pray. Three times Jesus fervently beseeched the one who had sent Him for a reprieve from the sacrificial death on a cross. Three times Jesus agreed in His prayer to carry out His mission. And three times He discovered His closest companions could not even stay awake for Him.

As expected, Judas came with a group sent by the religious leaders to point out Jesus. Although Jesus was never given to violence, the gang seizing Jesus came armed. Additional ironies surfaced when Jesus was hauled before the temple authorities who had contrived to have Him taken. They were so determined to convict Him that they even resorted to false witnesses. The supreme irony, however, was accomplished when these men, the leaders of the religious life of the nation, decreed that Jesus was guilty of blasphemy and therefore sentenced to die. Jesus was rejected by those who, more than any others, should have recognized the truth of His claims.

NOTES ON THE PRINTED TEXT

In 1992, workmen creating a water park in the neighborhood of Abu

Tor, near Jerusalem's Peace Forest, stumbled upon an old cave. What surprised the officers of the Antiquities Authority was the discovery of twelve ossuaries. These receptacles for bones were in a burial cave. Inscriptions on two of them indicated that this was the burial chamber of the Caiaphas family. One of the ossuaries may have held the remains of the high priest who interrogated Jesus.

Then those who had seized Jesus led him to Caiaphas the high priest, where the scribes and the elders had gathered (26:57). After Jesus' arrest, the temple police led Him to a hearing before a group of the religious authorities who were members of the Sanhedrin. The law stated that the Sanhedrin could not meet at night or in a place other than the Hall of Hewn Stone, and that no trial that required a second session could begin before a sabbath or a feast day. Technically therefore, Jesus' appearance was not a formal trial. It was an informal hearing. The accusers sought a charge that was serious enough to warrant the death penalty. Therefore, the authorities needed to conduct an investigation.

Peter followed him at a distance, as far as the courtyard . . . and going inside he sat with the guards (26:58). Peter had doggedly followed the arresting party to the house of the high priest. As it was a chilly, Judean evening, a fire had been prepared in the courtyard. The temple police and some servants had gathered around it to keep warm, and Peter slipped into the courtyard and sat with this group to wait and see what would happen to Jesus.

Now the chief priests and the whole counsel sought false testimony against Jesus (26:59). A formal hearing before the Sanhedrin followed strict guidelines. Evidence against the accused was weighed strictly and fairly. But since this was not a formal hearing, the court did not protect Jesus as the accused. The assembly acted as prosecutor and judge. It accepted false and inadmissible evidence since no evidence had been prepared in advance. The court had, in effect, prejudged Jesus as guilty.

Witnesses were sought in an effort to fabricate charges. Although *many false witnesses came forward* (26:60), nothing presented warranted the death penalty; no two witnesses agreed. Finally, two witnesses came forward. This was the least number that could sustain any charge by giving evidence. They should have been cross-examined separately but were not. Instead, they testified together. *This fellow said, "I am able to destroy the temple of God, and to build it in three days"* (26:61). Jesus had spoken about the destruction of the temple, figuratively referring to His own body.

Trying to prod more information that might convict Jesus, the high priest interrogated Jesus, even though this was strictly forbidden by law. *Have you no answer to make? What is it that these men testify against you?* (26:62).

In response, *Jesus was silent* (26:63). Jesus was fulfilling a prophecy (see Isa. 53:7 and Ps. 38:12-14).

I adjure you by the living God, tell us if you are the Christ, the Son of God (26:63). So far, the hearing had gone poorly. The evidence against Jesus was worthless. The high priest asked Jesus another direct question. This was illegal, since the accused could not be asked questions which, when answered, might incriminate him.

Jesus answered unequivocally. *You have said so. But I tell you, here-*

after you will see the Son of man seated at the right hand of Power, and coming on the clouds of heaven (26:64). He admitted that He was the Messiah, although He carefully avoided using the title. To be guilty of blasphemy, the accused had to use the divine name. Jesus used "Power" instead of the name "God." He should have been exonerated of the charges; however, He spoke of His exaltation. He described a regal and triumphant arrival and enthronement at God's side. To the hearers, this was blasphemy.

Following a prescribed practice when blasphemy was heard, the horrified judge tore his robes. *The high priest tore his robes, and said, "He has uttered blasphemy. Why do we still need witnesses? You have now heard his blasphemy"* (26:65). Overjoyed, Caiaphas finally had a charge against Jesus. The crime was punishable by death.

What is your judgment? (26:66). Although it was illegal, the high priest had presented the charges and pressed for conviction. *He deserves death* (26:66). The death sentence could not be passed immediately. Twenty-four hours should have elapsed in order to contemplate the charges. Only then would an individual poll be taken and the final vote made. In this case, a hurried voice vote convicted Jesus.

Finally, Jesus was subjected to various indignities, such as verbal and physical abuse. Although it was illegal to touch a prisoner, Jesus was spat upon and hit. He was mocked and insulted as He was slapped. *Prophesy to us, you Christ! Who is it that struck you?* (26:68). In the judgment of the council, the Messiah should have had prophetic power to discern who was abusing him.

SUGGESTIONS TO TEACHERS

Everyone in your class has experienced the pain of being misunderstood and rejected. Without turning the lesson into a "pity party," you could open your time together by asking a few to share about their times of hurt through rejection. This may help everyone to identify with what Jesus went through.

1. PLEA FOR COMPANIONSHIP. Start with Jesus' agony in Gethsemane. Help your people see that He was rejected even by those trusted disciples whom He had asked to sit with Him during the lonely hours. Remind students that these people rejected Him simply by drifting off to sleep. Rejection does not always mean deliberately turning one's back on the Lord. A person can reject Him by indifference, by carelessness, and even by plain laziness.

2. PETITION FOR RELEASE. Don't skip over the prayer reflecting Jesus' anguish. Jesus was not morbidly seeking martyrdom, nor was He depressed and suicidal. Furthermore, He knew the terrible disgrace and staggering physical agony that being nailed to a cross would bring, and a crucifixion would seem like the failure of His cause to onlookers. So Jesus pleaded earnestly in prayer to be relieved of this final act of His assignment.

Here is prayer portrayed in its starkest terms: a showdown with the Almighty. Jesus, three times requesting to be saved from having to take the cup of rejection and suffering, finally accepts the will of the Father.

Take some time to talk about prayer as such a struggle between human will and the divine will.

3. PRODUCT OF REJECTION. Among the many rejections felt by Jesus during those final hours in His earthly ministry was the rejection by Judas. This must have hurt Jesus. Nonetheless, when Judas approached to identify Jesus with the familiar greeting of a kiss, Jesus did not denounce Judas for his treachery or for his hypocrisy. Even at this point, Jesus addressed Judas with the word "friend" (Matt. 26:50). Was Jesus still holding out hope for Judas and extending His loving mercy to him in spite of the betrayal?

4. PRONOUNCEMENT OF SENTENCE. Invite your group members to review the details of Jesus' appearance before Caiaphas and his henchmen. Although these men had sworn to uphold the precepts of their religion, they abandoned these in order to frame Jesus. The final rejection of Jesus came at the hands of the very persons who should have gladly received Him as Messiah. Ironically, the temple leaders, entrusted with the spiritual health of Jesus' people, were the ones who condemned Him.

TOPIC FOR ADULTS
EXPERIENCING REJECTION

Rejection Slips. Jesus experienced rejection, and so do we. Writers also know the sense of loneliness and failure when they are rejected. Rudyard Kipling received the following rejection slip: "I am sorry, Mr. Kipling, but you just don't know how to use the English language."

Fifty years later, George Orwell's *Animal Farm* was turned down with the note: "It is impossible to sell animal stories in the U.S.A." A publisher turned down Pearl Buck's best-seller, *The Good Earth,* stating, "Regret that the American public is not interested in anything in China." Norman Maclean's masterpiece, *A River Runs Through It,* was sent back with the curt note, "These stories have trees in them." One editor looking at the manuscript of *The Diary of Anne Frank* tossed it aside, commenting, "The girl doesn't, it seems to me, have a special perception or feeling which would lift that book above the 'curiosity' level." The editor of John Le Carre's *The Spy Who Came in from the Cold* predicted, "You're welcome to Le Carre—he hasn't got any future."

People thought the same about Jesus. The temple leaders and the Roman authority rejected Him and believed they could silence Him permanently. Jesus knew what it was to be spurned and despised.

Dismissed as a Crackpot. W. Edwards Deming may not be a household name to most Americans, but the effects of his teachings are evident in almost every household worldwide. W. Edwards Deming was the production genius who helped create Japan's immense manufacturing power following World War II. He remained ignored by U.S. officials and industrialists who failed to heed his advice for more than forty years.

In the late 1940s and early 1950s, Deming was dismayed by what he realized were increasingly inept managerial methods and wasteful production practices in factories in the United States. He tried to interest American companies and leaders in adopting his proposals for a teamwork approach and rigid quality control at all levels of production. Although

Deming had great credentials as a quality-control specialist, his skills and warnings were brushed aside. Deming himself was dismissed as a crank or a fool.

Rejected in his own country, Deming went to Japan to test his theories. With its industrial capacities in ruins from the war, the Japanese were having to rebuild. Deming found a receptive audience for his radical ideas about quality control and competitiveness. He lectured to Japan's top industrialists. The Japanese soon found that Deming's ideas brought astonishing improvements. No longer did "Made in Japan" indicate a shoddy imitation of an American original. The phenomenal industrial resurgence of Japan followed, and Deming himself became revered as an oracle.

Edward Deming finally returned to the U.S. but continued to be ignored. Although he lived in Washington, D.C., he was never asked for advice by an American president. Belatedly, the production specialist who was rejected by his own people is now being recognized. But the continuing trade and budget deficits are the heavy price that Americans are paying for rejecting one of its authentic geniuses.

Hurtful Rejection. Elizabeth Barrett married the poet Robert Browning against her parents' wishes. In fact, they objected so strenuously to her marriage that they disowned her. As everyone knows, her marriage was a beautiful, happy relationship for both Elizabeth and Robert. In spite of the hurt of being rejected by her family, however, Elizabeth Barrett Browning continued to write regularly to them. In each letter, she told her father and mother how much she continued to love them. She received no response. Then, after total silence for ten years from her parents, a large package arrived. Elizabeth Barrett Browning eagerly opened it. The box contained all of the letters that she had written them since her marriage to Robert. Not one had been opened.

Sometimes the hardest forms of rejection to accept are from our own family members and loved ones—those expected to stand by us and accept us. This is the kind of rejection that Jesus knew.

Questions for Students on the Next Lesson. 1. How did the soldiers treat Jesus after His conviction? 2. Who was Simon of Cyrene? Why was he in Jerusalem? 3. Why did Jesus refuse to drink the wine mixed with gall? 4. How did the chief priests and the crowd mock Jesus? 5. How do you deal with the fact that sometimes the innocent suffer?

TOPIC FOR YOUTH
SUFFERING REJECTION

Rejected. A seven-year-old girl and her eleven-year-old brother were returned to the court, terminating the adoption procedure. Gary and Alma Knight of Miami, Florida, gave the two children back after their home was destroyed by Hurricane Andrew in the early fall of 1992. The Knights said that the losses during the hurricane were only a catalyst, the final straw, and maintained that the boy had enormous behavioral problems while the girl was withdrawn and had repeatedly run away.

Prior to the adoption, the two children had been abused by their biological parents. The Department of Health and Rehabilitation Services had cared for them in foster homes for several years. They had finally been adopted by the Knights.

Following the Knights' termination of their relationship, the children were placed with Joe and Pat Reddick by Dade County juvenile judge Adele S. Faske, who said that the two children had been rejected twice in their lives and should not be expected to take any more.

The two obviously knew what rejection was like. Like Jesus they knew abuse, sadness, and pain. Hopefully, the two will experience God's healing love through the Reddicks.

The Cost of Lying. In William Shakespeare's *Othello,* Iago insidiously, malevolently, and falsely poisoned Othello's mind against his faithful wife, Desdemona. He led Othello to believe that his virtuous and loving wife had been unfaithful by taking Cassio as her lover. Ultimately, his lies led Othello to murder Desdemona. These were lies that caused harm. These are the lies that people fear and resent most; they deceive individuals and cause ruin.

Many suffer because of such lies and false testimony. Jesus was wrongly accused. People lied or manipulated words against Him, and ultimately they ordered Him killed.

Still the record of Matthew shows a confident and calm Jesus. The Gospel story ends with His vindication and victory. The truth triumphed.

Fear to Fortitude. Tom was finally told by his parents that he had AIDS. He had secretly suspected and had feared that he had the disease. A hemophiliac since birth, he had had many blood transfusions.

Tom was afraid to tell anyone. He knew that people would be afraid to be near him, that friends would reject him, afraid they might contract the disease. He was nervous that people would say he was a homosexual or a drug user. For two years, he wrestled with his fears.

Finally, with great courage, Tom shared his secret with his school and his friends. He spoke at an assembly about his condition, and he began to educate his school on AIDS and its effects. He was able to share his story and start a support group within his school.

Like Tom, you can stand with equal confidence, calmness, and control knowing that you are not helpless. God gives you the strength and fortitude to overcome fear and to remain in His loving care.

Questions for Students on the Next Lesson. 1. What events took place before and during the Crucifixion? 2. Has anyone ever suffered for you? Who? When? 3. What was the charge against Jesus? Was this true? 4. How do people mock and crucify Jesus today? 5. What does the Crucifixion and the Cross mean to you?

LESSON 12—FEBRUARY 19

JESUS IS MOCKED AND CRUCIFIED

Background Scripture: Matthew 27:1-16
Devotional Reading: John 3:14-21

KING JAMES VERSION

MATTHEW 27:27 Then the soldiers of the governor took Jesus into the common hall, and gathered unto him the whole band of soldiers.

28 And they stripped him, and put on him a scarlet robe.

29 And when they had platted a crown of thorns, they put it upon his head, and a reed in his right hand: and they bowed the knee before him, and mocked him, saying, Hail, King of the Jews!

30 And they spit upon him, and took the reed, and smote him on the head.

31 And after that they had mocked him, they took the robe off from him, and put his own raiment on him, and led him away to crucify him.

32 And as they came out, they found a man of Cyrene, Simon by name: him they compelled to bear his cross.

33 And when they were come unto a place called Golgotha, that is to say, a place of a skull,

34 They gave him vinegar to drink mingled with gall: and when he had tasted thereof, he would not drink.

35 And they crucified him, and parted his garments, casting lots: that it might be fulfilled which was spoken by the prophet, They parted my garments among them, and upon my vesture did they cast lots.

36 And sitting down they watched him there;

37 And set up over his head his accusation written, THIS IS JESUS THE KING OF THE JEWS.

38 Then were there two thieves crucified with him, one on the right hand, and another on the left.

39 And they that passed by reviled him, wagging their heads,

40 And saying, Thou that destroyest the temple, and buildest it in three days, save thyself. If thou be the Son of God, come down from the cross.

41 Likewise also the chief priests mocking him, with the scribes and elders, said,

42 He saved others; himself he cannot save. If he be the King of Israel, let him now come down from the cross, and we will believe him.

REVISED STANDARD VERSION

MATTHEW 27:27 Then the soldiers of the governor took Jesus into the praetorium, and they gathered the whole battalion before him. 28 And they stripped him and put a scarlet robe upon him, 29 and plaiting a crown of thorns they put it on his head, and put a reed in his right hand. And kneeling before him they mocked him, saying, "Hail, King of the Jews!" 30 And they spat upon him, and took the reed and struck him on the head. 31 And when they had mocked him, they stripped him of the robe, and put his own clothes on him, and led him away to crucify him.

32 As they went out, they came upon a man of Cyrene, Simon by name; this man they compelled to carry his cross. 33 And when they came to a place called Golgotha (which means the place of a skull), 34 they offered him wine to drink, mingled with gall; but when he tasted it, he would not drink it. 35 And when they had crucified him, they divided his garments among them by casting lots; 36 then they sat down and kept watch over him there. 37 And over his head they put the charge against him, which read, "This is Jesus the King of the Jews." 38 Then two robbers were crucified with him, one on the right and one on the left. 39 And those who passed by derided him, wagging their heads 40 and saying, "You who would destroy the temple and build it in three days, save yourself! If you are the Son of God, come down from the cross." 41 So also the chief priests, with the scribes and elders, mocked him, saying, 42 "He saved others; he cannot save himself. He is the King of Israel; let him come down now from the cross, and we will believe in him. 43 He trusts in God; let God deliver him now, if he desires him; for he said, 'I am the Son of God.'" 44 And the robbers who were crucified with him also reviled him in the same way.

43 He trusted in God; let him deliver him
now, if he will have him: for he said, I am
the Son of God.

44 The thieves also, which were crucified
with him, cast the same in his teeth.

*KEY VERSE: Those who passed by derided him, wagging their heads and
saying, "You who would destroy the temple and build it in three days, save
yourself! If you are the Son of God, come down from the cross."*
Matthew 27:39, 40.

HOME DAILY BIBLE READINGS

Feb.	*13*	*M.*	Matthew 27:1-10	*Jesus Is Taken to Pilate;*
				Judas's Death
Feb.	*14*	*T.*	Matthew 27:11-20	*Jesus Is Silent before Pilate*
Feb.	*15*	*W.*	Matthew 27:21-26	*Jesus Condemned and Barabbas*
				Released
Feb.	*16*	*T.*	Matthew 27:27-31	*Jesus Is Mocked and Led Away*
Feb.	*17*	*F.*	Matthew 27:32-44	*The Crucifixion*
Feb.	*18*	*S.*	Matthew 27:45-54	*The Death of Jesus*
Feb.	*19*	*S.*	Matthew 27:55-61	*The Burial of Jesus*

BACKGROUND

After Jesus was arrested, He was dragged before an assembly of the
temple leaders. Technically, what followed in Caiaphas's residence was a
hearing, not a formal trial. But the outcome was the same as a trial verdict: Jesus was judged guilty of blasphemy and therefore condemned to
die. The problem for the religious leaders was to get the death sentence
carried out. At that time, Judea was a Roman province and, therefore,
subject to Roman laws regarding capital punishment. The temple authorities realized that they could not execute Jesus without the approval of
Pilate, the Roman governor. Furthermore, they preferred to have Pilate do
their dirty work because they wanted to avoid stirring up support for a
martyred Jesus.

Meanwhile, Judas apparently was near enough to learn what was happening. Suddenly overwhelmed with anguish and remorse in hearing that
Jesus was being rushed to His death by crucifixion, the betrayer had a
change of heart and tried to return the money he had received from the
temple leaders. He was rebuffed. Filled with remorse, realizing that he
could not undo the effects of his treachery, his guilt destroyed him. Judas
took his own life.

Pilate, a career army officer, had the unpleasant assignment of serving
as procurator, or financial agent, in Judea and Samaria from A.D. 26–36.
He never tried to understand Jewish ways or the situation in Jerusalem.
Each year, during Passover season, he traveled up from his comfortable
Mediterranean headquarters at Caesarea, with its Roman-style chariot
races and theater entertainments, to the holy city to make sure nothing
got out of hand when the thousands of Passover pilgrims poured in. Revolt
had been simmering, his informers reported, and the possibility of an
uprising by fanatic nationalists was increasing. He kept a battalion of

crack legionnaires with him in the grim governor's fortress in Jerusalem overlooking the temple area.

Pilate was unable to make sense of the charges Jesus' accusers brought against Him. Blasphemy meant nothing to this Roman, so Jesus' accusers rephrased their charge—hinting at the military and political dimensions to Jesus' claims of being "King of the Jews." Pilate's cross-examination of Jesus, however, provided no evidence of any guilt. Moreover, he found the prisoner strangely calm and also strangely silent. In addition, Pilate was puzzled by the disquieting dream his wife had experienced.

Hoping to placate the priests and the temple party, Pilate offered to release any prisoner of their choice. His lack of moral courage in avoiding a just decision in Jesus' case was obvious. The leaders realized that they could manipulate him and stirred the mob of bystanders to chant for the release of a brigand named Barabbas. Ironically, the name of this man means "son of the father." Perhaps the authorities thought to taunt Jesus, who Himself had spoken of being the Son of the Father, by screaming for Barabbas's release.

Pilate, now at the mercy of the mob, asked what he should do with Jesus. When he heard the shouts, "Crucify!" he feebly tried to reason that Jesus was innocent. The crowd sensed that Pilate was in retreat and grew more menacing. Pilate didn't want the mob to get out of control, so he handed Jesus over to be executed.

NOTES ON THE PRINTED TEXT

Then the soldiers of the governor took Jesus into the praetorium, and they gathered the whole battalion before him (27:27). Following His trial and scourging before Pilate, a battered, bruised, dehydrated, and exhausted Jesus was handed over to the Roman soldiers. They took Him to Pilate's residence, which was also their barracks.

Today, inscribed on the floor of the Fortress Antonia in the Sisters of Zion Convent in Jerusalem, can still be found a game board. It was a game called "basilica" or the "game of the king" in which soldiers made a straw dummy (or often dressed up a condemned prisoner to represent their commanding officer) which would then be roughed up. Pilate's soldiers stripped Jesus and *put a scarlet robe upon him* (27:28). This was probably the *sagum,* or the Roman soldier's scarlet cloak. They plaited a *crown of thorns* (27:29) woven of hawthorn branches to be a painful reminder of His claim to be a king. For a royal scepter, the soldiers placed a reed (27:29), probably a staff, in Jesus' right hand. Then the soldiers played the "game of the king." They mocked Jesus. *"Hail, King of the Jews!" And they spat upon him, and took the reed and struck him on the head* (27:29, 30). The soldiers knew Jesus was condemned to death for plotting to be a king. To their way of thinking, He was a weakling and a pretender.

After mocking and abusing Jesus, the soldiers tired of the game. They dressed Jesus in His own clothes again and led Him off to be crucified. *When they had mocked him, they stripped him of the robe, and put his own clothes on him, and led him away to crucify him* (27:31).

The condemned prisoner was forced to carry the crosspiece since the upright portion of the cross was already at the execution site. Weakened by shock and loss of blood from the scourging and beating, Jesus stumbled and fell. The soldiers selected a North African pilgrim to carry the cross. As they were marching out, *they came upon a man of Cyrene, Simon . . . this man they compelled to carry his cross* (27:32).

They came to a place called Golgotha (which means the place of a skull) (27:33). The soldiers marched the prisoner outside of the north city wall to a small hill. Perhaps, because of its resemblance to a human cranium, or because of a burial plot that had been discovered there, it was commonly called "the skull."

They offered him wine to drink, mingled with gall (27:34). The soldiers offered Jesus wine mixed with a narcotic or analgesic to dull His senses to the pain. Jesus tasted it but refused to drink it. He preferred to face the coming suffering and death fully conscious.

Simon dropped the crosspiece, and the cross was quickly assembled. It was probably no more than six feet in height. Jesus was quickly thrown backward upon it. A soldier drove a heavy, square, wrought-iron nail through the depression of His wrist, deep into the wood. The other wrist was also secured. Then His legs were bent and twisted to one side, and an iron nail was driven through His heels. The soldiers threw dice, a practice called "rolling the bones." Dice were made of bone, and dice rolling was a popular entertainment among Roman troops. They did this to divide Jesus' clothing among them as their extra pay for this unpleasant duty. Finally, they sat down and guarded the cross to prevent any rescue attempt.

This is Jesus the King of the Jews (27:37). The crime for which the victim had been executed hung above His head. It told that Jesus was killed for claiming to be a king.

Two robbers were crucified with him, one on the right and one on the left (27:38). Were these two bandits executed to discredit Jesus further, or did Pilate simply take advantage of the occasion to empty death row? Jesus was crucified between two common criminals.

The execution included those who took a sickening pleasure in the suffering of others. Passersby insulted Jesus. These were not simply traveling pedestrians ignorant of Jesus and the charges against Him. They repeated the charges. *You who would destroy the temple and build it in three days, save yourself! If you are the Son of God, come down from the cross* (27:40).

The presence of the chief priests, elders, and scribes at the Crucifixion during Passover was unusual. They, too, insulted Jesus. *He saved others; he cannot save himself. He is the King of Israel; let him come down now from the cross, and we will believe in him* (27:42). In addition, the bandits insulted Jesus.

SUGGESTIONS TO TEACHERS

The late writer and filmmaker Pier Paolo Pasolini produced a movie several years ago called "The Gospel According to Matthew" in which Jesus reflected Pasolini's radical Marxist views. Pasolini failed to stick to the report of Jesus' life and death that we've been studying in the biblical account by the writer Matthew. But he did perceive that Jesus was a revolutionary. Jesus posed such a threat that the powerful people finally resorted to killing Him.

Be sure that you bring out in your lesson how Jesus upset the status quo and disturbed the rulers. Emphasize that Jesus must never be brushed aside as a harmless, irrelevant back number. Jesus continues to upset and threaten our values and notions about God, others, life, even ourselves.

1. COLLAPSED BETRAYER. Matthew mentions the terrible guilt and despair Judas felt. Matthew even reported that Judas "repented" (27:3), using a verb meaning "to change his mind." But the damage was done. Judas's rash act in selling out could not be undone. The anguish and remorse finally destroyed the man. Guilt can kill.

2. CONFRONTED BY PILATE. Without spending too much time discussing Judas, move on to Jesus' hearing before Pilate. Ask why Jesus chose to remain silent, for the most part. Are there not times when the Lord seems to have nothing to say when a person treats Him with disrespect? To those unwilling to accept His claims, Jesus will give no answer.

3. CONCOCTED ACCUSATIONS. Look at the charges that Jesus' accusers leveled at Him before Pilate: a claim to be King of the Jews. However, the priests twisted Jesus' teachings about His messiahship to imply dangerous political plans. Talk with your class members about how Jesus challenges the values of our society today. Point out that Jesus continues to oppose greedy self-interest, those advocating violence, and those degrading humanity through, for example, injustice, pornography, and other forms of exploitation.

4. COUNTED INNOCENT. Pilate couldn't find anything with which to convict Jesus, so he should have thrown the case out of court. Part of the irony of the scene is that Jesus was unfairly sentenced by a representative of the most enlightened government in the ancient world at the request of religious leaders who claimed a righteous and loving personal God.

5. CONTRIVED COMPROMISES. Point out the shabby ways Pilate tried to evade his responsibility and compromised justice. Yet all of us show the same traits and actions from time to time as this Roman governor. We find it easy to go along with the cries of the crowd. After all, we don't like to be criticized. Pilate's question, "Then what shall I do with Jesus who is called Christ?" (27:22) is ours every time we feel the pressures to mute Jesus' message or to turn away from involvement in the lives of the hurting.

6. CONVICTED CRIMINAL. A crucifixion holds little horror for most moderns. A cross has become a pretty piece of costume jewelry at the end of a gold chain, or a decorative ornament between some candles on the altar. Help your students appreciate the rejection, the disgrace, the torture, and the terror associated with dying on a cross in Jesus' day. Jesus knew the cost of carrying out His mission. Yet He willingly suffered for others, including us.

TOPIC FOR ADULTS
SUFFERING FOR OTHERS

Sacrificing for a Chopper Crew. When Captain Max Cleland served in Vietnam, one day in 1967 he jumped from a hovering helicopter, then ran quickly to clear the whirring blades. He turned to watch the chopper take off. Suddenly, to his horror, he noticed that a live grenade had fallen from his pack and had rolled underneath the helicopter. Cleland realized instantly that the crew would be killed if the grenade exploded where it was, so he quickly reached for the grenade and was just beginning to throw it away from him when it exploded. Max Cleland saved the lives of the chopper crew but sacrificed an arm and both legs because of his act of valor.

The medics did not think he could survive, but, miraculously, he did. Ten years later, President Jimmy Carter appointed Cleland to be administrator of the Veterans' Administration. Cleland's willingness to suffer for the sake of others echoes the example of Jesus.

For True Belief: The Possibility of Doubt. Graham Greene has a character named Quixote, a naive, old priest who, by a series of flukes, is honored by the church and made an archbishop. His bishop is furious and sends the old man away on a leave of absence. The old priest realizes his life has apparently been a failure, and he feels the venom of the institution he has tried to serve. He goes off in disgrace and sadness.

One day he has a dream. The dream is of the Crucifixion. All the biblical characters are present—the soldiers, the crowd, the mother of Jesus. But in the dream, Jesus doesn't die. Instead, He appeals to a legion of angels and they come down and rescue Him. Jesus steps down dramatically from the cross. He is triumphant and acclaimed. The Roman legionnaires kneel in homage. The crowd falls to its knees to honor Him. The people of Jerusalem rush up the hill of Calvary to worship Him. The disciples cheerfully move forward and cluster about Him. Everyone knows for certain that Jesus is the Christ, the Son of God. There is no grim death, no gasping, "My God, my God, why have You forsaken me?" No broken corpse dragged to a borrowed tomb, no heavy stone to be rolled away, no darkness, no tears, no waiting, no questioning.

Greene adds, "There was no ambiguity, no room for doubt, and no room for faith at all . . . the whole world knew with certainty that Christ was the Son of God." But the story continues. Father Quixote woke with "the chill of despair felt by a man . . . who must continue to live in a kind of Saharan desert without doubt or faith . . . He found himself whispering, 'God save me from such a belief.' "—Graham Greene, *Monsignor Quixote* (Simon & Schuster, 1962), pp. 118-119.

We must enter into the mystery of the Cross. God makes Himself vulnerable. He and His people suffer together. He takes us seriously. So seriously that He joins in our struggles of being weak and wounded, hurt and humiliated, sometimes doubting.

Suffering Where You Are. A group of Christian ministers visited Mother Theresa in Calcutta. Deeply impressed with her work among the destitute and dying in India, several spoke at length about her sacrificial work. This dedicated woman waved her hand and looked intently at the visitors, replying, "No, you are the ones who are sacrificing." The ministers looked surprised. Mother Theresa continued, "You don't understand. You see, here people want me and my sisters. But where you come from, people don't seem to want Christ. You are the ones who must make the sacrifice by serving where they don't seem to care if you're there."

Questions for Students on the Next Lesson. 1. Who were the first to visit the tomb, according to Matthew? 2. What did the angel tell these first visitors? 3. Where did the eleven disciples first encounter the risen Lord? 4. What was Jesus' commission to the disciples when He met them in Galilee? 5. What effect has the news of the Resurrection had on your life?

TOPIC FOR YOUTH
SUFFERING FOR OTHERS

Wimps or Winners? They have been called "wimps." Some people have gone so far as to say they are "bad for sports." Others have questioned their "intensity." Critics have argued that they put a "low priority on winning."

Who are these individuals who are being ridiculed and questioned? The answer is that they are professional baseball players who are also committed Christians. They are men like Andy Van Slyke, Brett Butler, Sid Bream, Orel Hershiser, Darryl Strawberry, and Randy Tomlin. Their beliefs are shared by professional golfers like Steve Jones and Betsy King and professional football players like Reggie White and Jeff Siemon.

You will be ridiculed and suffer some abuse for your beliefs and the way in which you live. However, with conviction like Christ's, you can ultimately trust in victory.

Sacrificing Success. Take 6 is a gospel-jazz group of six musicians. Each of the sextet is a devout Christian. None of the Take 6 drinks, smokes, does drugs, or uses obscene language. In every appearance, the group members testify that they take their faith seriously. The Christian group became known for its distinctive a cappella harmonies several years ago when all six were students at Oakwood College, a Baptist institution in Alabama.

Recording companies and others in the music industry urged them to mute their Christian message and to exhibit a swinging life-style, to use lyrics with four-letter words and to forget their responsibility as role models. The six members of Take 6 refused. "Experts" in the entertainment industry warned that the group would never become successful unless it gave up its Christian code of values. The sextet insisted on sacrificing "success" for the sake of others. One of the group, Cedric Dent, says, "We feel a responsibility to say something and do something positive for young people."

After several years of singing on the gospel circuit under the name "Alliance," the six were finally signed by Reprise Records in Nashville.

Sanity Test. A certain hospital treating the emotionally and mentally disturbed has come up with an interesting way of helping the staff to decide whether patients are able to leave the hospital and move into the real world. The person under consideration for discharge is ushered toward a certain room. Upon entering, the patient sees that the sink in the corner has the water turned on, and the water is overflowing onto the floor. Beside the sink stands a mop and bucket.

If the patient turns off the faucet, unstops the sink, and begins to mop up the water on the floor, the doctors take these actions as a sign that the patient is thinking of others and is able to leave the institution. If the patient seems disinclined to concern himself with the mess and makes no effort to help clean up for others, the staff interprets this as an indication that the person is not ready to go back into society.

Only those who put themselves out for the sake of others are truly healthy, emotionally and mentally. Our example is Jesus Himself—the most sane person who ever lived.

Questions for Students on the Next Lesson 1. What would have happened if Jesus really had not been raised from the dead? Why? 2. Did the women believe that Jesus was resurrected? Why? 3. What authority does Jesus have over you? 4. What has Jesus commissioned you to do? 5. What assurance do you have that you will succeed in carrying out His commands?

LESSON 13—FEBRUARY 26

THE RISEN CHRIST COMMISSIONS DISCIPLES

Background Scripture: Matthew 27:62—28:20
Devotional Reading: Acts 10:34-48

KING JAMES VERSION

MATTHEW 28:1 In the end of the sabbath, as it began to dawn toward the first day of the week, came Mary Magdalene and the other Mary to see the sepulchre.

2 And, behold, there was a great earthquake: for the angel of the Lord descended from heaven, and came and rolled back the stone from the door, and sat upon it.

3 His countenance was like lightning, and his raiment white as snow:

4 And for fear of him the keepers did shake, and became as dead men.

5 And the angel answered and said unto the women, Fear not ye: for I know that ye seek Jesus, which was crucified.

6 He is not here: for he is risen, as he said. Come, see the place where the Lord lay.

7 And go quickly, and tell his disciples that he is risen from the dead; and, behold, he goeth before you into Galilee; there shall ye see him: lo, I have told you.

8 And they departed quickly from the sepulchre with fear and great joy; and did run to bring his disciples word.

9 And as they went to tell his disciples, behold, Jesus met them, saying, All hail. And they came and held him by the feet, and worshipped him.

10 Then said Jesus unto them, Be not afraid: go tell my brethren that they go into Galilee, and there shall they see me. . . .

16 Then the eleven disciples went away into Galilee, into a mountain where Jesus had appointed them.

17 And when they saw him, they worshipped him: but some doubted.

18 And Jesus came and spake unto them, saying, All power is given unto me in heaven and in earth.

19 Go ye therefore, and teach all nations, baptizing them in the name of the Father, and of the Son, and of the Holy Ghost:

20 Teaching them to observe all things whatsoever I have commanded you: and, lo, I am with you alway, even unto the end of the world. Amen.

REVISED STANDARD VERSION

MATTHEW 28:1 Now after the sabbath, toward the dawn of the first day of the week, Mary Magdalene and the other Mary went to see the sepulchre. 2 And behold, there was a great earthquake; for an angel of the Lord descended from heaven and came and rolled back the stone, and sat upon it. 3 His appearance was like lightning, and his raiment white as snow. 4 And for fear of him the guards trembled and became like dead men. 5 But the angel said to the women, "Do not be afraid; for I know that you seek Jesus who was crucified. 6 He is not here; for he has risen, as he said. Come, see the place where he lay. 7 Then go quickly and tell his disciples that he has risen from the dead, and behold, he is going before you to Galilee; there you will see him. Lo, I have told you." 8 So they departed quickly from the tomb with fear and great joy, and ran to tell his disciples. 9 And behold, Jesus met them and said, "Hail!" And they came up and took hold of his feet and worshiped him. 10 Then Jesus said to them, "Do not be afraid; go and tell my brethren to go to Galilee, and there they will see me.". . .

16 Now the eleven disciples went to Galilee, to the mountain to which Jesus had directed them. 17 And when they saw him they worshiped him; but some doubted. 18 And Jesus came and said to them, "All authority in heaven and on earth has been given to me. 19 Go therefore and make disciples of all nations, baptizing them in the name of the Father and of the Son and of the Holy Spirit, 20 teaching them to observe all that I have commanded you; and lo, I am with you always, to the close of the age."

KEY VERSE: *Go therefore and make disciples of all nations, baptizing them in the name of the Father and of the Son and of the Holy Spirit, teaching them to observe all that I have commanded you; and lo, I am with you always, to the close of the age.* Matthew 28:19, 20.

HOME DAILY BIBLE READINGS

Feb.	20	M.	Acts 10:34-43	*Witness to Jesus' Resurrection*
Feb.	21	T.	Matthew 27:62-66	*A Guarded Tomb*
Feb.	22	W.	Matthew 28:1-7	*The Empty Tomb*
Feb.	23	T.	Matthew 28:8-15	*Jesus' Resurrection Discounted*
Feb.	24	F.	Mark 16:1-8	*He Has Risen*
Feb.	25	S.	John 20:1, 11-23	*Jesus Appears to Mary and His Disciples*
Feb.	26	S.	Matthew 28:16-20	*Jesus' Commission to His Disciples*

BACKGROUND

The report that Jesus was raised from the dead and appeared alive to His followers startled everyone who heard it. Jesus had been brutally executed. Roman death squads knew their business and carried out their grim job with ruthless efficiency. No one doubted that Jesus had died.

But from earliest times, opponents to Christianity have tried to discredit the news of the Resurrection. One rumor was that disciples had snatched Jesus' body from the tomb and then reported that He had risen. Matthew, alone of the Gospel writers, deliberately refuted that lie by including the account of Pilate posting guards at the tomb at the request of the priestly party. Matthew also reported the terror the guards felt when the stone was rolled back and the angelic messenger made a dazzling appearance. Moreover, Matthew recorded that these guards finally recovered from their shock and fright and told the incredible story of the empty tomb to the temple authorities—but were bribed to spread the tale that Jesus' disciples had spirited away the mangled remains of their leader. Matthew went out of his way to convince his reader's that the news of the Resurrection was no hoax, but pure fact.

The fact that Jesus was raised alive is the basis for Matthew's writings. Without the Resurrection, this writer rightly recognized that there would be no community of faith. Only Matthew stated that the risen Lord first appeared to the eleven disciples in Galilee. According to Matthew the resurrected Jesus encountered the group in their old familiar haunts on the mountain near the Sea of Galilee. There, they recognized that He had the authority to claim their service for the rest of their lives. They finally realized that Jesus had no rivals; He was the universal Lord for all persons, for all times.

NOTES ON THE PRINTED TEXT

Toward the dawn of the first day of the week, Mary Magdalene and the other Mary went to see the sepulchre (28:1). On the first day of the week, at dawn on Sunday, Mary Magdalene and the other Mary went to the tomb. The two women had seen Jesus' death on the cross and His burial. There was no doubt in their minds that Jesus was dead. They wanted to pay their last respects at the tomb.

There was a great earthquake; for an angel of the Lord descended from heaven and came and rolled back the stone, and sat upon it (28:2). Palestine's geological structure made, and still makes, earthquakes common. One occurred on Friday at Jesus' death. On Sunday, the aftershock followed. Many people rightly understood the event as a miraculous manifestation; God was actively present and at work. An angel rolled away the great stone that blocked the tomb's entrance. (Such a stone, still at the entrance to the tomb of Queen Helena in Jerusalem, is about three to four feet in diameter and almost a foot wide. It would require the effort of several men to move it.) The angel, whose appearance was bright and dazzling, sat on the stone.

The guards trembled and became like dead men (28:4). Pilate, at the request of the Jewish leaders, had a guard posted. The Roman soldiers sealed the tomb. Everyone knew that Jesus was dead and buried. Until the angel's arrival, no one had tampered with the tomb. With the coming of the angel, though, these tough and disciplined soldiers were absolutely terrified.

The angel reassured the women. *Do not be afraid; for I know that you seek Jesus who was crucified* (28:5). The angel made a startling announcement. *He is not here; for he has risen, as he said. Come, see the place where he lay* (28:6). Even more surprising to the women was the invitation to examine the tomb. The messenger wanted the ladies to know that Jesus was alive.

Then go quickly and tell his disciples that he has risen from the dead, and behold, he is going before you to Galilee; there you will see him (28:7). The angel gave them an order. They were to hurry and make the announcement of Jesus' resurrection to the disciples. Convinced and overjoyed, the women rushed off to Jerusalem to find the disciples and share the glad news.

As the women departed to tell the disciples the good news, Jesus met them. *Hail!* (28:9). They recognized Him instantly, fell to their knees before Him, grasped His feet, and worshiped Him. The women met the risen Lord. He reassured them. *Do not be afraid* (28:10). The risen Christ also gave them a command. *Go and tell my brethren to go to Galilee, and there they will see me* (28:10). The Lord instructed the women to tell His disciples to meet Him in Galilee.

The eleven disciples met Jesus in Galilee. They had been directed to meet Him on a specific mountain. Most of the disciples recognized and worshiped Jesus. *When they saw him they worshiped him* (28:17). Matthew honestly noted that *some doubted* (28:17). Some of those present hesitated in fully believing. They had a few questions.

All authority in heaven and on earth has been given to me (28:18). Because of His death and resurrection, Jesus had been exalted. He now had dominion over everything. Naturally, Jesus had the authority to commission His disciples. They were to carry out His mission, proclaiming Jesus' lordship. *Go therefore and make disciples of all nations, baptizing them* (28:19). The disciples were to go into the world to teach and convert others to Jesus Christ. The disciples were ordered to baptize their converts and to teach and observe all that Jesus had taught them. All of this was for the purpose of bringing others into obedience to Jesus.

Finally, Jesus gave the disciples the promise of His eternal presence. *Lo, I am with you always, to the close of the age* (28:20).

SUGGESTIONS TO TEACHERS

Some students in your class may be surprised that you are teaching a class about the Resurrection today. After all, they may think, Easter doesn't come until April 16th. You may remind them that every Sunday is intended to celebrate the news that Jesus is risen and known to be alive in our midst. Every Sunday is a mini-Easter, in which we recognize the presence of the risen Lord and His commission to all of us who believe.

1. SECURING THE SEPULCHRE. The report of Jesus' being raised seemed too incredible to believe for some in Matthew's time. Therefore, the Gospel writer took pains to refute any alternative explanations by foes of the faith. The most obvious lie, of course, was that the disciples had stolen Jesus' body at night, then merely claimed that He had risen. In your lesson, you may take a few minutes to clear the air by pointing out that all attempts to explain away the Resurrection eventually fall flat, including this "body snatch" theory.

2. SEEKING THE BODY. Without all the fuss and stress of Easter Sunday, today is a good time to look at Matthew's account of the visit to the tomb by the women. Some think it is significant that women were the first to understand the wondrous news of Jesus' coming, and that women were the first to learn the momentous news of Jesus' resurrection. Point out that the women were coming to properly prepare Jesus' body. The resurrection news was God's unexpected act of deliverance.

3. STATING THE NEWS. The startling announcement by the angelic messenger stunned the hearers: "He is not here; for he has risen as he said." Appropriately, these words are inscribed on the site in the ancient church building in Jerusalem marking the traditional site of the tomb where Jesus' corpse had been laid.

4. SHARING THE ANNOUNCEMENT. The women were not permitted to keep this glorious news to themselves. The angel instructed them to share the report of the Resurrection to others. We also must tell it!

5. SALUTING HIS FOLLOWERS. The Easter message, however, is more than a report. Easter is meant to be a personal encounter with the risen Christ. The Lord met the women that first Easter and later hailed His eleven disciples in Galilee. Emphasize to the class that we do not worship a departed hero or refer to Jesus in the past tense. Nor do we consider Easter a piece of history that occurred two thousand years ago to some obscure Middle Easterners. The living Jesus Christ continues to present Himself to His followers—He lives within them, and His Spirit pervades the life of the church.

6. SENDING ALL DISCIPLES. With the authority of God Himself, Jesus Christ commissions every follower to go out into the world in His power. The main emphasis of this lesson is the Great Commission in Matthew 28:19, 20. Give plenty of lesson time to looking at each portion of this command. Remind your students of the assurance that the living Lord goes with all followers: "I am with you always . . ." (28:20).

TOPIC FOR ADULTS
FOLLOW THE LEADER

Red Jacket's Counsel. When a missionary was sent from Boston to the Mohawk Indians in New York State in the 1820s, Red Jacket was chosen to represent the tribe. After talking with the clergyman, Red Jacket ended the interview by saying:

"These things are difficult for the red men to understand. But if my father would go and repeat them to our nearest neighbors, the white men, and if the result of his preaching is to prevent the white men from stealing our land and our herds as they are doing every day, my father can come back to the red men and will find their ears more open."

Lives Again. The motion picture *Gandhi* starred Ben Kingsley as the central character. Rarely has an actor made so impressive a film debut as did Kingsley in *Gandhi.* He spent months preparing for the role, visiting Indian locales Gandhi had frequented. He even learned to spin cotton thread on a wooden wheel, as the Mahatma did, while holding conversations.

The physical resemblance between Gandhi and Kingsley proved startling. After filming a scene in a village south of Delhi, Kingsley stepped out of a car and an elderly peasant knelt to touch his feet. Embarrassed, Kingsley explained that he was merely an actor playing the Mahatma. "We know," replied the villager, "but through you he will surely live again."

Do others recognize anything of Jesus Christ when they encounter us? As Jesus Christ's followers, we know we are commissioned to continue His ministry. We will be the only glimpse of the risen Lord many will ever see.

Questions for Students on the Next Lesson. 1. Why did Paul write to the Corinthians? 2. What had happened between Paul and the Corinthians before he wrote this letter? 3. What were some of the problems in the Corinthian church? 4. What did Paul have to say about wisdom and foolishness? What does Paul insist is true wisdom? Foolishness? 5. What is the role of the Spirit, according to Paul?

TOPIC FOR YOUTH
ACCEPTING THE CHALLENGE

Reward or Punishment? Based on your life as it is today, do you expect to go to heaven or to hell when you die? This was the substance of a poll conducted on West Virginians by the West Virginia Poll.

Of those polled, 82 percent believed that they would see heaven, while 7 percent expected to see hell. Eleven percent did not know or chose not to answer.

Strangely, young adults expected eternal damnation, some 12 percent of people in the survey. This group was followed by young parents, from thirty-five to forty years old, who made up 10 percent of the respondents.

God in Christ offers to each of you forgiveness and the assurance of eternal life. This is the news of the Resurrection. Believe the news of salvation. And then live it in your life.

Passed Along. Astronomers claim that light travels 186,000 miles per second. If that is too hard to imagine, think of it another way: The starlight shining in your window left the star about the time Shakespeare was writing his plays. The light has been traveling all that time to reach you and provide its light.

The work of the first disciples still influences you. Centuries ago, men and women were commissioned to make disciples of all nations. Although they have been dead for almost two thousand years, the effect of their work has traveled through history and touched us. It is felt in our lives and in our churches today.

Like these disciples, are you willing to pass this story along to others?

Understanding. Some time ago, television's "Mr. Rogers' Neighborhood" made a program that focused on the death of a goldfish and a dog when the host, Fred Rogers, was a boy. The staff was later flooded with parents' requests to make copies of the program available because so many of these parents were trying to help their children understand about death.

Many people can accept loved ones dying, but it is hard to talk with children about death. Many children and youth have had little personal experience with death, funerals, and cemeteries.

Because of this, Fred Rogers, an ordained Christian minister, and his staff wrote a series of television shows, chapters of a book, and a pamphlet on talking with children about death.

Perhaps you have had little personal experience with death. Today you are to understand that fear of death and the hold of death has been broken by Jesus' rising from the grave. Jesus died and rose to bring you salvation and eternal life that continues after the grave.

Questions for Students on the Next Lesson. 1. What qualities make for good preaching? 2. What should a good sermon include? 3. What kind of preacher was Paul? 4. What kind of wisdom does Paul speak of to the Corinthians? 5. What roles does the Holy Spirit play in preaching?

MARCH, APRIL, MAY 1995

CHRISTIAN LIVING IN COMMUNITY

LESSON 1—MARCH 5

SPEAKING THE TRUTH PLAINLY

Background Scripture: I Corinthians 1:18—2:16
Devotional Reading: I Corinthians 1:18-25

KING JAMES VERSION	REVISED STANDARD VERSION

I CORINTHIANS 2:1 And I, brethren, when I came to you, came not with excellency of speech or of wisdom, declaring unto you the testimony of God.

2 For I determined not to know any thing among you, save Jesus Christ, and him crucified.

3 And I was with you in weakness, and in fear, and in much trembling.

4 And my speech and my preaching was not with enticing words of man's wisdom, but in demonstration of the Spirit and of power:

5 That your faith should not stand in the wisdom of men, but in the power of God.

6 Howbeit we speak wisdom among them that are perfect: yet not the wisdom of this world, nor of the princes of this world, that come to nought:

7 But we speak the wisdom of God in a mystery, even the hidden wisdom, which God ordained before the world unto our glory:

8 Which none of the princes of this world knew: for had they known it, they would not have crucified the Lord of glory.

9 But as it is written, Eye hath not seen, nor ear heard, neither have entered into the heart of man, the things which God hath prepared for them that love him.

10 But God hath revealed them unto us by his Spirit: for the Spirit searcheth all things, yea, the deep things of God.

11 For what man knoweth the things of a man, save the spirit of man which is in him? even so the things of God knoweth no man, but the Spirit of God.

12 Now we have received, not the spirit of the world, but the spirit which is of God; that we might know the things that are freely given to us of God.

13 Which things also we speak, not in the

I CORINTHIANS 2:1 When I came to you, brethren, I did not come proclaiming to you the testimony of God in lofty words or wisdom. 2 For I decided to know nothing among you except Jesus Christ and him crucified. 3 And I was with you in weakness and in much fear and trembling; 4 and my speech and my message were not in plausible words of wisdom, but in demonstration of the Spirit and of power, 5 that your faith might not rest in the wisdom of men but in the power of God.

6 Yet among the mature we do impart wisdom, although it is not a wisdom of this age or of the rulers of this age, who are doomed to pass away. 7 But we impart a secret and hidden wisdom of God, which God decreed before the ages for our glorification. 8 None of the rulers of this age understood this; for if they had, they would not have crucified the Lord of glory. 9 But, as it is written,

"What no eye has seen, nor ear heard, nor the heart of man conceived, what God has prepared for those who love him,"

10 God has revealed to us through the Spirit. For the Spirit searches everything, even the depths of God. 11 For what person knows a man's thoughts except the spirit of the man which is in him? So also no one comprehends the thoughts of God except the Spirit of God. 12 Now we have received not the spirit of the world, but the Spirit which is from God, that we might understand the gifts bestowed on us by God. 13 And we impart this in words not taught by human wisdom but taught by the Spirit, interpreting spiritual truths to those who possess the Spirit.

words which man's wisdom teacheth, but which the Holy Ghost teacheth; comparing spiritual things with spiritual.

KEY VERSE: I decided to know nothing among you except Jesus Christ and him crucified. I Corinthians 2:2.

HOME DAILY BIBLE READINGS

Feb. 27	M.	I Corinthians 1:17-25	*The Power of Christ's Cross*
Feb. 28	T.	I Corinthians 1:26-31	*God's Wisdom Revealed in Christ*
Mar. 1	W.	I Corinthians 2:1-9	*God's Power Is Faith's Foundation*
Mar. 2	T.	I Corinthians 2:10-16	*God's Spirit Gives Understanding*
Mar. 3	F.	I Peter 3:8-18	*Honor Christ as Lord*
Mar. 4	S.	Romans 8:12-25	*Live as Children of God*
Mar. 5	S.	Colossians 3:1-7	*Firm Counsel for Christian Living*

BACKGROUND

The city of Corinth lay on the southern end of the narrow isthmus joining the Peloponnesus to the rest of Greece. In ancient times, sailors avoided the open sea and tried to keep in sight of land. Since the long voyage around the Peloponnesus was risky, most cargo going from the Adriatic to the Aegean, and vice versa, was unloaded and carried across the isthmus, then reloaded on another vessel. Often, the ship itself was pulled across the isthmus on rollers (the Corinth ship canal was only completed in 1893). Corinth flourished as a strategic commercial and military city.

Corinth also hosted the great Isthmian Games, the famous athletic competitions, second only to the Olympics, held every other year. Corinth's bronze foundries and craftsmen turned out exceptionally fine products that brought additional wealth to the city.

The inhabitants were noted for their immorality and paganism, and even the easygoing Greeks and Romans were shocked at the debauchery of the Corinthians. The term "Corinthianize" in the first century referred to lurid depravity, and theaters always portrayed a person from Corinth as a drunk. The place also attracted every cult and religion, some so disgusting that the Romans refused to license them. Therefore, it would seem that Corinth was the least promising site for a Christian community. Yet Paul established a congregation there, staying eighteen months before being forced by a riot to move on.

In Ephesus, Paul began to receive disturbing reports about the congregation he had founded in Corinth. When some of the members wrote to ask advice about certain problems they were having, Paul wrote a response. His letter reveals the dismaying sins and weaknesses besetting the Corinthian church. The congregation was split into factions, and many leaders were unfairly lording it over others. Many church members were tolerating gross immorality among them. Disputes between church people had grown so intense that they were suing each other in the civil courts. Some were openly visiting prostitutes or flirting with idolatry. Worship had degenerated into a bedlam of competing voices, and members even got drunk at the Lord's Supper. Some self-appointed teachers had gone so far as to deny Christ's resurrection, undermining the faith of others. Yet Paul continued to be patient with this group. He even began his letter to these folks by addressing them as "saints," giving thanks for them as those who had been called and commissioned by God.

NOTES ON THE PRINTED TEXT

The church in Corinth was Paul's problem church. Among the various problems facing the church was severe disunity among the members. Boastful groups argued about the merits of their teachers and falsely prided themselves upon their wisdom. Paul responded to the Corinthian faction that exalted its wisdom. *When I came to you, brethren, I did not come proclaiming to you the testimony of God in lofty words or wisdom* (2:1). Paul reminded the Corinthians that they were not people of great wisdom. When he arrived in Corinth, he presented the Gospel without great eloquence or so-called wisdom. He used no clever words, skilled argumentation, or fancy rhetoric. Simply and plainly, he had preached what God had done through the crucifixion and resurrection of Jesus Christ.

For I decided to know nothing among you except Jesus Christ and him crucified (2:2). Paul preached nothing but the Cross. This was shocking to his listeners. Never had a crucified person been considered a god! Crucifixion was abhorred and hated. However, this was the simple proclamation Paul made to the Corinthians. The proclamation was made *in weakness and in much fear and trembling* (2:3). Did this mean that Paul preached with humility, or was Paul referring to a physical condition that made a smooth presentation difficult? Whatever the answer, Paul acknowledged that his preaching was not what had moved the Corinthians to believe. Rather, it was the power of the Holy Spirit that made them believe. God's power moved the believers to obedience and commitment. *My speech and my message were not in plausible words of wisdom, but in demonstration of the Spirit and of power* (2:4).

Paul's preaching was not the basis of the Corinthians' faith; God's power was. Human preaching that depended on logic and fancy rhetoric would not produce lasting faith because it was built merely on human logic. Real faith came to life through God's power alone. Preaching based on God's power produced faith. So Paul's preaching was marked by the power of God rather than by human wisdom in order that the Corinthians' *faith might not rest in the wisdom of men but in the power of God* (2:5).

Yet among the mature we do impart wisdom, although it is not a wisdom of this age (2:6). Paul preached Jesus crucified. Later, as believers matured, he added new understanding to their knowledge. Christ crucified was God's real, mature wisdom, which was contrary to human or worldly wisdom. Human wisdom, the *wisdom of this age or of the rulers of this age* (2:6), was human-centered and in opposition to God.

Paul imparted to the mature listeners the secrets and hidden wisdom of God as contrasted by the world's wisdom. *But we impart a secret and hid-*

den wisdom of God, which God decreed before the ages for our glorification (2:7). God's wisdom centered in the Cross and in Jesus Christ. Mature listeners were those who accepted this message. From the beginning, God wanted to redeem humankind through Christ. This was His purpose, and glory awaited each believer in the age to come.

The wisdom of God was not understood by the rulers of this age because they never recognized or understood God's plan for the salvation of the world. They didn't know what they were doing by crucifying Jesus. *None of the rulers of this age understood this; for if they had, they would not have crucified the Lord of glory* (2:8). To support his statements, Paul either quoted generally from memory a combination of passages from Isaiah, or he used a translation different from the one that we possess. Whatever the case, divine wisdom conceived a plan that human wisdom could never understand.

The plan was revealed by the Holy Spirit to those who loved God. *God has revealed to us through the Spirit* (2:10). Humankind could not know God's purpose. Only what was revealed by the Spirit could be known and understood. *For the Spirit searches everything, even the depths of God* (2:10).

Just as only a human being could understand what was truly human, only the Spirit of God could comprehend God's being. *For what person knows a man's thoughts except the spirit of the man which is in him? So also no one comprehends the thoughts of God except the Spirit of God* (2:11).

Paul explained the work of the Spirit. *Now we have received not the spirit of the world, but the Spirit which is from God, that we might understand the gifts bestowed on us by God* (2:12). God gave believers the Spirit to give them understanding and to help them communicate spiritual truths to others. Without the Spirit, humans would be ignorant of God. *And we impart this in words not taught by human wisdom but taught by the Spirit, interpreting spiritual truths to those who possess the Spirit* (2:13).

SUGGESTIONS TO TEACHERS

If you could assign homework to members of your class, you could instruct them to write a letter to your congregation and to bring their letters with them to class. Suppose you took up this assignment yourself. What would you put in a letter to your church?

Such a letter-writing exercise would be a helpful way to get into Paul's epistles to the Corinthian Christian community. You and your class will be surprised and edified as you discover Paul writing to groups of believers who were facing challenges and opportunities similar to those confronting your own congregation.

Today's lesson starts this important series dealing with the Corinthian church. Proclaiming the truth of the Gospel clearly and in the Spirit's power, Paul spoke plainly to Christians in Corinth and he speaks powerfully to us, too.

1. UNCONQUERABLE CHRIST. The Corinthian church was torn by the claims of various leaders and parties, each group insisting it had

greater wisdom than the others. The Greeks, who esteemed the Athenian sophists who debated high-blown ideas, fancied themselves as wise philosophers, and this conceited thinking infiltrated the minds of the Corinthian Christians.

Everyone knew that the Romans crucified only the worst slaves and criminals. Therefore, talk of Christ's death on a cross seemed absurd. The message of an obscure rabbi dying in such a disgraceful way to bring life and hope appeared to the cultivated Greeks to be laughable. Their philosophies had no place for suffering. Yet Paul countered this thinking with the startling claim that the crucified, risen Lord was the summation of all wisdom. Discuss with your class how the idea about the absurdity of a suffering Savior continues to flavor the thinking of many, even today.

2. UNCONVENTIONAL CHOICE. Paul bluntly reminded the Corinthians that God had not chosen them because of their worldly attainments. They were not the richest nor the wisest, yet they had been called to be the Lord's special instrument. Take enough time to consider with your students the fact that every person in your congregation could be regarded as an unconventional choice for the kingdom of God. Why, you may ask, would the Lord choose this group of people?

3. UNEQUIVOCAL CHALLENGE. One of the many problems afflicting the Corinthian church was the number of people boasting about their own abilities or achievements. In particular, many spoke loftily of their wisdom. Paul's counsel could well be stenciled on the wall of every room in your church: "Let him who boasts, boast of the Lord" (I Cor. 1:31).

4. UNCOMPROMISING CHAMPION. Some of Paul's critics in Corinth accused him of being weak because he did not project a powerful image through his speech or his appearance. Paul replied that he came among them only to tell them about the crucified Lord (I Cor. 2:1-5). Paul serves as a model of what to look for in a Christian leader. The best preacher or teacher comes humbly, relying not on persuasive charm or eloquent wisdom but offering the words of life "in demonstration of the Spirit and [in God's] power."

5. UNCHANGING CHARTER. Devote plenty of the lesson time to the theme of the wisdom of God. Learned discussions and intellectual seminars cannot fathom the depth of God's intentions. The Corinthians, with their love of human arguments and skillful discourse, eagerly examined new fads of thought. These Christians often got caught up in human speculation. Look carefully with your class at Paul's words about wisdom and folly, power and weakness from God's viewpoint and from society's viewpoint.

TOPIC FOR ADULTS
SPEAKING SPIRITUAL TRUTH

More Than a Touch-up. A Chicago art dealer noticed a painting in an antique shop and bought it for $450. When he took it to an art expert for appraisal, he and the art critic were astonished to find that it was an original da Vinci! Unfortunately, some amateur painter had decided to touch up the original masterpiece. The clumsy restorer had merely covered up the work of the great da Vinci so that only an expert could detect the actual worth of the masterpiece. Careful work removed the layers of paint daubed on by the person trying to fix up the original, and the painting was later sold for over one million dollars.

The apostle Paul, writing to the Corinthians, stated that men and women in their human "wisdom" thought they could touch up their lives. But all they had done was to obscure the real worth and beauty of God's creation. Through Jesus Christ, however, God has restored human life to what He intended it to be. Human pride and willfulness may have covered over the significance of the divine masterpiece, but the Master has worked to bring back in Christ what had been cheapened.

Back to Basics! The minister had called the youngsters forward for the children's sermon. Smiling benignly, he looked out upon the gathering of kids and asked brightly, "What is small and grey, has a bushy tail, sits up in the tree, and likes to eat acorns and nuts?" Momentary silence. Then a loud little voice called, "Jesus!" After a brief moment of consternation, the pastor recovered his composure and the titters of laughter died down in the congregation. "Let me ask again," he continued. "What sits up in a tree that has a bushy tail, is grey and furry, and eats nuts and acorns?" Again the same insistent little boy promptly answered, "Jesus!" The minister was disconcerted and asked the youngster why he had answered "Jesus."

"Yeah, I know it's a squirrel," the boy replied.

"But why didn't you say that?"

"Because you're supposed to tell us about Jesus, not about squirrels," came the response.

The answer of that little boy chastens us all. For we as the church must always remember that we come together in worship and fellowship mainly to talk about Jesus. Paul, writing to the Corinthians, like that youngster, forcefully reminded his congregation that the main topic was Jesus Christ. Paul intended to present Jesus and not human ideas.

Color Him Green. A class of youngsters in a Christian school in Korea was drawing colored illustrations of Bible stories. One child, portraying his version of the healing of a sick man, startled the teacher by coloring the figure of Jesus' face, hands, and clothes a brilliant green, while leaving the sick man a plain white. Puzzled by the unusual colors, the teacher asked the child for an explanation. To the child, it was obvious. Green meant life, as with trees and grass, and because Jesus is full of creative, life-giving power, the child associated green with Jesus. White, on the other hand, meant an absence of life. "Jesus," the boy explained, pointing to his picture, "is coming to give this sick man new life."

Paul, who would have understood the green Jesus, spoke the same kind of message to the Corinthians, and also to us. God made Jesus "our wisdom, our righteousness and sanctification and redemption" (I Cor. 1:30). When we understand this, we know we are instructed by the Spirit and have true wisdom.

Questions for Students on the Next Lesson. 1. Why did the Corinthians feel that Paul was unimpressive? 2. Who was Apollos? 3. Why did Paul have to admonish the Corinthian church? 4. How were Christian leaders to regard themselves, according to Paul? 5. Why were some Corinthians boasting?

TOPIC FOR YOUTH
SPEAKING TRUTHFULLY

A Shocking Method. The Reverend Dwight Rymer, a Baptist minister in Grand Rapids, Michigan, used electric shocks to teach the Bible to children. Children sat on a stool that was wired to a 6-volt lantern battery. They would receive a shock when quoting a memory verse incorrectly. Rymer apparently wanted to demonstrate that God could shock a person into hearing and speaking His Word.

Poor Rev. Rymer missed Paul's point. Electric shocks do not lead a person to hear or speak God's Word. The power of the Holy Spirit will do that. The Spirit moves believers to hear and truthfully present God's Word. Without the Spirit, there can be no understanding, no hearing, and no effective speaking!

Speaking Plainly. The great Swiss theologian, Karl Barth, was responding to a group of young people who were questioning him about his faith. He was asked to summarize what he felt was the most important truth of his faith.

The old theologian and professor had long criticized the cumbersome jargon and multi-syllable words that many preachers used. He felt such an approach masked shallow thought, and he urged his own students to preach simply and plainly. The professor who had many books to his credit reflected for a moment and then responded: "I think it would be what my mother taught me: 'Jesus loves me, this I know, for the Bible tells me so.' "

You may be impressed by spectacular orators and eloquent preachers as the Corinthians were. But Paul urged the church to communicate the riches of God's truth simply and effectively by telling the story of God's love in plain language.

Understood. An eleven-year-old girl overheard her parents speaking about their brilliant new minister. She, too, had heard him preach.

"Daddy," she said, "that man isn't so smart. I understand everything he says."

That preacher had apparently followed the example of Jesus and Paul, preaching in a language and a style that everyone, including an eleven year old, could understand.

In speaking of God's love, you do not need to be flashy or spectacular. You are simply to tell the story of God's love in Christ as plainly and truthfully as you can.

Questions for Students on the Next Lesson. 1. What model of leadership does your pastor utilize? 2. What quality or qualities should a Christian leader possess? 3. Can a Christian leader really minimize his or her importance? 4. Who ultimately judges a Christian leader? 5. Do you have a role model? If so, who? Why?

LESSON 2—MARCH 12

BEING FAITHFUL UNDER STRESS

Background Scripture: I Corinthians 4
Devotional Reading: Romans 12:1-10

KING JAMES VERSION

I CORINTHIANS 4:1 Let a man so account of us, as of the ministers of Christ, and stewards of the mysteries of God.

2 Moreover it is required in stewards, that a man be found faithful. . . .

6 And these things, brethren, I have in a figure transferred to myself and to Apollos for your sakes; that ye might learn in us not to think of men above that which is written, that no one of you be puffed up for one against another.

7 For who maketh thee to differ from another? and what hast thou that thou didst not receive? now if thou didst receive it, why dost thou glory, as if thou hadst not received it?

8 Now ye are full, now ye are rich, ye have reigned as kings without us: and I would to God ye did reign, that we also might reign with you.

9 For I think that God hath set forth us the apostles last, as it were appointed to death: for we are made a spectacle unto the world, and to angels, and to men.

10 We are fools for Christ's sake, but ye are wise in Christ; we are weak, but ye are strong; ye are honourable, but we are despised.

11 Even unto this present hour we both hunger, and thirst, and are naked, and are buffeted, and have no certain dwellingplace;

12 And labour, working with our own hands: being reviled, we bless; being persecuted, we suffer it:

13 Being defamed, we intreat: we are made as the filth of the world, and are the offscouring of all things unto this day.

14 I write not these things to shame you, but as my beloved sons I warn you.

15 For though ye have ten thousand instructers in Christ, yet have ye not many fathers: for in Christ Jesus I have begotten you through the gospel.

16 Wherefore I beseech you, be ye followers of me.

REVISED STANDARD VERSION

I CORINTHIANS 4:1 This is how one should regard us, as servants of Christ and stewards of the mysteries of God.

2 Moreover it is required of stewards that they be found trustworthy. . . .

6 I have applied all this to myself and Apollos for your benefit, brethren, that you may learn by us not to go beyond what is written, that none of you may be puffed up in favor of one against another. 7 For who sees anything different in you? What have you that you did not receive? If then you received it, why do you boast as if it were not a gift?

8 Already you are filled! Already you have become rich! Without us you have become kings! And would that you did reign, so that we might share the rule with you! 9 For I think that God has exhibited us apostles as last of all, like men sentenced to death; because we have become a spectacle to the world, to angels and to men. 10 We are fools for Christ's sake, but you are wise in Christ. We are weak, but you are strong. You are held in honor, but we in disrepute. 11 To the present hour we hunger and thirst, we are ill-clad and buffeted and homeless, 12 and we labor, working with our own hands. When reviled, we bless; when persecuted, we endure; 13 when slandered, we try to conciliate; we have become, and are now, as the refuse of the world, the offscouring of all things.

14 I do not write this to make you ashamed, but to admonish you as my beloved children. 15 For though you have countless guides in Christ, you do not have many fathers. For I became your father in Christ Jesus through the gospel. 16 I urge you, then, be imitators of me.

KEY VERSE: It is required of stewards that they be found trustworthy.
I Corinthians 4:2.

HOME DAILY BIBLE READINGS

Mar.	*6*	*M.*	I Corinthians 3:18-23	*Warning against Relying on Human Wisdom*
Mar.	*7*	*T.*	I Corinthians 4:1-7	*Ministers of Christ*
Mar.	*8*	*W.*	I Corinthians 4:8-13	*Faithfulness in Hard Times*
Mar.	*9*	*T.*	I Corinthians 4:14-21	*Fatherly Admonition*
Mar.	*10*	*F.*	Romans 12:11-21	*Christian Conduct in Adversity*
Mar.	*11*	*S.*	James 1:1-8	*Meet Trials with Steadfast Faith*
Mar.	*12*	*S.*	I Thessalonians 5:1-11	*Comfort for Christians*

BACKGROUND

Paul spent eighteen months in Corinth, preaching first in the synagogue, and, after being expelled, in the home of Titius Justus. He presented his message of Jesus Christ without the rhetorical flourishes that most Greek teacher-philosophers liked to display. Nevertheless, his presentation of the Gospel affected many in Corinth, especially people from the lower class, but also those from among the wealthy. Paul left for Ephesus and Syria after a mob stirred up by disgruntled synagogue members threatened to make it difficult for all new Christians.

Other leaders visited the Corinthian congregation. Apollos worked in Corinth; probably Peter did also. Unfortunately, many church members began to build personality cults around these various leaders. In some instances, these Corinthians pounced on some distinctive part of the message of one of these visiting Christian leaders and made it into a rallying cry against all other believers. The result was a spirit of rivalry that pitted leader against leader, faction against faction.

One unfortunate result of this squabbling was that some denounced Paul and accused him of not having the appeal and authority of a deep-thinking apostle. Paul was hurt by the slander but answered the critics by stating that he had tried to lay the only foundation possible for a Christian community, namely the good news of Jesus Christ. Others built on that foundation. The important thing was to realize that God was constructing a community of love and trust based on the grace of God through Christ. Personality cults and divisions do not belong in the church.

Compounding the problems in the Corinthian church, many leaders and members imagined they had "arrived" as mature believers and proudly told this to others. In the letter we call I Corinthians, Paul stated that these Corinthians were "puffed up," using that expression six times. He tried to bring them to their senses by reminding them that all they had was the gift of God's grace.

NOTES ON THE PRINTED TEXT

This is how one should regard us, as servants of Christ and stewards of the mysteries of God (4:1). Paul concluded his criticism of the party strife within the Corinthian church. Christian leaders were to be regarded as servants of Christ and stewards of God's mysteries. The servant was simply an assistant who completed the work of the master. The steward was a manager who had the responsibility for directing the workers. Similarly, the function of Christian leaders was to render assistance to Christ as His representatives. Paul mentioned an important quality for leaders. *Moreover it is required of stewards that they be found trustworthy* (4:2). A leader must be loyal, faithful, and honest.

I have applied all this to myself and Apollos for your benefit, brethren, that you may learn by us not to go beyond what is written, that none of you may be puffed up in favor of one against another (4:6). Paul used as an example the partnership he had with Apollos. Apollos was an eloquent Alexandrian Jew who converted to Christianity. Paul warned the Corinthians against pride or boasting in favor of one leader as opposed to another; no leader's importance must be exaggerated, because a leader's abilities came from God. Each must see himself as a coworker laboring in harmony with others. Favoritism would split the church.

Paul asked a series of sharp, rhetorical questions to help focus the Corinthians on Christian living. *For who sees anything different in you?* (4:7). Whether Paul was addressing the divisive leaders or their followers, both should have answered that they were no different than anyone else. All were forgiven sinners. *What have you that you did not receive?* (4:7). Once again, the answer was nothing. Everything had been received from God. *If then you received it, why do you boast as if it were not a gift?* (4:7). The gifts and abilities of all people were given to them by God alone.

Already you are filled! Already you have become rich! Without us you have become kings! (4:8). Sarcastically, Paul wrote that the Corinthians felt very important. In fact, they were acting as if the kingdom of God had already fully arrived. They were sharing rulership with Christ. They were assuming Christ's exclusive right to evaluate the worth of God's servants. The coming of the fullness of God's kingdom would indeed be pleasant, Paul wrote. *And would that you did reign, so that we might share the rule with you!* (4:8). However, that fulfillment had not as yet taken place.

Paul used the apostles as examples. The apostles might have been able to claim some special privileges; instead, they lived humbly, almost on the brink of death. Instead of basking in respect, power, and wealth, they were insulted, harassed, and hated. While others had abundance and an easy life, the apostle's life was one of hard work and suffering. *For I think that God has exhibited us apostles as last of all, like men sentenced to death; because we have become a spectacle to the world, to angels and to men* (4:9).

Paul continued, saying that those who proclaim the Gospel were *fools for Christ's sake* (4:10). In the world's wisdom, Paul looked foolish and was markedly different from the Corinthian Christians who claimed to be *wise in Christ.* (4:10). They looked down on him. He appeared *weak* (4:10), and they appeared *strong* (4:10). He was held in dishonor or disrepute while they were held in *honor* (4:10).

Paul also added a bleak picture of the life of an apostle. In stark contrast to the comfort and safety of the Corinthian Christians, apostles endured hunger and thirst. *We are ill-clad and buffeted and homeless, and we labor, working with our own hands* (4:11, 12). Hunger, thirst, nakedness, homelessness, physical and mental abuse on the long missionary journeys—all were part of an apostle's life. Paul reminded the Corinthians that he and other Christian witnesses had supported themselves. When faced with antagonism, insults, persecution, and slander, Paul and others responded as Jesus had instructed. *When reviled, we bless; when persecuted, we endure; when slandered, we try to conciliate* (4:12, 13).

Paul and his coworkers were considered the scum of the earth. They had received the world's dirt. However, they were actually the world's cleaning agent. They took upon themselves and absorbed the world's hatred and evil without any vengeance. They responded like Christ and continued His work. *We have become, and are now, as the refuse of the world, the offscouring of all things* (4:13).

I do not write this to make you ashamed, but to admonish you as my beloved children (4:14). Paul wrote not to shame the Corinthians but to admonish them. He had established the church; he had the authority to speak; he lovingly referred to them as his children and saw himself as their father who provided their conception in Christ Jesus. *For though you have countless guides in Christ, you do not have many fathers. For I became your father in Christ Jesus through the gospel* (4:15).

Paul then urged his readers to imitate him. His life could be an example of how to live and act. *I urge you, then, be imitators of me* (4:16).

SUGGESTIONS TO TEACHERS

Paul certainly had a stormy relationship with the Corinthian church. He endured great criticism because he apparently did not come across as a leader with wonderful rhetorical skills, exuding a sense of importance. Yet Paul's comments in his letter to the Corinthian church provide excellent insights into the ways Christian leaders should regard themselves and the ways Christians can deal with stressful situations.

1. PRONOUNCEMENT OF GOD'S PURPOSE. Paul wrote that Christian leaders should be considered "servants of Christ" and "stewards of the mysteries of God." Have your class members explore the meaning of both of these phrases. Both have to do with carrying out the wishes of the master of a household. In other words, Christians, whether leaders or not, must regard themselves as being under the orders of Christ. Above all, such a steward or member of the staff must "be found trustworthy," serving faithfully even under stress. This is how Paul saw himself.

2. PRESUMPTION OF THE PROUD. Move to verses 8-13 of chapter 4. Note Paul's sarcasm as he comments on the smug conceit of the Corinthians who believe they have attained a state of spiritual perfection, deserving everyone's applause. Paul firmly puts these proud people in their place by pointing out the irony of their bragging about how strong and smart they are. Paul contrasts this boastfulness with the suffering he had to endure. Talk with your students about what it means to be faithful under stress in everyday life.

3. PLEA OF A PARENT. Paul changed his tone and adopted the plea of a loving parent to a disobedient child. In spite of their sin and arrogance, these Corinthian Christians were still Paul's "beloved children" (vs. 14). Being faithful in stress means being loving throughout all the ups and downs of relating to others.

4. PLACE OF POWER. The Corinthian church was filled with big talkers who liked to boast about themselves and their spiritual wisdom. Paul's

words set them—and us—straight: "For the kingdom of God does not consist in talk but in power" (vs. 20). God empowers those who live trustingly and obediently as His servants. He enables us to keep the faith and live lovingly even in situations of stress and suffering.

TOPIC FOR ADULTS
FAITHFULNESS IN DIFFICULT TIMES

Fatal Addiction. The commander of Mexico's army in the early days of that country's independence was a tall, broad-shouldered leader named Antonio López de Santa Anna. Santa Anna. had made himself a national hero when he stopped the last attempt by Spain to regain control of its former colony. Then Santa Anna. seized power from a dictator who had grabbed control of the new national government. Posing as a champion of democracy, Santa Anna. was swept into power as the president.

The new president proved as adept in politics as in war, but Santa Anna. was also a devious libertine. He used his handsome looks and popularity to take whatever woman suited his fancy at the moment. He also enjoyed pomp and indulged in intrigue and murder. He used opium. Betrayed Mexicans were horrified at his brutal ways. When two Mexican states rose in revolt, Santa Anna. crushed their forces with terrible cruelty. He proudly advanced into the area of Mexico we now know as the state of Texas, determined to suppress any signs of rebellion there, crushing the valiant defenders at the Alamo.

Santa Anna was finally defeated by Sam Houston and a small force of Texans. His real problem had not been the rebellious Mexican provinces but his consuming addiction to power. "If they could make me God," he boasted, "I would still want something higher."

Paul warned against such boastful pride. He knew that such an addiction to power would destroy a leader and the group he led. In the Christian church, Paul realized, this fatal power-addiction indicated a desire to replace Christ with one's self. Such conceit ends in destruction.

Amateur's Guide to Saintliness. Basil Hume wrote a book full of hints for better living, which has been described as an "amateur's guide to saintliness." This British church leader's set of simple steps to holiness appear in *To Be a Pilgrim*. He suggests that it is harder to endure being bored by someone's conversation than to give up sugar in tea or coffee. Other people "can provide us with excellent opportunities for self-denial."

Hume says people should "thank heaven for pretty girls" and for music and the pleasures of life. It was "false spirituality" to regard pleasure as evil or dismiss the good things of the world as wrong in themselves.

Interestingly, he deals with the experience of unfair criticism, of being snubbed or ignored. The victim, he suggests, should just mutter, "Thanks be to God."

"You will go on feeling furious, but that prayer, said when you are churched up and upset, is extraordinarily valuable: and it does bring a deep peace—eventually," he says. He then quotes a friend who has a technique for handling difficult people. He asks himself: "What would I do if I really liked this person?" He then does it.

Hume's final "hint on holiness" is to "remain a little person." One should smile at oneself, at one's failures. "It does not matter if others do not take one seriously. God will. If you become holy, it is because God has made you so. You will not know it anyway."

The Helping Hand. During the American Revolution, a group of soldiers were busy trying to raise a heavy log to the top of a high wall. There were not enough men to do the job and it was going slowly. A corporal stood at the side shouting orders but offering no help. Soon an officer in civilian clothes rode up and surveyed the situation. "Why don't you give the men a hand?" he asked.

"I am a corporal," answered the man pompously.

"Oh, I'm sorry, I didn't see your rank," said the officer. Dismounting, he pitched in and struggled with the men until the log was in place. As he dusted off his coat and climbed back on his horse, he turned to the corporal and said courteously, "The next time you have a big job and too few men, call on your commander in chief. I will come again and assist you." With that General George Washington rode off, leaving an open-mouthed corporal staring after him.

Questions for Students on the Next Lesson. 1. Does everyone face temptation, or are some saintly persons exempt? 2. What was the evil of idolatry that Paul warned the Corinthians against? 3. What were some of the temptations confronting the Corinthians? 4. What did Paul say to those who thought they were above temptation? 5. What counsel did Paul offer to those facing temptation?

TOPIC FOR YOUTH
BEING FAITHFUL UNDER PRESSURE

Role Relationships. Yale Professor Daniel Levinson wrote in *The Seasons of a Man's Life* that a young person often attaches himself or herself to a mentor. This mentor is normally a half generation older, too young to be viewed as a parent, but too old to be seen as a peer. The young adult views this individual as a role model.

Levinson also noted that later, in most mentor-mentoree relationships, the young person comes to a point at which he or she pushes the older person away or even criticizes that person. Levinson feels that this is a sign of healthy individualism. Still later, the younger person usually reestablishes that relationship with the mentor.

If Levinson is correct and each person does look for a role model or a mentor, there should be a warning attached to this developing relationship. Paul cautioned that spiritual immaturity led the believers to find their own identities wrapped up in their mentors, role models, or leaders. Paul urged believers not to be so consumed with the leaders but to see themselves as coworkers for Jesus Christ.

Relieving Pressure? Members of rock music groups work hard. They seldom see their homes because of rugged road tours that sometimes include 250 concerts spread over three hundred days. One group, Lynard Skynard, performed 88 one-night concerts in a ninety-five-day stretch. Such tours inevitably produce pressure, and band members often turn to drugs and alcohol in an attempt to relieve the stress. Band members have even resorted to violence. In the case of Lynard Skynard, police records report arrests and fines for assaulting police officers and trashing hotel rooms by breaking tables, televisions, doors, and chairs.

Paul sketched a brief picture of life on the road as an evangelist. Along with hunger and homelessness, there was constant danger and actual physical abuse. Yet, in spite of all this, Paul never succumbed to the pressures of life on the road.

How did Paul handle the pressure? He wrote that he became like Christ. He urged the Corinthians and us to live as Jesus lived. Paul himself followed his own advice. Heed his message. Imitate both Paul and your Lord.

Money, or Ministry? Bill was a youth representative on the church's search committee for a new Christian education director. The committee interviewed several candidates who had impressive resumes. The final candidate seemed to have the best list of credentials. He came with a varied background of church work. He claimed to have created marvelous programs for the youth groups of churches that he had served. Everyone anticipated interviewing this candidate.

However, most of the candidate's questions to the committee centered on the financial package the church was offering—the salary, days off, benefits, and the perks that went with the job. The committee was surprised that he knew very little about the job itself and had no questions concerning the work of a Christian education director.

After the candidate left the interview room, the committee members voiced their feelings about his potential. Bill said that as far as he could see, the only thing the candidate was interested in was money.

Paul reminded his church that they should look for the spirit of servanthood in their leaders. Leaders were to live humbly, providing the necessary teaching and training for the church to prosper.

Questions for Students on the Next Lesson. 1. Is it possible for a Christian to be overconfident when facing temptation? 2. How can we withstand temptation? 3. What warnings did Paul offer regarding idolatry? Why? 4. Is there a limit to your Christian liberty? 5. Why is understanding the Old Testament important to understanding the New Testament?

LESSON 3—MARCH 19

RESISTING TEMPTATION

Background Scripture: I Corinthians 10:1-17
Devotional Reading: Ephesians 6:10-18

KING JAMES VERSION

I CORINTHIANS 10:1 Moreover, brethren, I would not that ye should be ignorant, how that all our fathers were under the cloud, and all passed through the sea;

2 And were all baptized unto Moses in the cloud and in the sea;

3 And did all eat the same spiritual meat;

4 And did all drink the same spiritual drink: for they drank of that spiritual Rock that followed them: and that Rock was Christ.

5 But with many of them God was not well pleased: for they were overthrown in the wilderness.

6 Now these things were our examples, to the intent we should not lust after evil things, as they also lusted.

7 Neither be ye idolaters, as were some of them; as it is written, The people sat down to eat and drink, and rose up to play.

8 Neither let us commit fornication, as some of them committed, and fell in one day three and twenty thousand.

9 Neither let us tempt Christ, as some of them also tempted, and were destroyed of serpents.

10 Neither murmur ye, as some of them also murmured, and were destroyed of the destroyer.

11 Now all these things happened unto them for ensamples: and they are written for our admonition, upon whom the ends of the world are come.

12 Wherefore let him that thinketh he standeth take heed lest he fall.

13 There hath no temptation taken you but such as is common to man: but God is faithful, who will not suffer you to be tempted above that ye are able; but will with the temptation also make a way to escape, that ye may be able to bear it.

14 Wherefore, my dearly beloved, flee from idolatry.

15 I speak as to wise men; judge ye what I say.

16 The cup of blessing which we bless, is it not the communion of the blood of Christ? The bread which we break, is it not the communion of the body of Christ?

17 For we being many are one bread, and one body: for we are all partakers of that one bread.

REVISED STANDARD VERSION

I CORINTHIANS 10:1 I want you to know, brethren, that our fathers were all under the cloud, and all passed through the sea, 2 and all were baptized into Moses in the cloud and in the sea, 3 and all ate the same supernatural food 4 and all drank the same supernatural drink. For they drank from the supernatural Rock which followed them, and the Rock was Christ. 5 Nevertheless with most of them God was not pleased; for they were overthrown in the wilderness.

6 Now these things are warnings for us, not to desire evil as they did. 7 Do not be idolaters as some of them were; as it is written, "The people sat down to eat and drink and rose up to dance." 8 We must not indulge in immorality as some of them did, and twenty-three thousand fell in a single day. 9 We must not put the Lord to the test, as some of them did and were destroyed by serpents; 10 nor grumble, as some of them did and were destroyed by the Destroyer. 11 Now these things happened to them as a warning, but they were written down for our instruction, upon whom the end of the ages has come. 12 Therefore let any one who thinks that he stands take heed lest he fall. 13 No temptation has overtaken you that is not common to man. God is faithful, and he will not let you be tempted beyond your strength, but with the temptation will also provide the way of escape, that you may be able to endure it.

14 Therefore, my beloved, shun the worship of idols. 15 I speak as to sensible men; judge for yourselves what I say. 16 The cup of blessing which we bless, is it not a participation in the blood of Christ? The bread which we break, is it not a participation in the body of Christ? 17 Because there is one bread, we who are many are one body, for we all partake of the one bread.

KEY VERSE: No temptation has overtaken you that is not common to man. God is faithful, and he will not let you be tempted beyond your strength, but with the temptation will also provide the way of escape, that you may be able to endure it. I Corinthians 10:13.

HOME DAILY BIBLE READINGS

Mar. 13	M.	Ephesians 6:10-18	*God's Armor for Protection from Evil*
Mar. 14	T.	I Corinthians 10:1-10	*Warning against Overconfidence*
Mar. 15	W.	I Corinthians 10:11-17	*Do Not Worship Idols*
Mar. 16	T.	I Timothy 6:9-19	*Pursue Righteousness*
Mar. 17	F.	I Peter 5:6-11	*Be Watchful and Firm in Faith*
Mar. 18	S.	James 4:4-12	*God Helps Those Who Resist Evil*
Mar. 19	S.	Psalm 24:1-6	*Purity of Heart Is Blessed*

BACKGROUND

One of the vexing problems plaguing the Corinthian church had to do with eating meat. The issue had nothing to do with animal rights or vegetarianism but with the fact that nearly all meat offered for sale in the market came from pagan shrines. Corinth, like most Mediterranean cities, boasted many temples dedicated to various deities. Part of the ritual ceremony in many of these temples called for sacrificing an animal. After a portion of meat was sliced off and presented to the pagan priests, the rest of the meat was sold. Since the main source of fresh meat was the heathen temples, those wanting it had to patronize the shrine meat market.

Some Christians had strong scruples about eating meat originally sacrificed to pagan gods. To these people, such meat was tainted with idolatry. Many of the Corinthian Christians had come out of the pagan cults, and eating such meat for them meant condoning the former system that they had left behind. Many of these Christians also strongly felt the temptation to return to the old way of life and were afraid of slipping back into their former practices. Often these new Christians were battling social pressures to conform to the ways of old friends and family members.

On the other hand, there were other Christians in Corinth who scoffed at these fellow believers, deriding them for their overconcern. After all, meat is merely meat, these "enlightened" church people insisted. Besides, they demanded, where else can anyone buy a roast or steaks? The Christians in this camp loudly announced that they were liberated from legalistic rules through the grace of the Gospel. They could quote Paul about being saved by faith in God's grace, not by human activities. If others in the Corinthian church got so worked up over eating meat coming from pagan shrines, these "liberated" intellectuals arrogantly stated, that was no concern of theirs.

Paul realized that both groups were beset by temptations that could prove destructive. One group, those upset over touching meat associated with pagan rituals, fought the temptation to slide back to the life from which Christ had rescued them. The other faction, convinced that eating meat had nothing to do with the faith, faced the temptations of intellectual pride in "knowing" everything to be known about theology.

NOTES ON THE PRINTED TEXT

Corinthian Christians were concerned about purchasing meat that had first been offered to idols. Excavations at Corinth have revealed an inscription identifying an ancient meat market at a large commercial building on the north side of the marketplace. Another site may have been on the west side of the marketplace where a row of shops stood. Each had a deep shaft that led to an underground water tunnel that might have provided a cooling place for the perishable meats. An inscription reading "Lucius the butcher" was also discovered here. In addition, several temples, one to Apollo, were nearby and might have provided the shops with sacrificed meat.

During his discussion on Christian freedom specifically built around food offered to idols, Paul called for self-control and discipline. He also reminded those who were confident of their loyalty to God that there were no guarantees against temptation. In fact, earlier Paul had written of his own vulnerability. Everyone, no matter how strong, would be tempted. He illustrated this point with an event from the history of ancient Israel, one that he assumed the Corinthian church would understand.

I want you to know, brethren, that our fathers were all under the cloud, and all passed through the sea, and all were baptized into Moses in the cloud and in the sea (10:1, 2). Paul recalled the Exodus. The passage through the Red Sea was a type of baptism, as was being under the cloud. Thus, Israel had undergone baptism with Moses.

In addition to baptism, Israel had its own sacred meal. *All ate the same supernatural food and all drank the same supernatural drink* (10:3, 4). Israel's eating the manna (and the quails) and drinking water from the rock was similar to eating and drinking the Lord's Supper. *For they drank from the supernatural Rock which followed them, and the Rock was Christ* (10:4). Paul reminded his readers that during the wandering in the wilderness, ancient Israel was supplied by God with the same benefits and supernatural blessings of Christ that the Corinthians were experiencing.

Israel enjoyed a privilege. Israel should have trusted God and expressed its gratitude, but Israel became religiously and morally lax. God became angry, and because of Israel's sins, the people died. *Nevertheless with most of them God was not pleased; for they were overthrown in the wilderness* (10:5).

Now these things are warnings for us, not to desire evil as they did (10:6). Paul sounded the warning. People convinced of their own strength and spiritual privilege can fall to temptation. So-called good people with a high degree of self-confidence can lust after evil things as easily as so-called bad people.

Do not be idolaters (10:7). Idolatry almost always involved sexual immorality. Paul reminded those self-confident Corinthians of the ancient Israelites. When the golden calf was created, Israel sat down to a huge feast that ultimately degenerated into a drunken orgy. Some three thousand Israelites were killed as punishment (see Exod. 32:28). Paul also recalled the twenty-four thousand individuals killed for having sexual relations with foreign women (see Num. 25:1-9). *We must not indulge in immorality as some of them did, and twenty-three thousand fell in a single day* (10:8).

Paul reminded his readers of other desert stories from the Exodus. Certain discontented Israelites challenged God to provide the necessary food. As punishment, God sent fiery serpents whose bites were fatal. Moses interceded and made a bronze serpent to save the people (see Num. 21:1-9). *We must not put the Lord to the test, as some of them did and were destroyed by serpents* (10:9).

Paul wrote that people must not complain, *nor grumble, as some of them did and were destroyed by the Destroyer* (10:10). Israel complained throughout the Exodus. Israel also believed in a special destroying angel who was the agent of punishment.

Now these things happened to them as a warning, but they were written down for our instruction, upon whom the end of the ages has come (10:11). Paul also pointed out that departure from God's way only brought destruction. These written accounts were a warning for the Corinthians. The believers must be faithful only to Christ, who had brought into being the final stage of history.

Therefore let any one who thinks that he stands take heed lest he fall (10:12). The Corinthians must understand that if the Israelites who were the chosen people and so highly favored by God stumbled into sin and were ultimately destroyed, they themselves must be careful about their spiritual standing. No one was totally secure; the proud should protect themselves for they might fall. In Paul's judgment they had not withstood anything out of the ordinary. *No temptation has overtaken you that is not common to man* (10:13). The temptations that confronted the Corinthians were ordinary ones.

God is faithful, and he will not let you be tempted beyond your strength (10:13). Paul reassured the church that while everyone would face temptation, God would give the power to endure. Hope rested on God's faithfulness. In addition, God guaranteed deliverance; there would always be a way to escape. *With the temptation* [God] *will also provide the way of escape, that you may be able to endure it* (10:13).

Paul repeated his call. *Therefore, my beloved, shun the worship of idols* (10:14). He told the Corinthians to run away from any occasion involving idol worship.

I speak as to sensible men; judge for yourselves what I say (10:15). The Corinthians considered themselves sensible and discriminating, so Paul urged them to use their common sense and wisdom.

The cup of blessing which we bless, is it not a participation in the blood of Christ? The bread which we break, is it not a participation in the body of Christ? (10:16). In the ancient world, eating established a fellowship. People who ate together were understood to be bound together in a special bond. Paul encouraged the Corinthians to share in the benefits of Christ through participation in Christian worship and fellowship. At the close of the meal at the Passover, a blessing was offered. Paul urged the Corinthians to remember the Lord and the benefits of His death in that blessing. The meal had been dedicated to the Lord who originally gave it. Likewise, at the Jewish meal, a loaf of bread was broken and passed to the guests. Paul saw the sharing of the bread as a means for the Corinthians to share in the body of Christ.

Paul then explained his view on partnership. *Because there is one bread, we who are many are one body, for we all partake of the one bread* (10:17). Since Christ was the bread, people were united in His body. They formed a fellowship with Him. The congregation became the body of Christ because all were united through His presence and through the benefits of His death.

SUGGESTIONS TO TEACHERS

The temptations facing the Corinthian Christians may seem strange to us. None of us will get worked up about meat offered to idols, but every one of us struggles with some form of temptation. As you work with the material in today's lesson, focus on the issue of resisting temptation in the Christian life.

1. WARNING. Paul's words warn against imagining that any believer is above temptation. He offered the example of the Israelite ancestors in the wilderness. Those people fell to the temptation to participate in pagan revelry by erecting the golden calf, and, later, by consorting with prostitutes. Paul's point is that no one is immune from temptation. Each Christian must avoid the arrogant notion of certain Corinthian church people who may have indicated that because they had been baptized, temptation was not a problem.

2. WEAKNESS. Paul further admonished everyone to face up to his or her weak points—the areas in life in which he or she might find it most difficult to withstand temptation. Each Christian must recognize where he or she is apt to be vulnerable when life's pressures build up. If you and your class members could be comfortable with it, ask for a sharing of some of the toughest temptations confronting adult Christians today. Otherwise, encourage each class member to write his or her own private list of temptations.

3. WARRANTY. The Lord is able to strengthen a believer to cope with any form of temptation. Here it might be useful to talk about the "Twelve Step" program of Alcoholics Anonymous. Recovering alcoholics acknowledge helplessness and the need to depend on a source outside themselves. People in recovery wisely recognize that God's promise holds when they are tempted to fall back into old patterns of escape from inner pain.

4. WATCHFULNESS. The sin of idolatry threatened to claim some of the Corinthian Christians, and they were prepared to take strong measures to fight the temptation. Brainstorm with your class to come up with a list of some of the more appealing forms of idolatry in today's culture. What forms of idolatry seem to be most prevalent in your community and in your church?

5. WORSHIP. Paul stressed the connectedness of all the members of the Corinthian church. They belonged to Christ, and therefore, to each other. Although tempted to go their own ways, they needed to realize that they were joined as one family when they gathered around the Lord's table.

Worship meant a sense of oneness among God's people. Help your students gain new understanding of the importance of worship and the Lord's Supper for the health of the church.

TOPIC FOR ADULTS
RESISTING TEMPTATION

Overcoming Temptation. U.S. tennis champion Arthur Ashe underwent heart-bypass surgery in 1983. At that time, hospitals were not checking blood samples for H.I.V. Through a blood transfusion, Ashe contracted AIDS. He did not suspect the transfusion had transmitted the dread infection to him until 1988, when he had to have brain surgery after his right arm became paralyzed. The surgery revealed a parasitic infection that quickly led to a diagnosis of AIDS. Ashe had not planned to reveal his illness until the time came when he would be noticeably changed by the disease physically, and then would have to answer obvious questions. But *USA Today* demanded he confirm or deny the rumor that he had AIDS in 1992. The tennis star, ranked seventh in the world before he was forced to retire, bravely held a press conference and announced that through the transfusion he had become a victim of AIDS.

Ashe had to face the temptation to be angry or bitter for the rest of his life, but he triumphed because of his faith. As the lone black male tennis star in the 1960s and 1970s, Ashe carried a burden that sometimes made him uncomfortable, but he carried it with dignity. He was a role model and a source of inspiration to blacks as well as whites. The story is by now well known: how a youth from segregated Richmond rose swiftly through the ranks, sometimes being refused entry in junior tournaments held in the South, to triumph in the nearly all-white tennis world.

Being an AIDS victim through no fault of his (he was not gay and remained constantly faithful to his wife), Arthur Ashe managed even to surmount the temptation to rage at God. Speaking at the Niagara County Community College in the fall of 1992, he testified to the place Jesus Christ held in his life in dealing with temptations.

"I've had a religious faith, growing up in the South and black and having the church as a focal point of my life," Ashe said. "And I was reminded of something Jesus said on the cross: 'My God, my God, why hast thou forsaken me?' Remember, Jesus was poor, humble, and of a despised minority. I wasn't poor in that my father was a policeman, but we certainly weren't rich. And Jesus asked the question, in effect, of why must the innocent suffer. And I'm not so innocent—I mean, I'm hardly a perfect human being—but you ask about yourself, 'Why me?' And I think, 'Why NOT me?'

"Why should I be spared what some others have been inflicted with," he continued. "And I have to think of all the good of my life, of having a great wife and daughter, and family and friends, and winning Wimbledon and the U.S. Open and playing for and coaching the Davis Cup team, and getting a free scholarship to U.C.L.A.—all kinds of good things. You could also ask about this, 'Why me?' Sometimes there are no explanations for things, especially for the bad."

Tempted to Cheat on Claims. A man in Florida had survived Andrew, the hurricane that had swept through his state. He was flabbergasted when his neighbor asked him, "So what claims are you putting in?"

The man had not suffered any damage to his house or car from the Florida storm, so he answered, "None." The neighbor could not believe it. "Hey, here's your opportunity to collect a few bucks. The insurance companies are practically writing checks on the spot," he told the friend. "How could anyone pass up putting in a claim for $5,000 for wet carpeting or a damaged car?"

The neighbor's willingness to give in to the temptation to falsify a claim is not unusual. One-third of those sampled by the University of Florida's Insurance Research Center believe it's okay to falsify an insurance application. One half feel it's all right to shade the truth in order to save on out-of-pocket deductibles. The survey related to a study on auto fraud, but no matter. It clearly shows the willingness of everyday people to step out of line. This free-for-all attitude can be found in all sectors of the insurance business, whether it's health, life, or as we saw in the University of Florida study, auto insurance.

We all eventually pay for this attitude.

Overcoming Temptation. Martin Luther King, Jr., was sometimes tempted to give in to fear, especially when threats came to him and his family in the early days of his crusade for justice. One day, after many threatening phone calls, he went into his kitchen and closed the door. "I found myself praying out loud," he said, "and I laid my life bare. I remembered saying, 'I'm here taking a stand and I've come to the point where I can't face it alone.' From somewhere came the response, 'Stand for truth, stand for righteousness, God is at your side.'" Declared King, "I have not known fear since."

King experienced the grace of God that prepares us to "bring to completion" our faith. Grasped by such grace, people do not rest on their ingenuity but on the fact that they are instruments of God. They know that it is God who will "bring to completion at the day of Jesus Christ" (Phil. 1:6) the preparations He has made for them.

Questions for Students on the Next Lesson. 1. What were the causes of conflict in the Corinthian congregation? 2. What was causing conflict between the Corinthians and Paul? 3. How did Paul resolve the conflict between the Corinthians and himself? 4. What advice did Paul give the Corinthians about resolving the congregational conflict? 5. What active steps can you and your class take to deal with real or possible conflict in your church?

TOPIC FOR YOUTH
RESISTING TEMPTATION

What You Don't See. Why do you purchase that particular cola or brand of jeans? Chances are you don't base your choice on the quality of the product. Your decision might well be the result of a powerful, subtle motivation at work on a subconscious level. In his book *Subliminal Seduction: Ad Media's Manipulation of a Not So Innocent America,* Wilson Bryan Key noted that it is not what you see that sells you. Subliminal techniques, such as subtly embedded graffiti in ice cubes or sexually symbolic forms and shapes in the graphic arts, expose Americans to five hundred advertising messages per day. Key estimates that an individual consciously perceives only seventy-five out of every five hundred of these messages. This means that 85 percent of all ad messages are blocked. Still, 2.5 percent of the messages are acted upon as a result of these techniques.

Consider the enormous potential this gives the Evil One. Think how many ways Satan can tempt you or influence you without your being aware of it. Temptation does not always stare at you eyeball to eyeball. It might well be quite subtle. Be alert in order to resist temptation.

Idols. Speaking of idol worship tends to conjure up scenes of people paying homage to a clay, metal, or wooden statue. Few of us would consider bowing down before any such human creation. However, many of us do bow down to other kinds of idols.

Eric was an active member of his church. On Sundays, he usually attended Sunday school, worship service, and youth group. However, Eric was also a swimmer. As Eric went through middle school, his attendance at church activities became irregular due to extra swimming practices and special coaching sessions. By high school, Eric had developed into a very good swimmer. He had gained recognition throughout the state. He swam constantly. His family continued to take him for more and more practices and for coaching at a local university. Eric was seldom seen anymore at church activities, except for Christmas and Easter. Swimming had become Eric's life. He dreamed of the Olympics and literally worshiped that dream.

An idol is anything that takes the place of God in our priorities. An idol is anything that is worshiped, anything that becomes the center of our existence.

Watch the Ice. The farm pond was frozen, and a father and his son stood staring at it. Each held a pair of ice skates. The father shook his head, saying that the ice looked too thin to skate upon. The young boy said it looked fine and they should at least try it.

Paul reminded Christians that they should be cautious of life's thin ice. Some acts are morally and spiritually questionable. We may be tempted to go ahead, but a Christian must refrain from any activity that deviates from God's purpose. Call upon the Spirit in prayer to resist temptation.

Questions for Students on the Next Lesson. 1. If Christians are to live in love and unity, why are there divisions in the church? 2. What human qualities are usually associated with disunity in a church? 3. What images does Paul utilize in explaining spiritual maturity? 4. What increases the unity within a church? 5. How does your denomination and your local church deal with division?

LESSON 4—MARCH 26

DEALING WITH CONFLICT

Background Scripture: II Corinthians 12—13
Devotional Reading: Colossians 3:8-17

KING JAMES VERSION

II CORINTHIANS 12:19 Again, think ye that we excuse ourselves unto you? we speak before God in Christ: but we do all things, dearly beloved, for your edifying.

20 For I fear, lest, when I come, I shall not find you such as I would, and that I shall be found unto you such as ye would not: lest there be debates, envyings, wraths, strifes, backbitings, whisperings, swellings, tumults:

21 And lest, when I come again, my God will humble me among you, and that I shall bewail many which have sinned already, and have not repented of the uncleanness and fornication and lasciviousness which they have committed. . . .

13:5 Examine yourselves, whether ye be in the faith; prove your own selves. Know ye not your own selves, how that Jesus Christ is in you, except ye be reprobates?

6 But I trust that ye shall know that we are not reprobates.

7 Now I pray to God that ye do no evil; not that we should appear approved, but that ye should do that which is honest, though we be as reprobates.

8 For we can do nothing against the truth, but for the truth.

9 For we are glad, when we are weak, and ye are strong: and this also we wish, even your perfection.

10 Therefore I write these things being absent, lest being present I should use sharpness, according to the power which the Lord hath given me to edification, and not to destruction.

11 Finally, brethren, farewell. Be perfect, be of good comfort, be of one mind, live in peace; and the God of love and peace shall be with you.

12 Greet one another with an holy kiss.

13 All the saints salute you.

REVISED STANDARD VERSION

II CORINTHIANS 12:19 Have you been thinking all along that we have been defending ourselves before you? It is in the sight of God that we have been speaking in Christ, and all for your upbuilding, beloved. 20 For I fear that perhaps I may come and find you not what I wish, and that you may find me not what you wish; that perhaps there may be quarreling, jealousy, anger, selfishness, slander, gossip, conceit, and disorder. 21 I fear that when I come again my God may humble me before you, and I may have to mourn over many of those who sinned before and have not repented of the impurity, immorality, and licentiousness which they have practiced. . . .

13:5 Examine yourselves, to see whether you are holding to your faith. Test yourselves. Do you not realize that Jesus Christ is in you?—unless indeed you fail to meet the test! 6 I hope you will find out that we have not failed. 7 But we pray God that you may not do wrong—not that we may appear to have met the test, but that you may do what is right, though we may seem to have failed. 8 For we cannot do anything against the truth, but only for the truth. 9 For we are glad when we are weak and you are strong. What we pray for is your improvement. 10 I write this while I am away from you, in order that when I come I may not have to be severe in my use of the authority which the Lord has given me for building up and not for tearing down.

11 Finally, brethren, farewell. Mend your ways, heed my appeal, agree with one another, live in peace, and the God of love and peace will be with you. 12 Greet one another with a holy kiss. 13 All the saints greet you.

KEY VERSE: Mend your ways, heed my appeal, agree with one another, live in peace, and the God of love and peace will be with you.
II Corinthians 13:11.

HOME DAILY BIBLE READINGS

Mar. 20	*M.*	II Corinthians 10:1-12	*Confronting Opponents in the Church*
Mar. 21	*T.*	II Corinthians 10:13-18	*Boast Only of the Lord*
Mar. 22	*W.*	II Corinthians 11:7-15	*Refuting False Charges with the Truth*
Mar. 23	*T.*	II Corinthians 12:1-10	*Strength in Weakness*
Mar. 24	*F.*	II Corinthians 12:11-18	*Paul Justifies His Actions*
Mar. 25	*S.*	II Corinthians 12:19—13:4	*Admonition to End the Dissension*
Mar. 26	*S.*	II Corinthians 13:5-13	*Live in Peace with One Another*

BACKGROUND

One of the problems facing the early church was fake apostles. These self-styled evangelists wandered from city to city, posing cleverly as genuine teachers of the faith. Vain and pompous, they preyed on the gullibility of recent converts with claims to special revelations and knowledge.

Some of these quack preachers came to Corinth and quickly won a following in the Corinthian congregation. Their words sounded impressive. These impostors, however, soon began to undermine what Paul had taught about the faith. When they seemed to be at variance with Paul's teaching about the Cross and Resurrection as the cornerstone of the Christian life, these visiting "apostles" belittled Paul. In fact, they resorted to dismissing him as inferior, flawed, and unimportant. The phony leaders bragged that they had all the credentials and characteristics of true apostles, while Paul had none.

The teaching of these bogus apostles soon divided the Corinthian church. Factions developed. Squabbling broke out, threatening to split the church into warring cliques.

Paul's letters to the controversial Corinthians attempted to bring them back to their senses. In today's Scripture passage, Paul addressed the boastful "apostles" and their claims. Paul stated that if they wanted to play the game of bragging about their apostleship, he could beat them handsdown. He cooly reported some of the facts of his career, aware that they could never match his record. Paul could also claim visions and revelations, but he refused to claim special privileges from these. He admitted that he also had had mystical experiences, but he would not pull rank on others because of them. After apologizing for this brief bit of boasting, Paul wrote that he had been kept humble by a "thorn" in his flesh. What this incapacitating problem was, we do not know. But Paul insisted that in spite of the physical suffering and mental anguish the ailment caused, God's grace more than matched his needs.

In spite of the slander and stinging criticism from these crooked leaders, Paul was most concerned to bring healing to the Corinthian church. He acknowledged that he never acted like his vain, pompous critics, but nevertheless he did have the authority of a real apostle. He announced that he would exercise godly authority if necessary, adding that the purpose of his authority was to build up, not tear down.

NOTES ON THE PRINTED TEXT

Have you been thinking all along that we have been defending ourselves before you? (12:19). Paul had spent a great deal of time and space writing about himself. He feared that the wrong impression might have been given. He was not coming to Corinth to make excuses for himself or to further his own interests. He wanted to satisfy God's standards, not the Corinthians'. He was coming to build up his converts and their faith. *It is in the sight of God that we have been speaking in Christ, and all for your upbuilding, beloved* (12:19).

Paul wrote that he was coming because he was afraid the Corinthians were guilty of certain undesirable attributes that had broken the unity of the church. The existence of these qualities would make it a difficult visit for both parties. Paul specifically listed eight of these negative traits that surfaced when there was disagreement. *For I fear that perhaps I may come and find you not what I wish, and that you may find me not what you wish; that perhaps there may be quarreling, jealousy, anger, selfishness, slander, gossip, conceit, and disorder* (12:20). Paul's list indicated the extent of the disagreements and squabbling. There was direct quarreling and anger, which resulted in disorder. There was quiet intrigue, whispered scheming, and politicking between rival groups. Self-importance and envy were all too apparent.

I fear that when I come again my God may humble me before you, and I may have to mourn over many of those who sinned before and have not repented of the impurity, immorality, and licentiousness which they have practiced (12:21). As bad as the division caused by the party spirit was, there was another problem. Certain individuals were committing sexual sins. Coming from a morally lax culture, they had joined the congregation but had not given up their old attitudes and morality. Corinth had a long-standing, notorious reputation for immorality. The Roman geographer Strabo noted that one thousand cult prostitutes served the temple of Aphrodite, which overlooked the city.

Paul warned the Corinthians that he would take disciplinary action if the Corinthians did not repent. When he arrived, there would be a harsh reckoning. Rather than employ that discipline, however, he hoped that the Corinthians would repent. He urged them to put their faith to the test to see if it was genuine. *Examine yourselves, to see whether you are holding to your faith. Test yourselves* (13:5).

Paul knew the answer to the Corinthians' examination. They would be confident that Jesus was present in their midst. The church was the body of Christ. Jesus dwelt in that body. *Do you not realize that Jesus Christ is in you?—unless indeed you fail to meet the test!* (13:5).

If their self-examination revealed that they were faithless, then Paul's work was in vain. Paul wrote expectantly, *I hope you will find out that we have not failed* (13:6).

Paul prayed for his church to reform. He did not want it to experience God's judgment. He wanted the church to resist evil and to be obedient to God. *But we pray God that you may not do wrong . . . but that you may do what is right* (13:7). So long as the church was doing what was right, Paul was not concerned about his own reputation.

So sure was Paul of the validity of his mission that he wrote: *For we cannot do anything against the truth, but only for the truth* (13:8). The truth was the Gospel. Paul would not further his own reputation at the expense of the Gospel's truthfulness.

That was the reason Paul appeared so weak. His apparent weakness was an imitation of Christ's servanthood. Paul lived this way so the Corinthians could become strong. *For we are glad when we are weak and you are strong* (13:9). He hoped they would repent so that he would not be forced to exhibit strength. Explicitly clear, he called for repentance. *What we pray for is your improvement* (13:9).

If his appeal was rejected, Paul promised that he would exercise his authority (which was given by the Lord) when he came. *I write this while I am away from you, in order that when I come I may not have to be severe in my use of the authority which the Lord has given me for building up and not for tearing down* (13:10). Discipline would prove destructive. Paul much preferred to build up the church.

Paul closed by urging the Corinthians to pray for him, to agree with one another, and to live together in peace. *Finally, brethren, farewell. Mend your ways, heed my appeal, agree with one another, live in peace, and the God of love and peace will be with you* (13:11). The appeal was for unity and an end to quarrels. The believers were urged to offer each a *holy kiss* (13:12), which normally was given as a greeting on the brow. He concluded with a greeting from those who were with him. *All the saints greet you* (13:13).

SUGGESTIONS TO TEACHERS

Church fights can be nasty. The Corinthian congregation seemed to boil with such quarrels. The possibility of conflict exists, of course, in every group. But in Christ's family, the church, conflict can be particularly destructive. Today's lesson should have special meaning for your class, your congregation, your denomination, and the personal relationships of each class member.

1. ACCUSATIONS. Certain newcomers to the Corinthian church were masquerading as apostles, basing their claims on ecstatic visions and revelations. Paul's modesty kept him from parading his own intensely private spiritual experiences, and he mentioned that he was also kept from feeling superior by a "thorn." Many Corinthian Christians, however, were taken in by the glitz and glamor of the super-apostles' performances, delighting in splashy spirituality and shiny spectacles, such as speaking in tongues and dramatic "miracles." Paul was denounced.

Conflict escalates when charges fly, especially personal charges. Paul was able to separate the issues from personal criticism. In spite of the hurt he felt, he did not overreact defensively but saw that the important matter was to reflect the life of Christ.

2. ARROGANCE. Paul's accusers revealed a lack of love and respect for the truth. Among their charges was the absurd accusation that Paul had tricked the Corinthians! Paul's detractors whispered that he had deceived everyone by not taking money from them when he had lived in Corinth, whereas a true apostle would gladly have accepted generous personal gifts.

Conflict results when we neglect caring and honesty in our relationships. Only when our group cultivates the life of Christ will we overcome arrogant, unloving, untruthful attitudes.

3. ACCOUNTABILITY. Paul reminded his readers (including us) that all Christians and all churches are constantly "in the sight of God" (II Cor. 12:19). Being under God's surveillance means remembering that we are all accountable to the Lord.

4. ACCURACY. Every believer must check the accuracy of his or her faith in light of the Cross. Look at II Corinthians 13:5 together. Only Jesus Christ is the proper yardstick, not personal ideas, not human knowledge, not teachings of visiting so-called apostles. Discuss what it means to "examine yourselves, to see whether you are holding to your faith."

5. ACCEPTANCE. Throughout this long section dealing with conflict, Paul conveys the grace Christ brings. He closes with a summary-benediction in II Corinthians 13, telling how God's grace can transform every situation, including the most hurtful of conflicts.

TOPIC FOR ADULTS
DEALING WITH DIFFERENCES

More Than Fistfights. Samuel de Champlain, the seventeenth-century French explorer and founder of Quebec, reported back to the Old World on many of the wonders he encountered while journeying through Canada. In these writings, he told one story of a mixed Catholic and Huguenot community in Nova Scotia that was served by both a Roman priest and a Protestant pastor.

Champlain does not go into detail as to the content of the doctrinal disputes that arose between these two servants of the Gospel, but he explains the means by which they sought resolution of their differences. At regular intervals, apparently, the priest and the pastor engaged in public fistfights. According to the explorer, crowds of settlers, Native Americans, and voyagers who were passing through would gather at the center of the village to cheer on the combatants.

Although most Christians do not resolve their differences by slugging it out with their fists in public, many have not learned to deal constructively with conflict. Paul urges believers to handle their difficulties with one another in ways that will eventually bring reconciliation and harmony.

Too Big for Herself. A pampered society woman with too much money and too much ego went to a psychiatrist out of boredom. The doctor invited her to tell him all about herself. She was delighted to oblige and spent the hour describing herself. After an hour, the therapist said that she would need to return again. At her next appointment, the woman rattled on in great detail again about herself. The same thing happened for each visit. Finally, after a dozen visits, the psychiatrist said at the end of another wearying hour of listening to the matron's egotistical prattle, "Mrs. Smith, since I don't think I can be of further help to you at this time, I urge you to travel to Niagara Falls as soon as you can." The woman asked why. The doctor continued, "Because there I advise you to take a good look at something bigger than yourself!"

Most conflicts in churches arise when persons think they are more important than they are and see others as less important. Paul's advice, in a sense, was to have every Christian see himself or herself in the light of Christ, recognizing that the Lord is greater than all.

Dealing with Differences. "In recent years the sectarian impulse has reawakened with the emergence of organized opposition groups within mainline Protestant denominations. The sectarian impulse is a perfectionist yearning, often keenly perceptive of the flaws in established Christianity and eager either to correct them or to secede and form a purer society. . . . Christianity in the United States has suffered split after split as various factions have broken away to form new denominations. The sectarian impulse to secede and start a new church when the old one seems intractable is the next step following increasingly hostile exchanges. In our time, when considerable headway toward unity among denominations has been made, a resurgence of sectarianism threatens to fracture the denominations themselves.

"Each party to a church-dividing conflict has a certain inner logic and conviction. In such controversy, everyone contributes to the problem by taking a win-lose stance and honing the skills of combat rather than the skills of reconciliation. Furthermore, each party to church conflict can learn from one another when honest listening is facilitated. As long as groups and individuals are in opposition within the church, the only real defeat occurs when opponents give up on each other. Then schism triumphs over unity.

"Christians know all too well how to separate from one another. What we need to learn is the prior commitment to oneness in Jesus Christ. . . . Difficult though it is to resolve to love one another despite substantial disagreement, this is precisely what we must pray for the ability to do." — From a Pastoral Letter from the Mercersburg Society to several mainline denominations, published in the Newsletter of the Mercersburg Society, January, 1993.

Questions for Students on the Next Lesson. 1. How are church members to use their spiritual gifts? 2. What are some of the gifts of the Spirit listed by Paul? 3. Are any of these less important than others? 4. Do members of your church feel joy or pain in response to the joy or pain of others? 5. Does everyone in the church have some gift to share?

TOPIC FOR YOUTH
DEALING WITH DIFFERENCES

Family Feud. An Ohio congregation was almost destroyed by internal fighting. Many members had stopped attending. Some were worshiping at other churches. A few had transferred, and others were talking of leaving. Those who remained in the congregation had been drawn into opposing factions.

How did this upheaval start? Surprisingly, the cause was a slight change in the job description of the church organist. The woman who had been employed by the church for seventeen years took the change in her duties as a personal rebuke. Using her influence, she spread complaints and accusations so effectively that she created an angry protest group. The church's official board tried unsuccessfully to resolve the growing conflict.

Finally, the local denominational body stepped in to handle the problem. This group spent almost one year listening, then began the slow task of trying to reconcile the two parties. Fortunately, harmony was finally restored. This took place, however, only when each person in the opposing camps began to realize the unity that Christ could bring. Eventually, they all grew to understand that they all belonged to Christ, and therefore, to one another. Out of the hurts of the conflict, they grew to a deeper appreciation of the love of God and could begin to care for each other.

Utopia? One of the fastest-growing cities in Florida is Orlando. Parts of this boomtown city of the South imitate Disney World. The city's goal is to offer an escape and to eliminate stress and problems. Voluntary conformity is the norm in this city that pays smiling workers to pick up gum wrappers and cigarette butts from tree planters. It also attempts to provide a model of a moral, clean, and harmonious city. Every subdivision strives to offer a dreamlike quality so that residents do not know where Disney World begins and ends.

In spite of these utopian dreams, the city has had its difficulties. This haven for white middle-class families is serviced by a number of low income workers who live in the nearby community of Osceola. This obvious difference goes against everything for which the community was founded. The Disney magic has not permeated the lives of Orlando's residents.

Long before Disney or the developer's dreams, Paul indicated that Christ was the only true source of real community.

Breach of Love. Jan Bentson had a disagreement with her pastor, the Rev. Arni Jacobson of the People's Church in Salem, Oregon, over the decline in church membership during a five-year period. Jacobson considered her accusations to be those of a "gossipy troublemaker" and had the membership of Jan and her husband, Cliff, revoked. Jan continued to attend worship services at the church and was eventually slapped with a criminal trespass action by Jacobson.

Conflicts and differences will arise in a church. Sometimes individuals will try to force others with whom they disagree out of the church's fellowship. Other times, an individual will leave a church family filled with anger. All of this is tragic.

Paul wrote that differences show a lack of Christ's love and a break within the family of God.

Questions for Students on the Next Lesson. 1. What gifts does the Spirit give to believers? 2. How are these gifts used by the church? 3. What image does Paul use to illustrate the believers' unity? 4. Is it possible for believers to use their gifts only for themselves? Why, or why not? 5. Does your church utilize your gifts and the gifts of other youth?

LESSON 5—APRIL 2

BUILDING UP THE BODY

Background Scripture: I Corinthians 12
Devotional Reading: Ephesians 4:4-16

KING JAMES VERSION

I CORINTHIANS 12:4 Now there are diversities of gifts, but the same Spirit.

5 And there are differences of administrations, but the same Lord.

6 And there are diversities of operations, but it is the same God which worketh all in all.

7 But the manifestation of the Spirit is given to every man to profit withal.

8 For to one is given by the Spirit the word of wisdom; to another the word of knowledge by the same Spirit;

9 To another faith by the same Spirit; to another the gifts of healing by the same Spirit;

10 To another the working of miracles; to another prophecy; to another discerning of spirits; to another divers kinds of tongues; to another the interpretation of tongues:

11 But all these worketh that one and the selfsame Spirit, dividing to every man severally as he will.

12 For as the body is one, and hath many members, and all the members of that one body, being many, are one body: so also is Christ.

13 For by one Spirit are we all baptized into one body, whether we be Jews or Gentiles, whether we be bond or free; and have been all made to drink into one Spirit.

14 For the body is not one member, but many.

15 If the foot shall say, Because I am not the hand, I am not of the body; is it therefore not of the body?

16 And if the ear shall say, Because I am not the eye, I am not of the body; is it therefore not of the body?

17 If the whole body were an eye, where were the hearing? If the whole were hearing, where were the smelling?

18 But now hath God set the members every one of them in the body, as it hath pleased him.

19 And if they were all one member, where were the body?

20 But now are they many members, yet but one body. . . .

26 And whether one member suffer, all the members suffer with it; or one member be honoured, all the members rejoice with it.

REVISED STANDARD VERSION

I CORINTHIANS 12:4 Now there are varieties of gifts, but the same Spirit; 5 and there are varieties of service, but the same Lord; 6 and there are varieties of working, but it is the same God who inspires them all in every one. 7 To each is given the manifestation of the Spirit for the common good. 8 To one is given through the Spirit the utterance of wisdom, and to another the utterance of knowledge according to the same Spirit, 9 to another faith by the same Spirit, to another gifts of healing by the one Spirit, 10 to another the working of miracles, to another prophecy, to another the ability to distinguish between spirits, to another various kinds of tongues, to another the interpretation of tongues. 11 All these are inspired by one and the same Spirit, who apportions to each one individually as he wills.

12 For just as the body is one and has many members, and all the members of the body, though many, are one body, so it is with Christ. 13 For by one Spirit we were all baptized into one body—Jews or Greeks, slaves or free—and all were made to drink of one Spirit.

14 For the body does not consist of one member but of many. 15 If the foot should say, "Because I am not a hand, I do not belong to the body," that would not make it any less a part of the body. 16 And if the ear should say, "Because I am not an eye, I do not belong to the body," that would not make it any less a part of the body. 17 If the whole body were an eye, where would be the hearing? If the whole body were an ear, where would be the sense of smell? 18 But as it is, God arranged the organs of the body, each one of them, as he chose. 19 If all were a single organ, where would the body be? 20 As it is, there are many parts, yet one body. . . .

212

KEY VERSE: To each is given the manifestation of the Spirit for the common good. I Corinthians 12:7

HOME DAILY BIBLE READINGS

Mar. 27	*M.*	I Corinthians 12:1-6	*Spiritual Gifts Are Given by God*
Mar. 28	*T.*	I Corinthians 12:7-11	*Gifts Are for the Common Good*
Mar. 29	*W.*	I Corinthians 12:12-20	*Many Members, One Body*
Mar. 30	*T.*	I Corinthians 12:21-26	*Members Need One Another*
Mar. 31	*F.*	I Corinthians 12:27-31	*The Church Is Christ's Body*
Apr. 1	*S.*	Ephesians 4:1-7	*Live in Unity of Faith*
Apr. 2	*S.*	Ephesians 4:11-16	*Build Up the Body of Christ*

BACKGROUND

Among the many problems in the Corinthian church was the feeling that certain members were more important than others. Some members had set up a sort of pecking order based on people's spiritual gifts. The idea that certain spiritual gifts were vastly superior led those possessing such gifts to lord it over others. For example, the church members who could speak in tongues thought they were the elite and looked down on the others.

Needless to say, this attitude broke the fellowship into divided blocks. Those speaking in tongues prided themselves in being the most religious. Those unable to speak in tongues were made to feel less important and less blessed. A kind of hierarchy evolved in the Corinthian church based on how valuable each person's gift was thought to be. It finally got to the point that those with the "higher" gifts made the claim that theirs were the only gifts that mattered. The ones speaking in tongues insisted that this was the one essential gift of the Spirit and that no other was necessary for the church's well-being.

As elsewhere in his letters (see Rom. 12 and Eph. 4), Paul here used a vivid metaphor to describe the church. He insisted that all believers were bound together in a unity like the organs of a human body. As with a human body, many members are necessary. Many different organs and parts are required for the body to function well. Likewise, the church thrives when a variety of gifts are functioning. Even apparently insignificant gifts, like apparently insignificant body parts, are indispensable for the well-being of Christ's community or body, the church.

Paul emphasized that each member was gifted by the Spirit in some way. He further insisted that every member's spiritual gift was bestowed to build up the community of faith and its ministry.

NOTES ON THE PRINTED TEXT

Paul addressed a third question raised by the Corinthian church (7:1; 8:1; 12:1) regarding spiritual gifts. *Now there are varieties of gifts, but the same Spirit* (12:4). God had equipped the members of the church with various gifts given through the Holy Spirit. The gifts were abilities that church members were to use in the life of the church for mutual edification. The believers received these gifts from the Spirit.

Likewise, others received abilities to serve. *There are varieties of service, but the same Lord* (12:5). Paul never defined those services. Perhaps they were teaching or missionary activities. What was known, however, was that they were given by Christ.

There are varieties of working, but it is the same God who inspires them all in every one (12:6). The workings refer to how the ministries were carried out or accomplished. God provided the energy or inspiration for the completion of the ministry.

To each is given the manifestation of the Spirit for the common good (12:7). Each individual received a different gift. However, the gift was not to be used for the individual's advantage but for the whole church's well-being.

Paul itemized some of the spiritual gifts. *To one is given through the Spirit the utterance of wisdom* (12:8). God equipped some members to preach the Gospel of Jesus with great understanding or perhaps to teach the doctrines of the faith. To others the Spirit gave the ability to instruct with effective reason the truths of the Christian faith through discourse. *To another the utterance of knowledge according to the same Spirit* (12:8).

To another faith by the same Spirit (12:9). Certain individuals exhibited a spiritual gift through which God's power worked through them to accomplish great things. Some had the ability to work *miracles* (12:10). These individuals enabled God's healing to take place physically. Others exhibited the gift of *prophecy* (12:10). Perhaps this involved the ability to predict the future. More likely, it was mainly the ability to preach with power and to move people to repentance the way the ancient prophets did. Still others were given the gift to *distinguish between spirits* (12:10). When there were doubts as to whether individuals were really speaking by God's Spirit, certain church members had the ability to discriminate between the true Spirit and false spirits. Still other members could legitimately speak in *various kinds of tongues* (12:10). Often when this was done, the sounds were unintelligible. Therefore, some had the ability of *interpretation of tongues* (12:10). These individuals could translate the message, whether an ecstatic utterance or a true language.

Paul reminded the Corinthians that no matter what gifts each possessed, *all these are inspired by one and the same Spirit, who apportions to each one individually as he wills* (12:11). The Spirit gave the gifts; Christians did not choose their gifts. Taking personal pride in an individual gift, or rating the value of one gift above another, was clearly wrong.

Paul referred to the human body to represent the church. *For just as the body is one and has many members, and all the members of the body, though many, are one body, so it is with Christ* (12:12). The church was like a human body in that it had many members but was still one organism. It was brought into being through the Spirit who indwelt believers. The Spirit incorporated all into the body, *Jews or Greeks, slaves or free* (12:13).

Paul continued the imagery to prove the interrelatedness of the body's parts. Could the foot (regarded as the lowest part of the body because it was soiled with dust) be independent since it was not able to be a hand (considered important because it was an agent of work)? Could the ear secede from the body since it was not a beautiful eye? Such notions were absurd. In the body, each organ served a purpose. One organ could not do the work of the other. That was why God created each. *As it is, God arranged the organs in the body, each one of them, as he chose* (12:18).

Paul then reminded his readers that all persons in the body were important. No one was so important as to become the whole body. *If all were a single organ, where would the body be? As it is, there are many parts, yet one body* (12:19, 20).

All the parts of the body should care for one another. Just as the physical body was sensitized by the nerves to pain and suffering, so, too, the church's members must be sensitized to the suffering of others. *If one member suffers, all suffer together; if one member is honored, all rejoice together* (12:26).

SUGGESTIONS TO TEACHERS

When I was a boy, I thought that I had figured out who really counted as most important in our congregation. My father, the pastor, of course, was at the top of the chart I had in my mind. Mr. Bergmeyer, the head usher, was slightly below him, followed by Lewis Baker, the leading elder. Then came a cluster of less important figures, including some Sunday school teachers and a few other laypersons. But I also had a list of those who I assumed, in my childish ignorance, didn't count for anything. This list of the unimportant included some poor widows, a man with a severe speech impediment, and the shut-ins. Only later did I come to appreciate that each of these people was precious to the Lord and indispensable to the body of Christ.

It might be both amusing and edifying to have your class recall whether they, too, imagined such a hierarchy in their childhood experiences of church. Probably everyone continues to carry some sense that certain gifts are really needed and others are unimportant. This lesson, then, is a "must" for all!

1. COLLECTION OF GIFTS. Point out how gloriously varied the gifts of the Spirit are. Point to Paul's imagery of the human body, and remind your students that the body of Christ also is composed of many, many parts or gifts, each indispensable. Ask class members to mention some of the gifts that are at work in your own church. Are any of those gifts taken for granted or ignored? Do we esteem those who clean the kitchen and bathrooms, who take care of toddlers in the nursery, or who pray from a nursing home room?

2. CHARISMA OF BELIEVERS. Paul's word for "gift" in the Greek New Testament is *charisma*. He writes that every believer is given some *charisma*, or gift of the Spirit. Being "charismatic," then, does not strictly refer to speaking in tongues, according to I Corinthians 12, but it means realizing that you and every other Christian has been uniquely endowed with some spiritual gift. Each person's *charisma* is different; each is needed. No believer has a monopoly on spiritual gifts. And there is no clearcut list of gradations of importance of the Spirit's gifts to church members.

Devote time to asking students if they have any "clues" about what particular gifts can be found in their group.

3. COMMON GOOD OF GIFTS. The purpose of the *charisma* bestowed on each Christian is to share it with others in Christ's community. In fact, unless the spiritual gift is used for the "common good" in the church, it fails to carry out its intended purpose. How may the gifts your class has identified in each class member be better accepted and used in your church?

4. CONNECTEDNESS OF THE BODY. Paul stressed that the parts of the human body are interconnected and interdependent, and likewise that Christians belong to one another and are joined together by Christ. The analogy can be carried further. Just as a hand, for example, is useless if severed from the body, so each of us is useless to the Lord if not actively joined to the body of Christ, the church. Each is needed. The body of Christ is weakened or crippled whenever any church member cuts himself or herself off from the fellowship.

TOPIC FOR ADULTS
BUILDING UP THE BODY

It's Me That Hurts! Many years ago, I injured my right shoulder while playing football. It was my own stupidity and vanity in trying to be a sports hero that caused the painful series of shoulder separations. Surgery was finally required. That was over thirty-five years ago. Although the shoulder has never dislocated since that time, it is stiff and sore, arthritic and weak. That right shoulder lacks mobility, and often causes me inconvenience. But it's not merely the socket or the ligaments or the tendons or muscles that hurt. It's ME that hurts! And I cannot say to that shoulder, "I do not need you," and have it cut off, because that shoulder is still indispensable to me. In spite of its weakness, an arm, a hand, four fingers, and a thumb depend on that shoulder. Moreover, countless activities my body must carry out, from opening a door while carrying a load of firewood to shifting gears in my car, make that shoulder a very important part of me. I need that shoulder. It's part of ME.

So it is with each of us who are a vital part of Christ's body, the church. We may never say, "I don't need you" to any member. And when one member hurts, it's Christ's body—all of us—who also hurt. We all belong to each other.

Sacrificial Marathoner. At a marathon race for older men in California, in the spring of 1992, two friends, Tom and Ed, entered as contestants. At ten miles, however, Ed "hit the wall," as runners say. He felt he could not go on. Tom, who had an excellent chance of not only continuing the race but coming in as one of the winners, insisted on staying with Ed to encourage him to continue. Continually talking to Ed and coaching him to keep putting one foot in front of the other, Tom helped Ed to finish the race. Tom sacrificed his opportunity to come in first in the marathon just to bring encouragement to his friend.

That kind of concern for another is what Paul would have understood. In the church, we are called to remain with one another, even when it means sacrificing our own interests.

Lay Leadership Galvanizes a Congregation. The young minister had just graduated from seminary and had settled into his first church in Philadelphia. He was visited by a member of the congregation.

"Frankly, you are not a strong preacher," the man told the young minister, and added, "You will probably fail here."

The newly appointed minister felt defeated and stood crestfallen at the visitor's remark.

The man who came to call on the young minister, however, continued. "You should know that a small group of us have agreed to gather every Sunday morning to pray for you."

That small group grew. Eventually, more than one thousand people prayed each week for their new minister. The congregation flourished. And the minister grew. His name was J. Wilbur Chapman, who became one of the leading American preachers. Thankfully, some laypersons sensed their calling to build up the body of Christ together.

Questions for Students on the Next Lesson. 1. What was harming the worship at Corinth? 2. How may speaking in tongues become divisive? 3. What did Paul advise those wishing to speak in tongues to do? 4. How can worship preserve the elements of joy and spontaneity without becoming hopelessly disorderly? 5. What is the meaning of Paul's plea, "Let all things be done for edification (I Cor. 14:26)?

TOPIC FOR YOUTH
WE ARE IMPORTANT

Diversity Needed. Imagine that your local hospital is staffed with only brain surgeons. They are the finest surgeons in the nation and diagnose and operate with the latest technology and skills. They provide the best care possible. This makes your hospital the best institution for brain care because of the skilled and gifted professionals on the staff.

However, your older brother is complaining of a pain in his stomach. Your parents suspect appendicitis. They call the receptionist and are told the hospital has no internist. Meanwhile, your younger sister has fallen out of her crib. It appears as if she might have broken her arm. However, you are told at the emergency room that the hospital has no orthopedic surgeon to set the broken arm. Several years ago your mother had a kidney stone and now she's experiencing pain in her lower back. However, your hospital has no urologist to see her.

As important as brain surgeons are, a hospital needs a staff with a variety of gifted doctors. The human body has many parts that need attention. No one individual skill can meet the healing needs of the entire body.

The same diversity is needed in the church. Paul reminded the Corinthians and us that each person has a gift given by the Holy Spirit to use for the common good.

A True Family. There is quite a story behind the song "The Family of God" written by Bill and Gloria Gaither.

Ron and Darlene Garner and their three children attended the same Indiana church as the Gaithers. Ron, a mechanic at a local garage, had taken off work the Thursday before Good Friday so he could take his daughter for medical tests prior to her heart surgery. In order to make up for this time off and to earn some extra money to help pay for the upcoming hospital and doctor bills, Ron decided to go into work the Saturday after Good Friday. Ron was alone when the combustible materials with which he was working exploded. He managed to escape just before the building blew apart and turned into a raging inferno. However, he was severely burned over much of his body.

At the emergency room in Muncie, the news was hardly encouraging. Although alive, Ron was not expected to live through the night. Within minutes, a phone chain alerted members of his church family. Little groups began to come to church to pray for Ron. Other groups met in members' homes. People prayed over their phones, and some people prayed alone.

Saturday night came. The doctors were still pessimistic. They did not know how Ron was holding on to life. He had lived eight hours, though, and if he made it through the night there was a possibility that he might live. The church kept praying. Families prayed. Old people, young people, couples, teens, and children all prayed. The church remained open all night as more and more people came to pray together as a family for Ron.

The first rays of sun came through the window on Easter morning. The sanctuary was filled. However, there was no Easter finery. No new hats or new clothes were being worn. The congregation was red-eyed and weary. There was an intense feeling that a larger family of Christ's people was sharing the pain, hurt, and worry of some of its members.

Twenty minutes into the worship service, the pastor entered the church. He had been with the Garner family at the hospital throughout the long ordeal. He announced that Ron was out of danger and would recover. The doctors were going to begin treatment.

The church celebrated Easter like it had never celebrated Easter before. Tears of joy and praise mixed with their songs and prayers. The church family also pledged its help by assisting with the many hospital trips, by giving pints of blood for Ron's transfusions, by providing food for a tired family and money for hospital bills. The members promised to support the Garners through the months ahead that would involve skin grafting, rehabilitation, and months of healing.

Bill and Gloria Gaither were overwhelmed by what had happened. The sense of community was so great that one evening while Gloria was getting dinner ready, Bill sat down at the piano and began to play and sing. The song "The Family of God" almost wrote itself.

Ron went on to become a basketball coach, and his daughter, Diane, had her heart surgery. However, the family was sustained through it all by the church, the family of God.

Paul would certainly understand this story. After all, church members are to be sensitive to other members' pain and suffering. "If one member suffers, all suffer together" (12:26).

Questions for Students on the Next Lesson. 1. What happened at worship in Corinth? Why was this bad? 2. What is "speaking in tongues"? What did Paul have to say about this? Is it around today? 3. What is the purpose of worship? 4. Should worship always have a set format? Where does the Spirit's spontaneity enter? 5. How would you rate your worship service?

LESSON 6—APRIL 9

GROWING THROUGH WORSHIP

Background Scripture: I Corinthians 14:1-33a
Devotional Reading: Psalm 95:1-7

KING JAMES VERSION

I CORINTHIANS 14:20 Brethren, be not children in understanding: howbeit in malice be ye children, but in understanding be men.

21 In the law it is written, With men of other tongues and other lips will I speak unto this people; and yet for all that will they not hear me, saith the Lord.

22 Wherefore tongues are for a sign, not to them that believe, but to them that believe not: but prophesying serveth not for them that believe not, but for them which believe.

23 If therefore the whole church be come together into one place, and all speak with tongues, and there come in those that are unlearned, or unbelievers, will they not say that ye are mad?

24 But if all prophesy, and there come in one that believeth not, or one unlearned, he is convinced of all, he is judged of all:

25 And thus are the secrets of his heart made manifest; and so falling down on his face, he will worship God, and report that God is in you of a truth.

26 How is it then, brethren? when ye come together, every one of you hath a psalm, hath a doctrine, hath a tongue, hath a revelation, hath an interpretation. Let all things be done unto edifying.

27 If any man speak in an unknown tongue, let it be by two, or at the most by three, and that by course; and let one interpret.

28 But if there be no interpreter, let him keep silence in the church; and let him speak to himself, and to God.

29 Let the prophets speak two or three, and let the other judge.

30 If any thing be revealed to another that sitteth by, let the first hold his peace.

31 For ye may all prophesy one by one, that all may learn, and all may be comforted.

32 And the spirits of the prophets are subject to the prophets.

33 For God is not the author of confusion, but of peace, as in all churches of the saints.

REVISED STANDARD VERSION

I CORINTHIANS 14:20 Brethren, do not be children in your thinking; be babes in evil, but in thinking be mature. 21 In the law it is written, "By men of strange tongues and by the lips of foreigners will I speak to this people, and even then they will not listen to me, says the Lord." 22 Thus, tongues are a sign not for believers but for unbelievers, while prophecy is not for unbelievers but for believers. 23 If, therefore, the whole church assembles and all speak in tongues, and outsiders or unbelievers enter, will they not say that you are mad? 24 But if all prophesy, and an unbeliever or outsider enters, he is convicted by all, he is called to account by all, 25 the secrets of his heart are disclosed; and so, falling on his face, he will worship God and declare that God is really among you.

26 What then, brethren? When you come together, each one has a hymn, a lesson, a revelation, a tongue, or an interpretation. Let all things be done for edification. 27 If any speak in a tongue, let there be only two or at most three, and each in turn; and let one interpret. 28 But if there is no one to interpret, let each of them keep silence in church and speak to himself and to God. 29 Let two or three prophets speak, and let the others weigh what is said. 30 If a revelation is made to another sitting by, let the first be silent. 31 For you can all prophesy one by one, so that all may learn and all be encouraged; 32 and the spirits of prophets are subject to prophets. 33 For God is not a God of confusion but of peace.

KEY VERSE: When you come together, each one has a hymn, a lesson, a revelation, a tongue, or an interpretation. Let all things be done for edification. I Corinthians 14:26.

HOME DAILY BIBLE READINGS

BACKGROUND

An ancient version of the charismatic movement existed in the Corinthian church. Unfortunately, those who spoke in tongues upset the congregation. Evidently, those with the gift of *glossolalia*, or speaking in tongues, began to act as if their gift was the only spiritual gift that mattered and that speaking in tongues was the mark of a genuine Christian believer. These people made those who did not speak in tongues feel like Grade-B church members.

To make matters worse, the speakers in tongues were disrupting the worship services. Convinced that they were inspired by the Holy Spirit, they would break into their ecstatic outbursts without any regard for what others were saying or doing. Sometimes worship degenerated into a bedlam of noise with several people babbling at once.

Preaching the Word, of course, was impossible in such a situation. All sense of being together as a community was destroyed, as a selfish insistence on individual expression took over.

Worse, however, was the impression given to visitors or newcomers. Others in Corinth who were perhaps interested in hearing more about the good news of Jesus Christ were shocked and disgusted when they came to a worship service. How could they ever learn anything about God's grace through Christ when all they heard was a burst of voices, speaking in words they couldn't understand?

Paul, who knew what it was like to experience moments of spiritual ecstasy, recognized that the gift of speaking in tongues was a legitimate *charisma*. But he also realized that those possessing that gift had responsibilities to the rest of the church, especially during worship services.

After discussing the gifts of the Spirit in I Corinthians 12, Paul pointed out that the greatest gift is love. He developed this idea in I Corinthians 13. Returning to the problem of the disruptions caused by those speaking in tongues in Chapter 14, Paul wrote that the charismatics, along with everyone else in the congregation, must work together through worship to help the church to grow.

NOTES ON THE PRINTED TEXT

Apparently some Corinthians possessed the gift of speaking in tongues. Because of this, they considered themselves better than the other Christians. Paul was concerned enough about this attitude to continue his discussion on speaking in tongues. *Brethren, do not be children in your thinking; be babes in evil, but in thinking be mature* (14:20). These believers were acting like children. They were emphasizing the wrong thing. Like children they were interested in the spectacular, but Paul urged them to be more discriminating and mature. If they were not, God would judge their evil.

In support, Paul quoted Isaiah (28:11, 12), claiming his reference came from the law. *In the law it is written, "By men of strange tongues and by the lips of foreigners will I speak to this people, and even then they will not listen to me, says the Lord"* (14:21). The prophet reminded his nation that God would execute judgment for the peoples' refusal to listen to His message. The nation would hear only the strange speech of its enemies that had conquered the land. These people would speak but not be understood. Their speech would be a sign of God's judgment.

Paul then directed his thoughts back to the Corinthian church. *Thus, tongues are a sign not for believers but for unbelievers, while prophecy is not for unbelievers but for believers* (14:22). Speaking in tongues without any interpretation was meant to point to, or symbolize, God's power and mysterious presence to any listening unbelievers. Prophecy was for the believers who listened to God's message. *If, therefore, the whole church assembles and all speak in tongues, and outsiders or unbelievers enter, will they not say that you are mad?* (14:23). Paul asked: If an unbeliever were to attend a worship service and everyone present was speaking in tongues, would he not think everyone was crazy? The sign that was meant for judgment would have no effect! However, the unbeliever who listened to a clearly explained teaching that addressed the various sins of the people would understand and experience God's claim on his life. Perhaps he would sense personal guilt, repent, and accept God's salvation. *But if all prophesy, and an unbeliever or outsider enters, he is convicted by all, he is called to account by all, the secrets of his heart are disclosed; and so, falling on his face, he will worship God and declare that God is really among you* (14:24, 25).

Worship within the Corinthian church was not formal nor orderly. Any member might speak. Paul's list mentioned songs or hymns and teaching. Curiously, prayer was apparently neglected. Paul was comfortable with this as long as all that was spoken served to strengthen the Christian community. *When you come together, each one has a hymn, a lesson, a revelation, a tongue, or an interpretation. Let all things be done for edification* (14:26).

Paul continued to write about speaking in tongues. *If any speak in a tongue, let there be only two or at most three, and each in turn; and let one interpret* (14:27). As a way of ordering worship, Paul suggested that only a few speak. There should always be an interpretation. Paul also recommended that if there was no one to interpret, then worship should be quiet and private. *But if there is no one to interpret, let each of them keep silence in church and speak to himself and to God* (14:28).

Let two or three prophets speak, and let the others weigh what is said (14:29). Paul instructed that only a few should preach. As each spoke, those attending could determine whether the preaching was true or untrue. If a believer received a divine insight during a presentation, the speaker should yield the floor to this individual so that all could hear the most current message. *If a revelation is made to another sitting by, let the first be silent* (14:30).

All worshipers should have the opportunity to share their insights, but the meeting should be orderly. Everyone could give and receive encouragement. *For you can all prophesy one by one, so that all may learn and all be encouraged* (14:31).

Paul explained his thoughts regarding order. *The spirits of prophets are subject to prophets* (14:32). A prophet had control over the prophetic spirit. The Spirit may give him an insight, but each must have the intelligence and courtesy to share that insight at an appropriate moment.

Paul could then conclude, reminding his church that God fostered peace, not confusion. *For God is not a God of confusion but of peace* (14:33).

SUGGESTIONS TO TEACHERS

Palm Sunday, commemorating the triumphal entry of Jesus into Jerusalem, is also a suitable occasion to discuss what it means to celebrate His kingship. Worship is the heart of a Christian community.

Start your lesson by finding out how important worship is to those in your class. Ask what church activities are central in their list of priorities. The youth group? The couples' club? The Sunday school? The bowling league? The choir? The Bible study groups? The women's association? The annual stewardship campaign? Special Lenten programs? Or is the weekly gathering of God's people, as His community at worship, the most necessary and vitalizing activity in your church? (If not, why not?)

The Scripture material from I Corinthians 14 provides helpful insights into the "why" and the "how" of worship.

1. CORPORATE. Paul's teaching, consistent with all Scripture, states that worship is always done in the context of God's community. Even when a person may be praying alone, he is actually praying as part of Christ's family. Worship is to be understood as congregational, much more than a practice of private piety. Therefore, a worshiper must always remember that coming together requires congregational participation, not just private ecstasy.

2. CONSTRUCTIVE. Uncontrolled speaking in tongues in the worship service, Paul stated, does not help strengthen the life of Christ's community when it becomes the main goal of some members. "Strive to excel in building up the church," he wisely advises (14:12). When the purpose of worship is to develop the vitality of the entire congregation and not a special few, God's work flourishes.

3. COMPREHENSIBLE. Worship in the Corinthian church was hopelessly unintelligible because of the babble of many in tongues. Outsiders heard only gibberish. Paul insisted that in the gathering of Christians the Gospel must be proclaimed clearly and intelligibly. Those who spoke must present their message in a way that others could understand it. Worship must enlighten people about God's good news. Does your worship meet this standard?

4. CARING. Paul, always the evangelist and missionary, burned with a zeal to reach those who did not know the Gospel. With his concern for outsiders, he pointed out to the Corinthians that the hopeless confusion in their worship services could hardly interest unbelievers in Jesus Christ. Worship in Christ's church must not confuse those who have not understood God's life-giving act through Christ.

5. COOPERATIVE. Finally, Paul admonished members of his "problem church" at Corinth to work together and not compete with one another, especially during worship. When worshipers are trying to compete with one another, whether by reading aloud, preaching, rendering a musical selection, or performing any other act of worship, they are breaking down the oneness of the family of Christ's people. There can be no prima donnas in the church, not in the choir loft, not even in the pulpit.

TOPIC FOR ADULTS
GROWING THROUGH WORSHIP

Purpose of Worship. A visitor was being shown the Greek Orthodox Church in San Francisco. He met the caretaker of the building, and, noting the absence of chairs or pews in the place of worship, asked the man why they didn't provide comfortable seating for their worshipers.

The old man looked the visitor in the eye and calmly replied, "In the presence of God, there are only two positions a person can assume. One is on his knees praying, 'Lord be merciful to me, a sinner.' The other is on his feet saying, 'Here am I, Lord; send me!' "

True worship happens when we become aware of God's grace through Jesus Christ, and when we receive God's marching orders through the Holy Spirit.

Each Sunday, we gather to receive the hope and healing that comes from knowing that God accepts us. And each Sunday, we remember that the risen Lord sends us into the world to continue His ministry.

Question about Healing. A sign hanging in a hospital in Orange County, California, reads:

     DO YOU WANT TO GET EVEN, OR
     DO YOU WANT TO GET WELL?

That same sign could well be posted in every church. Competing against each other, trying to get even, and putting down others makes for a sick person and a sick congregation. On the other hand, getting well and being healthy, both as a Christian person and a Christian church, means forsaking pride and envy and concentrating on using spiritual gifts to help the whole group of Christians grow in Christ.

Outdoing Others. Some people insist on trying to outdo others in silly ways. Mark Gottlieb of Tacoma, Washington, set a record for playing the violin under water, and a couple in Des Moines sat in tubs of vanilla pudding for 24 hours, 34 minutes, and 20 seconds. A plumber named Ronnie Farmer ate one hundred hot jalapeño peppers in fifteen minutes, beating the old record of 94 in 111 minutes. Lang Martin of North Carolina holds the record for balancing golf balls vertically (he stacked up six). Arden Chapman, at Northeast Louisiana University caught the grape in his mouth thrown from the farthest distance (259 feet). The Guinness Book of World Records shows that people are obsessed with beating others.

In Corinth, this competitive attitude pervaded the congregation's worship. Some thought they were better than others. They tried to outdo others. Worship became a confusing babble of competing voices. The only way Christians may legitimately try to outdo each other is in showing love.

Questions for Students on the Next Lesson. 1. Why were the women coming to the tomb? 2. Were the women or the apostles expecting the Resurrection? 3. Why did Paul have to write to the Corinthian church about the Resurrection? 4. What does the Resurrection mean to us in respect to our own deaths? 5. How has the news of Easter comforted you when you lost a loved one?

TOPIC FOR YOUTH
USING ONE'S GIFTS

Confusion or Confession? Eleven-year-old Duffy Strode, seven-year-old Pepper Strode, and six-year-old Matthew Strode were told by their father that they should preach in their classrooms at school. The problem was that their preaching was a series of long hellfire-and-damnation sermons filled with words like "adulterer" and "fornication." The youngsters' classes were repeatedly disrupted by their preaching. After giving many warnings, the school principal reluctantly suspended the three Strode children from the Marion, North Carolina, school in 1992.

This situation was similar to the situation in Corinth in Paul's day when a group of speakers disrupted worship. In the case of both the Strode children and the Corinthian preachers, their actions led to confusion instead of exalting Christ.

Sharing His Gifts. Christians in Africa like to tell the story of an old African deacon who was respected for his devotion to the Lord. One morning, the elderly believer felt he had received a message during his prayers that he would see the Lord that day. The old gentleman got his house in order, then he sat and waited.

Before long, a young man came by, journeying to the city to visit his elderly mother. The old man gave him a cup of cool water. Then the old man sat and waited for the Lord. Before long, an old woman came by on her way to the market. Poor, barefooted, a heavy load upon her head, she was thankful when the old man gave her some shoes and invited her to rest in the shade of his tree before going on. Then the old man sat and waited for the Lord.

Soon a young girl ran by, anxious to get into the city to find a doctor for her dying child. The old man said, "Take my horse, for I don't use him much anymore." Then the old man sat and waited for the Lord. But the evening came, and the Lord never appeared. The old man was discouraged and disgusted with himself that he had been taken in by such nonsense. He said to God, "You said you would come by here today, but you never did. Why not?" God asked the old man what he had done that day. "I gave a cup of cool water to a young man. I gave my shoes to an old woman. I gave my horse to a young woman." "Indeed," God said, "on this day, you saw the Lord, for you gave of yourself to others."

Let us strive to see our Lord in everyone we serve, that they, too, might see the face of God in us.

Gift or Gibberish? Friends in another church invited Mike, a high school senior in a Kansas town, to attend a gathering of charismatic Christians held at Arrowhead Stadium in Kansas City a couple of years ago. Mike had never heard of "charismatics" but often attended a Sunday school class and worship services in his home congregation. He and his friends were among the forty-five thousand persons attending the gathering. Mike was uncertain how to respond when his friends shouted "Glory to God!" and "Jesus is Lord!" He enjoyed the music, and found himself swaying to the rhythm with the others. He noticed his friends raised their arms during the prayers.

During the "Holy Ghost Breaks," Mike and the others rose to stretch. Later, the stadium scoreboard flashed "JESUS IS LORD," and Mike heard people around him mumbling in ways he couldn't understand. To Mike, it was gibberish. "They're speaking in tongues," one of his friends whispered excitedly to Mike. Mike liked the singing and felt the warmth of the thousands of devoted people praising Jesus Christ. But he was not sure what to make of it. When his friends said they'd attend his church the following Sunday, Mike assumed they would wave their arms and break into "Praise the Lord!" during the service. He was embarrassed to have them come.

To his relief, his friends conducted themselves like everyone else in Mike's church. Afterward, Mike said to his friends from the charismatic group, "You know, I was a little afraid that you'd act like you did at Arrowhead Stadium. You know, with the . . . well, the chanting and the babbling and everything."

"Hey, look, Mike," one said. "It means a lot to us to praise the Lord that way. And sometimes, some of us even find ourselves speaking in tongues. But we know we shouldn't let our charismatic ways wreck worship for others. Besides, the most important gift of the Spirit, we're taught, is love."

Questions for Students on the Next Lesson. 1. What was the content of the first Christian sermon, and who preached it? 2. How did the disciples respond? 3. What are the implications if we deny Jesus' resurrection? 4. What does Christ's resurrection mean for you? Why? 5. Paul spoke of Christ's victory. What was that victory and how does it affect you, personally?

LESSON 7—APRIL 16

BEING A RESURRECTION PEOPLE

Background Scripture: Luke 24:1-11; I Corinthians 15
Devotional Reading: Philippians 2:1-11

KING JAMES VERSION

LUKE 24:1 Now upon the first day of the week, very early in the morning, they came unto the sepulchre, bringing the spices which they had prepared, and certain others with them.

2 And they found the stone rolled away from the sepulchre.

3 And they entered in, and found not the body of the Lord Jesus.

4 And it came to pass, as they were much perplexed thereabout, behold, two men stood by them in shining garments:

5 And as they were afraid, and bowed down their faces to the earth, they said unto them, Why seek ye the living among the dead?

6 He is not here, but is risen: remember how he spake unto you when he was yet in Galilee,

7 Saying, The Son of man must be delivered into the hands of sinful men, and be crucified, and the third day rise again.

8 And they remembered his words,

9 And returned from the sepulchre, and told all these things unto the eleven, and to all the rest.

10 It was Mary Magdalene, and Joanna, and Mary the mother of James, and other women that were with them, which told these things unto the apostles.

11 And their words seemed to them as idle tales, and they believed them not.

I CORINTHIANS 15:12 Now if Christ be preached that he rose from the dead, how say some among you that there is no resurrection of the dead?

13 But if there be no resurrection of the dead, then is Christ not risen:

14 And if Christ be not risen, then is our preaching vain, and your faith is also vain.

15 Yea, and we are found false witnesses of God; because we have testified of God that he raised up Christ: whom he raised not up, if so be that the dead rise not.

16 For if the dead rise not, then is not Christ raised:

17 And if Christ be not raised, your faith is vain; ye are yet in your sins. . . .

56 The sting of death is sin; and the strength of sin is the law.

REVISED STANDARD VERSION

LUKE 24:1 But on the first day of the week, at early dawn, they went to the tomb, taking the spices which they had prepared. 2 And they found the stone rolled away from the tomb, 3 but when they went in they did not find the body. 4 While they were perplexed about this, behold, two men stood by them in dazzling apparel; 5 and as they were frightened and bowed their faces to the ground, the men said to them, "Why do you seek the living among the dead? 6 Remember how he told you, while he was still in Galilee, 7 that the Son of man must be delivered into the hands of sinful men, and be crucified, and on the third day rise." 8 And they remembered his words, 9 and returning from the tomb they told all this to the eleven and to all the rest. 10 Now it was Mary Magdalene and Joanna and Mary the mother of James and the other women with them who told this to the apostles; 11 but these words seemed to them an idle tale, and they did not believe them.

I CORINTHIANS 15:12 Now if Christ is preached as raised from the dead, how can some of you say that there is no resurrection of the dead? 13 But if there is no resurrection of the dead, then Christ has not been raised; 14 if Christ has not been raised, then our preaching is in vain and your faith is in vain. 15 We are even found to be misrepresenting God, because we testified of God that he raised Christ, whom he did not raise if it is true that the dead are not raised. 16 For if the dead are not raised, then Christ has not been raised. 17 If Christ has not been raised, your faith is futile and you are still in your sins. . . .

56 The sting of death is sin, and the power of sin is the law. 57 But thanks be to God, who gives us the victory through our Lord Jesus Christ.

58 Therefore, my beloved brethren, be steadfast, immovable, always abounding in the work of the Lord, knowing that in the Lord your labor is not in vain.

57 But thanks be to God, which giveth us the victory through our Lord Jesus Christ.

58 Therefore, my beloved brethren, be ye stedfast, unmoveable, always abounding in the work of the Lord, forasmuch as ye know that your labour is not in vain in the Lord.

KEY VERSE: Be steadfast, immovable, always abounding in the work of the Lord, knowing that in the Lord your labor is not in vain. I Corinthians 15:58.

HOME DAILY BIBLE READINGS

Apr.	10	M.	Luke 24:1-11	*The First Easter*
Apr.	11	T.	I Corinthians 15:1-11	*Paul's Witness to the Resurrection*
Apr.	12	W.	I Corinthians 15:12-19	*Faith Is Futile without the Resurrection*
Apr.	13	T.	I Corinthians 15:20-28	*We Are Made Alive in Christ*
Apr.	14	F.	I Corinthians 15:35-44	*Resurrection of the Imperishable Body*
Apr.	15	S.	I Corinthians 15:45-50	*A Spiritual Inheritance*
Apr.	16	S.	I Corinthians 15:51-58	*Victory through the Risen Christ*

BACKGROUND

If Jesus Christ had not risen from the tomb, there would be no Christian church. The Resurrection is the central fact of the Christian experience. Upon the news that Jesus Christ lives rests everything else in Christian teaching. Take away the Resurrection, and you take away everything relating to Christianity, especially hope for the future.

Every New Testament writer realized the centrality of the Resurrection. The Gospel writers recorded their accounts of Jesus' life and teachings in the light of His death on the cross and His being raised from the dead. The news of anyone being raised to life after dying on a cross was as unbelievable to first-century hearers as it is to modern hearers. Therefore, Luke and Paul, like the other authors of New Testament writings, stressed the reports of Jesus' appearances after the crucifixion.

Luke's account of the pair of dejected followers tramping homeward after the terrible event of Jesus' death on the cross describes the reactions of two men who were not expecting ever to encounter Jesus alive. The story of Jesus presenting Himself to them as they trudged toward Emmaus, and their recognizing Him as He broke bread with them, illustrates how supremely important the Resurrection was to the early church. No resurrection of Jesus? Then no community transformed by the Good News and committed to continuing Christ's ministry.

Paul had to contend with doubters and deniers of the Resurrection among the church members in Corinth. The Corinthian Christians had backgrounds in the various cults and religions of Greece. Greek thought was steeped in the idea that humans had souls that were released from their bodies at death. If Corinthians thought much about the future life, they were inclined to think in terms of a person's soul leaving his or her body. So the idea of resurrection was especially unbelievable to the Greek mind. At Corinth, some within the church were scoffing at the report of Jesus' resurrection, dismissing it as unbelievable and unimportant.

Paul realized that the teachings of these doubters would quickly undercut the hope of believers in Corinth and ultimately destroy the congregation. His magnificent words in I Corinthians 15 called that church to remember that the Gospel hinges on the report that Jesus was raised alive and lives.

NOTES ON THE PRINTED TEXT

On the first day of the week, at early dawn, they went to the tomb, taking the spices which they had prepared (Luke 24:1). On Sunday, at the breaking of dawn, Mary Magdalene, Joanna, Mary the mother of James, and some other women went to the tomb. The women carried with them scented oils, perfumes, and spices. Likely the spices included frankincense, myrrh, aromatic gum resins, and aloes, which would be placed within the linen shroud. This was a final act of love that the women planned to perform for Jesus. Certainly none of the women expected what they discovered.

They found the stone rolled away from the tomb (24:2). Jesus' corpse had been laid on a stone shelf within a stone-hewn tomb. A large, heavy circular stone should have blocked the tomb's entrance. However, the stone had been rolled back and the tomb's entrance was exposed. When the women entered the tomb, they discovered that Jesus' body was missing. The women were shaken and confused. *They were perplexed* (24:4).

Why do you seek the living among the dead? (24:5). Two men dressed in white robes startled the women. Their shining appearances immediately led the women to understand that they were in the presence of God's messengers. The women immediately bowed their faces to the ground out of a mixture of fear and respect and also, perhaps, to shield their eyes from the brightness. The two men were surprised that the women were there. They told the women that Jesus was risen as He had promised while the women had been together in Galilee. *Remember how he told you, while he was still in Galilee, that the Son of man must be delivered into the hands of sinful men, and be crucified, and on the third day rise* (24:6, 7).

The women recalled Jesus' words. Together they hurried to Jerusalem to tell the eleven disciples that Jesus was risen. The disciples were skeptical; this news of a resurrection must have seemed like utter nonsense. *These words seemed to them an idle tale* (24:11). The disciples believed the women's announcement to be idle babbling or wishful gossip. Together they refused to believe the report.

Of course, the resurrection of Jesus became the Gospel story. Paul took that story of Christ's resurrection and wrote of its implications for the Corinthians. *Now if Christ is preached as raised from the dead, how can some of you say that there is no resurrection of the dead?* (I Cor. 15:12). Although Paul and the other evangelists preached the resurrected Christ, there were those who denied that the dead could rise. To deny the resurrection of the dead was to deny that Christ Himself had been raised. *But if there is no resurrection of the dead, then Christ has not been raised* (15:13). Paul then stated that if Christ was not raised, then all preaching and faith were worthless. *If Christ has not been raised, then our preaching is in vain and your faith is in vain* (15:14).

Paul also stated that if Christ had not been raised from the dead, then the apostles were liars. They had spread lies and false testimony against God. *We are even found to be misrepresenting God, because we testified of God that he raised Christ, whom he did not raise if it is true that the dead are not raised* (15:15).

If the Christian message was a lie and the dead were not raised, then Christ had not been raised. This was the next logical conclusion. *For if the dead are not raised, then Christ has not been raised* (15:16). The ultimate conclusion, then, was that faith is foolish. Faith should be abandoned because it could not deal with sin and death. No one would experience God's salvation. *If Christ has not been raised, your faith is futile and you are still in your sins* (15:17).

Paul digressed and explained the Resurrection and the resurrection body. Later, he returned to his previous thought. Having announced that death had no victory, he wrote, *The sting of death is sin, and the power of sin is the law* (15:56). Death's real sting and power were founded on sin and the law. Sin meant failing to fulfill God's purpose or refusing to lead the life He called the believer to live. This created an estrangement from God and led to guilt. Without this, death had no sting. Sin's power rested on the law, which made the individual aware of God and His demands. The law led to guilt because it convicted persons of falling short of God's perfection.

Victory over sin, guilt, and the law came through Christ. Having received forgiveness, believers need fear death no longer. *But thanks be to God, who gives us the victory through our Lord Jesus Christ* (15:57).

Paul concluded by writing that the Resurrection provided encouragement and hope to believers as they did the work of the Lord. Because of the Resurrection, life now and yet to come had meaning. *Therefore, my beloved brethren, be steadfast, immovable, always abounding in the work of the Lord, knowing that in the Lord your labor is not in vain* (15:58).

SUGGESTIONS TO TEACHERS

Today is the high point of the Christian year—Easter, the celebration of the Resurrection. Your church is filled today, the choirs are presenting special music, and the sanctuary is beautifully decorated. The worship service features the response "Christ the Lord is risen! He is risen indeed!" But what about next Sunday?

Actually, every worship on every Sunday is a celebration of the Resurrection. One of the earliest names believers gave to themselves was "the Resurrection people." They gathered weekly to celebrate the glad news that God had raised up Christ from death.

Today's lesson can help your students deepen their sense of belonging in the Resurrection community. Encourage them to live each day in fellowship with the risen Lord as resurrected persons themselves.

1. RESURRECTION TIDINGS. Read carefully both the Luke 24 report

and the I Corinthians 15 account. Note how central to the faith the Resurrection is. Note also what good news the Resurrection was to the two disciples on their way to Emmaus and to the apostle Paul. Emphasize that the Easter message is more than a secondhand report; the Resurrection is meant to be a firsthand experience.

2. RELIABLE TESTIMONY. Focus on the details of Luke 24, asking group members to ponder the eyewitness report of the two followers heading to Emmaus. Remind students that these two were not expecting to see Jesus ever again. The Resurrection was not a hoax or hallucination. The testimony of these folks—and others—must be taken seriously. The only "explanation" for the early Christians' astonishingly heroic lives is that they had truly met the risen Christ.

3. RADIANT TRIUMPH. Paul was concerned about those who denied the Resurrection and, therefore, denied any hope after death. Paul's words ring out like a trumpet blast, calling Christians to get up and live with joy and hope because Christ lives. Even death will not thwart God's power or love. The God who raised up Christ will also overcome our deaths. In your lesson, make the distinction between the Greek philosophers' idea of "immortality of the soul" and the Bible's doctrine of the resurrection. Our hope rests on God's promise of resurrection, not in the continuation of an immortal soul.

4. REPRESENTATIVE TRAITS. Discuss the characteristics of the Christlike life as suggested by I Corinthians 15. We are the Resurrection people, having died to pure self-interest and having been raised with Christ to become new persons. Instead of despair, we have hope. Instead of guilt, we know forgiveness. In place of the finality of death, we live knowing that nothing, not even the grave, can separate us from God's love.

TOPIC FOR ADULTS
BECOMING A RESURRECTION PEOPLE

Cornerstone of Life. Our Scripture today lays out the argument in blunt terms: If you deny the resurrection of Jesus Christ, you end with a Jesus who is a minor footnote in history. No Resurrection, no faith to live by. No Resurrection, no hope to die with.

Without the Resurrection, there would be no New Testament. We would have no memory of Jesus' teachings, such as the Lord's Prayer or the Sermon on the Mount.

If there had been no Resurrection, there would not be a church. If His followers had not had an encounter with the risen Lord, it is likely there would have been no dynamic, faith-filled community of joyful Christians. No Resurrection: no church!

If the Resurrection had not occurred, history would have taken a radically different course. Western civilization as we know it would never have developed: no Chartres Cathedral, no rose window in Notre Dame; no "B-Minor Mass" by Bach or "Messiah" by Handel; no masterpieces in marble, such as the Pieta [pee-ay-TAH], or in frescoes, such as the ceiling of the Sistine chapel.

Historians point out that there would have been no voyage by Columbus, no group of Pilgrims in Plymouth; no colony in Massachusetts.

No Resurrection: no Harvard or Yale or Princeton or many other schools, since these were all originally established to train Christian ministers. There would be no community of believers, no Christian fellowship, no congregation where you live. The resurrection of Jesus Christ is the very cornerstone of your life.

Putting On Christ. Although Christians are a tiny minority in Japan, barely 2 percent of the population, their influence far outweighs their numbers. The Bible is a best-seller in Japan, and Japanese Christian authors are winning prizes for their Christian writings. Novelist Shusaku Endo reports that for him to become a Christian was like putting on an ill-fitting foreign set of clothes for the first time. Endo states that he felt very uncomfortable in this new suit.

Endo, whose novels have won literary acclaim in Japan, goes on to say that if he were not wearing that strange suit he would be even more uncomfortable. After all, he announces, he does not want to be left spiritually naked, and following the resurrected Lord is the best-fitting faith he can find. Endo, in effect, has "put on Christ." Like us, he is part of the Resurrection community, the church.

Mini-Easters Weekly. One of my favorite cartoons portrays a portly woman confronting a minister at the door of the church after worship. She complains, "Why is it every time I come to church you're always singing that same hymn, 'Christ the Lord Is Risen Today'?"

Obviously, that woman only showed up on Easter. But she ought to be hearing that hymn more often than on Easter Sunday. The reason is that every Sunday is meant to be celebrated as a mini-Easter. In fact, occasionally I have deliberately used "Christ the Lord Is Risen Today" for worship services other than Easter to emphasize that the resurrection of Christ should be central every week. Easter is more than a date on the calendar.

The early Christians intended every Sunday to be a celebration of the resurrection of Jesus Christ. It was meant to be commemorated weekly. And why Sunday? Because God raised up Jesus Christ on the first day of the week, that day we call Sunday. We don't need to wait until April 16th; we can wish each other "Happy Easter" every Sunday.

Questions for Students on the Next Lesson. 1. Why was the issue of eating food offered to idols such a divisive issue in Corinth? 2. What did Paul say to those who claimed liberty to eat what they wanted? 3. How do you define Christian freedom? 4. Why is our example before others so important?

TOPIC FOR YOUTH
WHAT COMES NEXT?

Pay Respects. On January 19, 1993, Jeff Jerome and nine other men spent the night in the cemetery of Westminster Church in Baltimore. Jerome was the curator of the city's Edgar Allen Poe House and Museum. On this same day each year, in a tradition that dated back to 1949, a mystery man visited the gravesite of Edgar Allen Poe, knelt briefly, and left three red roses and a bottle of cognac at the foot of the grave. He always came before 6 a.m. So Jerome and the others patiently waited. Just when they were convinced that there would be no visit this year, a man dressed in a black hat and a long dark coat came through the gate. The man knelt, left the gifts, and departed.

Over nineteen hundred years ago, others prepared to go to a grave and offer their gifts to a storyteller and author. Like this mystery man, these visitors planned to slip into the cemetery in the early morning, make their offering, and silently depart.

However, the visitors to the Jerusalem grave were surprised. The great Author of Life was alive! For the women, Easter became the experience of meeting the risen Lord. Easter brought the understanding that there was life after death.

For us, Easter is not a quick visit to the grave to pay our respects. Rather it is the experience of God introducing Himself to us through His risen Son.

Resurrection of the Soul. Eunice Azule was the young wife of a Puma Indian chief's son. Her husband's father, the chief, had sent his son on a mission against the Apache Indians. In that mission, Eunice's husband was killed. On learning of his death, Eunice vowed revenge; she would kill an Apache warrior with her own hands. Soon thereafter, she was granted special permission to lead a war party into the Arizona mountain country of the Apaches.

The Pumas were successful in capturing a large number of Apache warriors and their families. The children were spared. However, Eunice ordered the slaughter of the warriors and all the women except one warrior. With her own club, she killed the remaining Apache warrior in revenge for the death of her husband.

Many years later, Eunice heard the Gospel and became a Christian. She was overwhelmed by guilt for how hateful and unjust she had been in murdering the Apaches, even if they had been her enemies. When Eunice committed her life to Christ, she learned that her old soul had died and a new soul had been raised up. She lived under a new law.

Easter is the announcement that a new self has sprung from death. The chains of evil and sin are broken, bringing about a new beginning.

Disappointed, Depressed, and Hopeless. Teen suicide has grown into one of America's greatest and most repeated tragedies. Each year, over six thousand of America's young people commit suicide. During the same period, almost half a million attempt suicide.

A scientific survey has revealed that even thinking about suicide has become frighteningly common. Experts are quick to point out that most of these suicidal teens have lives that are not typical. The kids are often disappointed, depressed, and believe they have no hope. They see no future and see little value in their lives. Life means only a continuation of disappointment.

However, the resurrection of Jesus assures us that we need not be disappointed, depressed, or hopeless. The best is yet to come!

Questions for Students on the Next Lesson. 1. Why was eating meat a problem for some Corinthians? 2. According to Paul, was it wrong to eat meat dedicated to idols? 3. What was Paul's response to those who supported Christian liberty? 4. How is it a sin against Christ if we wound a believer's conscience? 5. Have you ever had to sacrifice your rights for another's faith? If so, when?

LESSON 8—APRIL 23

EXERCISING LIBERTY WISELY

Background Scripture: I Corinthians 8
Devotional Reading: Romans 15:1-13

KING JAMES VERSION

I CORINTHIANS 8:1 Now as touching things offered unto idols, we know that we all have knowledge. Knowledge puffeth up, but charity edifieth.

2 And if any man think that he knoweth any thing, he knoweth nothing yet as he ought to know.

3 But if any man love God, the same is known of him.

4 As concerning therefore the eating of those things that are offered in sacrifice unto idols, we know that an idol is nothing in the world, and that there is none other God but one.

5 For though there be that are called gods, whether in heaven or in earth, (as there be gods many, and lords many,)

6 But to us there is but one God, the Father, of whom are all things, and we in him; and one Lord Jesus Christ, by whom are all things, and we by him.

7 Howbeit there is not in every man that knowledge: for some with conscience of the idol unto this hour eat it as a thing offered unto an idol; and their conscience being weak is defiled.

8 But meat commendeth us not to God: for neither, if we eat, are we the better; neither, if we eat not, are we the worse.

9 But take heed lest by any means this liberty of your's become a stumblingblock to them that are weak.

10 For if any man see thee which hast knowledge sit at meat in the idol's temple, shall not the conscience of him which is weak be emboldened to eat those things which are offered to idols;

11 And through thy knowledge shall the weak brother perish, for whom Christ died?

12 But when ye sin so against the brethren, and wound their weak conscience, ye sin against Christ.

13 Wherefore, if meat make my brother to offend, I will eat no flesh while the world standeth, lest I make my brother to offend.

REVISED STANDARD VERSION

I CORINTHIANS 8:1 Now concerning food offered to idols: we know that "all of us possess knowledge." "Knowledge" puffs up, but love builds up. 2 If any one imagines that he knows something, he does not yet know as he ought to know. 3 But if one loves God, one is known by him.

4 Hence, as to the eating of food offered to idols, we know that "an idol has no real existence," and that "there is no God but one." 5 For although there may be so-called gods in heaven or on earth—as indeed there are many "gods" and many "lords"—6 yet for us there is one God, the Father, from whom are all things and for whom we exist, and one Lord, Jesus Christ, through whom are all things and through whom we exist.

7 However, not all possess this knowledge. But some, through being hitherto accustomed to idols, eat food as really offered to an idol; and their conscience, being weak, is defiled. 8 Food will not commend us to God. We are no worse off if we do not eat, and no better off if we do. 9 Only take care lest this liberty of yours somehow become a stumbling block to the weak. 10 For if any one sees you, a man of knowledge, at table in an idol's temple, might he not be encouraged, if his conscience is weak, to eat food offered to idols? 11 And so by your knowledge this weak man is destroyed, the brother for whom Christ died. 12 Thus, sinning against your brethren and wounding their conscience when it is weak, you sin against Christ. 13 Therefore, if food is a cause of my brother's falling, I will never eat meat, lest I cause my brother to fall.

KEY VERSE: Only take care lest this liberty of yours somehow become a stumbling block to the weak. I Corinthians 8:9.

HOME DAILY BIBLE READINGS

Apr.	17	M.	Romans 14:1-9	*Avoid Disputes over Opinions*
Apr.	18	T.	Romans 14:10-18	*Refrain from Passing Judgment*
Apr.	19	W.	Romans 14:19-23	*Seek Peace and Mutual Edification*
Apr.	20	T.	Romans 15:1-6	*Bear with the Weak*
Apr.	21	F.	Romans 15:7-13	*Receive One Another in Christ*
Apr.	22	S.	I Corinthians 8:1-6	*Love,Nnot Knowledge, Aids Christian Growth*
Apr.	23	S.	I Corinthians 8:7-13	*Use One's Christian Liberty with Care*

BACKGROUND

Paul was the champion of Christian liberty. More than any other first-century thinker in the church, he realized that trust in God's grace through Jesus Christ freed a believer from trying to appease the Lord by keeping a lot of rules. His insistence on the sufficiency of grace alone for salvation often brought him into conflict with other early professed Christians. He emphasized liberty so much that he was suspected of advocating a "do what you please" morality. Tradition-minded Christians who came out of Judaism were incensed when Paul admitted the uncircumcised to church membership and ignored Old Testament dietary laws. Paul steadfastly maintained that a Christian is liberated from a religion of regulations.

In Corinth, however, some Christians carried the notion of Christian liberty too far, insisting that they were free to eat whatever they wanted without regard to the scruples of any other believer. This created a serious problem.

The meat for sale in the markets, as we have learned, usually came from pagan shrines. Many Christians had formerly been involved with the idol worship and ceremonies of these shrines. These new converts to the Christian faith were offended when fellow Christians flaunted their freedom by patronizing the shrines' meat markets. Some felt tempted to go back to their old pagan practices or decided that they could dabble in the idolatrous cults because of the meat-eating Christians.

The "liberty" group dismissed the complaints of those claiming to be offended. These church people proclaimed themselves not only liberated from rules but also filled with "knowledge." Lamentably, their "knowledge" made them conceited as they pointed out that meat from the pagan shrines carried no taint of idolatry; meat was simply meat.

Paul wrote, asking those with guilt-free consciences to remember the weaker brothers and sisters who were upset by the meat eating. Paul pleaded with the "knowledgeable" believers to have a concern for those whose consciences would not allow them to patronize the pagan meat markets. Liberty should not be a stumbling block for others.

"Knowing" is not enough. Caring is most important. Christians must exercise liberty as a means of building up the faith of others in the church. Every Christian has a responsibility to be an encouraging example to other Christians. In this case, Paul suggests, the strong in faith should abstain from meat out of concern for those whose faith is shaky.

NOTES ON THE PRINTED TEXT

Now concerning food offered to idols (8:1). The Corinthians lived in a culture dominated by the worship of pagan gods and goddesses. Their devotion to such gods even determined what and how they would eat. Meals were dedicated to a god by placing a portion of food on an altar. On various occasions, it was customary for the pagan worshipers to offer a sacrifice in the temple. At this time, the legs and entrails of an animal were burned as an offering, and the remaining meat would be sold in the meat market attached to the temple. Paul addressed this subject, because Christians had to decide whether or not to buy the meat that had been sacrificed to idols.

We know that "all of us possess knowledge" (8:1). Paul and many of his readers knew the Jewish prohibitions about eating meat that had been offered to idols. He and his readers also knew that their acceptance of Christ allowed them to eat any food with thankfulness. Yet those with such liberty looked down on other believers who felt guilty about eating meat offered to idols. Their arrogance "puffed them up" with pride and disrupted the unity in the church.

Paul offered an alternative way to relate to one another. *Love builds up* (8:1). Love and concern for others must temper knowledge and liberty. Human knowledge was limited and partial. Anyone confident enough to believe that his or her knowledge on this issue was infallible was not truly wise. *If any one imagines that he knows something, he does not yet know as he ought to know* (8:2). In addition, love should lead to action. Mere knowledge about God was not enough. Love of God was to be demonstrated in the way church members dealt with one another. *But if one loves God, one is known by him* (8:3).

Paul then applied knowledge and love to the question of eating food offered to idols. Paul stressed that *"an idol has no real existence,"* and that *"there is no God but one"* (8:4). A god or goddess was the creation of human artisans. Paul affirmed the one God's existence, referring to the *Shema* [sh-MAH], Israel's earliest confession of faith. *There may be so-called gods in heaven or on earth—as indeed there are many "gods" and many "lords"* (8:5). Paul acknowledged the worship of many false divinities considered lords by their devotees. However, Christians had only one God and one Lord, Jesus Christ. *Yet for us there is one God, the Father, from whom are all things and for whom we exist, and one Lord, Jesus Christ, through whom are all things and through whom we exist* (8:6). The Christian God was the Creator of the entire universe, the almighty Father. Jesus was God's revelation of Himself.

Paul directly applied his points to the food question. *Some, through being hitherto accustomed to idols, eat food as really offered to an idol; and their conscience, being weak, is defiled* (8:7). Some Christians still looked upon food dedicated to an idol as sacred in some way. They simply could not give up that notion. To them, it seemed wrong to eat the food. To Paul, these believers had a weak conscience. *Food will not commend us to God.*

We are no worse off if we do not eat, and no better off if we do (8:8). Eating or not eating certain foods did not affect a believer's standing with God. Nothing was gained or lost by eating or abstaining from food offered to idols.

Yet, while Christians had the freedom to eat food sacrificed to idols, they were to put the needs and sensitivities of other Christians ahead of their own freedom. *Only take care lest this liberty of yours somehow become a stumbling block to the weak* (8:9). Paul offered an example. *For if any one sees you, a man of knowledge, at table in an idol's temple, might he not be encouraged, if his conscience is weak, to eat food offered to idols? And so by your knowledge this weak man is destroyed* (8:10, 11). Paul pictured a strong Christian, who believed in the existence of the one true God, partaking of a meal in the temple of an idol. Since these temple restaurants featured the best cuts of meat found in the city, it was a common practice for some Christians to eat in them, too. Suppose another Christian, who truly believed that these meats should not be eaten, saw the first Christian eating in the temple. Perhaps the second Christian would conclude that the first believer trusted in the pagan idol and had converted back to his pagan worship practices.

Paul wrote that to wound a believer's conscience was to sin against Christ. *Thus, sinning against your brethren and wounding their conscience when it is weak, you sin against Christ* (8:12).

Paul concluded by writing to the Corinthians that he would never eat meat if, by eating meat, he would be causing a fellow believer to fall back into old ways. *Therefore, if food is a cause of my brother's falling, I will never eat meat, lest I cause my brother to fall* (8:13).

SUGGESTIONS TO TEACHERS

Some of us were raised in homes where "religion" was primarily a set of rules to keep. In my boyhood days, for instance, being a good Christian meant strictly observing the first day of the week as a day of rest, which meant no movies or sports on Sunday. As a youngster, I naively assumed that anyone caught in a ball park or theater on a Sunday, or anyone who took a sip of any fermented juice, was committing serious sin and probably would not be saved. Therefore, I childishly thought I was irresistibly good in God's eyes because I observed these rules. Later, of course, I learned otherwise. Faith in Jesus Christ liberates a believer from trying to save himself or herself by a rule book.

But being granted liberty as a Christian lays on its own burdens. I may be free from rules, but I am not free to ignore the feelings and the sensitivities of fellow church members. I must use my freedom wisely and lovingly. This is the point of today's lesson.

1. THE KNOWLEDGE THAT EDIFIES. As teacher, help your class members understand the distinction between two types of knowledge. One kind of knowing recognizes that rightness with God does not come from being "a good person" or keeping rules. But this kind of knowledge is not a license to do as one pleases. There is another kind of knowledge—knowing that each Christian is responsible for helping brothers and sisters grow in the faith. In this kind of knowledge, a person uses what he or she knows to

strengthen the faith community.

2. THE LOVE THAT EXCELS. Impress on your students that persons are more important than precepts. The truth of Christian liberty is a prized doctrine, but Christian love takes precedence. In the case of the Corinthians, those aware of their liberty were called to act in love toward the weaker church members.

3. THE FAITH THAT AFFIRMS. In I Corinthians 8:4-6 Paul discusses "gods" and the "one God, the Father, from whom are all things and for whom we exist" (vs. 6). Talk with your class about the gods in our culture. Discuss why these gods are allowed by some to become substitutes for the one true God.

4. THE BELIEVER WHO ABSTAINS. Ask the class to think of times when concern for others might take priority over one's own freedom. For example, some Christians believe they are free to drink alcohol but they deliberately abstain out of concern for those who have alcohol addictions or who might be offended for other reasons.

TOPIC FOR ADULTS
EXERCISING CHRISTIAN FREEDOM

Amish Auction. Occasionally, an auction will be held in Amish country in rural eastern Pennsylvania. The Amish auction is unique. Usually an improvised fence, fashioned from a long piece of rope, encloses all the items to be auctioned. Inside the roped-off area will be quilts, blankets, blanket chests, oak chairs and tables, pine hutches, walnut corner cupboards, sets of dishes, and other household articles. A small sign states that this is a private auction; only members of the Amish community are allowed to bid on the items inside the roped enclosure. All of the goods might change hands, therefore, but none will leave the community.

The Amish know that in an open auction, one of the quilts could bring $500 or more. But they are also aware that the freedom to get that price would probably deprive a young Amish couple of having warm bedding. Although aware that they have the freedom to make a handsome profit on their goods by selling to dealers, collectors, decorators, and bidders, these Amish folk remember their responsibility to their own community.

What's It Matter? A man was sitting in his boat with several fishing companions. He took out his knife, since nothing was happening, and began boring a hole under his seat. The others looked on in surprise, knowing that it was his boat. As the knife carved deeper, one of them yelled at the man to stop. The man merely glanced toward the others and remarked, "What's it matter? I am only making the hole under my seat."

Freedom also carries responsibility! Christians are all in the same boat together.

Escaping Responsibilities. A genuine beeper used by physicians and others who must respond to emergencies costs at least $100. A couple of years ago, some enterprising manufacturers began selling "fake beepers."

Instead of calling you away from an enjoyable activity, the fake beeper works the other way around. By pressing a button, you can summon yourself away from an activity you don't like. Suppose you face a responsibility you want to avoid or a person you find boring . . . you push the button.

Twenty-five seconds later, the beeper goes off, giving you an excellent excuse to escape whatever you may dislike at the moment. Such freedom may sound attractive to many, but in the Christian life our freedom comes packaged with our responsibility to others.

Questions for Students on the Next Lesson. 1. What does II Corinthians 1 say about the way God comforts people in their afflictions? 2. What did Paul say about the purpose of the sufferings he and Timothy were experiencing? 3. What has comforted you in your times of suffering and affliction? 4. Whose perseverance has given you hope and inspiration in suffering? 5. How does prayer for others help them in their times of trial?

TOPIC FOR YOUTH
CULTURAL BELIEFS

Where's the Beef? In 1993, McDonald's, home of the golden arches, was finally invited to India. This invitation culminated years of trying to obtain the required license. The firm planned to invest over twenty million dollars in the deal. However, it had to agree not to sell any hamburger products.

Beef is taboo to the Hindus who make up 83 percent of India's 875 million people. The cow is sacred to them. In addition, Muslims, who comprise 12 percent of the nation's population, do not eat pork.

How could McDonald's, a company that made its millions by selling the famous hamburger, respect the cultural and religious beliefs of these people? It made plans to market chicken burgers, lamb burgers, and lentil burgers.

If the corporate world can respect other people's beliefs, shouldn't Christians do the same within the church? Naturally, we will speak for the truth; but in the "gray areas" let's pledge ourselves to caring for one another's spiritual growth.

Long-reaching Consequences. Bahvin was from Pakistan. He came to an American seminary to learn and to grow in his faith so that he could return home to better serve the church in Pakistan.

He was an outgoing fellow who became a favorite among his classmates. They enjoyed taking him out in the evenings for pizza and beer; they liked giving him beer because he would get silly after a couple of drinks.

The seminary class graduated, and the American students all went on to serve their Lord in churches across the United States. But Bahvin never returned to Pakistan as he had planned, but stayed in the United States. He also did not go on to serve his Lord in the church. Bahvin had developed quite a drinking problem during his years at the seminary. He ended up panhandling on the streets of New York City, trying to get enough money to buy another drink.

The American seminary students had caused the weaker brother to stumble. If they had been more sensitive and responsible in dealing with Bahvin, the outcome might have been quite different.

Only One God. Sid Bream, first baseman for the Atlanta Braves, utilized every opportunity to introduce individuals to his Lord. While most major league players just signed their names on baseball cards, Sid added to his autograph a Scripture reference, such as Romans 5:8 (his favorite).

On one autographing occasion, a youngster grumbled that this Scripture reference detracted from the baseball card's value. He asked Sid to please leave it off. However, Sid explained that he was committed to sharing His faith with others. This was one way he could do it.

Perhaps this youngster was in danger of elevating baseball cards to an idol. Sid, like Paul, certainly understood that people could be enticed to worship many and varying gods. Christians, however, have only one God and one Lord, Jesus Christ. That commitment carries responsibility. Do you carry your responsibility with as much conviction as Sid Bream?

Questions for Students on the Next Lesson. 1. Why was God's comfort and mercy so important to the Corinthians? 2. How do Christians share in Christ's suffering? 3. Do you feel that you share in Christ's comfort, as Paul and Timothy did? 4. Why did Paul ask the Corinthians to pray for him? 5. How effective is faithful praying?

LESSON 9—APRIL 30

CARING FOR ONE ANOTHER

Background Scripture: II Corinthians 1:1-14
Devotional Reading: Galatians 6:1-10

KING JAMES VERSION

II CORINTHIANS 1:3 Blessed be God, even the Father of our Lord Jesus Christ, the Father of mercies, and the God of all comfort;

4 Who comforteth us in all our tribulation, that we may be able to comfort them which are in any trouble, by the comfort wherewith we ourselves are comforted of God.

5 For as the sufferings of Christ abound in us, so our consolation also aboundeth by Christ.

6 And whether we be afflicted, it is for your consolation and salvation, which is effectual in the enduring of the same sufferings which we also suffer: or whether we be comforted, it is for your consolation and salvation.

7 And our hope of you is stedfast, knowing, that as ye are partakers of the sufferings, so shall ye be also of the consolation.

8 For we would not, brethren, have you ignorant of our trouble which came to us in Asia, that we were pressed out of measure, above strength, insomuch that we despaired even of life:

9 But we had the sentence of death in ourselves, that we should not trust in ourselves, but in God which raiseth the dead:

10 Who delivered us from so great a death, and doth deliver: in whom we trust that he will yet deliver us;

11 Ye also helping together by prayer for us, that for the gift bestowed upon us by the means of many persons thanks may be given by many on our behalf.

12 For our rejoicing is this, the testimony of our conscience, that in simplicity and godly sincerity, not with fleshly wisdom, but by the grace of God, we have had our conversation in the world, and more abundantly to you-ward.

13 For we write none other things unto you, than what ye read or acknowledge; and I trust ye shall acknowledge even to the end;

14 As also ye have acknowledged us in part, that we are your rejoicing, even as ye also are our's in the day of the Lord Jesus.

REVISED STANDARD VERSION

II CORINTHIANS 1:3 Blessed be the God and Father of our Lord Jesus Christ, the Father of mercies and God of all comfort, 4 who comforts us in all our affliction, so that we may be able to comfort those who are in any affliction, with the comfort with which we ourselves are comforted by God. 5 For as we share abundantly in Christ's sufferings, so through Christ we share abundantly in comfort too. 6 If we are afflicted, it is for your comfort and salvation; and if we are comforted, it is for your comfort, which you experience when you patiently endure the same sufferings that we suffer. 7 Our hope for you is unshaken; for we know that as you share in our sufferings, you will also share in our comfort.

8 For we do not want you to be ignorant, brethren, of the affliction we experienced in Asia; for we were so utterly, unbearably crushed that we despaired of life itself. 9 Why, we felt that we had received the sentence of death; but that was to make us rely not on ourselves but on God who raises the dead; 10 he delivered us from so deadly a peril, and he will deliver us; on him we have set our hope that he will deliver us again. 11 You also must help us by prayer, so that many will give thanks on our behalf for the blessing granted us in answer to many prayers.

12 For our boast is this, the testimony of our conscience that we have behaved in the world, and still more toward you, with holiness and godly sincerity, not by earthly wisdom but by the grace of God. 13 For we write you nothing but what you can read and understand; I hope that you will understand fully, 14 as you have understood in part, that you can be proud of us as we can be of you, on the day of the Lord Jesus.

KEY VERSE: *Blessed be the God and Father of our Lord Jesus Christ . . . who comforts us in all our affliction, so that we may be able to comfort those who are in any affliction.* II Corinthians 1:3, 4a.

HOME DAILY BIBLE READINGS

Apr. 24	M.	II Corinthians 1:1-7	Sharing Both Suffering and Comfort
Apr. 25	T.	II Corinthians 1:8-14	A Request for Prayer
Apr. 26	W.	Romans 1:8-15	Thankfulness for Faithful Christians
Apr. 27	T.	Galatians 6:1-5	Give Support to One Another
Apr. 28	F.	Galatians 6:6-10	Persevere in Doing Good
Apr. 29	S.	Ephesians 4:25-32	Be Kind to One Another
Apr. 30	S.	Mark 2:1-5	Active Caring for a Friend

BACKGROUND

The Corinthian congregation proved to be Paul's main "problem church." Recent converts, fresh from pagan cults and immersed in the unsavory culture of a city renowned for vice and drunkenness, did not take readily to the ways of a Christian community.

In addition to trying to advise about the internal problems threatening to tear apart the young church in Corinth, Paul had faced a stormy relationship with many of the Corinthian church leaders and members. Some of the members challenged his spiritual authority and questioned his apostleship. Worse, he had to endure savage personal attacks on his character. Critics in Corinth spread false accusations against him. Although Paul must have been deeply hurt by the stinging charges, he continued to treat the Corinthians as fellow members of Christ's family. He was far from them, across the Aegean in Ephesus, but he persisted in building his relationship with them.

The portions of the New Testament we now know as I and II Corinthians are a part of the correspondence that Paul had with that troubled church. If you have read I Corinthians carefully, you would have noticed (in I Cor. 5:9) that Paul stated he had written a previous letter. We don't know what happened to that letter. In any case, our I Corinthians is probably not the earliest piece of correspondence from Paul to Corinth.

After this letter was sent, however, the situation deteriorated further between the Corinthians and Paul. Paul apparently made a quick trip back to Corinth from Ephesus to try to mend the relationship. From references in II Corinthians, we know that this visit was painful for Paul. The problems remained.

Apparently, Paul sent another letter. Paul wrote this letter in anguish and later regretted that he had caused the Corinthians to grieve because of his stern tone. Some scholars think that parts of this "stern" letter are found in II Corinthians 10—13. The stern letter had its intended result, however, because the Corinthians did indeed repent. The church in Corinth and Paul were reconciled. The power of Christ's love prevailed.

NOTES ON THE PRINTED TEXT

Blessed be the God and Father of our Lord Jesus Christ, the Father of mercies and God of all comfort (1:3). Most ancient letters included a prayer of thanksgiving. Paul used a Jewish form of prayer and adapted it to Christian use. Here he described God as merciful and comforting. This was particularly important since the Corinthians were suffering. (Perhaps they were being victimized during a riot, or had had their businesses and homes vandalized, or had been falsely accused in court.)

God *comforts us in all our affliction, so that we may be able to comfort those who are in any affliction, with the comfort with which we ourselves are comforted by God* (1:4). Paul affirmed that God provided comfort in the midst of suffering so that the comforted would be able to comfort others. Paul himself had received comfort from other Christians. Comfort was transferred from one to another as each had received and experienced comfort from God.

Paul also reminded the Corinthian Christians that as they shared in Christ's sufferings they also shared in Christ's consolation. Paul believed that he shared in Christ's suffering (see Col. 1:24), though not in Christ's uniquely vicarious suffering for our sins. Perhaps he also held the belief, prevalent among many Jews of the day, that prior to the Messiah's coming (for Paul, Jesus' second coming), there would be a period of suffering for those who anticipated Him. Yet Paul, as a member of the body of Christ, also experienced God's comfort. *For as we share abundantly in Christ's sufferings, so through Christ we share abundantly in comfort too* (1:5).

Paul wrote that he and Timothy suffered for the benefit of the Corinthian Christians. Through their sufferings, the Corinthians had been comforted. *If we are afflicted, it is for your comfort and salvation; and if we are comforted, it is for your comfort, which you experience when you patiently endure the same sufferings that we suffer* (1:6). The Christians' comfort and salvation were also intermixed with their suffering. Paul then could write, *Our hope for you is unshaken; for we know that as you share in our sufferings, you will also share in our comfort* (1:7).

Paul used an autobiographical example. *For we do not want you to be ignorant . . . of the affliction we experienced in Asia; for we were so utterly, unbearably crushed that we despaired of life itself* (1:8). For Christians of today, Paul's reference is puzzling. Apparently the Corinthians were well aware of what had happened to Paul. He had been in serious danger of losing his life. His life might have been endangered by a lynch mob, by an arrest and execution, or by the threat of capture and possible murder by thieves. However, many scholars feel that the danger lay in a serious illness. Whatever the case, Paul felt despair. *We felt that we had received the sentence of death* (1:9).

However, in the midst of extreme danger, Paul and Timothy experienced God's providence. When no options seemed available in Paul's mind, God's power was still available. *That was to make us rely not on ourselves but on God who raises the dead* (1:9). Paul trusted that his hope lay in life eternal through his own resurrection.

God acted to deliver Paul. Again, the Corinthians must have known the story of his deliverance while we do not. *He delivered us from so deadly a peril, and he will deliver us; on him we have set our hope that he will deliver us again* (1:10). Paul trusted that he would be delivered from other dangers he faced in his mission efforts.

Paul learned that he could trust God to deliver him from all trying circumstances. God would not abandon him. So too, the Corinthians must not abandon him. Paul asked his readers to intercede for him and Timothy in prayer. *You also must help us by prayer, so that many will give thanks on our behalf for the blessing granted us in answer to many prayers* (1:11). Paul directed the Corinthians to pray for them so that God's plan could unfold and thanksgiving result.

Paul assured his readers that he had been utterly sincere with them. He had no doubts that his conduct and motives were sincere. *For our boast is this, the testimony of our conscience that we have behaved in the world, and still more toward you, with holiness and godly sincerity, not by earthly wisdom but by the grace of God* (1:12). Paul was confident that they would eventually clear up their misunderstandings and come to a full understanding. *For we write you nothing but what you can read and understand; I hope you will understand fully, as you have understood in part, that you can be proud of us as we can be of you, on the day of the Lord Jesus* (1:13, 14).

SUGGESTIONS TO TEACHERS

You undoubtedly have a few scars from wounds you have received from fellow church members over the years. Most people in your class probably also carry some painful memories of things said or done in the past by others in a congregation. Part of the reason why the pain is acute is that expectations are higher in the church.

Paul did not let slander and false accusations produce bitter feelings in him. Instead, he wrote movingly of caring for one another. His letter has deep relevance for every Christian and every congregation today.

1. POWER OF GOD. Paul speaks of "the Father of mercies and God of all comfort, who comforts us in all our affliction" (1:3, 4), emphasizing the compassion and love of the Lord. Paul knew from personal experience God's gracious deliverance from perils. He reminded his readers that they also had received divine mercy and comfort. Ask your students to share their experiences of knowing that mercy and comfort.

2. PURPOSE OF COMFORT. God gives comfort and mercy not only to soothe us. He comforts us so that we may comfort others, in turn. The Greek word here for "comfort" has the same root as the word *paraclete*, meaning "to call someone alongside." This word is used in John 14 and elsewhere to designate the Holy Spirit as Comforter. God stands alongside of us in our difficulties. In turn, He sends us to stand alongside of fellow believers when they are in difficulty. Emphasize this meaning of "comfort" for your class.

3. PATIENCE IN SUFFERING. Sharing each other's suffering is a form of sharing Christ's suffering. Suffering is part of being a human. We may try to avoid it, but we will encounter times of despair, pain, and loneliness, especially if we are involved in close relationships with others. We also know that the closer we are to others, the more we will feel the hurts they may be suffering. One of the reasons we are called to a community of faith

is that we might learn to care enough for each other to share each other's sufferings.

4. PERIL IN LIFE. Paul gives us a glimpse of some of his own sufferings. Apparently his pain and problems were so severe that he and his companions felt the situation was hopeless ("we despaired of life itself," he wrote in 1:8). He and his friends used the experience as a lesson: they must not rely on themselves but on the one who raised up Christ from the dead. God delivered them from death also, Paul stated. This same God provides new life in the midst of the most hopeless situations.

5. PRAYER FOR DELIVERANCE. Paul pleaded with the Corinthians to pray for him and his colleagues. Prayers for them would strengthen their resolve and their efforts, Paul knew. Invite your group members to think about prayer as a way of caring for others. Are you involved in a praying congregation? Are the members of your class praying for one another? Praying for each other is a way of sharing each other's pain.

TOPIC FOR ADULTS
SHARING ONE ANOTHER'S PAIN

On to the Finish Line. One of the most memorable events in the 1992 Olympics came during a 400-meter race. Derek Redmond, a British track man, ripped his right hamstring muscle in the early part of the race. Tearing a hamstring in one's leg is not only incredibly painful but also crippling. Redmond suddenly tumbled onto the cinder track. The injury apparently meant that he would not complete the race. But Derek got up and started hopping toward the tape. The other runners, of course, streaked ahead and finished the race. But Derek Redmond, his face contorted with agony, continued hopping slowly toward the finish line. He tottered. It appeared that he would collapse.

Suddenly a man appeared beside the crippled runner. It was Derek's father. His father had rushed down from the stands and hurried onto the track to help his son. The elder Redmond clasped the boy in his arms. The younger Redmond wept for a moment on his dad's shoulder. The two then continued, with the father supporting the son, as the young runner hobbled to the finish line and completed the race.

In the person of Jesus, the Gospel tells us, God the Father has come to us, His people, lovingly supporting us and encouraging us. We may be at the point of falling in pain and discouragement, but He walks the course of life with us and will do so until we finish the race. We are loved by this gracious one.

This same God who is with us in our pain and disappointments in the person of Jesus Christ also sends us to share the pain and disappointments of others.

Sharing the Pain. A few years ago, when Paul Vrablic had a heart attack on the Saturday before Thanksgiving, he figured his gas station would go out of business.

"Just lock it up and forget it," he told his wife, Ann, in the emergency room of the Allentown Sacred Heart Hospital Center.

Vrablic knew that if the small station closed, the customers he'd been serving for fifteen years would go elsewhere and he'd have trouble getting them back when he recovered.

The operator of the small service station saw no alternative. But his friends did. His only part-time employee, Charles Kerstetter, sent word that he'd keep working without pay as long as needed. George Prebula, a customer of Vrablic's, organized friends and neighbors to put in time, mostly pumping gasoline, which wouldn't make Vrablic prosper but would keep the station going. Jim Quier, who got off the night shift at Kraft Foods, went directly to the station for a couple of hours. Most of those helping out weren't mechanics. Some could do little more than pump gas. But because of his caring friends, Paul Vrablic was able to keep his business going. This is sharing another's pain!

Royal Indifference. In marriage, perhaps more than in any other human relationship, we must learn to share one another's hurts and needs. The world sighed when Prince Charles and Princess Diana, the couple blessed with so much, split in 1992. Some, however, were not surprised. One royal observer overheard the engaged couple conversing during his 1981 trip to New Zealand. Lonely and missing her fiance, Princess Di murmured, "I miss you, darling."

Charles's reply, in a matter-of-fact voice: "Yes, I know." Period. Nothing more. No words of endearment. No sharing of concern. No wonder the royal couple had marital problems.

Questions for Students on the Next Lesson. 1. In what ways did Paul identify with others? 2. Why did Paul state that he was willing to forgo his rights and freedom? 3. Why were the Corinthians so critical of Paul? 4. In what ways are you showing commitment and self-discipline as a Christian? 5. When is it appropriate for a Christian not to stand up for his rights?

TOPIC FOR YOUTH
FACING HARD TIMES

Cardboard Love. The announcer at the baseball card show was brief. A Youth and Family Services program in Milford, Connecticut, Boys Village, needed sports trading cards. People at the show were asked to drop their unwanted cards in a box at the door.

A seventy-six-year-old man approached the announcer. He held up a stack of 1988 Team USA baseball cards of Charles Nagy, the current right-handed pitcher for the Cleveland Indians. All had been autographed! The man was Charles E. Nagy, the uncle of Charles Nagy. He explained that he and Charles wanted the kids at the Boys Village to have the cards.

These cards became a prized possession of the youngsters, who were trying to discover love and to change their attitudes. The cards became tangible reminders of how God's comfort and love can be conveyed through others.

Sharing Christ's Story. In 1956 five American missionaries were lost in the jungles of Ecuador, the land of the Auca Indians. The bodies of the five men were eventually recovered. They had been brutally killed by the Aucas.

Thirty-seven years later, Don Johnson, a tall, blond, linguistic missionary stood amidst the Aucas, honoring the fallen missionaries. The majority of the Aucas were now Christians and stood as a moving testimony to the work of the many missionaries, like Johnson, who continued to live with these primitive natives.

Johnson and other missionaries lived with the tribal people and developed an alphabet for their language, eventually producing reading primers, health books, and a translation of the New Testament. Johnson began his work by merely being sensitive to the Aucas' feelings. Accepting the inherent risks and the rugged life-style, Johnson succeeded in sharing the story of God's love in Christ.

Paul might have identified with Johnson. Both faced death and triumphed by sharing the Gospel. Could you do the same?

Shared God's Love. Seventeen-year-old Toni lost some of her high school friends because she supported a recommendation made by the National Transportation Safety Board. In an effort to crack down on teenage traffic fatalities, the NTSB promoted a nighttime curfew on teenage drivers. The agency also supported an automatic license suspension for adolescents caught driving with any amount of alcohol in their blood.

In a debate sponsored by Students Against Drunk Driving, Toni argued that teens often do drink and drive. She felt teenagers were often inexperienced drivers and were prone to taking risks. Toni also cited statistics that showed that fifteen to twenty year olds accounted for 15 percent of all traffic fatalities even though this group comprised only 7 percent of all licensed drivers. Of these fatalities, 20 percent were at night, and 30 percent involved alcohol. Toni concluded by urging that the NTSB recommendation be adopted and that the local SADD group support the 1984 law requiring all states to make the minimum drinking age twenty-one or lose their federal highway aid.

As a result, Toni faced some harsh verbal abuse from friends, fellow students, and parents. However, she was willing to face hard times rather than risk losing the life of a friend. She wanted to share God-honoring principles through her actions.

In a small way, Toni shared in Christ's sufferings. She also shared in His comfort, knowing that her temporary suffering would ultimately benefit all people.

Questions for Students on the next Lesson. 1. Does a more mature believer have some privileges that an immature believer lacks? 2. What financial support does your church provide your pastor? 3. What images did Paul utilize when he spoke of financial support? 4. Why should we be willing to abridge our freedom for the sake of others? 5. What images did Paul use when he spoke of commitment and discipline?

LESSON 10—MAY 7

LIVING IN CHRISTIAN FREEDOM

Background Scripture: I Corinthians 9
Devotional Reading: Galatians 5:13-26

KING JAMES VERSION

I CORINTHIANS 9:1 Am I not an apostle? am I not free? have I not seen Jesus Christ our Lord? are not ye my work in the Lord?

2 If I be not an apostle unto others, yet doubtless I am to you: for the seal of mine apostleship are ye in the Lord.

3 Mine answer to them that do examine me is this,

4 Have we not power to eat and to drink?

5 Have we not power to lead about a sister, a wife, as well as other apostles, and as the brethren of the Lord, and Cephas?

6 Or I only and Barnabas, have not we power to forbear working?

7 Who goeth a warfare any time at his own charges? who planteth a vineyard, and eateth not of the fruit thereof? or who feedeth a flock, and eateth not of the milk of the flock? . . .

19 For though I be free from all men, yet have I made myself servant unto all, that I might gain the more.

20 And unto the Jews I became as a Jew, that I might gain the Jews; to them that are under the law, as under the law, that I might gain them that are under the law;

21 To them that are without law, as without law, (being not without law to God, but under the law to Christ,) that I might gain them that are without law.

22 To the weak became I as weak, that I might gain the weak: I am made all things to all men, that I might by all means save some.

23 And this I do for the gospel's sake, that I might be partaker thereof with you.

24 Know ye not that they which run in a race run all, but one receiveth the prize? So run, that ye may obtain.

25 And every man that striveth for the mastery is temperate in all things. Now they do it to obtain a corruptible crown; but we an incorruptible.

26 I therefore so run, not as uncertainly; so fight I, not as one that beateth the air:

27 But I keep under my body, and bring it into subjection: lest that by any means, when I have preached to others, I myself should be a castaway.

REVISED STANDARD VERSION

I CORINTHIANS 9:1 Am I not free? Am I not an apostle? Have I not seen Jesus our Lord? Are not you my workmanship in the Lord? 2 If to others I am not an apostle, at least I am to you; for you are the seal of my apostleship in the Lord.

3 This is my defense to those who would examine me. 4 Do we not have the right to our food and drink? 5 Do we not have the right to be accompanied by a wife, as the other apostles and the brothers of the Lord and Cephas? 6 Or is it only Barnabas and I who have no right to refrain from working for a living? 7 Who serves as a soldier at his own expense? Who plants a vineyard without eating any of its fruit? Who tends a flock without getting some of the milk? . . .

19 For though I am free from all men, I have made myself a slave to all, that I might win the more. 20 To the Jews I became as a Jew, in order to win Jews; to those under the law I became as one under the law—though not being myself under the law—that I might win those under the law. 21 To those outside the law I became as one outside the law—not being without law toward God but under the law of Christ—that I might win those outside the law. 22 To the weak I became weak, that I might win the weak. I have become all things to all men, that I might by all means save some. 23 I do it all for the sake of the gospel, that I may share in its blessings.

24 Do you not know that in a race all the runners compete, but only one receives the prize? So run that you may obtain it. 25 Every athlete exercises self-control in all things. They do it to receive a perishable wreath, but we an imperishable. 26 Well, I do not run aimlessly, I do not box as one beating the air; 27 But I pommel my body and subdue it, lest after preaching to others I myself should be disqualified.

KEY VERSE: For though I am free from all men, I have made myself a slave to all, that I might win the more. I Corinthians 9:19.

HOME DAILY BIBLE READINGS

May	1	M.	Galatians 5:13-21	*Live by the Spirit*
May	2	T.	Galatians 5:22-26	*Fruit of the Spirit*
May	3	W.	I Corinthians 9:1-7	*Rights of an Apostle*
May	4	T.	I Corinthians 9:8-18	*Refusing to Claim One's Rights*
May	5	F.	I Corinthians 9:19-27	*Free to Adapt for Christ's Sake*
May	6	S.	II Corinthians 3:12-18	*The Lord's Spirit Gives Freedom*
May	7	S.	Romans 8:1-11	*Christ Frees Us from Condemnation*

BACKGROUND

Earlier, we saw how Paul advised those tempted to flaunt their freedom to eat meat from pagan shrines. He told them not to abuse their freedom if eating that meat offended others. Paul then gave an example of the principle he was trying to establish. He insisted that it was more than a matter of roasts and steaks. His point was that freedom must never be allowed to become a stumbling block for less mature Christians, tempting them to return to a former life-style. For Paul, the primary issue was not a question of which foods to eat, but a question of how one believer's actions might affect the spiritual growth of another believer. "Are my actions helping or harming their relationship to Christ and to me?" To illustrate this, Paul discussed the fact that he had restricted himself from exercising all the rights normally extended to an apostle.

Like everyone, the apostles had to have money to buy groceries. None were wealthy. Apparently most were supported by freewill offerings from churches. Paul, however, did not stand on his rights as an apostle and accept such cash gifts as a rule. He pointed out to the Corinthians that he could have chosen to do what other missionaries did. He even mentioned that Peter received expense money both for himself and for his wife, and that this was appropriate. Every worker is entitled to receive a fair payment for services, and that even the temple priests made their living from the offerings.

However, Paul continued, in his own case he chose not to exercise his right to accept offerings for his ministry. Although he was free to receive support from churches, Paul deliberately turned down that freedom. As is well known, Paul paid his own expenses by working as a tentmaker. Why did Paul curtail his freedom in this way? Because, he stated, he did not want anyone to think that he was preaching Christ merely because he was getting paid to do it.

Paul acknowledged it was not easy to minister and earn money at the same time. He had to forsake personal comfort and live an austere, disciplined life, just as an athlete has to maintain strict training to keep his or her body in top condition. But forsaking his right to offerings, Paul maintained, meant no one could accuse him of being greedy or of being obligated to anyone except Christ.

NOTES ON THE PRINTED TEXT

As a Christian deepens his or her faith, he or she realizes that freedom must always be tempered with love for others. The more advanced a committed believer becomes, the greater the responsibility that believer has for others. Paul spoke to the Corinthians of his own life-style decisions. He outlined all the rights and privileges he could have exercised.

Am I not free? Am I not an apostle? (9:1). Paul was able to choose how he would live. This was a sign of freedom. Also, as an apostle, he had special status and could have accepted special privileges. *Have I not seen Jesus our Lord?* (9:1). Paul's authority centered in his having met the risen Lord on the Damascus road. Paul reminded the Corinthian Christians that their own Christian faith was evidence of his apostleship. *Are not you my workmanship in the Lord?* (9:1). The very existence of a Corinthian church was evidence of his calling as an apostle. *If to others I am not an apostle, at least I am to you; for you are the seal of my apostleship in the Lord* (9:2).

Replying to questions, or possibly responding to attacks against himself and his authority, Paul wrote, *This is my defense to those who would examine me* (9:3). Paul then responded to the Corinthians, stating the specific rights that were the privilege of any full-time Christian worker. He defended those rights. He had the right to any food and drink, regardless of Old Testament dietary laws. Christ had set him free from those legalistic laws. *Do we not have the right to our food and drink?* (9:4).

Paul also had the right to be accompanied by a wife as were other apostles. This was his privilege. Being celibate and single were not requirements for Christian service. *Do we not have the right to be accompanied by a wife, as the other apostles and the brothers of the Lord and Cephas?* (9:5).

He had the right to refrain from secular work in order to make money. Other apostles and itinerant preachers depended upon the Christians they served for their financial support. Yet Paul worked as a tentmaker. He reminded the Corinthians that he and Barnabas were exceptions in this regard. *Or is it only Barnabas and I who have no right to refrain from working for a living?* (9:6).

Paul then made a case for Christian workers being financially supported by their fellow believers. To reinforce his case, he used the analogies of a soldier, a landowning planter, a shepherd, and others from the Old Testament. *Who serves as a soldier at his own expense?* (9:7). A soldier did not serve his country at his own expense.

While Paul could have claimed many privileges, he did not exercise them. He surrendered his freedom in favor of servanthood, all in order to win others to Christ. *For though I am free from all men, I have made myself a slave to all, that I might win the more* (9:19).

Paul used a strategy of identification. He was willing to identify with all sorts of people in order to share the Gospel's blessing with them. *To the Jews I became as a Jew, in order to win Jews* (9:20). When Paul was with the Jews, he acted like the Jews in order to help them see Christ in him. He would not subject himself to the Law, but he would live under it in order to lead those who lived under the Law to Christ. Then, when living in a Gentile region, he acted like the Gentiles in order to reach them, too, with Christ's claim on their lives. *To those outside the law I became as one outside the law* (9:21). To those *weak* (9:22), or squeamish about eating food offered to idols, Paul was willing to abstain from eating meat in order to win them to Christ.

Paul concluded by declaring that a Gospel laborer must exercise discipline. He used an athletic illustration. *Do you not know that in a race all the runners compete, but only one receives the prize? So run that you may obtain it. Every athlete exercises self-control in all things. They do it to receive a perishable wreath, but we an imperishable* (9:24, 25).

Corinth was known for its athletic competitions. Every second year the city hosted the Isthmian Games in honor of the god Poseidon. Track and field events predominated. Since only one individual could win an event, the contestants trained very hard in order to win a crown of laurel leaves. Paul stressed that a Christian must be dedicated to a disciplined life in order to win an imperishable prize.

Paul encouraged the Corinthian church to exercise the same commitment and self-control in their efforts to share the Gospel. They were to focus on the finish line and move toward it. *Do not run aimlessly* (9:26). In addition, he reminded his readers that life was a battle. Paul knew he was not shadowboxing an imaginary opponent. Instead, he faithfully disciplined himself and prepared so that he could witness with power. *I do not box as one beating the air; but I pommel my body and subdue it, lest after preaching to others I myself should be disqualified* (9:26, 27).

SUGGESTIONS TO TEACHERS

A church staff member decided to start a part-time business selling cosmetics from her home. Some of the church members felt that they had to patronize her for fear of offending her. Others resented the sense of pressure they thought the staff member was putting on church members to become customers. A few others, who also made their living by selling cosmetics, were unhappy that the staff member was competing with them for trade. The woman dismissed all the criticism, insisting that she had the right to do what she wanted in her free time, as long as she was not doing anything immoral or illegal.

How would your class resolve this issue in that congregation? What about other instances in which a Christian feels free to do something that might cause other believers to be offended? Today's lesson from I Corinthians 9 gives us insights into how a believer is to live out his or her Christian freedom.

1. RENOUNCING PRIVILEGES. Paul offers the example of his own refusal to take payment to show that Christians may sometimes give up rights and privileges for the sake of others. The note of humility and concern in this act should illustrate how freedom for a Christian is not a license to do one's own thing, but a freedom to care for others. Remind your students that the perfect role model for living in freedom is Jesus.

2. RECEIVING PAYMENT. At the same time, Paul points out that just as the Roman emperor's soldiers get paid, Christ's servants deserve financial support. This suggests that your minister should receive an adequate salary. Often, church people take for granted that pastors and other leaders have enough to live on.

3. RESPECTING PRECEPTS. Have the class explore the meaning of I Corinthians 9:8-14, in which Paul shows that Christians are bound by a new and higher law than the old Mosaic code, namely the law of love. Christ's command of love is more demanding than any set of rules. Help your students understand why loving others is harder than keeping regulations.

4. REFUSING PREFERENCE. Paul turns down the perks and benefits of apostleship in order to be free to serve every kind of person. He means to become a "slave to all" (9:19) by putting limits on his personal freedom. What experiences in the lives of your class members have suggested the practical need for such limits?

5. RECEIVING THE PRIZE. Words like "sacrifice" and "discipline" are not fashionable nowadays, even for many Christians. Paul lifts vivid images out of the world of sports to describe the way believers must constantly keep spiritually fit in the rigorous service of Christ. No "I can do my own thing" or "If I feel like it" attitudes for a Christian!

TOPIC FOR ADULTS
COMMITTED TO SERVE

Disciplined. Olympic gold medalist and world record holder Jackie Joyner-Kersee had to excel in seven different events to win the women's heptathalon. The event required strength and endurance in the 100-meter hurdles, shot put, high jump, 200-meter run, long jump, javelin throw, and the 800-meter run.

Jackie became the gold medalist because of hard work and a lot of discipline. After years of hard training, she had to continue to train five to six hours a day, five days each week, in order just to stay competitive. She did this gladly.

Paul spoke of the disciplined athlete and a disciplined Christian. If people are willing to make such sacrifices for something as fleeting as the fame that accompanies winning the Olympics, how much more should a Christian discipline himself or herself for the prize of winning others into God's kingdom?

Free to Serve. Would you climb into an old yellow school bus filled with medical and agricultural supplies, and twenty other people, and drive over four thousand miles from your cozy home in Massachusetts to one of the poorest countries on earth? Barbara West did.

For most of us, one hour on the Massachusetts turnpike is more than we could probably take—bouncing around in those tiny seats, that deafening school bus hum echoing in our ears. But ten straight days of driving? Much of it on rough, unfinished roads in Mexico and Guatemala? Thank you very much. . . .

For Barbara West and a dedicated group of volunteers from the Heifer Project over twenty years ago, a school bus was the only way to go. With a limited budget, they had little choice. They were delivering desperately needed supplies and training to Guatemalan farmers, to help them pull themselves out of their impoverished condition.

The basic premise of the Heifer Project appealed to Barbara from the start—helping poor farmers in the U.S. and overseas learn to help themselves, giving them livestock, tools, a little know-how, and a push. Not just throwing them some money and a quick "hasta luego." And over the years, the Heifer Project's approach has worked, due in large part to the commitment of volunteers like Barbara.—Ted Scheu, United Church News, May, 1992.

Stood on Their Rights. In Scotland, in 1656, the two ministers of the lovely old Church of the Holy Rood quarrelled over their rights and authority. Each claimed to have the freedom to run the church as he saw fit. Each demanded the respect of the other and the entire congregation. Sadly, the insistence on "rights" and "freedom" brought such bitterness between the two that the congregation became divided. Eventually, the historic church was split. A wall was erected in the middle of the beautiful sanctuary to create two separate congregations. The Rev. James Guthrie took his people to one end, and his erstwhile colleague, the Rev. Matthew Simpson, took his part of the church to the other. The two headstrong ministers standing on their claims brought about a separation of the church that did not end until almost three hundred years later!

Questions for Students on the Next Lesson. 1. What does the word "reconciliation" mean to you? 2. What did Paul mean when he wrote that all in Christ are new creations? 3. How are we motivated to work for reconciliation? 4. What does it mean to be an "ambassador" for Christ? 5. Where in your community and in your world do you see the greatest need for reconciliation?

TOPIC FOR YOUTH
FREE TO SERVE

Free to Sacrifice. While Paul could have demanded many rights and privileges, he was willing to sacrifice them, subordinating himself so that he could serve others. Are you willing to make a similar sacrifice?

Imagine it is the ninth inning in a very close play-off baseball game, and the bases are loaded. The strongest and best batter comes to the plate. He looks at the third base coach and is given the bunt sign.

How is that batter going to react? Here is a certified league leader in hitting being told to bunt. Perhaps he figures that he should swing for the bleachers. He certainly has the potential for the grand slam. Perhaps he momentarily thinks of the prestige a home run would give him. Perhaps he thinks of his batting average statistics. However, the manager has called for a sacrifice bunt, knowing that the batter will be thrown out at first base. This will enable the third-base runner to score, tieing the game and leaving two more outs to possibly score the winning run.

The batter understands that this is what the game of baseball is all about—not individual glory, but winning the game as a team. In the church, too, personal sacrifice accomplishes great things.

Sacrificial Service. North Charles Street in Pittsburgh's Brighton Heights is a center of despair. It is a long stretch of nineteenth-century row houses that have been converted into apartments. It is one of the inner city's poorest areas. Sidewalks are often ankle deep in trash, buildings are boarded up, and the nights are filled with the sounds of rowdy teenagers.

Charles Street is hardly the place one would expect to find a white, retired CEO of a bank working tirelessly with teens. Yet, Charles Ott, retired chief executive officer of the Laurel Savings Association and a deacon of a white suburban church, has worked in this area for three years through Y.O.U. (Youth Opportunities Unlimited).

Over one thousand children pass through the Y.O.U. center each year. Ott teaches math and reading and delivers furniture and household goods to the needy.

At first, Ott found the work difficult. He could only work with one teen at a time. Eventually, some of his first students returned and helped Ott to help even more teens. They shared their new outlook on life with the younger children of their neighborhood.

Ott could have stayed at home, but he chose to identify with, and serve, others. He wanted to show the love of Christ in his actions. Through Ott's help, young teens found something worthwhile in which to invest their lives. Perhaps you can do the same.

Is It Mine? The sixteen-year-old son in a family with financial problems took his earnings and bought a pair of "scientifically designed and engineered" athletic shoes costing $150. The parents, struggling to provide basic household necessities, protested. The boy argued that it was his money and he could do whatever he wanted with his own money. Although bothered by the son's extravagance, the parents finally felt they had to remain silent.

Some observers think that this is the problem with American society. It's too easy for one person to run away from the family in a $150 pair of sneakers. Parents should ask whether one individual's wishes are more important than the needs of the social unit. Can parents not teach their children how to spend their money wisely? Are we turning into selfish consumers responsible to nobody but ourselves, no matter how bizarre our desires may be? Is the rugged individualism of our culture making us so preoccupied with personal pleasure, professional advancement, and private concerns that we forget our lives are always lived in community with others?

Paul's words to the Corinthians remind us that the phrase "It's mine, isn't it?" simply does not apply within Christ's family.

Questions for Students on the Next Lesson. 1. What is your motivation for Christian work? 2. What motivated Paul to the Christian ministry? 3. How does God bring about "new creations"? 4. What does reconciliation mean? How can you fulfill your duties as an "ambassador of Christ"?

LESSON 11—MAY 14

WORKING FOR RECONCILIATION

Background Scripture: II Corinthians 5
Devotional Reading: I John 4:7-21

KING JAMES VERSION

II CORINTHIANS 5:11 Knowing therefore the terror of the Lord, we persuade men; but we are made manifest unto God; and I trust also are made manifest in your consciences.

12 For we commend not ourselves again unto you, but give you occasion to glory on our behalf, that ye may have somewhat to answer them which glory in appearance, and not in heart.

13 For whether we be beside ourselves, it is to God: or whether we be sober, it is for your cause.

14 For the love of Christ constraineth us; because we thus judge, that if one died for all, then were all dead:

15 And that he died for all, that they which live should not henceforth live unto themselves, but unto him which died for them, and rose again.

16 Wherefore henceforth know we no man after the flesh: yea, though we have known Christ after the flesh, yet now henceforth know we him no more.

17 Therefore if any man be in Christ, he is a new creature: old things are passed away; behold, all things are become new.

18 And all things are of God, who hath reconciled us to himself by Jesus Christ, and hath given to us the ministry of reconciliation;

19 To wit, that God was in Christ, reconciling the world unto himself, not imputing their trespasses unto them; and hath committed unto us the word of reconciliation.

20 Now then we are ambassadors for Christ, as though God did beseech you by us: we pray you in Christ's stead, be ye reconciled to God.

21 For he hath made him to be sin for us, who knew no sin; that we might be made the righteousness of God in him.

REVISED STANDARD VERSION

II CORINTHIANS 5:11 Therefore, knowing the fear of the Lord, we persuade men; but what we are is known to God, and I hope it is known also to your conscience. 12 We are not commending ourselves to you again but giving you cause to be proud of us, so that you may be able to answer those who pride themselves on a man's position and not on his heart. 13 For if we are beside ourselves, it is for God; if we are in our right mind, it is for you. 14 For the love of Christ controls us, because we are convinced that one has died for all; therefore all have died. 15 And he died for all, that those who live might live no longer for themselves but for him who for their sake died and was raised.

16 From now on, therefore, we regard no one from a human point of view; even though we once regarded Christ from a human point of view, we regard him thus no longer. 17 Therefore, if any one is in Christ, he is a new creation; the old has passed away, behold, the new has come. 18 All this is from God, who through Christ reconciled us to himself and gave us the ministry of reconciliation; 19 that is, in Christ God was reconciling the world to himself, not counting their trespasses against them, and entrusting to us the message of reconciliation. 20 So we are ambassadors for Christ, God making his appeal through us. We beseech you on behalf of Christ, be reconciled to God. 21 For our sake he made him to be sin who knew no sin, so that in him we might become the righteousness of God.

KEY VERSE: God . . . reconciled us to himself and gave us the ministry of reconciliation. II Corinthians 5:18.

HOME DAILY BIBLE READINGS

May	8	M.	I John 4:1-7	*One Who Loves Knows God*
May	9	*T.*	I John 4:13-21	*We Love Because God Loves Us*
May	10	*W.*	II Corinthians 5:1-5	*God's Spirit Sustains Us*
May	11	*T.*	II Corinthians 5:6-10	*Aim to Please God*
May	12	*F.*	II Corinthians 5:11-15	*Christ's Love Constrains Us*
May	13	*S.*	II Corinthians 5:16-21	*The Ministry of Reconciliation*
May	14	*S.*	Matthew 5:21-26	*Seek Reconciliation before Worshiping*

BACKGROUND

Corinth had not been fertile soil for church planting. The city was notorious for its bars and brothels. Living in a bustling seaport and commercial center, Corinth's inhabitants were not only used to vice and depravity but also wise about the world's way of doing business. The group of Corinthians making up the Christian community founded by Paul seemed to carry over the attitudes and values of the culture around them. Most had come out of paganism and, therefore, lacked the foundation in morality that characterized persons who came from Jewish backgrounds. These new believers, unfortunately, also continued to be extremely competitive, just as most of their fellow Corinthians were. Ugly squabbles caused sharp divisions and hard feelings within the congregation. Slanderous talk, sometimes stirred up by other preachers who wandered into town, threatened to undermine Paul's authority and alienate the Corinthians from him.

Other leaders might have written off the Corinthian church as a hopeless situation. But not Paul. Like a parent, he persisted in trying to help these new converts to mature. His letters to Corinth pleaded, scolded, encouraged, and challenged. Throughout the relationship, Paul continued to love the Corinthians.

In this section of II Corinthians, a portion of what was probably Paul's final letter in a series of epistles to the Corinthian church, Paul gave a beautiful summary of the Christian faith and the Christian's calling. He reminded his readers that they were Christ's persons, and if they had anything to do with Christ, they must realize that God was bringing about a new creation in them. They were not the same as they had been before and certainly not the same as those in a society that did not recognize Christ.

NOTES ON THE PRINTED TEXT

Therefore, knowing the fear of the Lord, we persuade men: but what we are is known to God, and I hope it is known also to your conscience (5:11). Because Paul had been criticized for selfish behavior, he wrote to the Corinthians reminding them that he took God's ultimate judgment seriously. Knowing how seriously he took this judgment, they must realize how seriously he took his responsibility to lead others to faith in Christ. He reminded his readers that he had been a responsible leader, and they should be able to judge him for themselves.

We are not commending ourselves to you again but giving you cause to be proud of us, so that you may be able to answer those who pride themselves on a man's position and not on his heart (5:12). Paul would not boast nor ingratiate himself to the church for what he had accomplished. The Corinthians should have been proud of Paul and his accomplishments with them.

For if we are beside ourselves, it is for God; if we are in our right mind, it is for you (5:13). Paul assured the Corinthians that if his behavior seemed strange or outrageous, it came from his devotion and commitment to God. He was a rational and sensible individual who wanted the believers to be proud of him.

The real motivation in Paul's life was Christ's love. It motivated all that Paul did. *For the love of Christ controls us, because we are convinced that one has died for all; therefore all have died* (5:14). Love should control all that a believer does. The greatest example of love was Christ's willingness to die for sinners. This should motivate all believers to love others. *And he died for all, that those who live might live no longer for themselves but for him who for their sake died and was raised* (5:15).

As a consequence, Paul no longer regarded Christ from a human point of view as many others did. As a Christian, Paul had a new perspective in looking at others. *From now on, therefore, we regard no one from a human point of view; even though we once regarded Christ from a human point of view, we regard him thus no longer* (5:16). Led by the Spirit, Paul had new standards of judgment.

Another consequence of Christ's death was new life. People in Christ were new creations through His death and resurrection. *Therefore, if any one is in Christ, he is a new creation; the old has passed away, behold, the new has come* (5:17).

As a result of Christ's death, Christians were reconciled to God through Christ and were given the ministry of reconciliation. God forgave His people and drew them to Himself. Believers were to do the same toward others. *All this is from God, who through Christ reconciled us to himself and gave us the ministry of reconciliation* (5:18). Paul stated his belief more clearly. It detailed the work of Christ. *God was reconciling the world to himself, not counting their trespasses against them, and entrusting to us the message of reconciliation* (5:19). His theme also detailed a believer's work: they were to be committed to sharing the story of God's work.

Paul described his ministry. *We are ambassadors for Christ, God making his appeal through us* (5:20). Believers were to represent Jesus Christ just as an ambassador represented his country. Just as an ambassador could speak for the nation's leader, so Christians made an appeal on behalf of God. The need for reconciliation was the content of that appeal. *We beseech you on behalf of Christ, be reconciled to God* (5:20). Christians must be reconciled to God as well as to their neighbors.

God, though, had to establish reconciliation with His people. Sin separated the two parties. God made Christ to be sin for people so that people could have God's righteousness. Christ suffered unjustly and innocently in order to reconcile His people to God. *For our sake he made him to be sin who knew no sin, so that in him we might become the righteousness of God* (5:21).

SUGGESTIONS TO TEACHERS

We live in a fractured world. Although the Soviet Union and the United States no longer confront each other belligerently, much of the rest of the globe seethes with hatred and suffers from hostilities. Protestants and Catholics continue their murderous ways in Northern Ireland; Croats, Muslims, and Serbs fight in the rubble of Yugoslavia; and rival clans in Somalia have broken apart their nation. Hindu versus Muslim in India, Israeli versus Palestinian, Azerbaijanis against Armenians, Brooklyn Orthodox Jews and blacks in angry confrontations—the list goes on and on.

Even Christian denominations are not spared internal conflict. Hard feelings and dissension fester in many congregations. The brokenness extends to neighborhoods and families. Witness the appallingly high divorce rate, the huge incidence of child and spouse abuse, and the increasing antisocial behavior among teenagers.

Others in our society may sigh and throw up their hands in despair. The problems are so complex and daunting that many feel it is useless to try to do anything to remedy the brokenness. But Christians are different. We know that God cared so much about this world that He sent Jesus Christ among us. We also know that God is in the process of bringing about a transformation in each of our lives. Furthermore, we believers realize that we are sent out to bring the reconciliation among all peoples that God has brought between Himself and us.

1. CONFIDENT IN DEATH. Although the world may appear to be on a death trip, and although each of us knows the reality of eventual personal death, believers also have God's assurance through Christ that nothing, not even death, will be able to separate us from God's love.

2. COURAGEOUS IN DESPAIR. Society around us may despair of the world. We, like the apostles, may have to face crises and setbacks. Yet we may take hope from knowing God stands firm in His promises of victory. We may live courageously.

3. CONTROLLED BY DEVOTION. Our commitment to Christ means that we have been claimed by Him as His own. Focus on the words "For the love of Christ controls us" (5:14). In other words, we are not free to pursue our own agendas. We belong to Christ.

4. CREATED BY DESIGN. Have students probe the significance of Paul's words: "If any one is in Christ, he is a new creation" (5:17). What signs of transformation by God does your class think every Christian should exhibit?

5. CLAIMED FROM DIVISIVENESS. Because of God's great act of reconciliation in Christ, we know we are now accepted by God. This means being at one with each other and with the entire creation. Is your class and your church truly a community of reconciliation? Brainstorm for practical evidence.

6. CALLED AS DIPLOMATS. Play in your imagination with the word "ambassador" as it is used in this passage. An ambassador represents his government and is delegated authority to speak and act not just for himself but also for his country. An ambassador's task is risky (several have been killed in recent years). Apply these points about serving as an ambassador to the calling of every Christian.

TOPIC FOR ADULTS
MOTIVATED BY CHRIST'S LOVE

Ambassador to the Enemy. Led by legendary flier Jimmy Doolittle, sixteen U.S. Army B-25 bombers broke through Japanese defenses on April 18, 1942, to strike Tokyo and other cities in broad daylight. The daring and dramatic raid stunned Japan and revived American morale. After dropping their bombs, the planes continued toward the China coast, where they were supposed to land at designated airstrips. However, because of a series of snafus and lack of communications among various commands, no radio signals were beamed to guide the Doolittle raiders to safe landing places. Only one bomber managed a safe landing at an airfield. The others made crash landings, injuring most crew members. Plane No. 16, containing bombardier Jacob DeShazer and his four crew mates, crashed in Japanese-held territory, two hundred miles inside China.

For the rest of the war, DeShazer suffered as a prisoner. He was moved to Tokyo with seven other captured Doolittle fliers, handcuffed and leg-cuffed, and turned over to the infamous *Kempai Tai*, the Japanese army's notorious military police, who began hideous tortures. Sometimes as many as five guards worked over a single man. In June 1942, the prisoners, who had not been allowed to wash, shave, or change clothes since the time they had taken off for the raid, were transferred to a filthy lice- and rat-infested cell in Shanghai. The torture and maltreatment grew worse. Three of the surviving Americans were executed; DeShazer and the five others were shifted to Nanking and put in solitary confinement.

The captors told the fliers that they all would die in prison, because Japan was winning the war and would never release them. If, somehow, the Japanese lost, the prisoners would be beheaded. On December 1, 1943, one of the prisoners died of dysentery and beriberi. The cells were ice chambers in the winter and stifling ovens in the summer.

DeShazer, like the others, became weak from dysentery, covered with more than seventy boils on his body. He would get on his knees, face the cell door, and repeat passages from the Bible. From out of the depths of his suffering, DeShazer discovered the strength and mercy of Jesus Christ. "The way the Japanese treated me," he reflects, "I had to turn to Christ. No matter what they did to me, I prayed. I prayed for the strength to live. And I prayed for strength, somehow, to find forgiveness for what they were doing to me."

One morning in August, 1945, DeShazer felt the Lord urging him to pray, all that day, for an end to the war. DeShazer prayed, from seven in the morning until two in the afternoon. The date was August 9, the day on which an atomic bomb was dropped on Nagasaki. The following day Japan surrendered. Finally, on August 20, 1945, U.S. Army paratroopers rescued DeShazer and the other surviving fliers.

Jacob DeShazer knew that Christ meant him to be an agent of reconciliation, an "ambassador of Christ." He returned to Japan as a Christian missionary as soon as he could after the war. For the next thirty years, DeShazer effectively shared the news of God's work of reconciliation through Jesus Christ. Among others that he reached was Mitsuo Fuchida, the Japanese flier who had led the air attack on Pearl Harbor. Through

DeShazer, Fuchida became a Christian and went on to be ordained as a Christian minister.

Sympathetic Vibration. A well-known detective story is founded on the phenomenon of sympathetic vibration. A valuable violin was stolen and a detective had reason to believe that it might be hidden near the scene of the crime. Upon the assumption that the thief had not loosened the strings of the instrument, the detective walked through the building with another violin, playing its strings vigorously, then stopping the vibration while he listened. He was rewarded when he heard quiet tones coming from the stolen violin that had been locked in a cabinet.

It could have happened. Most of us have tried some experiments, in school or elsewhere, which demonstrate sympathetic vibration. It certainly happens in the spiritual world. Jesus has set up a "vibration" in the world that wins the response of people. Jesus Christ has been universal in His appeal. Men and women in all centuries, of all races, living in all nations, have responded to Him.

Questions for Students on the Next Lesson. 1. What was the purpose of Paul's offering? 2. What group of Christians did Paul hold up for commendation because of their generous response to his appeal for an offering? 3. What is the essence of Christian stewardship according to II Corinthians 8—9? 4. How had the Corinthians responded to Paul's request for the offering? 5. How do you think Paul would write to your church regarding the giving in your congregation?

TOPIC FOR YOUTH
WORKING FOR RECONCILIATION

Relatives Relieve Rifts. In the mid-1950s, author William Faulkner spoke to a University of Mississippi writing class. He told the class that author Ernest Hemingway lacked courage and was afraid to take chances in his fiction. However, by the time Faulkner's comment was printed, he was quoted as saying that Hemingway had a yellow streak when it came to danger. That caused a lot of hard feelings and a rift between the two authors that extended into their immediate families and relatives.

In March 1993, author-publisher Dean Faulkner Wells, niece of William Faulkner, worked together with Jack Hemingway, Ernest's son, to judge a literary competition in Los Angeles. At that time these two members of the feuding families learned that poor shorthand and editing had led to the misquote over forty years ago. They decided to work on bringing an end to the rift that existed between the two families.

Here were two individuals who worked to put an end to the differences that existed between their families and to reconcile the two families to each other. The two had become ambassadors who were living and enacting human reconciliation.

Still Reconciling. Jim Wallis, forty-four, is the founder of the Sojourners Community in Washington, D.C. He plans and works for a vision of justice by combining his biblical faith with social engagement.

At age thirteen, this church youth group leader, athlete, and Eagle Scout began to ask questions. He was curious about why blacks and whites did not worship together, attend school together, or live together in the same neighborhood. A committed Bible student and Christian, he asked his church's pastor and members for an explanation. He wasn't satisfied with their answers.

He went into the inner city of his hometown, Detroit, and spent time with African Americans, working and worshiping with them. While there, he discovered some other sides of American life, such as poverty and inequality.

From that time on, Wallis worked with the poor and the black church in a close relationship. From involvement in early civil rights marches and other activities in the 1960s, Wallis continued a long-standing commitment to combat racism in America and around the world.

Many young people are like Wallis. They are capable of long-term commitments to reconciliation of the world. You can do the same as an ambassador for Christ.

Blackballed. Dr. Pam Tronetti, a young doctor in Erie, Pennsylvania, hoped to become a member of The Erie Maennerchor Club. The club enjoyed a fine tradition in the Erie community, and she wanted the opportunity to be part of the club, the community, and the contacts that the club would offer. She was rejected by the club members by a vote of 66 to 42.

The 120-year-old club had no female members. Although the membership claimed that everyone was welcome and that everyone had a fifty-fifty chance of being received into membership, in reality the majority ruled and no women had been accepted. Five women had applied and had been rejected, including Erie Judge Stephanie Domitrovich.

Dr. Tronetti commented that she was disappointed.

Youth often experience similar kinds of rejection. We as Christians are called to be ambassadors who draw all people together as Christ has drawn us to Himself. We are to drop all distinctions that keep us apart and work so that everyone is joined to Christ and to one another.

God rejects no one. Neither should we. We must look upon others with a new perspective.

Questions for Students on the Next Lesson. 1. Why was Paul so concerned about stewardship? 2. What image does Paul use to illustrate his concern? 3. Do you give to your church cheerfully? 4. In what other ways could you exercise stewardship? 5. What is the "inexpressible gift of God"?

LESSON 12—MAY 21

SHARING BLESSING WITH OTHERS

Background Scripture: II Corinthians 8—9
Devotional Reading: Matthew 25:31-41

KING JAMES VERSION

II CORINTHIANS 9:1 For as touching the ministering to the saints, it is superfluous for me to write to you:

2 For I know the forwardness of your mind, for which I boast of you to them of Macedonia, that Achaia was ready a year ago; and your zeal hath provoked very many.

3 Yet have I sent the brethren, lest our boasting of you should be in vain in this behalf; that, as I said, ye may be ready:

4 Lest haply if they of Macedonia come with me, and find you unprepared, we (that we say not, ye) should be ashamed in this same confident boasting.

5 Therefore I thought it necessary to exhort the brethren, that they would go before unto you, and make up beforehand your bounty, whereof ye had notice before, that the same might be ready, as a matter of bounty, and not as of covetousness.

6 But this I say, He which soweth sparingly shall reap also sparingly; and he which soweth bountifully shall reap also bountifully.

7 Every man according as he purposeth in his heart, so let him give; not grudgingly, or of necessity: for God loveth a cheerful giver.

8 And God is able to make all grace abound toward you; that ye, always having all sufficiency in all things, may abound to every good work . . .

10 Now he that ministereth seed to the sower both minister bread for your food, and multiply your seed sown, and increase the fruits of your righteousness;)

11 Being enriched in every thing to all bountifulness, which causeth through us thanksgiving to God.

12 For the administration of this service not only supplieth the want of the saints, but is abundant also by many thanksgivings unto God;

13 Whiles by the experiment of this ministration they glorify God for your professed subjection unto the gospel of Christ, and for your liberal distribution unto them, and unto all men;

14 And by their prayer for you, which long after you for the exceeding grace of God in you.

15 Thanks be unto God for his unspeakable gift.

REVISED STANDARD VERSION

II CORINTHIANS 9:1 Now it is superfluous for me to write to you about the offering for the saints, 2 for I know your readiness, of which I boast about you to the people of Macedonia, saying that Achaia has been ready since last year; and your zeal has stirred up most of them. 3 But I am sending the brethren so that our boasting about you may not prove vain in this case, so that you may be ready, as I said you would be; 4 lest if some Macedonians come with me and find that you are not ready, we be humiliated—to say nothing of you—for being so confident. 5 So I thought it necessary to urge the brethren to go on to you before me, and arrange in advance for this gift you have promised, so that it may be ready not as an exaction but as a willing gift.

6 The point is this: he who sows sparingly will also reap sparingly, and he who sows bountifully will also reap bountifully. 7 Each one must do as he has made up his mind, not reluctantly or under compulsion, for God loves a cheerful giver. 8 And God is able to provide you with every blessing in abundance, so that you may always have enough of everything and may provide in abundance for every good work. . . .

10 He who supplies seed to the sower and bread for food will supply and multiply your resources and increase the harvest of your righteousness. 11 You will be enriched in every way for great generosity, which through us will produce thanksgiving to God; 12 for the rendering of this service not only supplies the wants of the saints but also overflows in many thanksgivings to God. 13 Under the test of this service, you will glorify God by your obedience in acknowledging the gospel of Christ, and by the generosity of your contribution for them and for all others; 14 while they long for you and pray for you, because of the surpassing grace of God in you. 15 Thanks be to God for his inexpressible gift!

KEY VERSE: He who sows sparingly will also reap sparingly, and he who sows bountifully will also reap bountifully. II Corinthians 9:6.

HOME DAILY BIBLE READINGS

May 15	M.	Matthew 25:31-41	*Works of Compassion Are Blessed*
May 16	T.	II Corinthians 8:1-7	*Give Freely to Help Others*
May 17	W.	II Corinthians 8:8-15	*Give in Proportion to One's Means*
May 18	T.	II Corinthians 8:16-24	*Responsible Accounting in the Church*
May 19	F.	II Corinthians 9:1-5	*Be Ready with One's Gifts*
May 20	S.	II Corinthians 9:6-10	*Share with Cheerfulness*
May 21	S.	II Corinthians 9:11-15	*Enriched by Generosity*

BACKGROUND

Christians in the Jerusalem area were primarily poor people. Bad weather, crop failures, and bad economic conditions brought hardship and suffering to the members of the mother church.

Before leaving the Jerusalem Conference described in Acts 15, Paul promised Peter and the other leaders that he would "remember the poor" (see Gal. 2:10). And Paul did remember. With characteristic energy, he made this a top-priority project. Along with his desire to show compassion for the hungry and destitute fellow Christians in Jerusalem, Paul also wanted to demonstrate the oneness of Christ's church. Paul believed with all his heart that through Jesus Christ God had united all believers into a community in which each member shared the pain of the other. Perhaps Paul felt his special relief offering would also show his Jewish-Christian skeptics back in Jerusalem that he was indeed concerned about them.

Paul made his appeal for his "Jerusalem Famine Fund" throughout the areas where he had preached and founded churches. The Gentile believers in Galatia and Macedonia responded by contributing generously. Although not well-off themselves, the Christians in Macedonia proved to be particularly generous.

On the other hand, the Corinthians had failed to give. Paul had referred to the special offering for those in poverty in Jerusalem in an earlier letter (see I Cor. 16:1-4), asking the Corinthian Christians to make a weekly contribution, probably at the worship service. But Paul's request had been ignored.

Knowing that the Corinthian church people were far better off financially than the Macedonian Christians, and also knowing that time was running out for raising the promised funds, Paul again reminded the Corinthians of their stewardship obligations. In II Corinthians 8 and 9, he outlined the responsibilities of Christians to share their money. Paul's words still provide believers with sound advice on budgetary and benevolent matters for their congregations.

NOTES ON THE PRINTED TEXT

Now it is superfluous for me to write to you about the offering for the saints, for I know your readiness, of which I boast about you to the people of Macedonia, saying that Achaia has been ready since last year; and your zeal has stirred up most of them (9:1, 2). Paul was taking a collection for the needy Christians in Jerusalem. The gift would alleviate some of the suffering and poverty of the Jewish Christians while solidifying the unity of the Christian churches. Corinth was the largest and one of the most important cities in Greece, and the Corinthian church had enthusiastically agreed to participate in the offering. Their initial excitement had allowed Paul to use them as an example to other churches.

But I am sending the brethren so that our boasting about you may not prove vain in this case, so that you may be ready, as I said you would be; lest if some Macedonians come with me and find that you are not ready, we be humiliated—to say nothing of you—for being so confident (9:3, 4). Paul wanted to stimulate giving and avoid embarrassment for himself and the Corinthians. Since some Macedonians might be accompanying him on the visit, he was sending some brothers ahead (perhaps Titus and others) to check on the Corinthians and ensure that the gift was ready. The word "gift" literally meant "blessing." Paul urged them to send not only a verbal blessing but also the tangible gift of money. *So I thought it necessary to urge the brethren to go on to you before me, and arrange in advance for this gift you have promised, so that it may be ready not as an exaction but as a willing gift* (9:5).

Like a good fund-raiser, Paul had a slogan and perhaps quoted an old proverb: *The point is this: he who sows sparingly will also reap sparingly, and he who sows bountifully will also reap bountifully* (9:6). The illustration was easily understood. A farmer who sowed only a few seeds would harvest little, while the farmer who sowed many seeds would harvest much. Paul reminded the Corinthians that those who gave generously would also receive generously.

Each one must do as he has made up his mind, not reluctantly or under compulsion, for God loves a cheerful giver (9:7). Paul taught that a giver should consider the need and, if moved, respond to the need. However, he added that the giver should give cheerfully. Giving that arose out of a desire for personal praise or that was pressured or coerced was not desirable. Paul said that giving should be offered with happiness and laughter.

Paul assured the Corinthians that God was able to meet their needs and would enable them to meet others' needs abundantly. *And God is able to provide you with every blessing in abundance, so that you may always have enough of everything and may provide in abundance for every good work* (9:8). The idea was echoed again when Paul reminded his readers that God supplied not only the seed but also the harvest. *He who supplies seed to the sower and bread for food will supply and multiply your resources and increase the harvest of your righteousness* (9:10). Paul summarized his thought: *You will be enriched in every way for great generosity* (9:11).

How would the believers be enriched? Paul saw three possibilities. First, the gift would *produce thanksgiving to God* (9:11). After receiving assistance and hearing who the benefactors were, the hungry and destitute people would praise God. Thus, the gift produced praise from both the giver and the receiver. Secondly, the gift would provide for the physical needs of those in Jerusalem. *For the rendering of this service not only supplies the wants of the saints but also overflows in many thanksgivings to God* (9:12). The Greek word for "service" has the same root as the word for "liturgy." Liturgy originally referred to the service that a wealthy individual provided to meet the needs of the community, or it could refer to the service a priest provided to meet the needs of a worshiping community. Paul wrote that the reason for all this generous service was to bring glory to God. *Under the test of this service, you will glorify God by your obedience in acknowledging the gospel of Christ, and by the generosity of your contribution for them and for all others* (9:13). Finally, when the Jerusalem church members saw the generosity of the Corinthians, they would glorify God and pray for those who made the gift. *They long for you and pray for you, because of the surpassing grace of God in you* (9:14).

With the prospect of such unity among believers, Paul thanked the Corinthian church and praised it. *Thanks be to God for his inexpressible gift!* (9:15).

SUGGESTIONS TO TEACHERS

During the annual fall pledging campaign, an irritated parishioner berated the pastor for "preaching on money and not sticking to the Bible." The church member was chagrined when the minister sat down and pointed out to him the many references to possessions and giving in the Gospels, and particularly the teaching on sharing money in I and II Corinthians.

As every worker in a church stewardship program knows, giving is the least popular subject for many church people. Some in your class, in fact, may resist any mention of pledging or tithing in the church. And the offering, more than almost any other subject, has often been the subject of unpleasant church jokes.

Today's lesson faces the topic of giving head-on. You need hesitate to discuss money. Paul introduces the subject for you in II Corinthians 8—9. Point to the Scripture and discover these important points:

1. GENEROUS IN POVERTY. Paul challenged his readers to ponder two examples, that of the Macedonian Christians and that of Jesus Christ. Out of their poverty, they gave so much.

Incidentally, those who continue to support the church most generously are not the rich and well-off but those in poor or modest circumstances. The widow's mites still support God's work most effectively. True stewardship does not require waiting until we are a millionaire before giving. It simply calls for systematically sharing from what we have.

2. GROUNDED IN PRIORITIES. Paul teaches us what true stewardship is. First, he says, we must dedicate ourselves, as the Macedonian believers did. "First they gave themselves to the Lord" (8:5). Stewardship is actually a matter of commitment more than a matter of cash.

3. GENUINE IN PROMISES. We can learn much about a Christian's faith by looking through his checkbook. How genuine is the love of Christ as indicated by the pledging and giving in your church? Like many congregations, are you faced with money problems? Perhaps careful attention to II Corinthians 8—9 will offer you and your class some clues about the connection between promises to serve Christ and performance in giving.

4. GRACIOUS IN PROVISION. Stress the portions in today's Scripture that tell how bountifully God provides for our needs and gives us resources for sharing. Giving enriches the givers. Sharing deepens our awareness of God's gift of grace to us. Through our giving we discover more deeply that God is THE Giver.

TOPIC FOR ADULTS
SHARING YOUR BLESSINGS

Each Enriched. An ancient folktale from Europe describes two brothers who had joint ownership of a farm and a mill. They agreed to share the flour evenly from the barley grown on their field and ground in their mill. One of the brothers was single. The other was married and had a large family to feed.

It occurred to the unmarried brother that it would be appropriate for him to give more of his share to his brother and family. Each night he crept out and carried some of his barley meal to his brother's storage bin. He said nothing to his brother, knowing that the brother would not want to accept more than his share.

Meanwhile, the married brother got to thinking about the fact that he had children to look after him in his old age, while the single brother would have no one. He decided to take some of his grain without mentioning it to his brother and quietly place it in the unmarried man's storage bin. Each brother was puzzled because the supply in his own bin seemed to be sufficient. Neither could figure out why, in spite of the secret sharing, there was enough.

One dark night, they encountered each other carrying a supply to place in the other's bin, and suddenly realized what had been happening. In their sharing, they discovered their love for each other in a deeper way.

Grace and Gratitude. We share with others because God has first shared with us. Grace brings gratitude. Country singer Barbara Mandrell attests to this. She says it was eight years before she returned to normal after a car wreck had left her with a brain injury.

"Until I was rehabilitated, until I was healed, Barbara Mandrell—the mommy to my children and wife to my husband—she was dead," Mandrell said.

The popular singer now devotes much of her time to speaking on behalf of those with brain injuries and the problems faced by their families. She frequently addresses groups on behalf of the victims of brain injury and has testified before a Tennessee legislative committee studying such problems. Grateful to the Lord for His grace in bringing her new health and life, Barbara Mandrell says, "I feel so fortunate and so blessed to have healed that I think it's the absolutely only Christian thing to do. If I'm needed, I'll go in and speak."

Willingly Sacrificed. In his book, *My Grandfather's War,* William D. Mathieson tells of a Canadian veteran of World War I who lost an arm in the trenches. Mathieson describes the old soldier walking down the main street in his hometown with one sleeve empty. A passerby stopped to commiserate with him for the loss of his arm. Standing proudly and looking the other in the eye, the one-armed veteran replied, "I did not lose it. I gave it!"

That attitude captures the spirit of a Christian giving his money.

Questions for Students on the Next Lesson. 1. What is the greatest spiritual gift? 2. How is this gift shown? 3. Who or what comes first in your life? 4. What kinds of relationships do you have in your family? 5. Is love mostly a matter of feelings?

TOPIC FOR YOUTH
SHARING YOUR BLESSINGS

To Help His Country. Larry Villella, a fourteen-year-old ninth grader from Fargo, North Dakota, was founder of "ConServe Products." His company marketed his new invention: a tree and shrub watering system made from recycled plastic tubing. By age fourteen, Larry had already earned over $50,000 for his efforts.

This young entrepreneur recognized the need to cut the federal deficit in order to help those who really needed financial support. To help decrease the debt, he sent President Clinton a check for $1,000. He further urged each American to help by donating $10.00 to the cause. Later, President Clinton personally called Larry to thank him for his contribution.

Like Larry, you, too, can share your blessings. Believing that his gift would ultimately help others, Larry gave generously. His gift produced thanksgiving and a good example for others to follow.

A Tradition of Caring. Little James Withers used to accompany his father, a family physician, on house calls in Hanover, Pennsylvania. He watched his father care for the sick, often free of charge.

James Withers's interest in public service grew, and he went on to become a doctor himself. He was accepted at Mercy Hospital in the inner city of Pittsburgh. The hospital had a tradition of community service. However, Dr. Withers felt that he wanted to be even more involved with the city's poor and needy.

By the age of thirty-five, Dr. Withers was making his most important rounds at night. These rounds took him more than five miles to visit patients with names like Caveman, Big Sue, and Gramps who lived in cardboard boxes, under plastic tarps, or on the banks of the Allegheny River. Their ailments ranged from head lice and chapped hands to gangrene and liver disease. Dr. Withers administered care to all of these patients, free of charge. He became known as the doctor to many of Pittsburgh's homeless street people.

Taking a concern that began as a boy while watching his father, Withers applied that concern to his life-style. He continued the tradition of caring for the needy that his father had taught him years earlier.

Paul would approve, knowing that Withers's sharing of his service ultimately produced thanksgiving to God as the needs of the community were met.

Gave As He Received. Tina Alvarez, supervisor of the Child Life Department, looked up from her desk at Children's Memorial Hospital in Chicago. She was surprised to see a young boy who had been a former patient standing in the doorway. Brian was holding a box of baseball cards in his hands.

The hospital had just begun a new program called Cards for Kids. Individuals and organizations donated baseball cards that were then distributed to young people suffering physically, emotionally, or socially. When Brian had been in the hospital, Tina had presented him with cards.

Brian told a suddenly tear-faced Tina how much he enjoyed receiving the cards and how important they were to his recovery. He had returned to say hello and to replenish her supply. He wanted other patients to receive what had been given to him.

That was the attitude Paul spoke about to the Corinthian church. He who sowed bountifully would also reap bountifully.

Questions for Students on the Next Lesson. 1. What is the most important spiritual gift a Christian can possess? 2. How does love relate to other spiritual gifts? 3. Define love. What does the word mean in our own culture? 4. How can we demonstrate Paul's concept of love in our own lives? 5. Is love really more important than faith and hope? Why, or why not?

LESSON 13—MAY 28

EXPRESSING LOVE TO ALL

Background Scripture: I Corinthians 13
Devotional Reading: John 15:9-17

KING JAMES VERSION

I CORINTHIANS 13:1 Though I speak with the tongues of men and of angels, and have not charity, I am become as sounding brass, or a tinkling cymbal.

2 And though I have the gift of prophecy, and understand all mysteries, and all knowledge; and though I have all faith, so that I could remove mountains, and have not charity, I am nothing.

3 And though I bestow all my goods to feed the poor, and though I give my body to be burned, and have not charity, it profiteth me nothing.

4 Charity suffereth long, and is kind; charity envieth not; charity vaunteth not itself, is not puffed up,

5 Doth not behave itself unseemly, seeketh not her own, is not easily provoked, thinketh no evil;

6 Rejoiceth not in iniquity, but rejoiceth in the truth;

7 Beareth all things, believeth all things, hopeth all things, endureth all things.

8 Charity never faileth: but whether there be prophecies, they shall fail; whether there be tongues, they shall cease; whether there be knowledge, it shall vanish away.

9 For we know in part, and we prophesy in part.

10 But when that which is perfect is come, then that which is in part shall be done away.

11 When I was a child, I spake as a child, I understood as a child, I thought as a child: but when I became a man, I put away childish things.

12 For now we see through a glass, darkly; but then face to face: now I know in part; but then shall I know even as also I am known.

13 And now abideth faith, hope, charity, these three; but the greatest of these is charity.

REVISED STANDARD VERSION

I CORINTHIANS 13:1 If I speak in the tongues of men and of angels, but have not love, I am a noisy gong or a clanging cymbal.

2 And if I have prophetic powers, and understand all mysteries and all knowledge, and if I have all faith, so as to remove mountains, but have not love, I am nothing. 3 If I give away all I have, and if I deliver my body to be burned, but have not love, I gain nothing.

4 Love is patient and kind; love is not jealous or boastful; 5 it is not arrogant or rude. Love does not insist on its own way; it is not irritable or resentful; 6 it does not rejoice at wrong, but rejoices in the right. 7 Loves bears all things, believes all things, hopes all things, endures all things.

8 Love never ends; as for prophecies, they will pass away; as for tongues, they will cease; as for knowledge, it will pass away. 9 For our knowledge is imperfect and our prophecy is imperfect; 10 but when the perfect comes, the imperfect will pass away. 11 When I was a child, I spoke like a child, I thought like a child, I reasoned like a child; when I became a man, I gave up childish ways. 12 For now we see in a mirror dimly, but then face to face. Now I know in part; then I shall understand fully, even as I have been fully understood. 13 So faith, hope, love abide, these three; but the greatest of these is love.

KEY VERSE: *Faith, hope, love abide, these three; but the greatest of these is love.* I Corinthians 13:13.

HOME DAILY BIBLE READINGS

May 22	M.	John 15:9-17	*Jesus' Commandment: Love One Another*
May 23	T.	I Corinthians 13:1-7	*The Way of Love*
May 24	W.	I Corinthians 13:8-13	*Love Is beyond All Spiritual Gifts*
May 25	T.	Ephesians 3:14-19	*Empowered by Christ's Love*
May 26	F.	Matthew 5:43-48	*Love Your Enemies*
May 27	S.	Luke 10:29-37	*Love Your Neighbor*
May 28	S.	James 2:1-7	*Love Shows No Partiality*

BACKGROUND

The Corinthian Christians mistakenly thought there was a hierarchy of spiritual gifts. Those with the gift of speaking in tongues prided themselves on having the most outstanding gift. Others, swollen with self-importance, felt privileged to have the gift of knowledge. Church members in Corinth disputed among themselves regarding whose gift counted the most.

We must remember that this squabbling over spiritual gifts was the context for Paul's great words in I Corinthians 13. Unfortunately, we sometimes rip this passage out of context and read it merely as a treatise on love. We must understand, however, that Paul was not writing some immortal prose on the general subject of love to be read at weddings. Rather, we need to recall that he was trying to teach some proud and obstinate Christians what the one most important gift is, and how every Christian is expected to share this gift.

The word for "love" in I Corinthians 13 is the Greek word *agape* (pronounced "ah-GAH-pay"). Unlike English, where the term "love" describes a variety of emotions, the Greek language has three main words sometimes translated "love." One is *eros*, referring primarily to sexual attraction and sensual pleasure. The second is *philia*, meaning friendship. The third, *agape*, means sacrificial caring.

Paul used *agape* to describe the way God has acted toward us in Jesus Christ. Agape also refers to the spiritual gift that God has bestowed on each person who responds to His love in Christ. Throughout this passage, Paul emphasized that sacrificial caring is the most important part of a Christian's life.

NOTES ON THE PRINTED TEXT

As important as all the spiritual gifts were, one was very important. Paul wrote that the greatest gift was love. *If I speak in the tongues of men and of angels, but have not love, I am a noisy gong or a clanging cymbal* (13:1). The early rabbis taught that there were seventy languages spoken by human beings, but the angels communicated only in Hebrew. Paul taught that speaking in tongues was not the supreme gift. Without love, the sound of speaking in tongues was only a noise like a clanking bronze gong. Corinth had its theaters and amphitheaters and Paul said that without love, the speaker was as empty as the acoustic amplifiers in these Greek theaters. The speaker would be full of sound but saying nothing.

And if I have prophetic powers, and understand all mysteries and all knowledge, and if I have all faith, so as to remove mountains, but have not love, I am nothing (13:2). Prophecy was the ability to speak and preach boldly for God (or, in some cases, to tell what God would do in the future). To understand all mysteries meant to be able to understand the meaning of the Scriptures and of God's nature. Other believers had a special faith and power that enabled them to accomplish great works. These gifts, as great as they were, became meaningless without love.

If I give away all I have, and if I deliver my body to be burned, but have not love, I gain nothing (13:3). If a believer sacrifices all and gives his or her possessions away to charity, the act will be ineffectual without love. Even if a believer allows himself or herself to be martyred, the act is meaningless without love.

Paul shifted his emphasis in order to define love. *Love is patient and kind; love is not jealous or boastful* (13:4). Love is willing to accept hurt without complaining. Love is willing to soothe another's pain, suffering, and anxiety. Love does not further one's own status. Love has no pride and does not brag. *It is not arrogant or rude* (13:5). Love considers the good of others. Love does not pursue its own advantage. *Love does not insist on its own way* (13:5). Love attempts to avoid resentment and retaliation. *Love is not irritable or resentful* (13:5). Love strives to recognize the difference between good and evil and to forgive wrongs. *It does not rejoice at wrong, but rejoices in the right* (13:6). Finally, love puts a cover over things. It keeps confidences where harm would result if they were made public. Love sees the possibilities in others. Love is resilient. *Love bears all things, believes all things, hopes all things, endures all things* (13:7).

Paul then spoke of the permanence of love. *Love never ends* (13:8). Love never ceases or fails, whereas other spiritual gifts, such as prophecies . . . tongues . . . and knowledge (13:8), would ultimately cease. Knowledge and prophecy were incomplete and imperfect. Such gifts were overvalued at the expense of love. Moving into a life of love was like moving from childhood to adulthood. *When I was a child, I spoke like a child, I thought like a child, I reasoned like a child; when I became a man, I gave up childish ways* (13:11).

Paul used the analogy of a mirror to show that a believer's knowledge was incomplete. Corinth was well known for its manufacture of bronze goods, and archaeologists have excavated three bronze foundries that made some brilliant bronze mirrors. The bronze had an unusually high tin content. Even so, the polished metal produced a far from clear reflection. The reflected image was indistinct. A believer's vision of God was indistinct too. But in the age yet to come, God would be clearly seen and known. *For now we see in a mirror dimly, but then face to face. Now I know in part; then I shall understand fully, even as I have been fully understood* (13:12). Human knowledge is partial, but someday it will be complete.

Paul concluded by writing of eternal attributes that come from God, the greatest being love. *So faith, hope, love abide, these three; but the greatest of these is love* (13:13).

SUGGESTIONS TO TEACHERS

"Love" is an overworked word in our society today. It has to signify preferences ("I love angel food cake"); it must apply to romantic feelings ("I think I'm in love with the checkout girl at the supermarket"). Reduced to the symbol of a red heart on a bumper sticker, it communicates our liking Cape Cod or New York. The word "love" has been so stretched and squeezed that it has lost its New Testament impact.

The first thing you will have to do in this lesson is clarify what love is in the Scripture for today. You might do this by asking class members to call out some of the ways we use the word "love" in our everyday speech ("I love angel food cake," etc.). You can get down to serious work in this lesson only when everyone realizes that love means more than mushy feelings or personal delights. Only when we consider the Cross and the Resurrection can we comprehend what the apostle Paul meant by love. Maybe the word you should use in this lesson is "caring"—the kind of caring God has shown toward us in Jesus Christ.

1. CONTRAST TO OTHER GIFTS. As you study I Corinthians 13, remember the reason Paul was writing these great verses. He was not composing an ode to "love in general." Rather, he was commenting on the gifts of the Spirit to the noisy, pushy Corinthians who claimed superior gifts. Tongues, prophecy, knowledge, faith, generosity, good works, even martyrdom counted for absolutely nothing as gifts unless they were enveloped in love. Without love, no gift meant a thing. The greatest gift of the Spirit is love.

2. CHARACTERISTICS OF THE GIFT. Delve into Paul's list of the qualities of Christian love. To keep this from mere theory, try inserting your name and the names of your class members before each phrase in verses 4 through 7. Say, for example, "John Doe is patient and kind," or reverse the meaning of the sentence and apply it: "John Doe is jealous and boastful, is arrogant and rude." "I am sometimes irritable and resentful," etc. This personal touch will illuminate the practical meaning of love.

3. CONSTANCY OF THIS GIFT. Love is permanent. Love endures. All other gifts are temporary. Remark about the fact that acts of caring (in contrast with giftedness) have eternal value.

4. CULMINATION OF THIS GIFT. The mature person is the loving person. We all need to mature or "grow up" as Christians. Life with Christ means leaving the childish demand for our own way and responding to God's love by caring for others.

5. CHARACTER OF GOD. Love describes the very being of God. Faith is what we do. Hope is what we have. Love—*agape*—is God's kind of sacrificial self-giving. Our human attempts at love will always be stained with self-interest. Make sure that your class realizes what God's kind of unconditional love means for them personally.

TOPIC FOR ADULTS
SERVING WITH LOVE

Love as Sacrifice. The earthquake that killed an estimated fifty-five thousand people in 1989 brought tragedy and sorrow to countless Armenians. Many stories of courage have emerged from the earthquake in

Armenia, but few, if any, are as touching or harrowing as the tale Susanna Petrosyan told. She and her daughter were entombed in eternal night, and their only food, a jar of jam, was gone. Tons of smashed concrete around them had become their prison. "Mommy, I'm so thirsty, I want to drink," cried the four-year-old girl.

Susanna Petrosyan said she was trapped flat on her back. A prefabricated concrete panel eighteen inches above her head, and a crumpled water pipe above her shoulders, kept her from standing. She wore only a slip, and it was horribly cold.

Beside her in the darkness lay the lifeless body of her sister-in-law, Karine. She had been crushed by the falling walls.

"Mommy, I need to drink," sobbed Mrs. Petrosyan's daughter, Gayaney. "Please give me something."

"I thought my child was going to die of thirst," Mrs. Petrosyan recalled. "I had no water, no fruit juice, no liquids. It was then I remembered that I had my own blood."

Although she was trapped in darkness, she could slide on her back from side to side. Her groping fingers, numb from the cold, found a shattered glass. She sliced open her left index finger with a shard and gave it to her daughter to suckle.

The drops of blood weren't enough. "Please, Mommy, some more. Cut another finger," Mrs. Petrosyan remembers her daughter saying. The woman made more cuts in her flesh, feeling nothing because of the bitter cold. She put her hand to her child's mouth, squeezing her fingers to make more blood come.

"I knew I was going to die," Mrs. Petrosyan said. "But I wanted my daughter to live."

Losing track of time because of the unchanging darkness, Mrs. Petrosyan doesn't know what day she cut open her fingers, or how many times she used the method to feed her daughter.

On the eighth day of their captivity, rescue workers opened a small hole that let in a shaft of light. "We're saved!" Mrs. Petrosyan cried.

Love is like that! Through the sacrifice of Christ's blood on the Cross, we have experienced the life-giving power of God's love.

Not Even a Little Rose. The great Moravian leader, Count von Zinzendorf, understood the meaning of I Corinthians 13 as well as anyone. Emphasizing the supreme gift of Christian love in a sermon one Sunday at Herrnhut, the saintly preacher stated, "Even if somebody converted all Turks and Chinese into Christians, he would not earn even a little rose from the paradise."

How Clear is the Message? We Christians are called to present the message of God's love clearly. Sometimes we garble the message, and those in the world get the wrong word.

Recall the days when U.S. forces first landed in Mogadishu, Somalia, in December 1992. The Marines were given leaflets to hand out to win over the Somali people. On one side of the leaflet was a drawing of a black American soldier and a Somali shaking hands, with a helicopter and Humvee in the background. On the other side was a picture of the flags of the United Nations and the United States with a message written below. The aim was to assure Somalis that the Americans had come as friends to protect relief shipments to starving people under U.N. auspices. However, the message was completely mangled and lost on all Somali readers. Instead of using the correct Somali word "aduunka" for "world" in the phrase "world forces," the leaflet used "adoonka," which means, roughly, "slave." The Somalis who read the leaflet found the message to be contrary to what the United Nations and U.S. leaders desired.

The only message from God that many in the world around us will ever see or hear is the life we Christians live. Is the word "love" being translated into caring actions that our neighbors can understand?

Questions for Students on the Next Lesson. 1. Who was Rehoboam? 2. Why did the northern tribes break away from his kingdom? 3. Whose advice did Rehoboam reject and whose did he heed? 4. Who was Jeroboam? 5. Do our national leaders seek to hear and satisfy the grievances of the oppressed?

TOPIC FOR YOUTH
LIVING A LIFE OF LOVE

Looking for Love. "Hello, I'm home alone." The caller is a nine-year-old boy. He is one of the ten million latchkey children in the United States. These children stay home alone while a parent or parents are at work. Statistics tell us that about 42 percent of American children between the ages of five and nine, and 77 percent of older children, fall into this category. Many of these children have adapted well. However, some feel alone and scared, calling volunteer services such as PhoneFriend in order to talk with someone who seems to care.

Like the nine-year-old boy, many youth are seeking love in its many forms. You, as a Christian, are called to live a life of love. True love requires much more than basking in warm sentiments. Love must be demonstrated. Paul offered his church a good definition. Follow it, and there will be fewer children like the ones calling PhoneFriend.

Loved Enough to Act. Eleven-year-old Ashley Jarrett is a fifth grader at Lemington Elementary School in Pittsburgh. When Ashley returned from school on February 25, 1993, she found her mother smoking crack cocaine in her bedroom. The two began to argue. Her mother, Trudy Smith, slapped her several times, threw her against the door, and finally ordered her to leave the house.

Ashley, though, was worried about her four-year-old sister, Keshia, who was also home. Ashley refused to leave. In desperation, her mother called the police.

When the police arrived, Ashley (who had recently completed a drug-awareness program) told the officers that her mother had a drug problem. She gave them a pipe and some crack cocaine. She then took the police into her mother's bedroom and gave them a mirror and two knives that contained cocaine residue. Finally, she lifted the mattress to show the officers where her mother hid her drugs.

This young, quiet, levelheaded girl knew her mother had a drug problem. She loved her mother and sister enough to make a difficult choice. She acted in love so her family ultimately could live once again in love.

Incomplete to Complete Understanding. Bill was given his father's old single lens reflex camera to use. After several years of use, the camera needed to be repaired. The shutter no longer operated as it should. While Bill was surprised, his father was shocked when the two were told by the camera repairman that the camera was too old to repair. Parts were no longer available.

The repairman went on to explain that the camera had been made in a different era. Since that time, men had walked on the moon. Science and technology had advanced. While Bill's camera was once the top of the line, better ones were now available. Increased knowledge had made this particular one obsolete.

Our knowledge is imperfect and incomplete. We have only partial knowledge and understanding of God. However, Paul reminds us that the day will come when our incomplete knowledge will become a complete and full knowledge of Jesus Christ.

Questions for Students on the Next Lesson. 1. Why did the ten northern tribes confront Rehoboam? 2. What advice did the two opposing groups offer to the uncrowned king? 3. How did the would-be king respond? 4. What was the end result of Rehoboam's decision? 5. Who do you turn to for advice? Why?

JUNE, JULY, AUGUST 1995

A NATION TURNS TO GOD

LESSON 1—JUNE 4

WHEN POWER IS MISUSED

Background Scripture: I Kings 11:26—12:24
Devotional Reading: Psalm 14

KING JAMES VERSION

I KINGS 12:6 And king Rehoboam consulted with the old men, that stood before Solomon his father while he yet lived, and said, How do ye advise that I may answer this people?

7 And they spake unto him, saying, If thou wilt be a servant unto this people this day, and wilt serve them, and answer them, and speak good words to them, then they will be thy servants for ever.

8 But he forsook the counsel of the old men, which they had given him, and consulted with the young men that were grown up with him, and which stood before him:

9 And he said unto them, What counsel give ye that we may answer this people, who have spoken to me, saying, Make the yoke which thy father did put upon us lighter?

10 And the young men that were grown up with him spake unto him, saying, Thus shalt thou speak unto this people that spake unto thee, saying, Thy father made our yoke heavy, but make thou it lighter unto us; thus shalt thou say unto them, My little finger shall be thicker than my father's loins.

11 And now whereas my father did lade you with a heavy yoke, I will add to your yoke: my father hath chastised you with whips, but I will chastise you with scorpions.

16 So when all Israel saw that the king hearkened not unto them, the people answered the king, saying, What portion have we in David? neither have we inheritance in the son of Jesse: to your tents, O Israel: now see to thine own house, David. So Israel departed unto their tents.

17 But as for the children of Israel which dwelt in the cities of Judah, Rehoboam reigned over them.

REVISED STANDARD VERSION

I KINGS 12:6 Then King Rehoboam took counsel with the old men, who had stood before Solomon his father while he was yet alive, saying, "How do you advise me to answer this people?" 7 And they said to him, "If you will be a servant to this people today and serve them, and speak good words to them when you answer them, then they will be your servants for ever." 8 But he forsook the counsel which the old men gave him, and took counsel with the young men who had grown up with him and stood before him. 9 And he said to them, "What do you advise that we answer this people who have said to me, 'Lighten the yoke that your father put upon us'?" 10 And the young men who had grown up with him said to him, "Thus shall you speak to this people who said to you, 'Your father made our yoke heavy, but do you lighten it for us'; thus shall you say to them, 'My little finger is thicker than my father's loins. 11 And now, whereas my father laid upon you a heavy yoke, I will add to your yoke. My father chastised you with whips, but I will chastise you with scorpions.' "

16 And when all Israel saw that the king did not hearken to them, the people answered the king, "What portion have we in David? We have no inheritance in the son of Jesse. To your tents, O Israel! Look now to your own house, David." So Israel departed to their tents. 17 But Rehoboam reigned over the people of Israel who dwelt in the cities of Judah.

KEY VERSE: If you will be a servant to this people today and serve them, and speak good words to them when you answer them, then they will be your servants for ever. I Kings 12:7.

HOME DAILY BIBLE READINGS

BACKGROUND

During this series of lessons, we will trace the story of Israel from its proudest moments under King Solomon to its destruction. This whole period was a time of struggle for political power and national security. Unfortunately, the centuries we will examine were also a time of injustice and oppression in which Israel violated its covenant with God. This study is crucial for us because it demonstrates that God reveals His will in historical events and in the prophets' interpretation of such events.

The series opens with the deaths of Solomon and his son, and the vain, stubborn Rehoboam beginning his reign. Solomon had built a magnificent capital city, spending lavishly. To carry out his ambitious building plans, he had resorted to forced labor gangs. To support his luxurious life-style and enormous household staff, he imposed heavy taxes. By the time of Solomon's final days, these burdens were becoming intolerable for the people of Israel. Revolts broke out in Edom and Syria. More ominously, the ten northern tribes were rumbling with dissatisfaction. These northerners had been brought into the state through David's political skills. Solomon's taxes and labor drafts became new grievances to these ten tribes, which had never been completely assimilated into the united kingdom.

Nevertheless, a new ruler with some sound political instincts would have lightened the tax load and shown a more compassionate attitude. Rehoboam could have kept his kingdom from splitting. Instead, displaying an arrogant unwillingness to listen to anyone except his youthful palace cronies, Rehoboam foolishly announced that he would levy even more onerous burdens on his weary, struggling subjects.

The restless northern tribes quickly found a hero in the person of an able young administrator named Jeroboam. Jeroboam headed the rebellion that erupted, and successfully seized control of most of the nation, leaving Rehoboam holding only Jerusalem and the territory of Judah.

NOTES ON THE PRINTED TEXT

Solomon's lavish spending, heavy taxes, and forced labor had been very unpopular, especially in northern Israel. Also, Solomon's cultivation of pagan faiths had been offensive to the north. With Solomon's death, his son Rehoboam sought to ascend to the throne of all Israel, and the elders of Judah did wish to anoint their son. The north, however, had another idea. Before Rehoboam was crowned king, certain policies would have to change. Rehoboam traveled north to Shechem to discuss the situation. At that meeting, the north summarized its grievances and asked for reforms. *Your father made our yoke heavy. Now therefore lighten the hard service of your father and his heavy yoke upon us, and we will serve you* (12:4). Rehoboam asked for three days to consider the north's request.

How do you advise me to answer this people? (12:6). Rehoboam first sought counsel from his father's advisers. Oddly, he failed to mention the north's petitions. Perhaps they were aware or suspected what had taken place. Whatever the situation was, the old counselors had seen the result of Solomon's policies. Loyalty and unity were worth the cost of a few concessions in taxes and labor obligations. They advised Rehoboam to be a responsive and responsible public servant. *If you will be a servant to this people today and serve them, and speak good words to them when you answer them, then they will be your servants for ever* (12:7).

Rehoboam also sought the advice of younger men with whom he had grown up. He fully briefed his friends on the political situation. *What do you advise that we answer this people who have said to me, "Lighten the yoke that your father put upon us"?* (12:9).

This group enjoyed power and wanted to preserve it. To make concessions was to show weakness. Perhaps they argued that they had already demonstrated weakness by journeying to Shechem. The northern elders should have come to Jerusalem. They counseled a strong, tough response that mocked the northern leaders' requests. *My little finger is thicker than my father's loins. And now, whereas my father laid upon you a heavy yoke, I will add to your yoke. My father chastised you with whips, but I will chastise you with scorpions* (12:10, 11).

Three days later, Rehoboam gave his answer. He arrogantly refused any reforms. In fact, he would make life tougher by increasing the peoples' burdens. He disregarded the advice of those experienced in government and took the advice of his younger friends, shattering any hope for unity. Muscle won out over wisdom.

Rehoboam's harsh response shocked the elders of the north. Hearing his decision, they rebelled. *What portion have we in David? We have no inheritance in the son of Jesse. To your tents, O Israel! Look now to your own house, David* (12:16). The north saw no reason to preserve any unity with the south. "To your tents" was a summons for the northerners to return home. They told Rehoboam that if he wished to rule, he could do it on his own, with the people of the south as his only subject. So Rehoboam reigned over only the southern area. His kingdom now included only the land of Judah and part of Benjamin.

SUGGESTIONS TO TEACHERS

You may not quite agree with old Henry Ford that "History is bunk." At the same time you may not be thrilled with the idea of spending thirteen lessons on the epoch of Israel's decline and fall. But recall Harvard philosopher George Santayana's famous saying: "Those who cannot remember the past are condemned to repeat it."

The story of Israel holds important lessons for the people of God in every generation. German Bible students use a theological word that gives insight into the important place of scriptural history in revealing God's saving actions to us: *Heilsgeschichte,* meaning "holy history" or "salvation story." Your teaching during these coming weeks is based on *God's story*, which means more than a collection of dreary ancient events. As you work with the material from "His-story", you will find the Lord relating also to *your* story—your story of salvation. After reading the Scripture passage for today, prepare your lesson to cover the following points:

1. AUTOCRATIC TYRANT. Examine Solomon's reign in its final days, particularly noting the way Solomon slipped from being the wise and godly ruler he once had been. His high-handed attitude and tactics were alienating his people, threatening the future of the nation. Use this example to discuss ways of relating to others, especially those over whom we have some form of authority. Autocratic leadership, whether carried out as a parent, a president, or a boss, breeds serious relationship problems.

2. AGGRESSIVE LEADER. In his early days, Rehoboam showed promising gifts as a leader. Later, he used these gifts to lead his kingdom into ways contrary to what God intended. How many other examples of wasted gifts (on the part of leaders) can you and your people give?

3. ANOINTING PROPHET. Ahijah saw the need for a new leader in the dreary, final days of Solomon's reign, so he anointed a man named Jeroboam (see I Kings 11:26-40). Sometimes, a godly man or woman sees the situation in a country or a congregation more clearly than anyone. Ahijah was willing to take the risk of anointing Jeroboam, trying to be faithful to his calling. Courage must go with godliness.

4. ABRASIVE ADVISERS. Rehoboam insisted on listening only to the circle of young admirers who told him what he wanted to hear. He ignored the moderating counsel of wiser heads. Whenever a person chooses to hear only whatever advice he or she likes to hear, the voice of the Spirit and wisdom will be muted. Rehoboam's so-called advisers advocated abrasive tactics that resulted in the young monarch's losing much of his kingdom.

5. ABUSIVE MONARCH. Rehoboam can serve as a case study in leadership. Since everyone in your class must act as a leader in some capacity, at least some of the time, examining Rehoboam's ways will be helpful. To whom do your group members turn for advice? What role does faith in God play in the life and work of your students when they act as leaders? How should a leader use his or her power?

TOPIC FOR ADULTS
WHEN POWER IS MISUSED

Misused Power Murders. Dmitri Volkogonov, a Russian scholar, managed to gain access to the archives of Joseph Stalin after they were finally made available a few years ago. Night after night, Volkogonov returned to his apartment deeply shaken by what he had read during the day. He recalled coming back home one evening after reviewing Stalin's activities on the day of December 12, 1938. Stalin had signed thirty lists of death sentences that day. Five thousand people, including many that were friends and others known to him personally, were on those lists detailing who would be shot.

What jarred Volkogonov most was not so much the signing of these documents but what Stalin did that evening. The callous dictator went to his personal movie theater that evening and watched a popular comedy, "Happy Guys," then retired to bed. Volkogonov could not understand how the dictator could watch such a movie after deciding the fate of five thousand human lives. Then Dmitri Volkogonov wrote in his book, *Stalin: Triumph and Tragedy*, that he began to understand that morality plays no role for dictators. Volkogonov began then to understand why his father was shot, why his mother died in exile, and why millions of innocent persons perished.

Power Corrupts. Few generalizations of human experience are more sure. And where is the temptation to misuse power more treacherous than in the parent-child relationship? Here even "Mr. Milquetoast," as father, can exercise lordly rule. Discipline dictated by selfish adult whim or convenience, exploitation of juvenile talent for parental gain, the cruelty of neglect, the equal cruelty of depersonalizing solicitude, the spoiling of a child because restraint demands time and care—any father or mother, with even a little self-criticism, could lengthen the catalog of parental egotisms almost endlessly. The results, if not redeemed by corresponding insights of penitence, can be disastrous. They provoke to anger. . . .

A child has a vivid sense of justice. To be in the discipline and instruction of the Lord, like all schooling in childhood and youth, may produce moods of rebellion or desire to escape. But the mood is on the surface. A child expects maturity. A youth is an amateur adult. To be cheated of instruction—with all the discipline and even punishment necessarily involved—can produce a lifelong anger.—Theodore A. Wedel in *The Interpreter's Bible: Ephesians.*

Recognized Dangers. Lionel Richie had a million-dollar career as a star performer, composer, and record producer in the mid-1980s. In 1984, he signed an $8 million deal with Pepsi Cola, and a year later cowrote "We Are the World" with Michael Jackson. An Oscar followed, then another hit, "Dancing on the Ceiling." Then, abruptly, Richie went home to Alabama, after sixteen years of movies, awards, tours, albums, and overall success. He had enjoyed immense power as one of the highest paid, most popular entertainers, but suddenly he learned that he lacked the power to hold his life together.

Richie started to have trouble with his vocal cords. His marriage fell apart, his father died, and he felt great inner turmoil. Richie realized that he was at the point in his career during which the power of success had led other artists to go astray. He remembered that at that critical time many associates had gotten into drugs and took to drinking. He recognized that he, like his artist friends, had huge egos, and that these egos made it difficult for them to listen to anyone who did not praise them.

Six years later, in 1992, Lionel Richie returned to the entertainment world a changed person. He had learned humility. Through an awareness of God's grace in Christ, he was finally able to realize what he had done wrong and experience forgiveness. He now attributes his gifts to the Lord and considers God his "cowriter." His vocal cords are good once more, and he works hard in the recording studio and on his concert tours. The power, fame, and money no longer threatens to destroy Richie, thanks to his faith.

Unlike Lionel Richie, Rehoboam followed his peers. In doing so, he made life miserable for himself and others.

Questions for Students on the Next Lesson. 1. What was Baal religion? 2. Why was Elijah vexed at King Ahab? 3. What was the challenge Elijah put to Ahab? 4. What was the outcome of that challenge? 5. How do you select the values you take most seriously?

TOPIC FOR YOUTH
POWER MISUSED

Foolish Action. Aaron Williams, or "Bubba," as he was known to his friends, seemed to have it made. The six-foot-two-inch, three-hundred-pound athlete graduated from Washington High School in Washington, Pennsylvania. During high school, this student-athlete had been an all-conference defensive tackle and held the school's best wrestling record. He had compiled an amazing 100-17-1 record and was third in the state in the heavyweight division. In his first year at college, he was good enough in wrestling to earn All-American honors by finishing eighth in the Division II National Tournament.

Then on February 19, 1993, he visited his aunt. Later in the evening, as the other family members watched him horse around as he usually did, Williams took a .357 Magnum pistol, emptied the chamber of the cartridges, then replaced one bullet in the chamber. He looked down the barrel and saw that the chamber lined up with the barrel was empty. Thinking that the gun would not fire, Williams pulled back the hammer. He put the gun to his head and pulled the trigger.

With a prank, Bubba killed himself. When he pulled the hammer, the chamber rotated, automatically clicking the bullet into place. His lack of knowledge about guns was fatal. Jovial, fun-loving Bubba had just been playing around. He had not considered the consequences of his playful actions.

Many young people do not think about the consequences of their actions. Rehoboam ignored the potential consequences of his decision to treat the Israelites ruthlessly. Instead of pondering the effects of his choice, he acted. He decision destroyed his kingdom.

Ignorant of Power. Many actors and actresses are aware of the power they wield. Their support behind an idea, issue, political candidate, or piece of legislation can draw public attention to a problem or situation. Many performers use this power responsibly, but others sadly misuse it.

Actress Melanie Griffith was put down by critics for her inept and flaky performance as an American spy during World War II in the film "Shining Through." To make the situation worse, when asked about the picture's historical context, she showed her ignorance of the Nazi Holocaust, in which six million Jews were killed! Flippantly she responded that she had not been born until 1957, therefore she would never have heard of the Holocaust.

This actress misused a wonderful opportunity to share the painful story of a brutal atrocity. She could have sensitized an ignorant world; instead, she showed her own ignorance and insensitivity while misusing the power she held in her hands.

Rehoboam and his friends made a similar mistake. Their insensitivity and misuse of power resulted in the division of a kingdom.

Power Misused. Minda Riley, a twenty-one-year-old political science major at the University of Alabama, decided to run for president of the Student Government Association. On January 31, 1993, Minda returned to her off-campus house in Tuscaloosa. She was tired after participating in a strategy session to plan for the final ten days of her campaign. The last thing she suspected as she entered her home was an attack.

An assailant greeted her by punching her and cutting her face with a knife. The attacker warned her not to run for president. The attack was another example of intimidation by the Machine, a clandestine campus organization that had gripped the campus for seventy years and was believed to have extended even into state politics. Traditionally, the Machine had dominated campus politics. Now, Minda was challenging that power.

Earlier a cross had been burned on her front lawn. Hate mail had been placed in her mailbox. The message in all these harassing actions was clear: Do not run! The Machine had already endorsed a male candidate.

Finally, the school administration postponed the election and dissolved the student government charter until a more representative system could be devised. As it stood, too much power stood in too few hands.

Like Rehoboam and his friends, the Machine had power. However, it never knew how to use that power wisely. Ultimately, all power was lost due to its misuse.

Questions for Students on the Next Lesson. 1. Who was Baal? What influence did he exert over Israel? 2. In Elijah's view, what danger did the worship of Baal pose to the nation? 3. What are some of the false gods this nation worships? 4. How did Elijah deal with Israel's false religion? 5. What was the effect of the contest on Mt. Carmel between the priests of Baal and Elijah?

LESSON 2—JUNE 11

THE DANGER OF FALSE RELIGION

Background Scripture: I Kings 18
Devotional Reading: Deuteronomy 6:5-15a

KING JAMES VERSION

I KINGS 18:30 And Elijah said unto all the people, Come near unto me. And all the people came near unto him. And he repaired the altar of the Lord that was broken down.

31 And Elijah took twelve stones, according to the number of the tribes of the sons of Jacob, unto whom the word of the Lord came, saying, Israel shall be thy name:

32 And with the stones he built an altar in the name of the Lord: and he made a trench about the altar, as great as would contain two measures of seed.

33 And he put the wood in order, and cut the bullock in pieces, and laid him on the wood, and said, Fill four barrels with water, and pour it on the burnt sacrifice, and on the wood.

34 And he said, Do it the second time. And they did it the second time. And he said, Do it the third time. And they did it the third time.

35 And the water ran round about the altar; and he filled the trench also with water.

36 And it came to pass at the time of the offering of the evening sacrifice, that Elijah the prophet came near, and said, Lord God of Abraham, Isaac, and of Israel, let it be known this day that thou art God in Israel, and that I am thy servant, and that I have done all these things at thy word.

37 Hear me, O Lord, hear me, that this people may know that thou art the Lord God, and that thou hast turned their heart back again.

38 Then the fire of the Lord fell, and consumed the burnt sacrifice, and the wood, and the stones, and the dust, and licked up the water that was in the trench.

39 And when all the people saw it, they fell on their faces: and they said, The Lord, he is the God; the Lord, he is the God.

REVISED STANDARD VERSION

I KINGS 18:30 Then Elijah said to all the people, "Come near to me"; and all the people came near to him. And he repaired the altar of the Lord that had been thrown down; 31 Elijah took twelve stones, according to the number of the tribes of the sons of Jacob, to whom the word of the Lord came, saying, "Israel shall be your name"; 32 and with the stones he built an altar in the name of the Lord. And he made a trench about the altar, as great as would contain two measures of seed. 33 And he put the wood in order, and cut the bull in pieces and laid it on the wood. And he said, "Fill four jars with water, and pour it on the burnt offering, and on the wood." 34 And he said, "Do it a second time"; and they did it a second time. And he said, "Do it a third time"; and they did it a third time. 35 And the water ran round about the altar, and filled the trench also with water.

36 And at the time of the offering of the oblation, Elijah the prophet came near and said, "O Lord, God of Abraham, Isaac, and Israel, let it be known this day that thou art God in Israel, and that I am thy servant, and that I have done all these things at thy word. 37 Answer me, O Lord, answer me, that this people may know that thou, O Lord, art God, and that thou hast turned their hearts back." 38 Then the fire of the Lord fell, and consumed the burnt offering, and the wood, and the stones, and the dust, and licked up the water that was in the trench. 39 And when all the people saw it, they fell on their faces; and they said, "The Lord, he is God; the Lord, he is God."

KEY VERSE: *How long will you go limping with two different opinions? If the Lord is God, follow him.* I Kings 18:21.

282

HOME DAILY BIBLE READINGS

June	*5*	*M.*	I Kings 18:1-6	*In the Third Year of Israel's Drought*
June	*6*	*T.*	I Kings 18:7-16	*Obadiah Carries Elijah's Message to Ahab*
June	*7*	*W.*	I Kings 18:17-21	*Command to Gather at Mount Carmel*
June	*8*	*T.*	I Kings 18:22-29	*Baal's Prophets Fail the Test*
June	*9*	*F.*	I Kings 18:30-35	*Elijah Prepares the Burnt Offering*
June	*10*	*S.*	I Kings 18:36-40	*God's Fire Consumes Elijah's Offering*
June	*11*	*S.*	I Kings 18:41-46	*God Ends the Drought*

BACKGROUND

We need to fill in a few details regarding the events after King Solomon died. We saw last week that Rehoboam, Solomon's son, refused to heed the advice of seasoned counselors, laying more severe taxes on his already heavily burdened subjects. The result was that the ten northern tribes revolted under Jeroboam and set up a separate nation. From this point, we will refer to the northern kingdom as Israel, and the southern as Judah, with its capital of Jerusalem.

Jeroboam ruled over Israel, the larger and more powerful of the two kingdoms. Knowing that the temple stood in Jerusalem in the southern kingdom, Jeroboam emphasized worship in ancient sanctuaries in his own realm. However, traces of pagan Canaanite religion clung to these old shrines, so Jeroboam was allowing his people to fall into practices that smacked of idolatry and superstition.

Upon Jeroboam's death, his son, Nadab, managed to hold the throne for only two years before he was killed in a coup led by an upstart named Baasha. A series of monotonously unfit rulers followed. Each change brought new turbulence. Finally, a powerful leader, Omri [AHM-rye], seized power and established a dynasty that lasted almost forty years. The House of Omri, as this dynasty was called, with its new capital of Samaria, became a typical Gentile absolute monarchy and exerted power in the ancient world for a couple of generations.

Omri's son, King Ahab, delighted in playing the part of a successful dictator. Although giving lip service to the Lord, Ahab dabbled in many of the popular religious cults. He married a strong-minded Phoenician princess, Jezebel, and permitted her to import her own god, Baal-Melqart.

Jezebel quickly caused the religious situation in Israel to degenerate further. In addition to allowing the ancient Canaanite fertility rites to continue, Jezebel zealously promoted her own Phoenician Baal worship. The moral tone of the nation quickly sagged. Those trying to remain faithful to the Lord found themselves persecuted.

God, however, continued to be master of history. He raised up a spokesman named Elijah to confront the evil Ahab and Jezebel and their army of Baal-prophets.

NOTES ON THE PRINTED TEXT

Elijah proposed a contest: The whole nation would witness a test of strength between the Lord and Baal. Ahab agreed and summoned the nation to Mount Carmel. The ridge of Mount Carmel towered over the Plain of Jezreel and abruptly broke into the coastal plain by jutting out into the Mediterranean. There, on top of the mountain, altars to the Hebrew God, Yahweh, and the Canaanite God, Baal stood side by side,

On the appointed day, the people climbed to the mountain's summit. There they met Elijah. Dressed in his leather loincloth and a cloak of woven hair, the tough, bearded prophet challenged the people. They were to choose who to follow. *How long will you go limping with two different opinions? If the Lord is God, follow him; but if Baal, then follow him* (18:21). The people refused to respond; they remained uncommitted. *The people did not answer him a word* (18:21).

Elijah outlined the contest. The odds would be stacked against the Lord. One prophet, Elijah, would represent the Lord while Baal's position would be represented by 450 prophets. Each group would take a bull, kill it, and place it upon a pile of wood. However, they would set no fires. Each party would call upon its respective deity to respond and set the pile of wood ablaze. This simple test would prove who was the true deity. Everyone agreed to the rules.

The prophets of Baal were given first choice of a bull and the chance to win a quick victory. They made their preparations, cutting down several oak trees for logs and kindling wood. They prepared a bonfire and then slaughtered a bull, hacked it to pieces, and placed it upon the wood atop the altar. All morning they prayed without any success. At noon Elijah taunted them. *Cry aloud, for he is a god; either he is musing, or he has gone aside, or he is on a journey, or perhaps he is asleep and must be awakened* (18:27). As the storm god, certainly Baal should have been able to produce lightning. Elijah deliberately mocked and insulted the prophets of Baal. This drove the prophets into a frenzy. They raved, danced, and even cut their bodies with swords and spears (a very typical ritual in this ecstatic form of worship) in an effort to get Baal's attention. Despite all they had done, nothing happened. Their time had run out.

Elijah called to the people to come near to him. Silently they gathered around and watched him rebuild the Lord's altar that had been destroyed. He again piled up the twelve large stones, each representing one of Israel's twelve tribes. Around the altar, he dug a deep trench. He then piled logs upon the stones. Upon the wood, he placed the pieces of his sacrificial bull. Next he ordered men to fill four huge clay jars with water and pour water over the pieces of meat and the wood. The process was repeated three times until the altar was soaked and water filled the trench.

His preparations methodically completed, Elijah prayed. *O Lord, God of Abraham, Isaac, and Israel, let it be known this day that thou art God in Israel. . . . Answer me, O Lord, answer me, that this people may know that thou, O Lord, art God, and that thou hast turned their hearts back* (18:36, 37).

Suddenly, a bolt of lightning (most likely) flashed from the sky. Flames instantly destroyed not only the sacrifice but the altar and the water as well. The astonished people screamed and respectfully fell to their faces. To a person, they acknowledged, *The Lord [Yahweh], he is God; the Lord, he is God* (18:39). They committed themselves to the Lord and shortly thereafter dragged the prophets of Baal to the brook Kishon and killed them.

SUGGESTIONS TO TEACHERS

Seldom has there been such a dramatic showdown between the Lord and the forces of evil as the one depicted in today's lesson. Elijah's victorious confrontation with the horde of pagan priests ranks as one of the most famous stories of history. Let this powerful narrative carry your lesson.

1. DESPERATE SITUATION. Remark about the conditions in Samaria at the time the story opens. A drought and famine had struck the land, causing hunger and hardship. Worse, a spiritual drought also afflicted the nation. The prophets of the Lord suffered persecution, and the faithful were demoralized. Explore with your class members how people of faith can cope during tough times.

2. DEVOUT SERVANT. Do a character study on Obadiah, "the servant of Yahweh." At great risk, this brave and devout man had saved the lives of one hundred of the Lord's prophets when Jezebel and Ahab threatened to have them killed. Faith sometimes calls for heroism and sacrifice, as Obadiah was willing to acknowledge. The obedient servant of the Lord is willing to take risks.

3. DEATH SENTENCE. Use some of your lesson time to portray King Ahab clearly. Describe the reasons for Ahab's hatred of Elijah. Then focus on the prophet Elijah. Make sure students know the background for Elijah's absence from the country.

Notice the dialogue between Ahab and Elijah. Ahab called Elijah a "troublemaker." Often God's people will be accused of being troublemakers by authorities. Jesus was so much a troublemaker that the religious leaders and state officials had Him silenced by nailing Him to a cross. Is your church ever causing this kind of sanctified "trouble" in your community? Or is it merely blessing the status quo?

4. DISOBEDIENT SOCIETY. Elijah insisted that King Ahab be accountable to God. As the ruler, as Elijah pointed out, Ahab set the tone and agenda for the nation. Even powerful monarchs were never to think of themselves as above God's law. Elijah boldly told Ahab that the palace's practices had made the people of God disobedient.

5. DRAMATIC SHOWDOWN. The heart of this lesson, of course, is the contest between the Lord and the forces of Baal on Mount Carmel. The fire of the Lord demonstrated conclusively that God was supreme. Elijah's bold challenge vindicated the Lord, and showed that the Lord, not the Canaanite or Phoenician gods, controlled the elements and brought rain. Remind your students that the life-or-death struggle between the people of God and the forces of evil continues to our day. Superstitions and cults abound. False religions, such as a self-righteous nationalism and a pleasure-loving hedonism, threaten us just as much as Jezebel's prophets threatened Israel.

TOPIC FOR ADULTS
WHOM WILL YOU FOLLOW?

Witness against False Religion. Christians in China have been quietly and heroically standing up for their faith during the past fifty years following the departure of foreign missionaries. One example was reported by the Hong Kong Office of the Amity News Service, an information outlet sponsored by the Amity Foundation, to report news of the China Christian Council. The Amity office received a handwritten note telling of the establishment of a new church in Henghu, Jiangxi Province. The story in the handwritten note, translated and summarized, tells this story of brave prophetic witness in the face of the false religion of Communist ideology and Chinese nationalism.

Until the time of the Cultural Revolution (1966–1976), there had never been Christians in the peasant community of Henghu. Then a Christian couple, Brother He Feng Ming and Sister Zhu Fengqi, were sent by the Christian community in Hunan Province to share the faith in Jiangxi Province. The couple began to hold secret worship gatherings with their neighbors. When some religious freedom began in the 1970s, the number of Christians began to increase, but it continued to be dangerous to profess faith in Christ. The Henghu home worship gathering was still not recognized because of the "Leftist" orientation of local party authorities ("cadres"). The cadres put all sorts of pressure on local Christians, and frequently called in Brother He for a "talk." They told him to change his ways and discontinue the worship meetings, suggesting that his job might be in jeopardy if he did not comply.

But Brother He and the local church held fast to their beliefs, and the number of Christians in Henghu continued to increase. They witnessed to the community through their deeds, and people began to take notice. Christian families were more enthusiastic in turning in their grain levies, they didn't cheat, they were helpful to others, and their family relations were harmonious. Sister Zhu and other Christians often helped the weakest members of their community.

This model behavior and beautiful witness eventually moved the local cadres, causing them to change their impression of the church. The cadres again studied the government's religious policy, and now made a special effort to abide by its spirit and uphold religious freedom. At one point, a local cadre even moved out of his house so that Christians would have a place to meet.

When Henghu Christians applied to build their own church—a new church building in a community which had never had one—they were immediately granted land by the local government. The Christians pooled their resources and prayed that they would have enough funds to build the church. Young and old, rich and poor, they all gave what they could.

Later, Henghu church leaders contacted the China Christian Council, for they still lacked resources. The Wonju Youngkang Church of South Korea learned of the story of the Christians of Henghu, and were so moved that the decision was made to give ten thousand U.S. dollars as a freewill offering to complete the building of the new church.

The church building, which seats three hundred people, was finally completed in mid-October, 1992. However, the Christian community in

Henghu now numbers more than a thousand; so many Christians continue to meet in their homes.—In *Monday Morning,* February 22, 1993.

Entertaining Pulpiteer. Occasionally a magazine article will highlight some preacher who attracts crowds with colorful stunts and a pleasant message. Often the preacher turns out to be a false prophet attracting a large following to a false religion. It's the prophets of Baal all over again. However, the subtle temptation presents itself to every person in the pulpit to please the folks and pack the sanctuary on Sunday.

Dr. Donald Miller, beloved professor and seminary president, told of the advice a crusty old seminary professor once gave a student. It seems an immature, young student was about to graduate and accept a call to a dying city congregation.

"Do you want to fill your church on Sunday?" the old prof asked.

"Oh, yes! Of course!" the young man eagerly responded.

"Then preach in your underwear" came the answer. "But what will you do next week?"

Falsifying Religion. Going through the motions of Christian worship does not make a person Christian. In fact, without the sense of repentance and a commitment to building God's kingdom rather than promoting one's personal agenda, the pretense of worship in a church can actually be a form of false religion. Take the case of Mobutu Sese Seko, dictator of Zaire. During over thirty years of absolute power, a tenure marked by the torture and killing of his opponents and corruption that has funneled much of his nation's wealth into his private pocket, Mobutu has attended worship each week, seldom missing a Sunday. He is the picture of piety, reverently clasping his hands and kneeling in prayer to receive Communion. But his attendance in his lavish private chapel each Sunday has not kept him from building a personal fortune of at least five billion dollars—mostly through pilfering the public resources, skimming the foreign funds, and demanding kickbacks from businesses.

Although most of his people live in disease, hunger, and poverty, Mobutu has bank accounts in Switzerland and elsewhere, palatial residences in Spain, Portugal, the French Riviera, Morocco, and Senegal, as well as an enormous presidential palace. His nation is bankrupt. Food and supplies are critically short, but Mobutu dines luxuriously with cronies on lobster and steak specially flown in on one of his Boeing jets in the presidential fleet. Leprosy, malaria, and other diseases are widespread in the slums and hinterland. His elite security forces ruthlessly have murdered or tortured those questioning his ways. Mobutu also enjoys taking whatever woman he fancies for his personal sexual pleasure, including the wives of political associates.

This leader falsifies the faith. His ways deny the Gospel. Yet Mobutu swears on his "honor as a Christian" that he is upright. His nation is in anarchy, and his rule is doomed.

Questions for Students on the Next Lesson. 1. Why did Naboth not want to sell his vineyard? 2. What did Queen Jezebel do to secure the vineyard for her husband? 3. What did Elijah do upon hearing of Jezebel's actions? 4. Does justice finally prevail in the world? 5. Is any person above being punished for evil behavior?

TOPIC FOR YOUTH
WHOM WILL YOU FOLLOW?

Misplaced Loyalty. Sixteen-year-old George Rudolph was strangled and left in a ravine. Though the Pittsburgh teenager's body was not discovered for seventeen days, the visitation prior to his funeral took a bizarre twist when gang members wanted to dress his corpse in the gang's colors.

Two dozen police were summoned to White Memorial Chapel on Thursday, March 25, 1993. Arriving at the scene police found thirty teenagers outside. Apparently some of the teens had attempted to remove the corpse from the coffin in order to redress the corpse in the gang's colors. In the resulting disturbance, five individuals were arrested.

Sometimes people attach their loyalty to the wrong things, such as loyalty to a gang. The gang becomes the family and its leader a god.

Elijah challenged his people to put their loyalty in the one, true, and living God. He called them to follow God and to live their lives as people committed to the true leader of Israel.

Who to Follow? Jennifer and her sister Kathy Andrade were searching for religious options. In a Bible class, they met a man who led them to David Koresh. Their spiritual search eventually took the girls to Waco, Texas, and the compound of the Branch Davidians, a secluded religious cult. Once there, the girls came more and more under the spell of Koresh and his preaching. Then on February 28, 1993, agents from the Bureau of Alcohol, Tobacco, and Firearms assaulted the compound. Four agents were killed and sixteen wounded. Thus began a fifty-one-day standoff that finally ended in the fiery death of eighty-six followers, including Koresh and the Andrade sisters.

Koresh claimed to be the Christ. He readied his followers for a final battle with unbelievers by stockpiling food and ammunition and storing his huge arsenal of automatic weapons in an armory. His teaching was a mixture of the Bible, end-times theology, and survivalism. To prepare his flock psychologically, he constantly replayed movies about the Vietnam War. Followers were required to undergo weight training and military drills. To prepare his followers for famine, Koresh enforced a strict vegetarian diet. Daily life consisted of work, drills, and Bible study. Celibacy was the norm.

Television was forbidden, as were birthday celebrations. Entertainment consisted of listening to Koresh's lectures on the Scriptures. Cult members donated all their money to the cult, and Koresh demanded absolute obedience, even if it meant sacrificing the welfare of a child. Ironically, Koresh himself ate meat, drank beer, watched TV, and fathered almost a dozen children by his nineteen wives.

There are people like the Andrade sisters who are looking for a leader. The sisters were but two young people who sought guidance and direction. However, they never learned that they are to be committed to God and not merely a person. You are to be committed to God through Jesus Christ. Long before Jesus, Elijah summoned the nation to follow God and commit itself to Him. His call still stands, and any other response to a false god ends in spiritual death.

Idol Worship. Tom bought his first automobile. It was a sky-blue 1988 Pontiac Grand Am. He spent hours washing the car, polishing the chrome, waxing the painted body, and cleaning the upholstery. He added a larger sound system. Judging by the hours he devoted to its care and the sacrifices that he made for the car, it could be argued that Tom worshiped the car.

Material objects can become idols. We can worship the wrong things and the wrong gods. The true God is a jealous God! He does not want anything to get between you and Him.

Questions for Students on the Next Lesson. 1. Why did Ahab desire Naboth's vineyard? 2. Why was Naboth unwilling to agree to King Ahab's request? 3. How was the vineyard acquired by the royal family? 4. What was Elijah's response to the acquisition and his verdict on Ahab? 5. What do you do when faced with corruption at school or in politics?

LESSON 3—JUNE 18

WHEN JUSTICE IS CORRUPTED

Background Scripture: I Kings 21
Devotional Reading: Micah 6:6-13

KING JAMES VERSION

I KINGS 21:1 And it came to pass after these things, that Naboth the Jezreelite had a vineyard, which was in Jezreel, hard by the palace of Ahab king of Samaria.

2 And Ahab spake unto Naboth, saying, Give me thy vineyard, that I may have it for a garden of herbs, because it is near unto my house: and I will give thee for it a better vineyard than it; or, if it seem good to thee, I will give thee the worth of it in money.

3 And Naboth said to Ahab, The Lord forbid it me, that I should give the inheritance of my fathers unto thee.

4 And Ahab came into his house heavy and displeased because of the word which Naboth the Jezreelite had spoken to him: for he had said, I will not give thee the inheritance of my fathers. And he laid him down upon his bed, and turned away his face, and would eat no bread. . . .

15 And it came to pass, when Jezebel heard that Naboth was stoned, and was dead, that Jezebel said to Ahab, Arise, take possession of the vineyard of Naboth the Jezreelite, which he refused to give thee for money: for Naboth is not alive, but dead.

16 And it came to pass, when Ahab heard that Naboth was dead, that Ahab rose up to go down to the vineyard of Naboth the Jezreelite, to take possession of it.

17 And the word of the Lord came to Elijah the Tishbite, saying,

18 Arise, go down to meet Ahab king of Israel, which is in Samaria: behold, he is in the vineyard of Naboth, whither he is gone down to possess it.

19 And thou shalt speak unto him, saying, Thus saith the Lord, Hast thou killed, and also taken possession? And thou shalt speak unto him, saying, Thus saith the Lord, In the place where dogs licked the blood of Naboth shall dogs lick thy blood, even thine.

20 And Ahab said to Elijah, Hast thou found me, O mine enemy? And he answered, I have found thee: because thou hast sold thyself to work evil in the sight of the Lord.

REVISED STANDARD VERSION

I KINGS 21:1 Now Naboth the Jezreelite had a vineyard in Jezreel, beside the palace of Ahab king of Samaria. 2 And after this Ahab said to Naboth, "Give me your vineyard, that I may have it for a vegetable garden, because it is near my house; and I will give you a better vineyard for it; or, if it seems good to you, I will give you its value in money." 3 But Naboth said to Ahab, "The Lord forbid that I should give you the inheritance of my fathers." 4 And Ahab went into his house vexed and sullen because of what Naboth the Jezreelite had said to him; for he had said, "I will not give you the inheritance of my fathers." And he lay down on his bed, and turned away his face, and would eat no food. . . .

15 As soon as Jezebel heard that Naboth had been stoned and was dead. Jezebel said to Ahab, "Arise, take possession of the vineyard of Naboth the Jezreelite, which he refused to give you for money; for Naboth is not alive, but dead." 16 And as soon as Ahab heard that Naboth was dead, Ahab arose to go down to the vineyard of Naboth the Jezreelite, to take possession of it.

17 Then the word of the Lord came to Elijah the Tishbite, saying, 18 "Arise, go down to meet Ahab king of Israel, who is in Samaria; behold, he is in the vineyard of Naboth, where he has gone to take possession. 19 And you shall say to him, 'Thus says the Lord, "Have you killed, and also taken possession?" ' And you shall say to him, 'Thus says the Lord: "In the place where dogs licked up the blood of Naboth shall dogs lick your own blood." ' "

20 Ahab said to Elijah, "Have you found me, O my enemy?" He answered, "I have found you, because you have sold yourself to do what is evil in the sight of the Lord."

KEY VERSE: You have sold yourself to do what is evil in the sight of the Lord. I Kings 21:20b.

HOME DAILY BIBLE READINGS

June 12	M.	Micah 6:6-13	*God Requires Justice and Faithfulness*
June 13	T.	I Kings 21:1-7	*Naboth Refuses to Sell His Vineyard*
June 14	W.	I Kings 21:8-14	*Jezebel Causes Naboth's Death*
June 15	T.	I Kings 21:15, 16	*Ahab Seizes Naboth's Vineyard*
June 16	F.	I Kings 21:17-24	*Elijah Judges Ahab and Jezebel*
June 17	S.	I Kings 21:25-29	*Ahab's Repentance Brings a Temporary Reprieve*
June 18	S.	Psalm 36	*Evildoers Do Not Revere God*

BACKGROUND

"Power corrupts; absolute power corrupts absolutely," wrote Lord Acton. The truth of the saying is illustrated by the rule of King Ahab of Israel. The nation of Israel was meant to be a theocracy in which God ruled as supreme head. The Old Testament Law clearly intended that the kings as well as all other inhabitants of Israel be subjects of the Lord and, therefore, constrained to obey the statutes of God's law. This type of government was different than other ancient regimes. In the other nations, the king was under no obligation to anyone but himself. In Israel, on the other hand, it was understood that the king was answerable to the Lord. The Israelites were to live in a monarchy that had limits to its powers. King Ahab, however, refused to accept those limits.

One of the most sacred and cherished parts of the Hebrew legal code had to do with the use of land. To this day, land ownership remains an issue of great importance and a cause of severe contention between the Palestinians and Israelis. Part of the reason, of course, is that good crop-growing land is so scarce in the Middle East. From ancient times to the present, families have regarded their land as a sacred trust from God to be used carefully, to be preserved and passed on to the next generation. Ancestral fields and vineyards had (and still have) a sacred significance. It was critically important, according to the Law (see Lev. 25 and Deut. 25) that inherited land remain in the family and not be casually sold.

Naboth [NAY-bahth], a faithful Israelite, observed and cherished the Hebrew law. He had inherited his vineyard from his father, who in turn had inherited it from his father, and so on back through many generations. Naboth had given his solemn promise to the Lord, in effect, to cherish this inheritance and hand it on to his children. Undoubtedly, this acreage of vines also represented countless hours of hard physical labor by Naboth and his forefathers—clearing stones, pruning vines, watering the shoots, and cultivating the rocky soil.

The king already held ample lands, but he coveted Naboth's vineyard. When Naboth turned down Ahab's offers, the monarch sulked. Queen Jezebel, who had no scruples about her husband's exercising absolute power or acting corruptly, engineered Naboth's death so Ahab could have the vineyard.

NOTES ON THE PRINTED TEXT

Now Naboth the Jezreelite had a vineyard in Jezreel, beside the palace of Ahab king of Samaria (21:1). The plain of Jezreel sloped down to the Jordan River. With terrace farming methods, vineyards were planted and cultivated; they produced an abundant harvest in the lush valley. Naboth's ancestors had worked this vineyard as would his descendants.

Then Ahab constructed a second palace, or winter palace, in Jezreel (his first palace was in Samaria). Ahab fostered a vision of grandeur for his new palace. He had an idea for better use of the land, Naboth's land. *Give me your vineyard, that I may have it for a vegetable garden, because it is near my house* (21:2). On a visit, Ahab offered to trade one of his better vineyards or to buy Naboth's vineyard outright. *I will give you a better vineyard for it; or, if it seems good to you, I will give you its value in money* (21:2). At this point, there was no royal pressure but apparently a fair offer made by the king.

The Lord forbid that I should give you the inheritance of my fathers (21:3). Naboth refused the king's offer; it was unthinkable. Long-established legal and religious obligations dictated that the land be passed down through the family. This was the Levitical law (see Deut. 25:5-10). While this law was sometimes ignored, Naboth had taken an oath to the Lord not to sell the land but to keep it within his family. He responded, *I will not give you the inheritance of my fathers* (21:4).

Ahab was depressed, even though he knew Naboth was right. He went to his royal bedchamber, lay down on his ivory-decorated bed, turned his face to the wall, and refused to get out of bed or to eat.

Hearing of Ahab's strange behavior, Queen Jezebel went to the royal bedchamber to soothe and calm Ahab, promising to handle the problem. After all, she pointed out to Ahab, he was the king! He had a right to the vineyard. Jezebel's Canaanite religion taught that power and might made the action right.

Carefully, Jezebel arranged a plot against Naboth. Signing Ahab's name, she wrote letters, stamped with the royal seal, to Jezreel's elders. Most likely these men were nobles loyal to Ahab and Jezebel. These elders were to proclaim a fast, signifying some kind of national crisis, which would require the people to meet together, apparently to discuss who among them might be responsible for God's displeasure. Naboth would be the principal character at the hearing. Two paid thugs were to be seated opposite him who would bring a charge of treason against him. The penalty for blasphemy against the Lord and the king was death. The elders were to carry out the sentence by stoning Naboth to death.

The orders were carried out to the letter, and Naboth and his family were killed. Since there were no heirs, the property now belonged to the king. Jezebel rushed to Ahab with the news. *Arise, take possession of the vineyard of Naboth the Jezreelite . . . for Naboth is not alive, but dead* (21:15). Hearing the news, Ahab happily rushed to the vineyard.

The murderous treachery had not gone unnoticed, however. God had orders for Elijah. He was to go to the vineyard and confront Ahab. Entering the vineyard, Elijah angrily shouted, *Have you killed, and also taken possession? . . . Thus says the Lord: "In the place where dogs licked up the blood of Naboth shall dogs lick your own blood"* (21:19). Just as the dogs had cleaned up what was left of Naboth, the same would happen to Ahab.

Initially, Ahab was unimpressed. He snapped, *Have you found me, O my enemy?* (21:20). To Ahab, Elijah the troublemaker was busy again.

Elijah thundered, *I have found you, because you have sold yourself to do what is evil in the sight of the Lord* (21:20). Then, he again spoke of God's judgment on Ahab and his family.

SUGGESTIONS TO TEACHERS

The Scripture in today's lesson has the majesty of a classic drama. You need no gimmicks to make it interesting or relevant. Let the story of greed and treachery unfold, and the applications will quickly become apparent to everyone in your class.

1. COVETOUS KING. You have already introduced Ahab to your class in last week's lesson. Ask students to comment on Ahab's character after reading the material in I Kings 21.

2. CONNIVING QUEEN. Likewise, invite students to offer adjectives describing Jezebel's personality. Remind your class members how easy it is for a person in power to exhibit traits like those of Ahab and Jezebel.

3. CONTEMPTIBLE CONSPIRACY. Discuss Jezebel's appalling scheme to seize Naboth's vineyard. Make the point that those refusing to acknowledge God's supremacy will ultimately place themselves above God. Jezebel and Ahab felt no obligation to the Lord; hence, they eventually experienced no sense of conscience or compassion, no awareness of covenant or commitment. Framing and murdering an innocent person was not a concern if it meant carrying out their wishes to grab a piece of property.

4. CORRUPT COURTIERS. Jezebel's and Ahab's cruel and greedy scheme could not be carried out by the two of them alone but required henchmen. The callous participants in the evil plot cooperated with the king and queen. They shared responsibility for Naboth's death and the perversion of justice.

Have your students offer examples of excuses that these courtiers might have used (for example: "Only following orders"; "Just doing my job"; "My country, right or wrong"; "Didn't want to stick my neck out and get in trouble"; etc.). Point out that complacent people merely "doing their job," who consider themselves respectable citizens, may often be party to acts of injustice in a society.

5. CALAMITOUS CONFRONTATION. Bring Elijah into the drama, and dwell on his words to Ahab. Make the point that God is never mocked. Nor is the Lord incapable of handling brutal dictators. Maltbie Babcock's words in his hymn "This Is My Father's World" always hold true: "Though the wrong seems oft so strong, God is the Ruler yet!"

TOPIC FOR ADULTS
JUSTICE CORRUPTED

Hearing Those around You. The Rev. Tom Wright of Worcester College, Oxford, described taking a group of his students to visit a monastery in Dorset. There, one of the friars explained the rule for singing in the chapel. The friar said that most people in church don't sing at all, or else try to sing so loudly that everyone else can hear them. The secret, the friar pointed out, is to sing in such a way that you can hear those around you. Dr. Wright preaches, "You must never order your life in such a manner that you can no longer hear those around you."

Justice is corrupted when we refuse to hear the voices of those around us, especially the oppressed and forgotten in society. Justice is corrupted when we listen only to our own selfish and insistent screech.

White House Inscription. The White House in Washington, D.C., was built during the late eighteenth century, completed in 1792. The first presidential occupant was John Adams. On his second night in the newly-finished residence, Adams wrote to his wife, Abigail:

"I pray heaven to bestow the best of blessings on this house and on all that shall hereafter inhabit it. May none but honest and wise men ever dwell under this roof."

One hundred forty-five years later, Franklin Delano Roosevelt had these words carved on the marble mantle of the State Dining Room: "When honest and wise men serve as Presidents, justice prevails in our nation."

Sadly, ancient Israel's kings neglected to live by the precepts contained in the Scriptures that influenced the words of President Adams to his wife.

Victim of Injustice. The great Michelangelo knew he was disliked by jealous, inferior artisans. In Florence, Michelangelo had won fame through his magnificent sculptures, being the undisputed master in the art of carving in marble. Petty fellow-sculptors, however, resented his fame and skill.

Most disappointing to Michelangelo, however, was being caught in the dirty politics of the church at that period of history. Julius II had summoned Michelangelo to Rome to design and build for him a dazzling tomb. Michelangelo spent the following eight months in the mountains, personally selecting the blocks of marble to be used, and arranging to have them shipped to Rome for the project. When he arrived back in Rome, Julius refused to see him and sent word that he must rebuild St. Peter's instead of the tomb.

Michelangelo learned that Bramante and Raphael had hatched a plan to persuade Julius to use his resources to carry out their pet project of St. Peter's and to cut Michelangelo out of any additional success. To discredit Michelangelo as much as possible and to remove him from competing with them, these other lesser artists schemed to have the ruling church leader assign Michelangelo to decorate the ceiling of a private chapel. This relatively obscure but incredibly difficult project, they knew, would discredit Michelangelo, since Michelangelo had no experience in coloring with fresco and had never exhibited any paintings.

The jealous Bramante and Raphael congratulated themselves on concocting a way to divert Michelangelo's energies from sculpture to a form of art that would supposedly show him unfavorably. They were confident that Michelangelo would be disgraced.

Michelangelo had never used color or worked in fresco. Nevertheless, in spite of the unjust way he was being treated by other artists and by the church, he took on the assignment. The ceiling was tunnel-vaulted, a curved surface broken up by eight windows that produced unmanageable triangles, presenting almost impossible challenges for design and execution. For the following four years, Michelangelo labored, designing and painting the ceiling himself. Most of the time, he had to work facing upward, which impaired his sight so badly that, for several months after completing the task, he could not read or look at drawings except with his head tilted far back.

In 1512, his work was unveiled. The result of the effort that his enemies had stage-managed to discredit him was the masterpiece known as the Sistine Chapel Ceiling. In the awkward curved space broken by the triangles, in a medium previously unknown to him, Michelangelo took the unjust treatment meted out to him by cruel critics and produced one of the world's greatest treasures!

Questions for Students on the Next Lesson. 1. Whom did the king of Israel blame for the siege of Samaria? 2. What did the Lord disclose to Elisha about the siege and famine? 3. What did the lepers discover when they came to the camp of the Arameans? 4. Have you ever experienced a time when you seemed to lose hope? 5. What does the sharing by the lepers suggest to you about sharing the good news of Jesus Christ?

TOPIC FOR YOUTH
JUSTICE CORRUPTED

Greed. Ask an older brother or sister, or your mother or father, to open his or her wallet. Count the number of credit cards in it. The national average is between eight and ten. Is your relative close, or maybe even over that average?

According to financial experts, most consumers have nine credit cards. These include bank credit cards, department store cards, and gasoline company cards. The total amount of credit available to the average individual is $20,000.

Les Kirschbaum, the president of Mid-Continent Agencies, Inc., a debt-collection agency in Glenview, Illinois, warns that access to an extensive line of credit encourages frivolous spending and leads to debt and possible bankruptcy. This is true for young and old.

Long before this warning, Elijah warned rulers and people of the perils of desiring things that were not theirs. Such covetousness and greed lead only to downfall, despair, and death.

Corruption in Government. The United States government has taken some strong human rights stands in the past twenty years. However, leaked classified CIA reports and the United Nations' Truth Commission Report on El Salvador indicated that our government learned in 1985 that two officers in El Salvador's armed forces were linked to the death squads that murdered thousands of suspected enemies. They were apparently involved in such atrocities as the Mozote massacre and the slaying of six Jesuit priests, their housekeeper, and her daughter.

In spite of this, our government concealed any knowledge of these men's involvement in the atrocities. Finally, the government nurtured the careers of these two officers by advancing them to the top echelons of the U.S.-backed armed forces!

You may be surprised, but our government also has blood on its hands. Corruption and immoral actions occur in our own government as much as it did in Ahab's. Consider what Elijah might say to our leaders! No earthly kingdom perfectly reflects God's kingdom.

Haves and Have-Nots. If the world's population could be shrunk to comprise a village of precisely one hundred people, and all the existing human ratios remained the same, the village would look something like this: Fifty percent of the entire world's wealth would be in the hands of 6 people. These 6 people would be Americans. Yet, 70 people would be unable to read, 50 would be malnourished, 80 would live in substandard houses, and only one would have a college education.

Make no mistake. Injustice exists everywhere. Elijah's message stands, and we know that God will judge every nation someday. We can and must act to influence our nation for the good.

Questions for Students on the Next Lesson. 1. Who was Elisha? 2. Why did the king of Israel blame Elisha for the famine? 3. Why did the Aramean army retreat? 4. How did the lepers respond to the discovery of the food? 5. How and why do you share joyous news?

LESSON 4—JUNE 25

A DAY OF GOOD NEWS

Background Scripture: II Kings 6:24—7:20
Devotional Reading: I Thessalonians 5:8-18

KING JAMES VERSION

II KINGS 7:1 Then Elisha said, Hear ye the word of the Lord; Thus saith the Lord, To morrow about this time shall a measure of fine flour be sold for a shekel, and two measures of barley for a shekel, in the gate of Samaria.

2 Then a lord on whose hand the king leaned answered the man of God, and said, Behold, if the Lord would make windows in heaven, might this thing be? And he said, Behold, thou shalt see it with thine eyes, but shalt not eat thereof.

3 And there were four leprous men at the entering in of the gate: and they said one to another, Why sit we here until we die?

4 If we say, We will enter into the city, then the famine is in the city, and we shall die there: and if we sit still here, we die also. Now therefore come, and let us fall unto the host of the Syrians: if they save us alive, we shall live; and if they kill us, we shall but die.

5 And they rose up in the twilight, to go unto the camp of the Syrians: and when they were come to the uttermost part of the camp of Syria, behold, there was no man there.

6 For the Lord had made the host of the Syrians to hear a noise of chariots, and a noise of horses, even the noise of a great host: and they said one to another, Lo, the king of Israel hath hired against us the kings of the Hittites, and the kings of the Egyptians, to come upon us.

7 Wherefore they arose and fled in the twilight, and left their tents, and their horses, and their asses, even the camp as it was, and fled for their life.

8 And when these lepers came to the uttermost part of the camp, they went into one tent, and did eat and drink, and carried thence silver, and gold, and raiment, and went and hid it; and came again, and entered into another tent, and carried thence also, and went and hid it.

9 Then they said one to another, We do not well: this day is a day of good tidings, and we hold our peace: if we tarry till the morning light, some mischief will come upon us: now therefore come, that we may go and tell the king's household.

REVISED STANDARD VERSION

II KINGS 7:1 But Elisha said, "Hear the word of the Lord: thus says the Lord, Tomorrow about this time a measure of fine meal shall be sold for a shekel, and two measures of barley for a shekel, at the gate of Samaria." 2 Then the captain on whose hand the king leaned said to the man of God, "If the Lord himself should make windows in heaven, could this thing be?" But he said, "You shall see it with your own eyes, but you shall not eat of it."

3 Now there were four men who were lepers at the entrance to the gate; and they said to one another, "Why do we sit here till we die? 4 If we say, 'Let us enter the city,' the famine is in the city, and we shall die there; and if we sit here, we die also. So now come, let us go over to the camp of the Syrians; if they spare our lives we shall live, and if they kill us we shall but die." 5 So they arose at twilight to go to the camp of the Syrians; but when they came to the edge of the camp of the Syrians, behold, there was no one there. 6 For the Lord had made the army of the Syrians hear the sound of chariots, and of horses, the sound of a great army, so that they said to one another, "Behold, the king of Israel has hired against us the kings of the Hittites and the kings of Egypt to come upon us." 7 So they fled away in the twilight and forsook their tents, their horses, and their asses, leaving the camp as it was, and fled for their lives. 8 And when these lepers came to the edge of the camp, they went into a tent, and ate and drank, and they carried off silver and gold and clothing, and went and hid them; then they came back, and entered another tent, and carried off things from it, and went and hid them.

9 Then they said to one another, "We are not doing right. This day is a day of good news; if we are silent and wait until the morning light, punishment will overtake us; now therefore come, let us go and tell the king's household."

KEY VERSE: This day is a day of good news . . . let us go and tell.
II Kings 7:9b.

HOME DAILY BIBLE READINGS

June	19	M.	Psalm 86:1-7	*A Prayer for God's Help*
June	20	T.	Psalm 86:8-17	*God Does Wondrous Things*
June	21	W.	II Kings 6:24-29	*Syria's Siege Brings Famine in Samaria*
June	22	T.	II Kings 6:30—7:2	*Elisha's Assurance of Imminent Relief*
June	23	F.	II Kings 7:3-8	*Lepers Find the Syrian Camp Abandoned*
June	24	S.	II Kings 7:9-15	*The Lepers Report the Good News*
June	25	S.	II Kings 7:16-20	*Relief from Siege and Famine*

BACKGROUND

Ahab and Jezebel, as predicted by Elijah, died without fanfare because of their lack of loyalty to God and their persistent evil practices. Old Elijah himself, the greatest of the Old Testament prophets, finally was carried into the presence of the Lord.

Meanwhile, relations between Israel and its northern neighbor, Syria, continued to worsen. Wars with the Syrians flared frequently. Ahab's father, Omri, had been forced to give up territory and commercial rights in the kingdom. Later, kings of Israel tried to reclaim land that had been lost in the northern Transjordan. Frequently, guerrilla bands from Syria roamed through Israel, raiding villages and keeping the nation on edge. Elisha, the prophet anointed by Elijah as his successor, finally intervened to put an end to the raiding parties.

A new crisis erupted. The Syrian army suddenly marched south and surrounded Israel's capital, Samaria. The city tried to hang on, but the stranglehold of the Syrian siege produced desperate conditions for the people inside the walls of Samaria. Various ancient historians have given us reports about the lives of the suffering populace during sieges. In Samaria, as in other sieges, food supplies gave out; prices soared; people even resorted to eating such repulsive things as doves' dung. Some stooped to cannibalism.

The king of Israel angrily swore that he would destroy the prophet Elisha for encouraging the nation to resist because of the assurance of God's intervention. As always, however, God had the last word. The king of Israel might have despaired of relying on the Lord and might have thought that bigger armored divisions were what counted in the world. But God writes the script for the human drama, as the people of Samaria discovered in the day when the siege was lifted and the Syrian army suddenly fled.

NOTES ON THE PRINTED TEXT

A state of war existed between Jehoram of Israel and Ben-hadad of Syria. The weak Israelites offered little resistance and were forced to retreat to the hilltop capital in Samaria. The Aramean invaders surrounded the city, preventing anything from going in or coming out. The elegant city was clogged with beggars and sick, dying, hungry people. So desperate was the situation that some people resorted to cannibalism.

King Jehoram was furious with Elisha. He blamed Elisha for the terrible famine and the conditions in the city. He felt the Lord's prophet should have protected the nation, and because Elisha had not done this, he sent a servant to murder Elisha. The servant could not gain entry through a door barred by an old man. Then the king arrived. Jehoram stood outside the door complaining that God had brought all of the trouble. How could he ever expect deliverance?

Hear the word of the Lord: . . . Tomorrow about this time a measure of fine meal shall be sold for a shekel, and two measures of barley for a shekel, at the gate of Samaria (7:1). Elisha responded by precisely giving the next day's farm market report. He offered the price of a bushel of wheat and barley sold at the city gate. Gates were the center of commercial activity and the site of the public market.

If the Lord himself should make windows in heaven, could this thing be? (7:2). The captain (likely the royal aide-de-camp) was doubtful. How could God change the famine conditions in the land and city so quickly? Would manna be provided? His skepticism was met with the announcement of doom. Elisha prophesied judgment. *You shall see it with your own eyes, but you shall not eat of it* (7:2).

Why do we sit here till we die? . . . Let us go over to the camp of the Syrians; if they spare our lives we shall live, and if they kill us we shall but die (7:3, 4). Four lepers (more likely they had a skin ailment rather than what we call leprosy, since they had access to the city) decided to desert to the Syrians. They reasoned that if they entered the city or stayed where they were, they would die of starvation. The very worst that could happen would be death at the hands of the enemy. Either way, they would die.

At early dawn, the lepers went to the Syrian camp to surrender. To their surprise, it was empty. *There was no one there* (7:5). The Syrians had fled.

The writer tells the reader, *For the Lord had made the army of the Syrians hear the sound of chariots, and of horses, the sound of a great army, so that they said to one another, "Behold, the king of Israel has hired against us the kings of the Hittites and the kings of Egypt to come upon us"* (7:6). The Syrians heard (at the Lord's initiation) what they believed to be horses and chariots. They believed the rumor that Israel had hired a mercenary army of Hittites and Egyptians. In panic, the Syrians fled, leaving their tents, provisions, equipment, gold, and silver.

The lepers were overwhelmed. They ate and drank until they were satisfied. They carried off clothing, gold, and silver before their consciences were awakened. Finally, they recognized that they must share this good news with the king so the famine would be relieved. *We are not doing right. This day is a day of good news; if we are silent and wait until the morning light, punishment will overtake us; now therefore come, let us go and tell the king's household* (7:9). Returning to the gate, they shouted up the news to the gatekeeper.

SUGGESTIONS TO TEACHERS

"We have decided we will never have a family," a couple told their minister. "This world is in such terrible condition that we don't see any future for children. Therefore, we refuse ever to have a baby."

This young husband and wife could not be convinced that God was still involved in the human scene. Some students in your class may not want to carry their pessimism quite as far as this couple, but nonetheless they may share the attitude about God's supposed powerlessness.

Today's lesson dramatically demonstrates that God still rules this universe. The Lord continues to bring days of good news.

1. SUFFERING CAPITAL. The Bible never looks at life through rose-colored lenses. It acknowledges the dark and terrible side of human existence. The scene of Samaria suffering under siege, described in II Kings 6, has been replicated in Sarajevo and Somalia in recent times. This presents an opportunity to discuss the cause of human suffering. Remind the class that human pride, human greed, human cruelty, human insensitivity—these are some causes of hunger, oppression, and bloodshed. Behind all these causes is the refusal of humans to live as faithful subjects of the Lord of Lords.

2. A CYNICAL KING. Kings, corporation presidents, committee members, and all others wielding some form of power (and that includes most of us) may be inclined to overestimate human power and underestimate divine authority. Some even try to blame God for all problems, as the king in Samaria did. Look again at his words: "It's the Lord who has brought this trouble on us. Why should I wait any longer for Him to do something?" (see II Kings 6:33). In other words, "Why wait for God? He's powerless. The situation is hopeless." Ask students how they might respond to this kind of thinking.

3. A STEADFAST COMMITMENT. Introduce the prophet Elisha, and focus on the words of this brave and committed believer. In spite of the bleak outlook, this man of God steadfastly continued to be confident in God's power and presence. God's people are "in spite of" believers: in spite of whatever may be happening in the world, God's people maintain that God has not given up on His creation.

4. THE SURPRISING CREATOR. Let the rest of the narrative of II Kings 6:24—7:20 unfold. God intervened. Samaria was saved at the time when everyone except Elisha had assumed there was no hope or future. How does this story apply to our time?

TOPIC FOR ADULTS
SHARING THE GOOD NEWS

Sufficient Summary. The young missionary finally arrived in the remote outpost, brimming with confidence from his seminary training. As he unloaded his belongings from the truck, the old missionary and the members of the tribe living near the mission station gathered. The veteran missionary suggested that it would be appropriate for the newcomer to say a few words of greeting to the gathered tribe, and said that he would translate the recently-arrived missionary's words from English into the local language. The young man eagerly accepted. Addressing the large group in front of him, he presented his remarks.

"The ecclesiastical and eschatological significance of this auspicious occasion causes one to ponder that the exigencies of the human condition in every cultural milieu precipitate each believer to a profound trinitarian doxological response."

The old missionary gasped. The young man paused, waiting for the translation. The experienced old-timer cleared his throat and smiled at the people of the tribe. "Dear friends," he said. "He wants you to know how much he loves you, and how pleased he is to be here with you."

Isn't this a pretty good summary of God's message to the world? He wants us to know He loves us, and is pleased to be here with us.

Why Do They Join? When we think of evangelism, we may think of huge rallies and slick television promotion. But mass evangelism techniques—attempts to "reach" every person through mass mailings, radio, or television—are not sufficient. Mass communication must be part of a plan that includes local programs and local people, says Donald K. Smith, professor of international communication at Western Seminary and director of the International Institute for Christian Communication in Portland, Oregon.

As a missionary in southern and eastern Africa, Smith saw how family and community patterns could support or detract from a mass-media message. He calls on churches to learn the same lesson—that interpersonal relationships influence how messages are understood.

This notion may challenge the popular picture of the successful evangelist as one who reaches large audiences, Smith acknowledges. But preachers such as Bakht Singh in India, John Wesley in England, and Dwight L. Moody in the U.S. (as well as the apostle Paul among Gentiles) also worked with small groups. More than 80 percent of Christian converts begin their pilgrimages through friends, Smith says.

Eighty percent start their journey with Christ because some friend shared the Good News! Have you shared the hope and joy that Jesus Christ brings as eagerly as those lepers shared the news that the siege had been lifted?

Sharing in the Stadium. Lay Christian Edwin Thate, Jr., believes he must share the good news of Christ. He is convinced that an effective way to tell others about the Gospel is to display banners at football games. When lay evangelist Thate tried to display two banners with biblical references at Washington's RFK Stadium during the Redskins-Falcons game on January 4, 1992, stadium officials removed the banners because they were concerned that some fans might be offended. Thate said he didn't set out to offend anybody, but he believed that he had a constitutional right to display his religious convictions at such an event.

Thate sought help from the Rutherford Institute, an organization in Charlottesville, Virginia, which defends religious freedom in the courts. The institute filed a suit against stadium officials and the District of Columbia Armory Board, which supervises the facility. U.S. District Judge Joyce Hens Green issued a preliminary injunction that allowed Thate and two other lay evangelists to display religious banners at the stadium. Green ruled that the banners are protected under the First Amendment and that fear of a disturbance "is not enough to overcome the right to freedom of expression."

Not everyone would agree that Mr. Thate's method of witnessing for his faith is the most effective, but nobody can fault him for his zeal in sharing the Good News. Tempted to scoff at Ed Thate, we might ask ourselves, "What have I, myself, done to share the Good News recently?"

Questions for Students on the Next Lesson. 1. Who was Amos, and what was his background? 2. Why did he cause such an uproar in Bethel? 3. What was the heart of Amos's message? 4. Why do some people seem unaware of the relationship between a nation's actions and the consequences of those actions? 5. How healthy is the moral environment of your community? Of this nation?

TOPIC FOR YOUTH
SHARING GOOD NEWS

Comparisons. "Operation Restore Hope" was a humanitarian effort spearheaded by the United States to alleviate hunger in Somalia. It began in December 1992. However, health officials discovered, to their horror, the difficulties in dealing with malnourished individuals.

Relief workers distributed unmilled wheat to the living skeletons. The wheat had to be pounded by the recipients in order to create an edible mush. The energy expended to create the food vastly exceeded the nutritional benefit. During the famine in Somalia, the average daily food intake dwindled from 1,700 calories per person to the hopelessly inadequate 200 calories.

This caused a majority of the children under the age of five to die. Those that survived would carry the scars for the rest of their lives. Some would go blind as a result of a lack of vitamin A. Many would never achieve their full height and many would be unable to conceive or bear children. Mental function would be impaired or severely retarded.

Meanwhile, children in the United States had more than enough to eat. School dumpsters contained plenty of uneaten food.

The lepers realized they had to share the food they discovered. This was their responsibility as people of God. Have you made a similar discovery and commitment?

Sharing Good Fortune. After the fall of the Philippines in 1942, the American POWs were interned at Camp O'Donnell. In May 1942, the fourteen thousand defenders of Corregidor began to arrive.

Seventeen-year-old Pvt. Adriano Olivar, Jr., arrived at Camp O'Donnell. The youth had had his leg amputated as a result of a shell exploding near him. He had survived the walk of eighty-five miles from Mariveles to San Fernando, the near suffocating forty-mile train ride to Capas, and the final few miles' hike to the camp. He was one of only six amputees that eventually survived the infamous Bataan Death March even though it had taken him several days longer since he had to hobble on his crutches.

Along the route, he had picked up a brown bottle of pills from the dust. He hid the bottle in his ragged shirt, planning to keep it until someone could solve the mystery of its contents.

Arriving at Camp O'Donnell, Olivar worked in the hospital. The haggard doctors assigned him to obtain whatever personal drugs the newly arrived POWs might have carried in with them. Olivar immediately handed over his large bottle of pills, unaware of its contents. The doctors were ecstatic! It was a bottle of sulfa pills, a drug desperately needed to treat pneumonia and intestinal infections.

Although the bottle rightfully belonged to Olivar, and he could have kept it for his own survival, he freely shared what he had. Some young people gladly share their good fortune. Our love is to be directed to all people. Rather than hoard what we have, we are called to share with others.

No Doubts about Helping. On December 23, 1972, an earthquake hit Nicaragua, killing 10,000 people, injuring 20,000, and leaving 250,000 homeless. Star outfielder and eventual Hall of Famer Roberto Clemente did not have to be asked to help with Puerto Rico's relief effort. He left many of his Christmas presents unopened and threw himself into the task with enormous energy. Being the last of seven children growing up in a Puerto Rican barrio, he had known tough times. He had watched a sister die when her dress caught fire and had seen his two brothers die of cancer. His older sister had died giving birth. He had no doubts that he would help.

Worried that previous shipments were not getting through, and worried about a small boy with artificial legs that he had befriended, he insisted on flying with the third planeload of relief supplies. On New Year's Eve, the plane lifted off from the runway, but the left engine caught fire. The plane banked and crashed into the sea, killing all on board.

Clemente's family took some consolation in the fact that Roberto never doubted that he was making the right decision to help. Neither did the lepers doubt that they were making the right decision in sharing the food with their fellow citizens.

Questions for Students on the Next Lesson. 1. Who was Amos? Where did he prophesy? 2. For what crimes were Judah and Israel judged? 3. Why were the listeners surprised? 4. Does God still condemn a nation's wrongdoing? 5. How would God judge this nation today?

LESSON 5—JULY 2

CONDEMNATION FOR NATIONAL WRONGDOING

Background Scripture: Amos 1:1—3:2
Devotional Reading: Psalm 82

KING JAMES VERSION

AMOS 2:4 Thus saith the Lord; For three transgressions of Judah, and for four, I will not turn away the punishment thereof; because they have despised the law of the Lord, and have not kept his commandments, and their lies caused them to err, after the which their fathers have walked:

5 But I will send a fire upon Judah, and it shall devour the palaces of Jerusalem.

6 Thus saith the Lord; For three transgressions of Israel, and for four, I will not turn away the punishment thereof; because they sold the righteous for silver, and the poor for a pair of shoes;

7 That pant after the dust of the earth on the head of the poor, and turn aside the way of the meek: and a man and his father will go in unto the same maid, to profane my holy name:

8 And they lay themselves down upon clothes laid to pledge by every altar, and they drink the wine of the condemned in the house of their god. . . .

3:1 Hear this word that the Lord hath spoken against you, O children of Israel, against the whole family which I brought up from the land of Egypt, saying,

2 You only have I known of all the families of the earth: therefore I will punish you for all your iniquities.

REVISED STANDARD VERSION

AMOS 2:4 Thus says the Lord: "For three transgressions of Judah, and for four, I will not revoke the punishment; because they have rejected the law of the Lord, and have not kept his statutes, but their lies have led them astray, after which their fathers walked. 5 So I will send a fire upon Judah, and it shall devour the strongholds of Jerusalem."

6 Thus says the Lord: "For three transgressions of Israel, and for four, I will not revoke the punishment; because they sell the righteous for silver, and the needy for a pair of shoes—7 they that trample the head of the poor into the dust of the earth, and turn aside the way of the afflicted; a man and his father go in to the same maiden, so that my holy name is profaned; 8 they lay themselves down beside every altar upon garments taken in pledge; and in the house of their God they drink the wine of those who have been fined. . . ."

3:1 Hear this word that the Lord has spoken against you, O people of Israel, against the whole family which I brought up out of the land of Egypt:

2 "You only have I known of all the families of the earth; therefore I will punish you for all your iniquities.

KEY VERSE: *You only have I known of all the families of the earth; therefore I will punish you for all your iniquities. Amos 3:2.*

HOME DAILY BIBLE READINGS

June 26	M.	Psalm 82	God Wants Justice in the World
June 27	T.	Amos 1:1-5	Amos Announces God's Judgment on Syria
June 28	W.	Amos 1:6-12	Judgment on Philistia, Tyre, and Edom
June 29	T.	Amos 1:13—2:3	Judgment on Ammon and Moab
June 30	F.	Amos 2:4-8	Judgment on Judah and Israel
July 1	S.	Amos 2:9-13	God's Mercy Was Ignored
July 2	S.	Amos 2:14—3:2	Punishment for Abusing God's Favor

BACKGROUND

In spite of bold confrontations with prophets like Elijah and Elisha, the kings of Israel persisted in idolatry and injustices. The dreary saga of evil rulers testing the patience of the gracious Lord continued. The nation of Israel seemed determined to turn its back on God and His ways.

Outwardly, everything appeared to be going well. The nation seemed to flourish for forty-one years (786–746 B.C.) during the reign of Jeroboam II. A lull in the wars with powerful neighboring nations, and a brief international power vacuum, brought a wave of prosperity. A new class of wealthy landowners appeared, and the upper classes prospered. Many lived luxuriously; however, large numbers of poor people appeared, creating a class of serfs who were exploited by the rich. So economic prosperity came at the cost of great suffering by the poor and by displaced small farmers. Meanwhile, Baal worship continued throughout the kingdom.

The king and the wealthy people offered lip service to the Lord. On festival days at the great shrines in Bethel and Samaria, crowds came to offer expensive sacrifices and perform elaborate ceremonies before God. But this show of faith was a sham. Faithful, perceptive people of God sensed that Israel and her leaders had abandoned the covenant relationship with God and were participating in corrupt practices. A day of reckoning was bound to come.

During one of the religious holidays at the great national shrine at Bethel, a street-corner preacher shouted dire warnings about the nation's sins. His name was Amos. He was not a northerner but came from the southern nation of Judah, which made him resented as an outsider interfering with Israel's affairs. Moreover, Amos was a shepherd, not a professional prophet. Since he carried none of the credentials of membership in the guild of prophets, the well-paid religious leaders of Israel sneered at him. But Amos insistently spoke God's message of justice, and his words still burn themselves into the conscience of everyone who hears or reads them.

NOTES ON THE PRINTED TEXT

Amos announced God's approaching judgment to the northern kingdom of Israel, proclaiming God's condemnation of all the nations' wrongdoings. One after another, Israel's seven neighbors, including Judah, were condemned for their sins.

Then the surprised audience heard Amos announce Israel's devastation. These comments about Israel were the longest and most blistering. While the oracle began with the same opening structure as the oracles about other nations, the crimes of Israel were given in great detail.

Thus says the Lord: "For three transgressions of Judah, and for four, I will not revoke the punishment" (2:4). Amos's oracles each began with a typical prophetic formula. The format remained the same, only the country changed. The consequence also remained the same: punishment.

Normally, a specific reason was given. Judah's crime was general. The nation's major crime was rejecting God's law and following false ways that led the nation astray. This usually meant that the nation was worshiping idols and false gods and neglecting all the moral teachings. *They have rejected the law of the Lord, and have not kept his statutes, but their lies have led them astray, after which their fathers walked* (2:4).

The punishment was specific. *I will send a fire upon Judah, and it shall devour the strongholds of Jerusalem* (2:5). It was exactly the same punishment as the other pagan nations received. God's standard was the same for all nations. He had no favorites. Even Jerusalem would be destroyed.

They sell the righteous for silver, and the needy for a pair of shoes (2:6). Amos indicted the nation for allowing innocent or poor people to be sold into slavery. Other people were sold into slavery for a very small debt, such as the price of a pair of sandals. Rich people were using the courts of law to drive poor people off their land and to take their money. The victims became slaves.

The rich and the creditors, *they that trample the head of the poor into the dust of the earth, and turn aside the way of the afflicted* (2:7), were condemned. The poor and those who had no standing in the nation should have been protected and their needs provided. Instead, they were further exploited, probably by the courts of law. Whole families worked together to systematically defraud the poor.

Amos blasted Israel's promiscuity and immorality, as well. *A man and his father go in to the same maiden, so that my holy name is profaned* (2:7). Perhaps Amos was referring to the use of cult prostitutes prevalent in the Canaanite fertility religion. Or perhaps he was condemning a father and son for using a female slave for sexual fulfillment. Whatever the case, the practices profaned God's name.

They lay themselves down beside every altar upon garments taken in pledge (2:8). Garments secured a debt. The borrower left his or her cloak as the guarantee of repayment. Law required that the cloak be returned at sunset so that the debtor could be warm while sleeping at night. The rich apparently had kept the cloaks and spread them out beside the altars for some quasi-religious purpose.

Other excesses took place in God's house. *In the house of their God they drink the wine of those who have been fined* (2:8). Payments of debts were made in kind, such as with wine. The rich reclined in God's house on the garments of the poor and ate and drank the profits of their perversion of justice. Israel had been unjust and cruel to the needy. The nation had broken God's law and despised its religious tradition.

Preparing Judah and Israel for God's judgment, Amos reminded the people of all they had received from God. God had removed the supposedly invincible Amorites. God had delivered the people from Egypt. God had provided prophets to guide the nations. However, because of their cruelty and irresponsibility in keeping God's covenant, God was going to punish the nation. *Hear this . . . O people of Israel . . . You only have I known of all the families of the earth; therefore I will punish you for all your iniquities* (3:1, 2).

SUGGESTIONS TO TEACHERS

With the July Fourth celebrations under way this weekend, today's lesson has a certain timeliness. The American nation, as our founders knew, is "under God" and therefore accountable to the Ruler of all nations. Amos addressed Israel, insisting that the nation was accountable to God. He offered a message that is relevant to every country and every citizen.

1. INDICTMENT OF NEIGHBORING DISTRICTS. Amos, spokesman for God, spared no nation. He pointed out the ways that all the countries had persisted in flaunting God's basic demands. With majestic sweep, the prophet turned toward all points of the compass to denounce the Syrians to the north, the Edomites to the east, the Philistines to the south, and the kingdoms of Ashkelon and Tyre to the west. Emphasize to your class that God is Lord of all, and holds every nation responsible.

2. INDICATION OF GOD'S DISPLEASURE. Amos's hearers might have smiled indulgently upon hearing him denounce other nations for their sin. But when he spoke about Israel's disobedience, the Israelites grew defensive and hostile. And isn't that the way we still react when we hear someone criticizing our own country?

Amos presented a catalog of Judah's sins. Topping the list was rampant injustice. Humans were hurting, being exploited. Oppression of another person or group, Amos proclaimed, mocked the most basic of God's requirements. The widespread immorality in society reflected the way the leaders and people had rejected God.

Amos spared no words. He "told it like it was" in describing the luxury and debauchery, the corruption, and other social evils in the kingdom. In the opinion of your students, what would Amos have to say about conditions in our nation?

3. IMPLICATIONS OF HUMAN DISOBEDIENCE. Israel's rejection of the Lord would inevitably result in the nation's destruction. This doom was being brought on by persistent disobedience and must be interpreted as divine punishment. Amos bluntly stated that Israel was held to a greater degree of accountability than others because of its unique relationship to God. The prophet stated, "You only have I known of all the families of the earth; therefore I will punish you for all your iniquities" (3:1, 2). Discuss with your class whether our nation, with its profession of being "under God" and standing for "liberty and justice for all," might be held to a stricter responsibility to its citizens than other countries. Is America answerable to God?

TOPIC FOR ADULTS
CONDEMNING FOR NATIONAL WRONGS

Ike's Warning. Richard L. Simon, president of the publishing firm of Simon & Schuster, had written President Dwight D. Eisenhower on March 28, 1956, calling attention to a newspaper column (by Joseph and Steward Alsop) that urged an immediate military buildup in response to the Soviet military threat.

This is Eisenhower's reply of April 4, 1956:

Dear Dick:

Thank you for your letter, which brings up subjects too vast to be discussed adequately in a letter. Suffice it to say here that I doubt that any columnist—and here I depend upon hearsay as I have no time to read them—is concerning himself with what is the true security problem of the day. That problem is not merely man against man or nation against nation. It is man against war.

I have spent my life in the study of military strength as a deterrent to war, and in the character of military armaments necessary to win a war. The study of the first of these questions is still profitable, but we are rapidly getting to the point that no war can be won. War implies a contest; when you get to the point that contest is no longer involved and the outlook comes close to destruction of the enemy and suicide for ourselves—an outlook that neither side can ignore—then arguments as to the exact amount of available strength as compared to somebody else's are no longer the vital issues.

When we get to the point, as we one day will, that both sides know that in any outbreak of general hostilities, regardless of the element of surprise, destruction will be both reciprocal and complete, possibly we will have sense enough to meet at the conference table with the understanding that the era of armaments has ended and the human race must conform its actions to this truth or die.

The fullness of this potentiality has not yet been attained, and I do not, by any means, decry the need for strength. That strength must be spiritual, economic, and military. All three are important and they are not mutually exclusive. They are all part of, and the product of, the American genius, the American will.

But already we have come to the point where safety cannot be assumed by arms alone. But I repeat that their usefulness becomes concentrated more and more in their characteristics as deterrents than in instruments with which to obtain victory over opponents, as in 1945. In this regard, today we are further separated from the end of World War II than the beginning of the century was separated from the beginning of the sixteenth century.

Naturally, I am not taking the time here to discuss the usefulness of available military strength in putting out "prairie fires"—spots where American interests are seriously jeopardized by unjustified outbreaks of minor wars. I have contented myself with a few observations on the implications of a major arms race.

Finally, I do not believe that I shall ever have to defend myself against the charge that I am indifferent to the fate of my countrymen, and I assure you that there are experts, technicians, philosophers, and advisers here who give far more intelligent attention to these matters than do the Alsops.

With warm regard, sincerely,
Dwight D. Eisenhower

The letter was marked "personal and confidential." But if ever there was a message that echoes across the decades to our own time, it is this one. In eight short paragraphs, the remarkable man who had led the Allied armies to victory over Hitler and served the nation as its last two-term president, distilled a lifetime of wisdom.

One sentence, in particular, deserves to be carved in stone. Just read it slowly—clause by clause—and think about it:

"When we get to the point, as we one day will, that both sides know that in any outbreak of general hostilities, regardless of the element of surprise, destruction will be both reciprocal and complete, possibly we will have sense enough to meet at the conference table with the understanding that the era of armaments has ended and the human race must conform its actions to this truth or die."

Recovering the Motto. A few years ago, someone got to digging around in the records and archives of the city of Glasgow. For years, the seal of Glasgow had carried the phrase "Let Glasgow Flourish," and it was assumed by everyone that those words constituted that great city's motto. The researcher discovered that Glasgow's motto originally was, "Let Glasgow Flourish by Preaching the Word." Glasgow's citizens were unexpectedly reminded that their city, like the Scottish nation itself, flourished because of the Word of God at work in the lives of its people.

Questions for Students on the Next Lesson. 1. Why had Israel's worship become offensive to God, according to Amos? 2. What did Amos mean by the words "the Day of the Lord"? 3. What were some of the analogies Amos used to point out the unexpectedness of God's judgment on His people? 4. Can religious observances ever substitute for justice, according to Amos? 5. What is your congregation doing to carry out God's mandate for peace and justice in the world?

TOPIC FOR YOUTH
CORRUPTION REIGNS

Intolerance Still Exists. When Slippery Rock University's Rhoades Hall Assistant-Resident, Lewis Williams, awoke on February 17, 1993, he found racial slurs written on his door in black marker. Another door down the hall, that of James Kenny and Darryl Carpenter, also had similar slurs. All three students were black.

Black students were angry and upset over the incident, which happened during Black History Month. It was a reminder that some people still judge others by the color of their skin and that racism is a continuing problem.

Sadly, such acts of intolerance are still happening on campuses all over the country. Youth and adults are victims of social injustice. Yet Amos's message remains the same: God will condemn and punish His people for all injustice.

Heroes or Heels? Eric Richardson, seventeen, and eight of his Lakewood High School friends were arrested and jailed for molesting and raping girls as young as ten. The Lakewood, California, youths were all part of a group called the Spur Posse. After several days in jail, all the unrepentant boys were released and returned to school as heroes.

Lakewood Mayor Marc Titel hoped the town would do some serious self-examination. The predominantly white, upper-class community was inclined to be lenient on these student-athletes and excuse their behavior. He called for an examination of the community's values, noting that teen promiscuity was one of the community's significant problems.

Mayor Titel was frustrated. The District Attorney would not prosecute the several incidents, stating that it was a social issue best left to the churches, schools, and parents. The parents, however, were boastful! Don Belman, father of two of the arrested boys, said his sons were "all man." He maintained that the boys were only being boys and that almost every male in America would be in jail if they were imprisoned for doing what his sons had done. Of the four thousand students at Lakewood High, a few were troubled. Most, though, defended the boys, to the embarrassment of the school administration.

Like the people before Amos, these young people and members of their community were indifferent to God's moral absolutes. Their lawlessness, corruption, and sin would be punished, Amos promised. And, of course, someday each boy will be held accountable for his actions.

Indifference. During the height of world concern about hunger and famine in Africa, a sports agreement was reached among certain African countries. U.S. advisers were to develop an aerobics training program for these countries that would coincide with the international effort to feed the hungry.

As millions starved, some groups saw an opportunity to line their wallets by attempting to train people to lose weight or control their weight. Amos would have had some sharp words of condemnation for these people and their nation.

Questions for Students on the Next Lesson. 1. Why did Amos condemn Israel's worship? 2. What was the significance of the Day of the Lord? 3. What did Amos announce about that Day? 4. Can worship be a substitute for justice? 5. What criteria does God use to judge His people?

LESSON 6—JULY 9

A CALL FOR JUSTICE AND RIGHTEOUSNESS

Background Scripture: Amos 4—5
Devotional Reading: Amos 5:6-15

KING JAMES VERSION	REVISED STANDARD VERSION
AMOS 4:4 Come to Bethel, and transgress; at Gilgal multiply transgression; and bring your sacrifices every morning, and your tithes after three years:	AMOS 4:4 "Come to Bethel, and transgress; to Gilgal, and multiply transgression; bring your sacrifices every morning, your tithes every three days; 5 offer a sacrifice of thanksgiving of that which is leavened, and proclaim freewill offerings, publish them; for so you love to do, O people of Israel!" says the Lord God. . . .
5 And offer a sacrifice of thanksgiving with leaven, and proclaim and publish the free offerings: for this liketh you, O ye children of Israel, saith the Lord God. . . .	
5:18 Woe unto you that desire the day of the Lord! to what end is it for you? the day of the Lord is darkness, and not light.	5:18 Woe to you who desire the day of the Lord! Why would you have the day of the Lord? It is darkness, and not light; 19 as if a man fled from a lion, and a bear met him; or went into the house and leaned with his hand against the wall, and a serpent bit him. 20 Is not the day of the Lord darkness, and not light, and gloom with no brightness in it?
19 As if a man did flee from a lion, and a bear met him; or went into the house, and leaned his hand on the wall, and a serpent bit him.	
20 Shall not the day of the Lord be darkness, and not light? even very dark, and no brightness in it?	
21 I hate, I despise your feast days, and I will not smell in your solemn assemblies.	21 "I hate, I despise your feasts, and I take no delight in your solemn assemblies. 22 Even though you offer me your burnt offerings and cereal offerings, I will not accept them, and the peace offerings of your fatted beasts I will not look upon. 23 Take away from me the noise of your songs; to the melody of your harps I will not listen. 24 But let justice roll down like waters, and righteousness like an everflowing stream.
22 Though ye offer me burnt offerings and your meat offerings, I will not accept them: neither will I regard the peace offerings of your fat beasts.	
23 Take thou away from me the noise of thy songs; for I will not hear the melody of thy viols.	
24 But let judgment run down as waters, and righteousness as a mighty stream.	

KEY VERSE: But let justice roll down like waters, and righteousness like an everflowing stream. Amos 5:24.

HOME DAILY BIBLE READINGS

July	3	M.	Amos 4:1-5	Israel's Vain Piety Will Be Punished
July	4	T.	Amos 4:6-11	God's Warnings Were Ignored
July	5	W.	Amos 4:12—5:3	God's Punishment Is at Hand
July	6	T.	Amos 5:4-9	There Is Still Time for Repentance
July	7	F.	Amos 5:10-15	Warning and Call to Seek God
July	8	S.	Amos 5:16-20	The Day of the Lord: Judgment
July	9	S.	Amos 5:21-27	God Wants Justice and Righteousness

BACKGROUND

The name of Tekoa, Amos's hometown, meant "the alarm trumpet" in Hebrew. Amos's message was, indeed, a trumpet sounding the alarm.

Amos had been a shepherd. As a shepherd, he probably had firsthand experience with predatory animals feeding on his sheep. He had seen how a wild beast could kill and devour a lamb, leaving only a few scraps of the carcass. In his sermon in Amos 3:12, the outspoken prophet from Tekoa stated that Assyria would pounce like a fierce lion, and that Israel's national carcass will have left only the equivalent of a couple of pieces of shin bone and the rag of an ear.

Needless to say, Amos was not a popular preacher in the great shrine city of Bethel. But Amos was determined to point out that God disciplines His people by means of events in history. Israel's disregard for God's commandments was bringing ruin. The basis for God's discipline is His love for His people and His demand for right living.

The Israelites clung to a sacrificial system in their worship that was understood to bring forgiveness of sins. Although they were also supposed to change their behavior, most worshipers assumed that carrying out the proper rituals was the only requirement. Therefore, the people failed to express true repentance. Worship turned into a kind of mechanical transaction to gain assurance of forgiveness. Amos vigorously protested this shallow understanding of God's mercy.

Furthermore, in Hebrew faith, devotion to God must always issue in concern for one's neighbor. When the prophets pleaded for a return to God, they always meant a recommitment to the covenant, which urged caring for the poor and powerless. The religious revivals that sometimes swept Israel before its collapse often had no relationship to biblical faith, with the people expressing little sense of social justice. Amos attacked the priests and religious leaders for their lack of moral sensitivity. He denounced the leaders for permitting the poor to be oppressed. In the oracles in today's lesson, Amos told all the worshipers at Bethel, in effect, "Come to Bethel and sin! Bring your impressive-sounding offerings and advertise them, for that's what you really love!"

Amos followed up these words by reciting the unheeded warnings he and other true prophets had given Israel. He announced that calamities to come would be God's way of trying to bring His people to their senses. The concluding portion of the Scripture in today's lesson, chapter 5, was announced in the form of a funeral lament over the nation.

NOTES ON THE PRINTED TEXT

During a great religious festival, Amos arrived at Bethel. The people had gathered to hear the priest and to make the appropriate sacrifices and offerings. Instead, Amos spoke. He himself assumed the role of the priest, summoning the people to worship. Speaking with bitter irony and sarcasm, he pointed out that Israel's worship had become offensive to God.

Come to Bethel, and transgress; to Gilgal, and multiply transgression (4:4). He summoned the people to the two most important religious shrines . . . to sin! Bethel had long been an important religious center. Jeroboam had made it one of two state shrines that could be used as alternatives to Jerusalem. Gilgal had traditions that went back to Joshua. The two places were considered places of worship to the Lord. People arriving at the shrine, offering their sacrifices to bring about forgiveness, atonement, and communion, were told that their worship had no spiritual content. It was offensive to God. Sarcastically, Amos summoned the people to come to church and sin.

Bring your sacrifices every morning, your tithes every three days (4:4). Worshipers offered a sacrifice to establish peace with God. Part of the animal was eaten as an expression of communion with God. The tithe was one-tenth of the yield, which Israel presented at the sanctuary. It was to be used in festival meals before God and was offered on the third day. On the first day a smaller offering was made. *Offer a sacrifice of thanksgiving of that which is leavened, and proclaim freewill offerings, publish them* (4:5). Worshipers were invited to make a thank offering. This was an offering of praise and thanks to God for blessings and answers to prayers. While leavened bread was used at sacred meals (except for Passover), it was forbidden as an offering by fire. A freewill offering was a voluntary, sacrificial gift, expressing a worshiper's devotion and commitment.

The people's faith had become diluted with empty ritual and gesturing, something they loved to do but which expressed no real commitment to God. *You love to do* (4:5). Amos also shattered another cherished belief. Israel trusted that the Day of the Lord would end all trouble. This end-time period of history would be a time of judgment and punishment for Israel's enemies and a time of deliverance and salvation for Israel. God would someday place Israel at the head of all the nations. Amos warned, however, that the Day of the Lord would be a day of judgment for the Israelite nation, too. *Woe to you who desire the day of the Lord! Why would you have the day of the Lord? It is darkness, and not light* (5:18).

God's coming would bring no security. Amos used several analogies to point out the unexpectedness of God's judgment on His people. Warning evildoers against complacency, he said they would be like a man who fled from a lion only to be attacked by a bear, or who entered his house, leaned against the wall, and was bitten by a snake. Again Amos challenged the people to realize that their confidence in the Day of the Lord was misplaced. *Is not the day of the Lord darkness, and not light, and gloom with no brightness in it?* (5:20).

Amos restated his condemnation of Israel's worship. He took each element, one after another, and announced God's rejection of each one. *I hate, I despise your feasts, and I take no delight in your solemn assemblies* (5:21). Israel's observance of festivals was rejected by God as were the sacrifices and ritual expressions of praise. These nauseated and disgusted God; they would not work as substitutes for justice.

What God desired was righteousness and justice. Amos called Israel to be just and righteous in its relationships in order to be acceptable to God. *Let justice roll down like waters, and righteousness like an everflowing stream* (5:24).

SUGGESTIONS TO TEACHERS

Imagine the reaction if a man in overalls stood out on the sidewalk in front of your church on Easter Sunday morning, loudly listing the social sins of this country and calling for repentance and justice. How would you and the people in your congregation react? Call the police? Try to ignore the man as a nuisance? Send your minister out to try to quiet him down and send him away?

Amos's appearance during a great festival at Bethel was roughly like the scene just pictured. His message, however, cannot be dismissed as the rantings of an eccentric. Amos's call for justice and righteousness must sound before every gathering of God's people. Make sure it is heard today in your class.

1. CONDEMNATION OF WEALTHY OPPRESSORS. Amos criticized the luxury-loving rich for their extravagance in the face of need and hunger. This points to the life-style of most of us. Discuss the need for greater simplicity and carefulness in our spending. Recall the saying "Live simply that others may simply live!" Explore with your students how a Christian can distinguish between needs and wants. How often we confuse the two, rationalizing our wants into needs.

Move the discussion also to the subject of worship. Amos scolded the people in Bethel for loving flashy religious ceremonies while they ignored the poor and powerless. Emphasize that love of God and love of neighbor go together. True piety requires acting on behalf of the hurting and oppressed.

2. CALAMITIES FROM REFUSALS. Refusing to live justly results in hardship for everyone. Amos proclaimed that drought, famine, and disease would come to Israel because of the nation's callousness toward the poor. Discuss whether God would permit this sort of thing to happen to us because of our failure to reach out to the poor and hungry, the homeless and forgotten in our society. Does God judge our country today?

3. CALL FOR REPENTANCE. Amos pleaded with Israel to return to God. "Seek the Lord and live" (5:6). "Seek good, and not evil, that you may live" (5:14). Note that the promise of life is offered to those who live with God and for God. And living with and for God, throughout the Bible, always means sharing His passionate concern for the persons who are suffering. Beginning with the Hebrews in Egyptian slavery, God has shown that He sides with the hurting and oppressed.

4. CRITICISM OF ASSUMPTIONS. Amos warned that God has no favorites, announcing that neither Israel nor any nation had an automatic exemption from obeying the Lord. Most Israelites assumed that because they were God's chosen ones they would always be vindicated. Discuss whether this type of thinking characterizes our churches and our nation.

TOPIC FOR ADULTS
WORKING FOR JUSTICE AND RIGHTEOUSNESS

A Rock of Justice. Former Supreme Court Justice Thurgood Marshall, who died January 24, 1993, from heart failure, was the legal architect of desegregation and the remedies necessary to achieve integration. His moral commitment to equality transcended the shifting sands of politics and public opinion. He began and ended his career in dissent, facing first the hostile and brutal world of segregated America and then retiring from the high court after twenty-four years of service, fighting the backlash against the civil rights gains he did so much to win.

Marshall, who retired in 1991, will be remembered chiefly as the

NAACP attorney who argued the 1954 *Brown* v. *Board of Education* case and as the first black named to the high court. The 1954 case scuttled the "separate but equal" doctrine for public education, enacted in 1896. But there were many other high points and fights for the high-spirited and scrappy Baltimore native. One of the first came when, as a fourteen-year-old boy, he confronted a white man who had called him "nigger."

In 1964, Marshall, as a lay delegate to the Episcopal Church's General Convention, staged a walkout at the session. Convention members had rejected a resolution allowing for civil disobedience to laws and customs that were "in basic conflict with the concept of human dignity." At the time Marshall was a member of St. Philip's Episcopal Church in Harlem and a member of the standing committee of his diocese.

During his funeral, Marshall was eulogized for making real the words inscribed above the entrance to the Supreme Court building: "Equal Justice for All." He was remembered as a man who "was chased by gangs and received by presidents."

A Righteous Alabamian. Civil rights leaders like Martin Luther King, Jr., got the headlines during the struggle for justice. But in increasing numbers in the 1950s and 1960s, such leaders stood before courageous judges who risked their lives to uphold the Constitution.

Foremost among these judges was Frank M. Johnson, Jr., of Alabama. A native of rural Winston County in northern Alabama, and a friend and classmate of George Wallace at the University of Alabama Law School, Judge Johnson overcame local defiance, including that of Governor Wallace himself, and, in the end, changed the face of the South. Appointed to the federal bench in Montgomery by President Dwight D. Eisenhower in 1955, Judge Johnson quickly found himself in the midst of the hurricane. In his very first opinion on civil rights, dealing with the Montgomery bus boycott, he declared segregation on Alabama city buses to be unconstitutional.

Most of his fellow white Alabamians were shocked that this son of the South should have gone over to the "enemy." To segregationists, Judge Johnson became the hated symbol of federal denial of states' rights. He soon found himself ostracized by most of white society. His mother's home was bombed; a cross was burned in his front yard; he received countless threatening phone calls and lived under the nearly constant protection of a Federal marshal.

In 1960, Judge Johnson became the first judge to draw up a court-ordered legislative reapportionment plan. His decisions would also desegregate Alabama schools, bus terminals, parks, museums, airports, libraries, state police, and correctional and mental institutions.

Johnson was always a step ahead in developing legal tools such as the civil rights injunction, an order preventing state officials from applying blatantly discriminatory voting laws against blacks attempting to register. In *United States* v. *Alabama* (1961), Judge Johnson found a deliberate pattern of discrimination against blacks in voter registration practices. His ruling freezing voter registration standards available to whites and extending them to blacks was one of the key principles incorporated into the Voting Rights Act of 1965. Judge Johnson's later circuit court decisions advanced the rights of women. This legendary judge, as Martin Luther

King, Jr., said, "gave true meaning to the word justice."

A Brave Stand. Fannie Lou Hamer was an unlikely leader for justice. Born in 1917 to a family that already had nineteen children, she began picking cotton at the age of six. She married Perry Hamer in 1944 and took up the hardscrabble life of a sharecropper farmer's wife. Her future, like that of millions of other poor, uneducated black women in Mississippi, looked like a continuing bleak struggle with poverty.

Fannie Lou Hamer tried to register to vote in 1962. She failed her registration test, as did virtually all blacks in the Jim Crow Mississippi of the early 1960s. But when the news of her having tried to register leaked out, she was fired from her job on the plantation and forced to move from the house she and her husband had lived in for eighteen years.

From this point on, Hamer dedicated her life to the civil rights movement. In a Mississippi that led the nation in recorded lynchings (581 between 1882 and 1968), she became living proof that the system could be defied. On her second trip to the courthouse, she even succeeded in getting on the voter rolls, convincing the local registrar that if he did not sign her up this time she would keep coming back until he did. A year later, however, her courage nearly cost her her life. On her way home from a civil rights meeting, she was arrested in Winona, Mississippi, and subjected to a beating by her jailers that left her with lifelong injuries.

Hamer's response to the beating was to plunge still further into civil rights work. She was a key participant in the Mississippi Summer Project of 1964, in which college students from all over the country aided local voter registration efforts, and that August she made national news at the Democratic National Convention in Atlantic City. At a televised credentials committee hearing, held to decide whether the integrated Mississippi Freedom Democratic Party or the all-white Mississippi delegation of party regulars should be seated, Hamer delivered the speech of her life. She described her beating in such moving terms that President Lyndon B. Johnson, who was watching the proceedings on television, worried that his reelection chances would be hurt by a Southern walkout over the Mississippi question. He actually tried to divert attention from her by calling an impromptu news conference while she was still speaking.

In less than two years, Fannie Lou Hamer had gone from a woman nearly beaten to death in a small Mississippi jail to someone who could worry a sitting president! She was never tempted to side with those who wanted to read whites out of the civil rights movement. "If we're trying to break down this barrier of segregation, we can't segregate ourselves," she declared at a 1963 S.N.C.C. meeting. Later she told an interviewer, "I am not fighting for an all-black world, just like I am not going to tolerate an all-white world." In his speech at the Democratic National Convention, Bill Clinton described Fannie Lou Hamer, who died in 1977, as a "great civil rights pioneer" whose commitment to social change is part of our heritage.

Questions for Students on the Next Lesson. 1. Who was Gomer, and what was she like? 2. Why did Hosea marry her? 3. What was the significance of the names of Hosea's and Gomer's children? 4. What was the heartbreak experienced by Hosea, and what did he do? 5. What did Hosea's story lead him to say about the Lord?

TOPIC FOR YOUTH
WORKING FOR JUSTICE AND RIGHTEOUSNESS

Analogies. Amos used several analogies appropriate to his audience. Equally appropriate and prophetic were the words of Peter Teeley, President Bush's representative to the Convention on the Rights of the Child, held in 1991 at the United Nations building in New York City. Teeley pointed out that if 40,000 spotted owls were dying every day, there would be a public outrage. However, 40,000 children die each day and no one notices. Later, he made another similar analogy. If 100 Boeing-747 airplanes, each one carrying 400 people, crashed every day, the government would take action. However, an equal number of deaths occur each day that involve children, and there is no comment from the government.

For all the emphasis on need in the world, the children are the most forgotten. Israel's lack of commitment to young and old was condemned by Amos. The prophet's words remain terribly relevant to people today.

Call to Justice. It is estimated that the number of the world's extremely underprivileged and street children is over one hundred million. How many children is that? If you were to count one street child per second, there would be sixty each minute, or 3,600 in an hour. In one twenty-four hour day, there would be 86,400. It would take twenty-three days, almost a month, to count to two million (the number of these children in Mexico City alone). To count to one hundred million would take 1,157 days, or three years and two months.

You are called to work for justice and righteousness. Your call is to bring people into a relationship with God so that the family of God has no outsiders in the street.

Worked for Justice. Daniel Trocme was a slender, steel-rim bespectacled, intellectual youth, who suffered from a heart ailment that made him short of breath. He lived in Le Chambon, France, at the beginning of World War II. This tiny village was perched in the Cévennes Mountains in southern France. It was populated by many impoverished Christians. Yet, even with the Germans only a dozen miles away, this tiny town saved the lives of thousands of Jewish refugees.

Daniel worked at two particular dwellings that housed young Jewish refugees. The Crickets was the residence for Jewish children between the ages of eight and twelve. The House of Rocks was for older boys. Daniel's job was to drag large bowls of soup up through the hills to the Crickets. This was dangerous for him because of his medical condition and because of the risk of detection by the Germans. He also was responsible for resoling the children's shoes with old tires.

One day, in the summer of 1943, the Gestapo raided the town. All the children in the House of Rocks were rounded up and detained in the three-story granite structure. The children were all roughly interrogated.

Daniel was brutally interrogated in a small room. Because he spoke fluent German, the Gestapo suspected that he was a German Jew. Under severe questioning, he spoke his conscience and defended the Jews. He stood his ground and spoke for justice and righteousness.

Daniel was led out with the other children to three buses. Knowing that he was going to a concentration camp, he called his second cousin, Magda, asking her to write to his parents to tell them not to worry about him—to remind them that he liked to travel!

For his stand on justice and righteousness for all peoples, Daniel was gassed and incinerated at Majdanek Death Camp on April 4, 1944. Like Amos, Daniel Trocme found that a stand for justice and righteousness could result in great personal sacrifice.

Questions for Students on the Next Lesson. 1. Who were Hosea and Gomer? 2. How would you characterize their marriage? 3. What did the names of their children mean? Why did Hosea give them such names? 4. Why did Hosea buy back Gomer? 5. Can a relationship ever really be restored?

LESSON 7—JULY 16

A PROPHET WHO LIVED HIS MESSAGE

Background Scripture: Hosea 1:1—3:5
Devotional Reading: Romans 5:1-11

KING JAMES VERSION

HOSEA 1:2 The beginning of the word of the Lord by Hosea. And the Lord said to Hosea, Go, take unto thee a wife of whoredoms and children of whoredoms: for the land hath committed great whoredom, departing from the Lord.

3 So he went and took Gomer the daughter of Diblaim; which conceived, and bare him a son.

4 And the Lord said unto him, Call his name Jezreel; for yet a little while, and I will avenge the blood of Jezreel upon the house of Jehu, and will cause to cease the kingdom of the house of Israel.

5 And it shall come to pass at that day, that I will break the bow of Israel in the valley of Jezreel.

6 And she conceived again, and bare a daughter. And God said unto him, Call her name Lo-ruhamah: for I will no more have mercy upon the house of Israel; but I will utterly take them away.

7 But I will have mercy upon the house of Judah, and will save them by the Lord their God, and will not save them by bow, nor by sword, nor by battle, by horses, nor by horsemen.

8 Now when she had weaned Lo-ruhamah, she conceived, and bare a son.

9 Then said God, Call his name Lo-ammi: for ye are not my people, and I will not be your God. . . .

3:1 Then said the Lord unto me, Go yet, love a woman beloved of her friend, yet an adulteress, according to the love of the Lord toward the children of Israel, who look to other gods, and love flagons of wine.

2 So I bought her to me for fifteen pieces of silver, and for an homer of barley, and an half homer of barley:

3 And I said unto her, Thou shalt abide for me many days; thou shalt not play the harlot, and thou shalt not be for another man: so will I also be for thee.

4 For the children of Israel shall abide many days without a king, and without a prince, and without a sacrifice, and without an image, and without an ephod, and without teraphim:

REVISED STANDARD VERSION

HOSEA 1:2 When the Lord first spoke through Hosea, the Lord said to Hosea, "Go, take to yourself a wife of harlotry and have children of harlotry, for the land commits great harlotry by forsaking the Lord." 3 So he went and took Gomer the daughter of Diblaim, and she conceived and bore him a son.

4 And the Lord said to him, "Call his name Jezreel; for yet a little while, and I will punish the house of Jehu for the blood of Jezreel, and I will put an end to the kingdom of the house of Israel. 5 And on that day, I will break the bow of Israel in the valley of Jezreel."

6 She conceived again and bore a daughter. And the Lord said to him, "Call her name Not pitied, for I will no more have pity on the house of Israel, to forgive them at all. 7 But I will have pity on the house of Judah, and I will deliver them by the Lord their God; I will not deliver them by bow, nor by sword, nor by war, nor by horses, nor by horsemen."

8 When she had weaned Not pitied, she conceived and bore a son. 9 And the Lord said, "Call his name Not my people, for you are not my people and I am not your God.". . .

3:1 And the Lord said to me, "Go again, love a woman who is beloved of a paramour and is an adulteress; even as the Lord loves the people of Israel, though they turn to other gods and love cakes of raisins." 2 So I bought her for fifteen shekels of silver and a homer and a lethech of barley. 3 And I said to her, "You must dwell as mine for many days; you shall not play the harlot, or belong to another man; so will I also be to you."

4 For the children of Israel shall dwell many days without king or prince, without sacrifice or pillar, without ephod or teraphim.

5 Afterward the children of Israel shall return and seek the Lord their God, and David their king; and they shall come in fear to the Lord and to his goodness in the latter days.

5 Afterward shall the children of Israel
return, and seek the Lord their God, and
David their king; and shall fear the Lord
and his goodness in the latter days.

KEY VERSE: *I will betroth you to me . . . in righteousness and in justice, in
steadfast love, and in mercy.* Hosea 2:19.

HOME DAILY BIBLE READINGS

July	10	M.	Romans 5:1-11	*Peace with God through Christ*
July	11	T.	Hosea 1:1-5	*God's Instructions to Hosea*
July	12	W.	Hosea 1:6—2:1	*Names for Hosea's Children*
July	13	T.	Hosea 2:2-13	*Shame and Hardship for Israel*
July	14	F.	Hosea 2:14-23	*God Will Woo Israel Back*
July	15	S.	Hosea 3	*God Will Restore Israel*
July	16	S.	Psalm 115:1-13	*The Lord Will Bless Us*

BACKGROUND

As Amos thundered his warnings of doom to the Israelites at Bethel,
another prophet was anguishing over Israel's unfaithfulness. This other
prophet, Hosea, had his heart broken when his beloved wife left him to
take up the adulterous ways of the Baal cults. Hosea recognized that his
situation seemed to parallel Israel's refusal to remain faithful to the Lord.
The writing of Hosea reflects both his own personal sorrow regarding his
wife and also God's sorrow and efforts to win back His beloved Israel.

Ancient Canaanite Baal worship persisted throughout Israel's history.
Its fertility ceremonies were a blend of magic and superstition. Practicing
these rituals was supposed to guarantee favorable harvests for one's crops
and healthy offspring for the animals and humans. The cults of these
nature gods flourished in "the high places," on hilltops and in groves of
trees in various places in Israel. The rites usually involved sexual orgies.
Sometimes women would turn themselves over as cult prostitutes in these
scandalous practices.

Hosea's wife, Gomer, had apparently turned into such a wayward
woman before he married her. At God's command, Hosea deliberately
chose a harlot for his wife. Hosea felt tenderly toward Gomer. Gomer produced three children. Some scholars interpret the text to mean that Hosea
was not the father. Nevertheless, Hosea accepted them and assigned them
strikingly prophetic names.

In spite of Hosea's caring, Gomer left him and insisted on resuming her
disgusting life as a cult prostitute. Yet the heartbroken prophet refused to
write her off. With immense love and patience, Hosea wooed and re-
claimed Gomer.

The Bible does not record Hosea's experience merely to provide us with
an intriguing soap-opera drama. Rather, Hosea told the story of his tender
concern for his wayward wife as an allegory to describe the relationship
between God and Israel. God had looked upon Israel as His "bride." Israel,
however, had deserted the Lord and had attached herself to the disgusting
Canaanite deities. God was determined to win Israel back.

NOTES ON THE PRINTED TEXT

Go, take to yourself a wife of harlotry and have children of harlotry, for the land commits great harlotry by forsaking the Lord (1:2). Hosea was a citizen of Israel, the only prophet from the northern kingdom. He clearly saw the dilution of the true faith of God by the fertility cult.

God ordered Hosea to marry a prostitute. Most likely she was more than a promiscuous woman, probably a cult prostitute dedicated to serving Baal. Hosea was also ordered to have children by this woman. His marriage was to symbolize God's love for Israel despite Israel's unfaithfulness.

So he went and took Gomer the daughter of Diblaim, and she conceived and bore him a son (1:3). Hosea selected and married Gomer. Whether her name was a derivative of the word for the Canaanite god, Pam, or a reference to fig cakes (this would suggest that Gomer's services could be bought for two fig cakes) is uncertain. Hosea, the Jewish prophet, did the unthinkable. He married the woman and produced a son.

Call his name Jezreel (1:4). Hosea's children were to be given names symbolic of God's decision about the future of Israel. Jezreel meant "God sows." The name indicated that God was about to sow judgment and doom. Jezreel, the valley between Samaria and Galilee, was a dark blot on Israel's history. Here Naboth had been murdered; here Jehu and his fanatics had butchered and exterminated the house of Omri. Now a similar fate would come to Jehu's descendants. God passed the death sentence on the dynasty of Jehu: *Yet a little while, and I will punish the house of Jehu for the blood of Jezreel, and I will put an end to the kingdom of the house of Israel* (1:4). What's more, all Israel would be punished. The country's military might would be broken. *And on that day, I will break the bow of Israel in the valley of Jezreel* (1:5).

Call her name Not pitied, for I will no more have pity on the house of Israel, to forgive them at all (1:6). The second child, a daughter, continued the prophetic symbolism. The little girl's name meant "unloved" or "disliked." Because of the nation's sins, God would withdraw His compassionate actions. Without love, there could be no forgiveness. The nation was in danger of being abandoned.

However, Judah would continue to be loved. *But I will have pity on the house of Judah, and I will deliver them by the Lord their God* (1:7).

Two or three years later (the time necessary to wean a child), Gomer gave birth to the couple's third child. The son was also given a symbolic name. *Call his name Not my people, for you are not my people and I am not your God* (1:9). To a people who considered themselves God's chosen people, Hosea announced that they were no longer God's people. The Lord had rejected them. He was no longer their God.

Apparently Gomer and Hosea were separated. Gomer returned to her promiscuous life as a prostitute. To show God's love for unfaithful Israel, God commanded Hosea to return to and love the unfaithful Gomer, who was now living with another man. *Go again, love a woman who is beloved of a paramour and is an adulteress; even as the Lord loves the people of Israel, though they turn to other gods and love cakes of raisins* (3:1). Symbolically, Hosea was demonstrating God's love. As Gomer had turned from Hosea, so the nation had left God for Baal. (Raisin cakes were made of pressed grapes and were offered at the cultic feasts of Baal as a sign of fertility.) Now God would try to reunite with His people.

Hosea legally bought Gomer. Did he itemize the cost because he had trouble finding the necessary funds and because times were hard? Seven ounces of silver and eight bushels of barley were not much. Perhaps the price was cheap because of the merchandise. A slave sold for thirty shekels.

You must dwell as mine for many days; you shall not play the harlot, or belong to another man; so will I also be to you (3:3). Back with Hosea, Gomer heard the stipulations of their relationship. She was to have no other man. Since Hosea could not command Gomer to love him, he would wait for her love in hope of reconciliation. Israel must turn from her sin and be faithful.

Like Gomer, Israel would undergo a period of spiritual discipline to nurture faithfulness to God. *For the children of Israel shall dwell many days without king or prince, without sacrifice or pillar, without ephod or teraphim* (3:4). Israel would be without a king and all of the religious techniques for discerning God's will. Hosea's new relationship with Gomer symbolized the possibility of Israel's relationship with God.

There was hope. Judgment would bring a new relationship with God. The nation would turn and seek God. *Afterward the children of Israel shall return and seek the Lord . . . and they shall come in fear to the Lord and to his goodness in the latter days* (3:5).

SUGGESTIONS TO TEACHERS

God, not Hosea, is the primary subject of your lesson today. Guard against concentrating solely on Hosea's relationship with his faithless wife, Gomer. Keep in mind that Hosea told about his personal heartbreak not to call attention to his own pain and problems but to illustrate the adulterous behavior of Israel. God loved His faithless nation.

1. PARABLE FOR ADULTEROUS ISRAEL. Set the facts of Hosea's marriage before the class and then tie in Israel's ways. Make sure your students understand the gravity of Israel's sin. Note how God's community belongs to Him in the way a human couple belong to one another in marriage. Israel had entered into a covenant with God, a pact similar to the sacred word-giving of a wife and husband at their wedding. But Israel, like a wife cheating on her husband, had carried on affairs with other lovers, or gods. Gomer's deserting Hosea to live like a prostitute is the way God's people insisted on running off with degenerate deities.

Bring all this down to 1995. Invite your group members to consider ways in which God's people seem to have abandoned their sacred commitments to the Lord and perhaps prostituted themselves. When we sell ourselves to please any other cause or interest more than pleasing the Lord, we become a community of Gomers.

2. PROPHET FOR A RIGHTEOUS GOD. Take a few minutes to look at the names Hosea gave his children. Discuss the significance of each: "God Sows," "Not Pitied," and "Not My People." Hosea was being obedient in trying to call Israel back to its original allegiance to God. In what practical ways can Christians today call each other and the church back to loyalty to Christ?

3. PUNISHMENT FOR A FAITHLESS PEOPLE. The wanton behavior

of running off with other gods eventually brings shame and disillusionment. Do not portray God as a mean-spirited tyrant, anxious to whip wayward subjects. Behind God's disciplining actions is always love.

4. PLAN OF THE LOVING LORD. God's wants a relationship of trust and caring between His people and Himself. That kind of relationship implies that His people live in community with each other in these ways and work to bring about that kind of society. Discuss the intentions of God toward us, as indicated in Hosea.

5. PURCHASE OF A LOST WIFE. The prophet took extraordinary steps to try to woo back Gomer. And he stated that God takes extraordinary measures to try to win back His people to the covenant relationship. Point out that we see God's ultimate act of undeserved love in action at the Cross. Through Christ's death, we Christians begin to appreciate how deeply God yearns to reclaim us as His own beloved.

TOPIC FOR ADULTS
DEMONSTRATING UNDESERVED LOVE

Unconditional Helper. The area around the Booker T. Washington High School in Memphis is not a place that strangers and white people usually go. Police advise people not to travel in the neighborhood without an escort. A couple of years ago, while workers were inside the school installing alarms, someone broke into their parked vans.

But another van, driven by Ken Bennett, a blond, bearded young white man, is never touched. Ken Bennett has won a place in the hearts of the students at Booker T. Washington High School. Asked whom they look up to most, many young black teenagers answer, "Ken Bennett." Ken Bennett, more than a father, teacher, coach, or preacher seems to be the role model most admired.

It never comes up that Kenneth Bennett is white and that every one of the forty-five hundred children under eighteen in the two projects where he works is black. It does not come up because of what Mr. Bennett has been doing for the last seven years. With a shoestring budget, a single assistant, and dozens of volunteers, he has created a job for himself as a role model, problem solver, and merchant of hope. He often stops to chat with schoolchildren, reminding them to come in for tutoring or asking about a sick parent. He shuttles young people to school football and basketball games, sometimes staying to cheer for the players. He goes to the school cafeterias most days to mix with the students at lunchtime.

In 1988, Ken Bennett established a service that he calls "Streets." He works mostly in two of the city's twenty-two housing projects, Foote Homes and Cleaborn Homes, with about fourteen hundred apartments. But he also draws young people from two other nearby projects, LeMoyne Gardens and Fowler Homes, and from nearby strips of bungalows.

Five churches in Memphis provide most of his $85,000 budget, which includes his annual salary of $24,000. About two hundred young people, mostly teenagers, take part in Streets programs, which include services twice a week of secular and religious songs and skits.

Each week scores of other people stop Bennett's van or come into the Streets headquarters, an old one-story brick factory building. He rustles up food, diapers, money for utilities, and transportation to work. And he passes out his business card with his office and home telephone numbers.

Thirty-five Vance Junior High School students, whom teachers deem promising but in need of help, go to Streets for tutoring one afternoon a week. The goal is to steer them toward college. The program is three years old, so it is too soon to say how well it succeeds.

From the churches that subsidize Streets, Bennett has recruited thirty-five volunteers, one for each student, to do the tutoring. These adults include a stockbroker, a computer specialist, two surgeons, an architect, two teachers, a construction engineer, a real estate agent, a basketball coach, and a marketing executive. Kenneth Bennett is thirty-seven years old, married to a teacher, and the father of an eighteen-month-old daughter. His father was a machinist, his mother a part-time cafeteria worker. He went to Memphis public schools and Memphis State University, and he has been a physical education teacher in Memphis schools and an alcohol and drug counselor at a Memphis hospital.

His faith motivates Ken Bennett, an evangelical Christian. "Faith without works is death," he says, paraphrasing James 2:17. "My faith calls me to do this, not in a romantic or martyrdom way. We have two cars and a house. We don't go without. We are about spreading the Gospel of Jesus Christ, but we're not conditional." Kids can take the Gospel or leave it, he says. "We'll continue to track with them."—Adapted from an article by Peter T. Kilborn, *New York Times,* January 31, 1993.

Clean Slate. Most states seal the records of juvenile offenders to protect them later in life. This is not the case with adults. Now, however, New Jersey convicts can utilize an eighteen-page manual entitled "Clearing the Record." This document details how a criminal record can be wiped clean under an "expungement" or deletion law.

The idea behind the novel law is that a criminal record can prevent an individual from gaining entry into a college, from obtaining financial credit, or even from getting a job. In addition, psychologists note that a criminal record can be psychologically haunting. People have an emotional desire to have an unblemished record. While critics of the new law charge this amounts to a cover-up, the hope is that individuals start fresh and again become law-abiding citizens.

Hosea reminded Israel that God does forgive His people and offers them fresh starts. God has expunged His people's sins through Jesus Christ so that we all can be represented by an unblemished record.

Questions for Students on the Next Lesson. 1. How did Hosea use the image of a parent raising a child to remind Israel of God's love? 2. What did Israel do to reject the Lord? 3. What did Hosea say that God would do to Israel as a result of its disobedience? 4. Can you recount occasions when you have received unconditional love? 5. How can we learn to show unconditional love to others?

TOPIC FOR YOUTH
UNDESERVED LOVE

Wanted and Loved? Eight-year-old Sergei Mayorov lived at the airport in St. Petersburg, Russia. He had been homeless since he was six. He was one of the twenty-five thousand homeless children in St. Petersburg who lived in basements, train stations, abandoned buildings, and sewers. He ran away from home because his alcoholic parents beat him, a common story among the homeless children. He existed by stealing and begging and relying on handouts from airport workers.

Sergei was one of Russia's "other children." These children were the unwanted children. When the nation went through the political changes in the early 1990s, the Russian economy sputtered and stalled. The children's shelters and orphanages were the first to feel the effects, and children were forced into the rough streets and quickly learned to survive in any way they could. All fully understood that they were unwanted and unloved.

The story of Hosea and Gomer is a love story. It demonstrates God's love for us as His children. It reminds us that we are both wanted and loved.

Uncommitted. Many young people voice a fear of marriage. Too many see marriages that end in divorce. Susan Littwin wrote in *The Generation Postponed* that committed, lasting relationships are a critical aspect of maturity.

Today's young people have more trouble with relationships than in any other area of their lives. Littwin feels there are several reasons for this. First, youth have difficulty with commitment in general. This, in her opinion, is a result of their reluctance to define themselves. Second, there are so many confusing choices. Third, we are now a society of individuals, not a society of families. The sum of all this is that adolescents keep commitment in limbo. The *New York Times* has dubbed today's youth as "the uncommitted generation," a generation where love is experienced alone, not together.

Through Gomer and Hosea, God defined commitment. Hosea did not speak of commitment, he lived it. And, as he lived it, he modeled God's love and commitment for us.

Cafeteria Demonstration. A school teacher in Seattle tells a story about an opportunity a junior high boy had to be a peacemaker. The story is about Peter, a popular student in the school where he teaches, and Eric, a retarded boy who had recently come to the junior high from a special school. On the first day of school, at lunch hour, Eric entered the lunchroom, sat on the floor, opened his bag lunch, and began to eat. After several days of doing this the other students began to laugh and make fun of Eric.

One day Peter asked Eric to join him and his friends at their lunch table. After hesitating, he did join them and continued to do so every day. Two weeks later, Peter was sick and was not in school. Eric again sat on the floor, took out his bag lunch and ate. This time some of the boys who sit at Peter's table asked Eric to join them. Eric did sit with them that day and each day after that. The other students stopped laughing and making fun of Eric. Through Peter's action, the good news of God's peace spread.

Questions for Students on the Next Lesson. 1. What image did Hosea utilize to picture God's love for Israel? 2. Does God demonstrate any feelings when He judges or punishes? 3. Does God ever give up on His people? 4. Have you ever rebelled against God? 5. Have you ever experienced true forgiveness?

LESSON 8—JULY 23

GOD'S LOVE FOR ISRAEL

Background Scripture: Hosea 11
Devotional Reading: Psalm 103:6-14

KING JAMES VERSION

HOSEA 11:1 When Israel was a child, then I loved him, and called my son out of Egypt.

2 As they called them, so they went from them: they sacrificed unto Baalim, and burned incense to graven images.

3 I taught Ephraim also to go, taking them by their arms; but they knew not that I healed them.

4 I drew them with cords of a man, with bands of love: and I was to them as they that take off the yoke on their jaws, and I laid meat unto them.

5 He shall not return into the land of Egypt, and the Assyrian shall be his king, because they refused to return.

6 And the sword shall abide on his cities, and shall consume his branches, and devour them, because of their own counsels.

7 And my people are bent to backsliding from me: though they called them to the most High, none at all would exalt him.

8 How shall I give thee up, Ephraim? how shall I deliver thee, Israel? how shall I make thee as Admah? how shall I set thee as Zeboim? mine heart is turned within me, my repentings are kindled together.

9 I will not execute the fierceness of mine anger, I will not return to destroy Ephraim: for I am God, and not man; the Holy One in the midst of thee: and I will not enter into the city.

REVISED STANDARD VERSION

HOSEA 11:1 When Israel was a child, I loved him, and out of Egypt I called my son.

2 The more I called them, the more they went from me; they kept sacrificing to the Baals, and burning incense to idols.

3 Yet it was I who taught Ephraim to walk, I took them up in my arms; but they did not know that I healed them. 4 I led them with cords of compassion, with the bands of love, and I became to them as one who eases the yoke on their jaws, and I bent down to them and fed them.

5 They shall return to the land of Egypt, and Assyria shall be their king, because they have refused to return to me. 6 The sword shall rage against their cities, consume the bars of their gates, and devour them in their fortresses. 7 My people are bent on turning away from me; so they are appointed to the yoke, and none shall remove it.

8 How can I give you up, O Ephraim! How can I hand you over, O Israel! How can I make you like Admah! How can I treat you like Zeboiim! My heart recoils within me, my compassion grows warm and tender. 9 I will not execute my fierce anger, I will not again destroy Ephraim; for I am God and not man, the Holy One in your midst, and I will not come to destroy.

KEY VERSE: *I will heal their faithlessness; I will love them freely, for my anger has turned from them.* Hosea 14:4.

HOME DAILY BIBLE READINGS

July	17	M.	Psalm 103:6-14	Mercy for Those Who Fear God
July	18	T.	Hosea 10:9-15	Punishment for Israel's Unfaithfulness
July	19	W.	Hosea 11:1-6	God's Love Was Rejected
July	20	T.	Hosea 11:7-12	God's Anger Is Restrained by Compassion
July	21	F.	Hosea 14	Israel Urged to Return to God
July	22	S.	Psalm 79:8-13	A Prayer for God's Forgiveness
July	23	S.	Psalm 130	God Forgives and Restores

BACKGROUND

Conditions in Israel had grown worse. The dreaded, all-powerful Assyrians had invaded. Some Israelites had already been carried off as captives, probably in the deportation of 733 B.C. (see II Kings 15:29-31). Although the cities of Israel had not yet been destroyed (but would be captured and burned shortly), the situation looked grim. The king of Israel had made an ill-advised alliance with the superpower to the south, Egypt, in the hopes of staving off the Assyrians (II Kings 17:4). Some Israelites had already fled to Egypt as refugees, but Hosea knew that it was only a matter of time before the Assyrian armies would take Samaria and the other cities of Israel. The prophet could see the time coming when the people of Israel would experience another period of captivity. Instead of being in Egypt under the pharaoh, the people would suffer a new captivity in Assyria.

As Hosea intimated, the unwise policies of Israel's kings, consisting of bad politics and poor diplomacy, were useless in preventing ruin. Under the mighty Assyrian emperor, Shalmaneser V, the Assyrian war machine swept through the land of Israel, and Samaria fell in 721 B.C. The people of the ten northern tribes were taken captive, known ever after as the "lost tribes of Israel."

The nation could come to an end, but not God's love. Hosea insisted that, in spite of the terrible conditions, the Lord continued to care. Israel's actions, like those of a willfully disobedient child, were bringing disastrous consequences. But the people remained loved by a God who grieved for them in their rebellious ways.

NOTES ON THE PRINTED TEXT

How can God's love be described? Hosea used the image of a parent rearing a child to remind Israel of God's love. Perhaps the idea was drawn from Hosea's own experience with his children.

When Israel was a child, I loved him, and out of Egypt I called my son (11:1). The word Hosea chose for love was unusual, a word that describes human love. The other prophets tended not to employ it. Isaiah used it once, while Amos and Micah used it twice. Hosea, on the other hand, used it nineteen times. God was described as an affectionate, tender, sentimental father who loved His young son, Israel. The child spent his youth in Egypt before God summoned him into a relationship.

God's love was persistent despite the child's unfaithfulness. *The more I called them, the more they went from me* (11:2). God continually called to the child, but the child was rebellious. Sinful and disobedient, he *kept sacrificing to the Baals, and burning incense to idols* (11:2). The more God loved Israel, the more Israel rejected God.

God declared His loving care toward Israel. A picture from ordinary family life describes the Lord teaching the toddler to walk, repeatedly steadying the child and helping him back onto his feet. *It was I who taught Ephraim to walk, I took them up in my arms; but they did not know that I healed them* (11:3). In spite of all fatherly care, Israel did not respond to God's love.

God continued to describe His care. While Israel had not been free to do as it pleased, neither had God been a tough disciplinarian. He was kind and compassionate. *I led them with cords of compassion, with the bands of love* (11:4). Here is a picture of a caring plowman who lovingly cared for his oxen. As he loosened the yoke so the oxen could eat, so the Lord tenderly fed His child.

They shall return to the land of Egypt, and Assyria shall be their king, because they have refused to return to me (11:5). Because of Israel's disobedience, God proclaimed a return to slavery. This time Assyria would be the slaveholder and taskmaster. Instead of being the nation's savior, Assyria would be the instrument of God's punishment. Israel's cities would be destroyed. The gates and walls of the fortified cities (symbols of strength and protection) would be reduced to rubble, something at which the Assyrian battering rams were quite effective.

My people are bent on turning away from me; so they are appointed to the yoke, and none shall remove it (11:7). Nothing would save Israel from its appointed end, a yoke of bondage. Perhaps this imagery referred to the herding of prisoners for deportation.

The fatherhood of God emerged again. He was grieved at the thought of rejecting Israel. *How can I give you up, O Ephraim! How can I hand you over, O Israel!* (11:8). The Father agonized over abandoning the child. How could He destroy His child as Admah and Zeboiim, two cities of the plain, had been annihilated with Sodom and Gomorrah?

The Parent drew back at such drastic punishment. *My heart recoils within me, my compassion grows warm and tender* (11:8). He still loved the child too much to punish him severely. In fact, God's love for Israel stayed His anger toward them. *I will not execute my fierce anger, I will not again destroy Ephraim* (11:9). Parental love prevailed. God would discipline but not destroy.

SUGGESTIONS TO TEACHERS

Hosea's imagery comes from his own experience. Last week we saw how he compared his love for his unfaithful wife, Gomer, to God's love for Israel. This week, we find the prophet presenting the unforgettable picture of a loving parent toward a disobedient child. Everyone can appreciate Hosea's memorable description of God's nurturing of His children.

1. REMEMBERING HIS CHILD. Draw attention to the touching way Hosea portrayed God remembering Israel, His chosen community, as a small child learning to walk. Hosea used the beautiful imagery of an attentive father or mother showing loving care for the little one. What a significant way to describe the personality and ways of the Lord!

2. REVIEWING ISRAEL'S WAYS. According to Hosea, Israel's disobedience would result in a new period of captivity and slavery, similar to the previous bondage in Egypt. Some in your class may wonder how God would let this happen to the people He claimed to love. Certainly, some in Israel were wondering about this too!

Consider bringing Hosea's imagery into a modern context. For example, a parent repeatedly warns her youngster not to run out into the busy street. The youngster defiantly refuses to listen. The parent pleads and warns, but to no avail. One day, the child recklessly decides to race out into the street. The disobedience brings terrible hurt, and the parent feels deeply disappointed that the child has rejected all instructions and brought on itself such damage. This is the way God reacts to Israel's rebelliousness—and to ours.

3. RESTRAINING HIS ANGER. No matter how bad a child may behave, a good parent cannot forget the potential he or she once saw in the child. Most fathers and mothers continue to have an unconditional love for their children, even when the children fail to return that love or to behave responsibly. Hosea 11:8, 9 tells us that our human love for our children can give us a glimpse of God's great love for us.

4. RESPONDING TO REPENTANCE. In spite of the heartbreak the Lord experienced over Israel's rebellious ways, He assured His people He would gladly receive them back into relationship if they would only turn around. Hosea's message was taught and enacted seven hundred years later through Jesus Christ. God's unconditional love to His children was demonstrated at the cross and in the resurrection of our Lord. But repentance must take place if that good news is to have any effect. Devote lesson time to the meaning of repentance. Talk together about what it means to experience unconditional love.

TOPIC FOR ADULTS
EXPERIENCING UNDESERVED LOVE

Experiencing Cookie Caring. The child's name was Annie, and she was confined to an institution because of her sometimes wild and sometimes withdrawn behavior. Her violent outbursts and long, sullen spells prevented the workers in the institution from communicating with the girl. The hospital personnel dismissed Annie as a hopeless case.

One elderly nurse, however, refused to give up hope for Annie. Each day, this nurse came and sat with Annie, even though Annie gave no response. The nurse could not even be sure that little Annie was aware of her presence. The older nurse also brought some cookies and left them beside Annie's bed.

For a long time, Annie seemed oblivious to the patient care and attention of the elderly nurse. But finally she smiled when the nurse appeared with the cookies one day. The doctors and other staff members of the institution were surprised to notice some change in little Annie's behavior. She became calmer and less given to sudden screaming tantrums or trancelike silences. The nurse persisted in the caring and cookies, and gradually little Annie was so improved that she was able to be discharged. The experience of undeserved love brought Annie healing.

But there is more to Annie's story. Having known what it was to be loved, Annie was determined to share that love with others. And how she did! Annie, whom we remember as Anne Sullivan, reached out to a wild, rebellious little girl who was blind, deaf, and unable to speak. Through Anne Sullivan, that child, Helen Keller, experienced undeserved love too. And Helen Keller became one of the great figures of our century. Thanks to the love shared by an elderly nurse, a chain reaction was set in place, helping others to experience undeserved love.

Charges Dropped. In 1972 newspapers carried the story from Salonika, Greece, that many pending trials could not be held as planned because mice had devoured files in the civil court archives. Imagine how those up for trial would rejoice if they knew that all records of their crimes had been permanently destroyed so that they could never be accused!

What rejoicing might one feel if he knew that all his sins—not only of the past year but for his whole life—had been blotted out so that he could never be accused in the tribunal of God! That is exactly the rejoicing that all may know who will come in humility to the Lord Jesus Christ. On the cross of Calvary He paid the penalty that our sins deserved. Now He bids us come to Him to receive undeserved love.

Hardest to Convince. Drawing on his extensive experience as a pastor, the distinguished church leader, Dr. Kenneth Chafin, has commented and written on the thing he has found most difficult for people to accept. Dr. Chafin, who works closely with Dr. Billy Graham, states that in his early days in the ministry, he tried to convict people of their sinfulness. He found many in his audiences rejected this idea, and he thought that the toughest task he had was to convince his hearers of their state of sin.

As he matured in the Christian faith, Dr. Chafin came to realize more deeply the meaning of the Gospel as the unconditional love of God through Jesus Christ. He now says that the hardest thing to get people to appreciate is that God truly loves them "as they are." God's undeserved love is such that He accepts them even though He does not approve of their sin. The most difficult part of preaching, Dr. Chafin claims, is to enable hearers to realize that God has poured out his unconditional, undeserved mercy on them personally.

Questions for Students on the Next Lesson. 1. Who was Micah; when did he live; and where did he prophesy? 2. Why did Micah criticize certain other prophets? 3. What did Micah say about the leaders and public officials? 4. What did Micah say about the future of Jerusalem? 5. When do you feel the pressure to compromise your integrity?

TOPIC FOR YOUTH
GOD'S ENDURING LOVE

Chic Rebellion. Very alarming things were happening in Biddeford, Maine. High school students were consulting Ouija boards and a spirit named "Charles" before planning their daily activities. There were suspicious fires in two churches and the high school. At the sites of these fires, satanic symbols were found. Alarmed parents demanded answers about teenagers and satanism.

Joe Vieira of Shatter the Dark Ministries reminded people that teenage satanism was a form of anti-parent and anti-society rebellion. Another expert noted that satanism was the chic way to rebel. It showed a desire for power, a godlike power.

Israel also rebelled against God's authority. The nation demonstrated the same power-grasping tendencies. Through the prophet, God reminded the nation of His love for them. Even when they rejected Him, He loved them. However, there were limits. Continued rejection and rebellion would ultimately end in judgment.

Looking for Love. A survey of 677 seventh, eighth, and ninth graders at a mostly white, lower middle class Indianapolis junior high school revealed that 55 percent had experienced sex. Sexually inexperienced girls by age fifteen were in the minority, while boys who were virgins at the age of thirteen were in the minority. The common denominator was a desire to find love.

But love is more than sex. Love is a commitment to a long-term, satisfying relationship of mutual caring. Christian love is a faithful and permanent relationship between two persons in which sex is only one facet. The real model of love can be seen in God's relationship with His people. True love demands faithfulness, caring, and commitment—not simply the physical aspect of love.

Forgot the Scars. John B. Gordon was an able Confederate general. He directed the last official action against the Union on a Sunday morning in April, 1865, at Appomattox when Lee surrendered to Grant.

Later Gordon became a candidate for the United States Senate. However, a man who had served under him became enraged over a political incident. As a member of the legislature, he vowed to do all that he could to defeat Gordon.

At the convention, this man stormed down the aisle to present his vote against Gordon in order to stop his bid for election. As he neared the platform upon which Gordon sat, he looked at his former commander. The once handsome face was now disfigured by battle scars. He recalled the actions in which Gordon had led the troops.

Overcome with emotion, tears fell from his cheeks. He declared to the assembly that he could not vote against Gordon. Then turning to Gordon, he asked the general's forgiveness. "Forgive me, General. I had forgotten the scars."

Although Israel had marched under God's banner, it never fathomed the depth of God's love. However, we who have seen the victory of Jesus and have acted against Him need to recall the extent of the love He displayed on the cross. Perhaps then we, too, would declare, "Forgive me. I had forgotten the scars."

Questions for Students on the Next Lesson. 1. Who was Micah? 2. What charge did he bring against the nation's leaders? 3. What is the definition of justice? 4. What responsibilities do our nation's leaders carry? 5. Can you list some examples of national greed?

LESSON 9—JULY 30

GREEDY LEADERS DENOUNCED

Background Scripture: Micah 1—3
Devotional Reading: Micah 2:1-7

KING JAMES VERSION

MICAH 3:5 Thus saith the Lord concerning the prophets that make my people err, that bite with their teeth, and cry, Peace; and he that putteth not into their mouths, they even prepare war against him.

6 Therefore night shall be unto you, that ye shall not have a vision; and it shall be dark unto you, that ye shall not divine; and the sun shall go down over the prophets, and the day shall be dark over them.

7 Then shall the seers be ashamed, and the diviners confounded: yea, they shall all cover their lips; for there is no answer of God.

8 But truly I am full of power by the spirit of the Lord, and of judgment, and of might, to declare unto Jacob his transgression, and to Israel his sin.

9 Hear this, I pray you, ye heads of the house of Jacob, and princes of the house of Israel, that abhor judgment, and pervert all equity.

10 They build up Zion with blood, and Jerusalem with iniquity.

11 The heads thereof judge for reward, and the priests thereof teach for hire, and the prophets thereof divine for money: yet will they lean upon the Lord, and say, Is not the Lord among us? none evil can come upon us.

12 Therefore shall Zion for your sake be plowed as a field, and Jerusalem shall become heaps, and the mountain of the house as the high places of the forest.

REVISED STANDARD VERSION

MICAH 3:5 Thus says the Lord concerning the prophets who lead my people astray, who cry "Peace" when they have something to eat, but declare war against him who puts nothing into their mouths. 6 Therefore it shall be night to you, without vision, and darkness to you, without divination. The sun shall go down upon the prophets, and the day shall be black over them; 7 the seers shall be disgraced, and the diviners put to shame; they shall all cover their lips, for there is no answer from God. 8 But as for me, I am filled with power, with the Spirit of the Lord, and with justice and might, to declare to Jacob his transgression and to Israel his sin.

9 Hear this, you heads of the house of Jacob and rulers of the house of Israel, who abhor justice and pervert all equity, 10 who build Zion with blood and Jerusalem with wrong. 11 Its heads give judgment for a bribe, its priests teach for hire, its prophets divine for money; yet they lean upon the Lord and say, "Is not the Lord in the midst of us? No evil shall come upon us." 12 Therefore because of you Zion shall be plowed as a field; Jerusalem shall become a heap of ruins, and the mountain of the house a wooded height.

KEY VERSE: Then they will cry to the Lord, but he will not answer them; he will hide his face from them at that time, because they have made their deeds evil. Micah 3:4.

HOME DAILY BIBLE READINGS

July	24	M.	Micah 1:1-7	*Judgment for Israel's Sins*
July	25	T.	Micah 1:8-16	*Lamentation for the Judgment on Israel*
July	26	W.	Micah 2:1-5	*Woe to Those Who Oppress Others*

BACKGROUND

Near the close of the eighth century B.C., the Assyrian armies returned repeatedly to the Middle East. Both the northern kingdom of Israel and the smaller, southern kingdom of Judah were compelled to pay tribute to Assyria. Both also tried to play the deadly game of international politics to protect themselves. The Assyrians took Samaria and cruelly deported much of its population. Amos and Hosea had prophesied in the northern kingdom during the tumultuous years before Israel's fall.

At the same time, another prophet was preaching in Judah in the south. His name, Micah, means "Who is like the Lord?" He came from the village of Moresheth, an insignificant town about twenty-five miles southwest of Jerusalem that had been established by King Rehoboam as a defense post. Most likely, Micah's family was part of the group that felt threatened by the social evils in Judah. He referred to those who were evicted from their homes as "my people" (2:9).

Micah lived in a period of international crises and domestic problems. During the eighth century, a kind of industrial revolution took place in which enormous social changes occurred. A wealthy class appeared. Poor villagers left their small farms to try to find jobs in the cities. Social and economic injustices became commonplace. Rich landowners devised schemes to increase their holdings by forcing small farmers to sell out. Poor families and widows were often left homeless. The political leaders engaged in costly building projects in Jerusalem that exploited the workers. The courts failed to bring compensation to those who were oppressed, and bribery and payoffs became widespread. Even the religious leaders were infected with the prevailing corruption. Paganism flourished openly, and many priests and prophets greedily sold their services to the nation's wealthy class. The few authentic voices for the Lord found themselves denounced. Micah, God's spokesman in his day, fearlessly criticized his country and grieved because of its inevitable coming doom.

NOTES ON THE PRINTED TEXT

Micah condemned Judah for many of the things that had previously drawn the ire of other prophets. One of these was the insincerity of the priests and the prophets' cozy relationship with the rulers. Perhaps the guild of prophets in Jerusalem had summoned Micah to appear before them. They questioned his legitimacy as God's spokesman. His words seemed to contradict their own. Conflict erupted.

Micah stood his ground and indicted the prophets for misleading the people. *Thus says the Lord concerning the prophets who lead my people astray, who cry "Peace" when they have something to eat, but declare war against him who puts nothing into their mouths* (3:5). They were corrupt. Their motivation was based on self-interest. The prophets promised peace *(shalom* meant a state of wholeness, security, and well-being, not just an absence of enemies) to those who paid them well. To those who did not support them they promised misfortune.

Micah announced their punishment. *Therefore it shall be night to you, without vision, and darkness to you, without divination. The sun shall go down upon the prophets, and the day shall be black over them* (3:6). The prophets would receive no visions. The gift they possessed would be taken away, and those who claimed the gift of vision would be humiliated. *The seers shall be disgraced, and the diviners put to shame* (3:7). The professional prophets would be ashamed in the absence of any answers from God. *They shall all cover their lips, for there is no answer from God* (3:7).

Then, to the assembled guild of prophets, Micah declared the basis of his own mission. *As for me, I am filled with power, with the Spirit of the Lord, and with justice and might* (3:8). The indwelling Spirit of God strengthened the true prophet with perseverance, courage, and a sense of what was right. These were his credentials.

His own mission was *to declare to Jacob his transgression and to Israel his sin* (3:8). He was to preach to the southern kingdom about its sin and coming judgment. Micah also addressed the nation's leaders who were responsible for protecting the rights of the poor and weak. However, the leaders had failed and had proven to be corrupt. The public officials had disregarded justice. *Hear this, you heads of the house of Jacob and rulers of the house of Israel, who abhor justice and pervert all equity* (3:9). Their crimes were unknown. Perhaps Micah referred to the greed of the leaders, who were not above committing murder in order to gain property to build their lavish homes. Whatever the case, Jerusalem was being built by bloodshed and violence. Micah gave several examples of corrupt city officials.

Its heads give judgment for a bribe (3:11). The judges disregarded the law, selling justice for a bribe. *Priests teach for hire* (3:11). Likely this was a condemnation of the priests charging for a legal verdict. Problems were brought to the priests in order to hear how God would instruct the parties on the issues. Now the priests were guilty of greed and perverting justice. Finally, *prophets divine for money* (3:11). Prophets were using their services for gain. Greed overrode a concern for God and others.

In addition, Micah condemned the leaders' belief that nothing bad would ever happen to the nation because they were God's chosen people. *Is not the Lord in the midst of us? No evil shall come upon us* (3:11).

Micah declared that God made no guarantee for the nation's safety. Jerusalem would become a pile of ruins, and the temple would become forest land because of the corruption of its leaders. *Therefore because of you Zion shall be plowed as a field; Jerusalem shall become a heap of ruins, and the mountain of the house a wooded height* (3:12).

SUGGESTIONS TO TEACHERS

Occasionally we hear someone criticize Christians for addressing evils and injustices in society. "Stick to the Gospel," these complainers say. Translation: "God isn't really concerned about people who are hurting, so don't mention issues like greed."

Much as some want to mute the biblical message and twist their faith into what could be called a "hot tub religion," the words of Micah and his successors in our generation must be heard. You may find it helpful to open this lesson by discussing frankly how a concern for social justice must always accompany personal piety. As George MacLeod of Scotland used to say, Christians must "pray and picket." Not one or the other, but both.

Looking at the material in Micah 1-3, note the following:

1. THE WOUND THAT IS INCURABLE. A nation experiences a self-inflicted wound on itself when it permits injustice to continue. If left unattended, this wound can prove fatal, as in the case of Judah and Israel, according to Micah. Think with your students about the wounds that threaten the body politic of our nation. If the 1980s were known as the "Decade of Greed," what were some of its effects?

2. THE RICH WHO ARE INSOLENT. Look at Micah 2:1-5, where the prophet denounced the powerful who grab the fields of small landowning farmers by forcing them to sell out at a loss. Who are some of the comparable insolent wealthy in our society? What about those who use leveraged buyouts or manipulate stock, sometimes forcing mergers or bankruptcies of companies and throwing helpless employees out of work? America has witnessed the effects of the greed of Ivan Boesky and Michael Milliken and Charles Keating during the past decade. Remind students that such greed can also corrupt "ordinary" people like us.

3. THE PROPHET WHO IS UNWELCOME. No society elects a person like Micah as "Man of the Year" or holds testimonial banquets for him. Comment about the pressures on persons of faith to speak pleasant, choice words that the public likes to hear. Ask if your class members and congregation's members support your minister when controversial issues of the day are addressed. Remind the class that each Christian is pressured to "go along" and "fit in" and "be popular." In one sense, being a prophet—one called by the Lord to speak up for God—is the calling of every believer.

4. THE LEADERS WHO ARE INHUMANE. Micah warned of those who "hate the good and love the evil" (3:2), thereby hurting the poor and powerless and corrupting the nation. Shady business practices, bribery, price-fixing to smother competition, and all other examples of greed in industry or government oppress others and are contrary to God's intentions. Discuss the comment of one Christian industrialist who opposed a questionable policy in his company: "It may be legal, but is it moral?"

5. THE CITY THAT IS INDEFENSIBLE. Micah warned that Jerusalem would become a heap of ruins if it continued on its path of greed. When leaders—even religious leaders—countenance a situation where people are hungry and homeless, a nation is in trouble, according to Micah.

TOPIC FOR ADULTS
BEWARE OF GREED

Everybody Does It? Claude Lochet, of Orleans, Massachusetts, showed such charm and inspired such trust as a stockbroker and financial planner that dozens of retired persons and elderly widows confidently invested their life savings with him. The thirty-four-year-old seemed to be the model of professionalism and propriety.

Suddenly, in December, 1991, Lochet disappeared. At first, foul play was suspected, but then it was learned that $1.7 million was missing from client accounts. Then Lochet's van, with stubs for plane tickets to Paris for himself and his girlfriend, was discovered in the parking area of Kennedy Airport in New York. Embezzlement and larceny charges were brought against Lochet, but he could not be found.

Meanwhile, people from whose accounts he had stolen the money were left with big losses. Most were older persons living on fixed incomes or modest pensions who had invested through Lochet. Finally, on the weekend of February 21, 1992, "Prime Suspect," a nationally syndicated television show that airs fugitive cases, described Lochet's case. Two callers from Los Angeles telephoned to report that a man fitting Lochet's description was living in their area. Lochet was arrested. None of the money was found. When Los Angeles Detective Carl Holmstrom asked Lochet why he stole $1.7 million from clients, the fugitive broker showed no remorse and said, "Everybody does it."

The "everybody does it" attitude threatens our society. Trust is broken. People are hurt, emotionally and financially. When greed takes over a career or a culture, the entire community is weakened.

A Better Investment. The leaders of St. Malchy's Parish on the west side of Chicago wondered what influence the Illinois State Lottery had upon its parishioners. It was decided that on Sunday, the members of the parish were to bring their losing lottery tickets for that week and place them in the offering plates. To their amazement they gathered more than $5,000 worth—quite a collection for a church whose weekly offering is about $300! Five thousand dollars, which brought nothing in return, compared to three hundred dollars that ministered to persons in the name of Jesus Christ.— First United Methodist Church, New Port Richey, Florida.

Micah's Influence. Micah's words continue to exert a powerful influence twenty-seven hundred years after they were first uttered. His vision still makes an impact on public life. In January 1977, when Jimmy Carter was inaugurated as president of the United States of America, he took his oath of office, with his hand on the Bible opened to Micah 6:8, and quoted the words "He hath shewed thee, O man, what is good; and what doth the Lord require of thee, but to do justly, and to love mercy, and to walk humbly with thy God?"

A few years earlier, in 1959, the Soviet Union presented a bronze statue to the United Nations. The piece of sculpture was of a man beating a sword into a plowshare. At the base of the nine-foot-high piece of art symbolizing Micah's vision (and also Isaiah's) of universal disarmament and lasting peace, the words paraphrasing Micah 4:3 are inscribed: "We shall beat our swords into plowshares." And this from a state that was denying the existence of God! But the message of God's prophet struck a chord even in the hearts of those communist leaders.

Questions for Students on the Next Lesson. 1. Who was Isaiah and what was his background? 2. What was happening in Judah at the time of Isaiah's call? 3. What were the significant aspects of Isaiah's experience in the temple when he received his call from the Lord? 4. What did Isaiah preach? 5. Do you ever struggle for a sense of direction and purpose for your life? Has your faith helped?

TOPIC FOR YOUTH
BEWARE OF GREED

Power of Greed. Seventy-two-year-old Mabel Sheehan lived alone in a working-class district of Philadelphia. It was rumored that the old woman had money stashed away in her modest row house. Some people said she had $35,000 while others believed she had more. Some claimed that she had as much as $45 million hoarded in her house!

The rumors continued to circulate and grow more extravagant. Finally a crowd of over three hundred gathered in front of her home. Poor Mabel fled to a nearby convent for safety after summoning police to protect her house from vandals. Over one hundred police, all in full riot gear, and others mounted on horses, rushed to the scene. The crowd refused to disperse. Even when told that Mabel had no money, one skeptical youth asked, "If there's no money in there, why are all these police here guarding the house?"

It took police one full day and nineteen arrests to convince the crowd to leave. Ironically, Mabel lived alone with her dog on her $247 monthly Social Security check. Her only savings was her prepaid burial plan. Such was the power of greed in Philadelphia.

A Right? Lightning struck two teens in Sequoia National Park, killing one and damaging the other's nervous system. It was a tragedy; however, the families filed a lawsuit against the National Park Service, demanding $1.6 million for the dead teen's family and $1 million for the disabled teen. Their contention was that the park management should have warned the victims against standing where lightning might strike.

If that sounds bizarre, realize that injured parties routinely sue others today. One reason is that consumer activists have made the public aware of possible claims. Another reason is the public's awareness that agencies, hospitals, physicians, companies, and institutions are vulnerable to lawsuits and that juries tend to be overly generous. Realizing this, the public has become greedy. The consensus seems to be, "I have a right to get everything I can!"

Does the public have a right to collect damages for accidents, or would Micah call this greed?

Prisoner of Greed. Eric Kimmel tells the tale of Hershel of Ostropol's efforts to light the menorah at the Jewish celebration of Hanukkah. To do so, Hershel must outwit a number of goblins. One of the methods he used was to put a jar of pickles on the table. One hungry goblin looked at the sour pickles longingly until Hershel gave him one. The hungry goblin ate it. Hershel then invited the goblin to take as many as he wanted. The greedy goblin stuck his claw into the jar and seized the whole jar full in his fist. However, he could not extract his hand from the jar. He cried that he was stuck! The goblin wailed and cried that he was under a spell!

Finally, Hershel decided to let the goblin go free. He told the goblin simply that he was a prisoner of greed and that all he needed to do was to let go of the pickles. The goblin did so and, of course, easily extracted his hand.

We are often like that goblin. We greedily grasp all that we can hold in our hands. Like that goblin, we become prisoners of our greed. Only when we open our hands and lovingly offer them to help others will we be truly free and responsible people before God.

The Facts of Greed. Fortune Magazine reported that 93 percent of teenage girls stated that shopping was their favorite pastime, even ahead of sixth-place dating. The magazine also reported that in 1967, 40 percent of American college freshmen indicated to pollsters that it was important to be well-off financially while 80 percent wanted to develop a meaningful philosophy. That has changed! Now 80 percent desire money while 40 percent want to serve or help others. What would Micah have to say in light of these findings?

Questions for Students on the Next Lesson. 1. Who was Isaiah? Why was he in the temple? 2. How did Isaiah react to God's call and his assignment? 3. Do you sense a need for forgiveness in your life? 4. Do you sense God has a purpose in mind for you? 5. Can you experience forgiveness only through religious ceremonies or is something else required?

LESSON 10—AUGUST 6

ISAIAH'S CALL AND MESSAGE

Background Scripture: Isaiah 6; 1 (in that order)
Devotional Reading: Isaiah 55:6-11

KING JAMES VERSION

ISAIAH 6:1 In the year that king Uzziah died I saw also the Lord sitting upon a throne, high and lifted up, and his train filled the temple.

2 Above it stood the seraphims: each one had six wings; with twain he covered his face, and with twain he covered his feet, and with twain he did fly.

3 And one cried unto another, and said, Holy, holy, holy, is the Lord of hosts: the whole earth is full of his glory.

4 And the posts of the door moved at the voice of him that cried, and the house was filled with smoke.

5 Then said I, Woe is me! for I am undone; because I am a man of unclean lips, and I dwell in the midst of a people of unclean lips: for mine eyes have seen the King, the Lord of hosts.

6 Then flew one of the seraphims unto me, having a live coal in his hand, which he had taken with the tongs from off the altar:

7 And he laid it upon my mouth, and said, Lo, this hath touched thy lips; and thine iniquity is taken away, and thy sin purged.

8 Also I heard the voice of the Lord, saying, Whom shall I send, and who will go for us? Then said I, Here am I; send me. . . .

1:14 Your new moons and your appointed feasts my soul hateth: they are a trouble unto me; I am weary to bear them.

15 And when ye spread forth your hands, I will hide mine eyes from you: yea, when ye make many prayers, I will not hear: your hands are full of blood.

16 Wash you, make you clean; put away the evil of your doings from before mine eyes; cease to do evil;

17 Learn to do well; seek judgment, relieve the oppressed, judge the fatherless, plead for the widow.

REVISED STANDARD VERSION

ISAIAH 6:1 In the year that King Uzziah died I saw the Lord sitting upon a throne, high and lifted up; and his train filled the temple. 2 Above him stood the seraphim; each had six wings: with two he covered his face, and with two he covered his feet, and with two he flew. 3 And one called to another and said: "Holy, holy, holy is the Lord of hosts; the whole earth is full of his glory." 4 And the foundations of the thresholds shook at the voice of him who called, and the house was filled with smoke. 5 And I said: "Woe is me! For I am lost; for I am a man of unclean lips, and I dwell in the midst of a people of unclean lips; for my eyes have seen the King, the Lord of hosts!"

6 Then flew one of the seraphim to me, having in his hand a burning coal which he had taken with tongs from the altar. 7 And he touched my mouth and said: "Behold, this has touched your lips; your guilt is taken away, and your sin forgiven." 8 And I heard the voice of the Lord saying, "Whom shall I send, and who will go for us?" Then I said, "Here am I! Send me." . . .

1:14 "Your new moons and your appointed feasts my soul hates; they have become a burden to me, I am weary of bearing them. 15 When you spread forth your hands, I will hide my eyes from you; even though you make many prayers, I will not listen; your hands are full of blood. 16 Wash yourselves; make yourselves clean; remove the evil of your doings from before my eyes; cease to do evil, 17 learn to do good; seek justice, correct oppression; defend the fatherless, plead for the widow."

KEY VERSE: I heard the voice of the Lord saying, "Whom shall I send, and who will go for us?" Then I said, "Here am I! Send me." Isaiah 6:8.

HOME DAILY BIBLE READINGS

July	31	M.	Isaiah 6:1-5	*Isaiah's Call and Plea of Unworthiness*
Aug.	1	T.	Isaiah 6:6-13	*A Forgiven Isaiah Accepts His Call*
Aug.	2	W.	Isaiah 1:1-6	*God's Message to Judah through Isaiah*
Aug.	3	T.	Isaiah 1:7-11	*Judah's Desolate Condition*
Aug.	4	F.	Isaiah 1:12-17	*Superficial Religion Is Offensive to God*
Aug.	5	S.	Isaiah 1:18-23	*God Expects Justice and Righteousness*
Aug.	6	S.	Isaiah 1:24-31	*Sinful Rebellion Must Be Punished*

BACKGROUND

The southern nation of Judah had been led by an effective leader, King Uzziah, during the turmoil in Israel when Amos and Hosea prophesied. Uzziah's reign for a half century brought a period of prosperity to Judah. He also successfully withstood the threats of a takeover by the powerful Assyrian kings. Judah lived uneasily through those tense times but was spared from invasion.

Uzziah's death brought new crises. He was followed by a series of weak kings in Judah. It was in this time of national anxiety and international unrest that God called a young man named Isaiah to serve as a prophet. The secure days of Uzziah's long reign were over. Judah as well as all of Palestine lay between the two superpowers of the day, Egypt and Assyria, each holding imperialistic designs on the entire Middle East.

Isaiah experienced an overwhelming awareness of God's presence one day in the temple in Jerusalem. The young man had a vision. He became acutely conscious of the awesome nearness and greatness of the Almighty. In his call, we are overhearing the confession of a sensitive man relating a very personal and life-changing experience. This dramatic manifestation of God, more than anything, meant that Isaiah realized the holiness of God.

God is THE Holy One, and no human may control Him. All must reverence this holy God. The words of our hymn, "Holy, Holy, Holy," are taken from this vision and describe in poetry form what Isaiah and every person encountered by the Lord must realize.

Whenever God confronts a person, He always assigns a task. Isaiah's experience in the temple was not merely an emotionally-charged sense of God's nearness and mercy, but was also a call to serve. Specifically, God called Isaiah to serve by speaking out for the Lord's ways. In Isaiah's day, as in every era, this was a terrible burden, and Isaiah knew it. However, for the next fifty years, from about 740 B.C. to 690 B.C., Isaiah responded to God's call and commission.

NOTES ON THE PRINTED TEXT

In the year that King Uzziah died (6:1). Isaiah received God's call in

740 B.C., the year leprosy-stricken Uzziah died. Jotham, Uzziah's son, was to be crowned king. Perhaps Isaiah waited with the priests and other worshipers at the eastern gates of the temple. The sun's light would pass directly through the opening and shine through the temple doors. Behind those cedar boards with their inlaid gold chains stood the ark of the covenant, God's throne. Cherubim, some fifteen feet tall and six feet across, stood on either side of the throne. Isaiah had an overpowering sense of God's presence. *And the foundations of the thresholds shook at the voice of him who called, and the house was filled with smoke* (6:4). Smoke escaped from the latticework windows as perhaps a great earthquake rocked Jerusalem. Even the great doors, their pivots set in the foundation stones, shook. Isaiah experienced a vision of God surrounded by the heavenly court who praised Him.

Woe is me! For I am lost; for I am a man of unclean lips, and I dwell in the midst of a people of unclean lips; for my eyes have seen the King, the Lord of hosts! (6:5). God's holy presence made Isaiah keenly aware of his own and his nation's guilt. Before God, all were unworthy sinners. Because he felt he could not even join in God's worship, he was reduced to silence. He expected only death, since he had looked upon God (see Exod. 33:20).

One of the seraphim, using a pair of tongs, removed a hot, glowing coal from the fire burning on the altar of incense. The altar was consecrated to God, and the coal could purify Isaiah. The seraphim touched Isaiah's mouth with the hot coal and declared, *Behold, this has touched your lips; your guilt is taken away, and your sin forgiven* (6:7). The contrite Isaiah received assurance of God's forgiveness.

Whom shall I send, and who will go for us? (6:8). The Lord desired a volunteer for a specific job. Isaiah volunteered. *Here am I! Send me* (6:8). Isaiah heard and accepted God's call. He was to take a message to the people of Judah that they were to return to God's covenant or face judgment.

Isaiah immediately accepted his new role, speaking to the political and religious leaders of God's judgment. He spoke as if in a courtroom, summoning all creation to be witnesses. The already angered hearers heard God's address through Isaiah. *Your new moons and your appointed feasts my soul hates; they have become a burden to me, I am weary of bearing them* (1:14). The hearers assumed that their sacrifices and observances of all the festivals were proof of their faithfulness to God. Isaiah declared otherwise; the religious rituals were unacceptable from people who perpetuated injustice. Sacrifices were worthless and an insult to God. They merely annoyed Him. *When you spread forth your hands, I will hide my eyes from you; even though you make many prayers, I will not listen; your hands are full of blood* (1:15).

Isaiah also offered the hope of a pardon. He called the people to repent and to cleanse themselves spiritually, and to stop doing evil. *Wash yourselves; make yourselves clean; remove the evil of your doings from before my eyes; cease to do evil* (1:16). Finally, the nation was summoned to do good. The people must practice righteousness. *Learn to do good; seek justice, correct oppression; defend the fatherless, plead for the widow* (1:17).

SUGGESTIONS TO TEACHERS

Although this lesson centers on the call of Isaiah, we must not treat it like a group of scientists examining a butterfly. We may be tempted to look at Isaiah's experience in the temple as an interesting specimen to be pinned to a board. But we must take the next step: to allow the Scripture here to give us a deeper sense of God's call and message to each of us.

1. AWED BY A SENSE OF THE HOLY. Isaiah felt a deep awe when he realized the presence of the Lord. No flippant, palsy-walsy relationship with God on Isaiah's part! Take some time to discuss the role of reverence toward God in the Christian life. Explore some of the ways worship has sometimes been allowed to turn into a "make me feel good" experience, in which a person demands an emotional high for himself or herself. This is a human-centered, not God-centered, exercise.

Furthermore, discuss with your students whether a sense of awe before the Lord must be recovered in worship. The chummy talk about God often implies that the Lord is not the almighty Creator and ruler of the universe but simply a genial buddy. Look carefully at Isaiah 6 for clues about worship and reverence in everyone's life.

2. AWARENESS OF ONE'S OWN SINFUL STANDING. *Whatever Became of Sin?* was the title of a book by Dr. Karl Menninger, the famous Topeka psychiatrist and founder of the great Menninger Clinic. Dr. Menninger, not a minister or theologian but a committed layperson, devoted an entire book to the way contemporary people—including church folks—have tried to ignore or downplay the sense of self-centeredness that separates them from God, from each other, and their own being. As Isaiah stated, an awareness of the presence of the Lord also brings an awareness of one's unworthiness and God's grace.

3. ACCEPTANCE BY GOD. Isaiah realized firsthand the cleansing power of divine mercy. Here is the opportunity for you and the class to discuss the forgiveness of God. Be sure to introduce the way we Christians understand that we are forgiven, namely through the costly price of Christ's blood.

4. ANSWER TO A CALL. Every time the Lord calls a person, that person is given a task. Isaiah's response, "Here am I! Send me" (6:8), revealed his wholehearted willingness to accept an assignment. Likewise, if you or anyone in your class has ever had any sense of God's goodness and nearness, you and they have also been called to serve. God bestows His love in order that it be shared. Spend time discussing ways in which each of us may respond to God's call. Stress that all believers have been "called" through knowing something of Christ.

TOPIC FOR ADULTS
RESPONDING TO GOD'S CALL

Highway Patrol to Pulpit. God's call comes in various ways to people. With Ed Jackson, it came in the course of his duties with the Ohio State Highway Patrol. He said he was a devout Christian but had become somewhat jaded after investigating murders, rapes, and other crimes. He left the patrol after an experience during a riot at Ohio State University in 1970.

"One of the rioters was injured very badly. I was in a position to help him. I wasn't so sure I wanted to," he said. "That man disgusted me. He had thrown bags of urine on me. He spit on me. He burnt my flag. I'm a patriot. Everything I love and cherished he attempted to destroy."

Then, he said, he recalled how Jesus died on the cross, forgiving those who persecuted him. That changed Jackson, and he decided to become a minister.

He gave up his job eight years before he could retire and collect a pension. He said his wife and children supported him in his decision. "I think people are finding that there is not a whole lot of fulfillment in material things," said Ed Jackson, who is one of the founders of the Grace Brethren Church in Columbus.

God's Game Plan for Player and Coach. Dan Reeves was a star athlete in his hometown of Americus, Georgia, and at the University of South Carolina. He went on to the pros to become a running back with the Dallas Cowboys from 1965 to 1972. In his last two seasons as a Cowboy player, Reeves also was a coach. Moving to Denver as the head coach of the Denver Broncos, Dan Reeves led that club to three Super Bowls. Reeves has also suffered disappointments, such as being fired at Denver. Whether as a player or as a coach, however, Reeves insists that character is more important than winning. Character, as the most important factor in his life and in the lives of his players, for this coach stems from an awareness of God's call and guidance. Looking back on the direction that God has given his life, from his childhood in Georgia to his new post as head coach of the Giants, Reeves states:

"I know I couldn't do the things that I do if God didn't give me the wisdom and the strength and the courage and the patience and all the things that I need and ask for. . . . When I got fired at Denver, it devastated me. But the reason I was able to handle it is that I have tremendous faith that God has a plan for me. I didn't know what it was going to be, but I knew I was one of His children and He was going to take care of me. He's always done that. This episode proved to me he does have a plan. I end up with the best job in the National Football League."—From an interview by Samantha Stevenson, as told in the *New York Times,* February 7, 1993.

Doctors on Call. Answering Christ's call to minister in His name, Dr. Richard Gieser, Dr. Ben Bacchi, and their staff at their Wheaton, Illinois, eye clinic pay their own way to spend twelve-hour unpaid workdays caring for persons with eye problems in forgotten areas of the globe. Dr. Gieser, Dr. Bacchi, and their colleagues have traveled to Nigeria, Mexico, Afghanistan, and most recently to China.

Their trip to the medical post in China required that they scrunch on hard seats as they traveled bad roads on an unheated bus for seventeen hours. The Christian Medical and Dental Society helps these physicians. They and their staff are fervent evangelicals, undertaking the risks and enduring the discomforts out of their sense of calling by Jesus Christ. These doctors who bring healing in Christ's name have responded to God's call to serve. In what ways are you responding to that call?

Questions for Students on the Next Lesson. 1. Why was King Ahaz frightened? 2. How did Isaiah try to reassure him that God should be heeded? 3. What was the sign God would offer the king? 4. What do you think is the greatest source of national security? 5. How can Isaiah's words help us deal with frightening circumstances?

TOPIC FOR YOUTH
RESPONDING TO GOD'S CALL

Responded. When defensive end Reggie White became a free agent, the bidding war for his talents began in earnest. White, a Baptist minister, announced that he would rely on God's guidance in deciding where to play.

Mike Holmgren, Coach of the Green Bay Packers, called White and left a message on his answering machine. "Reggie, this is God. Go to Green Bay." White signed a four-year deal with the Packers worth seventeen million dollars!

You may smile at this story, but it does illustrate that we are to respond to God's call to service. Isaiah understood that and so did White. The question is, will we respond sincerely and wisely?

Delivered. One dark night in the 1940s, the Goldbergers were suddenly sent to a spot near the coast, an hour from Copenhagen. They only had time to grab some clothing and family photos before leaving the apartment. Hiding in the low bushes along the beach in Dragor, on the island of Amager, they waited in the cold October night. The three-year-old boy had been given a sleeping pill to keep him quiet. Finally, a light flashed from the sea. The family walked almost forty yards out into the icy water that reached up to their necks. Mr. Goldberger carried his two small sons while his oldest son struggled to carry the family's two suitcases. The daughter helped her mother. They were hurriedly loaded into a concealed cargo space where they laid on their backs under a smelly canvas. Along with twenty other Jews, they crossed the open sea. A few hours later they were safe in Sweden.

While much of Europe was deaf and silent as the Jews were rounded up and sent to the death camps, the Danish underground rallied and saved many of their own by getting families, such as the Goldbergers, to Sweden. (Out of seventy-eight hundred Danish Jews, seventy-two hundred were saved!)

Denmark was one small nation that responded to God's call and acted. Instead of agreeing to injustice, the people acted justly.

Idol Threat. Guilt in the form of "feeling spooked" caused two thieves to return their loot and beg for forgiveness fifteen years later. In 1978 Jimmy Lee Hinton and Randall Doyle Morris stole two wooden ceremonial figurines, some pottery, and other artifacts from a cave used by the Hopi Indians in ancient tribal ceremonies. The two young men thought that they had gotten away with their theft and that they could hold on to their illegally-gathered Hopi materials. After all, they thought, the figurines were sort of like idols.

For the next fifteen years, Hinton and Morris claimed that they were plagued with strange happenings because of taking the Hopi valuables. Hinton said that at 2 a.m. every morning he heard little wind chimes, and kachinas (Hopi masked gods) would appear nightly in his dreams. In addition, he suffered kidney, liver, and gallbladder failure after the theft. Just months after stealing the idols, Morris was nearly killed in a motorcycle

KEY VERSE: Take heed, be quiet, do not fear. Isaiah 7:4a.

HOME DAILY BIBLE READINGS

Aug.	7	M.	Isaiah 7:1-9	*Isaiah Advises Ahaz to Trust God*
Aug.	8	T.	Isaiah 7:10-17	*A Sign for the Fearful King*
Aug.	9	W.	Isaiah 7:18-25	*Ahaz's Actions Will Bring Hard Times*
Aug.	10	T.	II Kings 16:1-6	*Ahaz Turns Away from God*
Aug.	11	F.	II Kings 16:7-9	*Ahaz Buys Help from Assyria*
Aug.	12	S.	II Kings 16:10-18	*Ahaz's New Altar*
Aug.	13	S.	Psalm 75	*God Will Judge Unrighteousness*

BACKGROUND

Isaiah's ministry in Judah took place during the height of the power of the mighty Assyrian Empire. Under some of the world's ablest and most fearsome military leaders, the Assyrian war machine ravaged and terrorized the Middle East. At one time or another, all the smaller countries, including Israel and Judah, were forced to pay tribute or become client states.

Periodically, these client states would try to declare their independence or stop paying off the Assyrians. One such episode occurred during the reign of King Ahaz of Judah. The king of Israel and the king of Damascus in Syria plotted to overthrow the Assyrians who were threatening them and costing them so much tribute money. These two leaders decided that Judah should be forced to join their coalition. They told King Ahaz to take up arms with them, or suffer the consequences.

King Ahaz and most of Jerusalem's population were as frightened "as the trees in the forest shake before the wind" (Isaiah 7:2) when the combined forces of Syria and Israel appeared at the gates. The only calm person amidst the panic was Isaiah, who confronted the shaken weakling of a king. The prophet challenged the ruler to heed God's message to "take heed, be quiet, do not fear" (7:4), assuring Ahaz that the threat to Judah by Samaria and Damascus would pass.

Isaiah instructed Ahaz to put his trust in the Lord, not in chariots. To confirm his faith in God, Ahaz was told that he could have a sign from the Lord: a child named Immanuel, which translates as "God is with us." Isaiah tried to convince the wavering Ahaz that God indeed was with His people. God would bring forth a child in the royal lineage who would be God's deliverer. Seven centuries later, Matthew, the Gospel writer, picked up this promise and stated that Jesus was its fulfillment. We know this passage in Isaiah as the Old Testament origin of the story of the virgin birth.

In spite of Isaiah's entreaties and the promises from God, Ahaz panicked. Foolishly he appealed to Assyria for help against Israel and Syria. The Assyrian emperor was happy to oblige—for a price. That price was a staggeringly heavy payment to Assyria. In effect, Ahaz sold out Judah for protection from two minor-league kings threatening him. And Assyria continued to demand tribute. Judah became a satellite state in the Assyrian

Empire, although it was permitted to retain its own kings as long as it kept the cash flowing to the Assyrian capital.

NOTES ON THE PRINTED TEXT

Jotham ruled Judah from 740–735 B.C. His policy had been to appease Assyria and not to offer her any military opposition. When he died, his son and successor, Ahaz, assumed the throne and continued his father's foreign policy. Judah would offer no offense to Assyria.

However, Israel and Syria formed an alliance against Assyria. Apparently they counted on Egyptian support. They wanted Ahaz to join them, but he refused. The two invaded Judah, planning to overthrow the government in Jerusalem and replace it with a Syrian named ben Tabeel. Ahaz and the nation panicked. They appealed to pagan gods and even sacrificed Ahaz's own son to the Canaanite god, Molech! *When the house of David was told, "Syria is in league with Ephraim," his heart and the heart of his people shook as the trees of the forest shake before the wind* (7:2).

Preparing for the siege of Jerusalem, Ahaz inspected the city's defenses. He was outside the city at the Gihon Spring with his advisers and army officers. This open air reservoir and water shaft was the city's water supply. Since water was essential, the men likely were discussing how to protect it. It was to this location that the Lord ordered Isaiah and his son to go. *Go forth to meet Ahaz, you and Shearjashub your son, at the end of the conduit of the upper pool on the highway to the Fuller's Field* (7:3).

Isaiah advised the king not to panic, but to stand fast and trust exclusively in God. The nation was told to do nothing but remain loyal to the Lord. *Take heed, be quiet, do not fear, and do not let your heart be faint because of these two smoldering stumps of firebrands* (7:4). Rezin's and Pekah's power was already spent. They were like a fire that now was almost extinguished, leaving only some smoking coals. Their attempt was doomed and would not succeed.

Apparently Isaiah was unable to convince Ahaz. At a later time, Isaiah again went to Ahaz. For a second time he urged the king to trust God, even offering a sign. It could come from the underworld or from heaven. *Ask a sign of the Lord your God; let it be deep as Sheol or high as heaven* (7:11).

Ahaz refused. Perhaps he remembered Moses' condemnation of the people in the wilderness or knew the Deuteronomic prohibition testing against God (see Deut. 6:16). *I will not ask, and I will not put the Lord to the test* (7:12). More likely, he was simply hiding his halfhearted commitment to God.

Isaiah was angry. Indignantly he criticized Ahaz's weakness and vacillation. Isaiah's patience had reached its limit. He realized that Ahaz would not trust God. *Hear then, O house of David! Is it too little for you to weary men, that you weary my God also?* (7:13).

God Himself would supply a sign. *A young woman* [in RSV; virgin in KJV or NIV] *shall conceive and bear a son, and shall call his name Immanuel* (7:14). Probably the context calls for both near- and far-range fulfillments. Isaiah proclaimed that the danger from the attack would disappear so quickly that a pregnant woman would thankfully name her son Immanuel, which meant "God with us." The greater, long-range fulfillment is seen in Matthew 1:21-23.

However, this sign of hope would also be a sign of doom. *He shall eat curds and honey when he knows how to refuse the evil and choose the good* (7:15). Before the child could properly distinguish between good and evil (about twenty years of age), he and the population would be eating the food of nomads and shepherds. Before the child reached his twentieth birthday, the two nations that Judah feared would be devastated. *For before the child knows how to refuse the evil and choose the good, the land before whose two kings you are in dread will be deserted* (7:16).

Isaiah prophesied that Ahaz's course of action would lead to difficult times for Judah. His reliance on Assyria, instead of God, would bring disaster. *The Lord will bring upon you and upon your people and upon your father's house such days as have not come since the day that Ephraim departed from Judah—the king of Assyria* (7:17).

SUGGESTIONS TO TEACHERS

When Mr. Rogers appeared as a guest on the Arsenio Hall program one night a few years ago, he and Arsenio talked about trying to help children and young people have a better sense of their intrinsic value as human beings loved by God. Arsenio told of a conversation he had had a few days earlier with a young man in Los Angeles who had been involved in drugs and petty crime. "Be good," Hall advised, "or you'll end up in a box."

"Don't make no difference," the youth replied. "I'm dead already."

The host of the late-night talk show tried to convince him otherwise.

Kids in the ghetto and kids in upper-class suburbs, and many, many adults share the sense of despair the young man in L.A. disclosed to Arsenio. Some may be in your class. Your lesson this Sunday is intended to be an antidote to those feelings of futility. Listen to the words of Isaiah.

1. SMOLDERING STUMPS. Isaiah dismissed the invasion forces as "smoldering stumps." He tried to convince the weak king that the futility he felt was not necessary. Ahaz was exaggerating their power. Most of all Ahaz had in effect given up on the Lord. Our feelings of hopelessness invariably result from our lack of trust in God.

2. SACRED SIGN. Isaiah promised King Ahaz that a child named "Immanuel" would be born into the royal family—as a sign from God. Move the topic of discussion to how Jesus is truly *the* promised "Immanuel." Jesus completely fulfills the meaning of the name "God is with us."

3. SINFUL SOVEREIGN. King Ahaz disregarded the advice of Isaiah. Furthermore, the king participated in the unsavory practices of the Canaanite cults, including child sacrifice. The superstitious monarch believed he had to appease malignant powers in the universe by having his own little boy killed on a pagan altar. Once the Lord is rejected, evil, superstitious rituals soon creep in. Remark how dark and destructive pseudo-religions continue to attract persons in our society. Mention that these false faiths inevitably fail, and worse, bring deterioration and even death.

4. STUPID SELLOUT. Ahaz's reliance on Assyria reduced Judah to being dependent on Assyria. The king's lack of faith in God and his sellout to the Assyrians practically bankrupted Judah. Ironically, the

Assyrian king went ahead and did what he had intended to do, and captured Damascus and Samaria. Sadly, Ahaz aped Assyrian ways, even to the design of the altar in the Jerusalem temple. This Judean king serves as an example of faithlessness and rejection of God for all generations.

TOPIC FOR ADULTS
ONLY GOD CAN PROTECT

The Greatest Dramatist. Ken Burns struggled for more than five years to produce his prize-winning documentary film on the history of the Civil War for public television. He visited more than 160 archives. He went to dozens of Civil War sites.

The research and filming proved more difficult than Burns had anticipated. He reported that toward the end of the making of his epic documentary he received a remarkable letter from the distinguished American Civil War historian Shelby Foote. Foote's letter, Burns stated, was filled with good suggestions about how to fix scenes that had been defying the touch of Burns and his staff, especially in blending a concern for the ordinary soldier with the more familiar history of generals and presidents.

What caught Ken Burns's attention the most in Dr. Foote's letter, however, was the stunning closing sentences. "Remember," Foote wrote, "that God is the greatest dramatist. Whenever the story seems to sag, along comes God (or History) and provides the extra kick, the ultimate turn of the screw." Burns reflected often afterward about how on one level Foote's advice helped make a better film. "God was the greatest dramatist. We jettisoned the arty flashbacks and stuck to chronology—God's drama—finally realizing that so much of history is destroyed by our present-day imposition of new ideas and structures and literary license. In short, we don't want to do anything to history to make it better, sexier, happier, safer, more relevant. We need only to listen to it, accept it, even its seemingly unbearable moments, and trust in its lessons."—From comments made by Ken Burns, February 2, 1993, at Ford's Theater, Washington, D.C.

Proud, Stubborn, and Silly. The person who refuses God usually refuses to be wrong. Since he or she has taken the place of God, that person must always be right. Such an attitude always brings silly, if not stupid, episodes. Take the case of the man who founded the *Indianapolis News,* John Holliday, a man convinced of his own infallibility.

One day, Holliday discovered that the word "height" was incorrectly spelled as "hight." Furious that such a mistake could be found in his paper, he stormed through the offices to track down the culprit who had left the letter "e" out of the word "height." It turned out that the person who had written the article and also proofread it with the offensive misspelling was John Holliday himself!

Holliday did not show any embarrassment. He announced stubbornly that if he had spelled "height" as "hight," then that was the way the word was properly written. Holliday could not permit himself ever to be seen doing anything incorrectly. He insisted that the right way to spell the word was without the "e." For the following thirty years, his newspaper therefore, always had the word written as "hight," exactly as John Holliday insisted. Holliday's words, "If I spelled it that way, that's the correct way!" betrayed an attitude that permeated the thinking of Judah's leaders, and, if widespread enough among the powerful, can wreck any society. Only God is infallible!

Questions for Students on the Next Lesson. 1. What did Isaiah have to say about those greedily acquiring lands? 2. Why was Isaiah so harsh toward his fellow countrymen who loved drinking and partying? 3. What did Isaiah warn about those perpetuating injustice? 4. How can the cynicism about our justice system be overcome? 5. Do you feel that pleasure-seeking practices in our society are weakening our nation's moral fiber? Why?

TOPIC FOR YOUTH
DANGER AHEAD

Not to Be Ignored. Antiochus IV was the youngest son of Antiochus III, leader of the Seleucid dynasty after the death of Alexander the Great. In 169 B.C. he became king. As a young man he had designs to expand his empire and, therefore, left his homeland of Syria and marched his army toward Egypt. In 167 B.C. he reached Egypt and sacked Memphis. Then he began to march toward Alexandria.

He was met by one man, Popilius Laenas, the Roman ambassador. Popilius announced to the surprised young man that Rome had had enough of his ambitions. Antiochus was to go home immediately and take his army with him. Young and rash, Antiochus asked for time to think the matter over. Using his staff, old Popilius drew a circle around Antiochus in the sand. He then told Antiochus not to step out of the circle until he had made his decision. If he did, he was at war with Rome!

Antiochus knew all too well of Roman might and power. The threat was not empty. To disobey was to invite disaster and defeat. Antiochus took his army and went home.

Antiochus had known that he was in a dangerous situation, and to have ignored the circle would have meant disaster. In the same way, Ahaz knew that he was in danger. When Isaiah came with a sign, it would have been foolish to ignore it.

Two Who Act. "Lead or Leave" is a group founded by Rob Nelson and Jon Cowan. The two are part of the twenty-something generation and college students who are worried about the economy and the burden that the huge national deficit will place on tomorrow's younger people. They actively lobby for a reduction in the federal deficit and for changes within the Social Security system.

They have been successful in gaining the support of Ross Perot, New Jersey Senator Bill Bradley, and Commerce Secretary Pete Petersen. They have carried their message to other young people through magazine and newspaper interviews as well as through morning and afternoon talk show circuits.

Here are two who do know how to deal with frightening circumstances that they face. Here are two who are trying to offer a course of action that would avert difficult times for their country. Here are two who act like Isaiah to lessen the future danger lying before their nation.

Reawakened Faith. The Boston Marathon threads its way through the city of Boston. One part of the course is a long, tortuous stretch known as "Heartbreak Hill." Thousands of spectators gather here to watch people struggling against this hill. As the better runners' chests heave and other runners consider dropping out, the people yell encouragement.

One young marathon runner "hit the wall" as he approached Heartbreak Hill. It appeared doubtful that he could go another step. Spectators yelled and shouted encouragement, but it did not help.

An older man, who was obviously in better shape than the younger man, came alongside the boy. He put his arm around him, put his hip under the young boy's hip, and spoke quietly to him. Together, slowly, they made their way up Heartbreak Hill. Encouragement was all that it took.

Isaiah spoke to a king who had hit the wall. Overwhelmed by discouragement, Isaiah offered Ahaz encouragement and hope. He awoke the faith of a king much like an older man reawakened a young runner's faith that he could finish a race.

Questions for Students on the Next Lesson. 1. What charges did Isaiah press against the people? 2. What were to be the consequences of sin? 3. Are there consequences to acquiring too much money or drinking too much alcohol or lying? If so, what? 4. Have you ever been guilty of such sins or do you know such people?

LESSON 12—AUGUST 20

JUDGMENT COMES ON ISRAEL

Background Scripture: Isaiah 9:8—10:4; 5
Devotional Reading: Psalm 2

KING JAMES VERSION

ISAIAH 5:8 Woe unto them that join house to house, that lay field to field, till there be no place, that they may be placed alone in the midst of the earth!

9 In mine ears said the Lord of hosts, Of a truth many houses shall be desolate, even great and fair, without inhabitant.

10 Yea, ten acres of vineyard shall yield one bath, and the seed of an homer shall yield an ephah.

11 Woe unto them that rise up early in the morning, that they may follow strong drink; that continue until night, till wine inflame them!

12 And the harp, and the viol, the tabret, and pipe, and wine, are in their feasts: but they regard not the work of the Lord, neither consider the operation of his hands. . . .

18 Woe unto them that draw iniquity with cords of vanity, and sin as it were with a cart rope:

19 That say, Let him make speed, and hasten his work, that we may see it: and let the counsel of the Holy One of Israel draw nigh and come, that we may know it!

20 Woe unto them that call evil good, and good evil; that put darkness for light, and light for darkness; that put bitter for sweet, and sweet for bitter!

21 Woe unto them that are wise in their own eyes, and prudent in their own sight!

22 Woe unto them that are mighty to drink wine, and men of strength to mingle strong drink:

23 Which justify the wicked for reward, and take away the righteousness of the righteous from him!

REVISED STANDARD VERSION

ISAIAH 5:8 Woe to those who join house to house, who add field to field, until there is no more room, and you are made to dwell alone in the midst of the land. 9 The Lord of hosts has sworn in my hearing: "Surely many houses shall be desolate, large and beautiful houses, without inhabitant. 10 For ten acres of vineyard shall yield but one bath, and a homer of seed shall yield but an ephah."

11 Woe to those who rise early in the morning, that they may run after strong drink, who tarry late into the evening till wine inflames them! 12 They have lyre and harp, timbrel and flute and wine at their feasts; but they do not regard the deeds of the Lord, or see the work of his hands.

18 Woe to those who draw iniquity with cords of falsehood, who draw sin as with cart ropes, 19 who say: "Let him make haste, let him speed his work that we may see it; let the purpose of the Holy One of Israel draw near, and let it come, that we may know it!" 20 Woe to those who call evil good and good evil, who put darkness for light and light for darkness, who put bitter for sweet and sweet for bitter! 21 Woe to those who are wise in their own eyes, and shrewd in their own sight! 22 Woe to those who are heroes at drinking wine, and valiant men in mixing strong drink, 23 who acquit the guilty for a bribe, and deprive the innocent of his right!

KEY VERSE: Remove the evil of your doings from before my eyes; cease to do evil, learn to do good; seek justice, correct oppression; defend the fatherless, plead for the widow. Isaiah 1:16, 17.

HOME DAILY BIBLE READINGS

| Aug. | 14 | M. | Isaiah 9:8-17 | Punishment for Proud and Corrupt Leaders |
| Aug. | 15 | T. | Isaiah 9:18—10:4 | Moral Decay and Injustice Are Judged |

Aug.	16	W.	Isaiah 5:1-7	*Israel and Judah as a Vineyard*
Aug.	17	T.	Isaiah 5:8-12	*Judgment on Greed and Selfish Indulgence*
Aug.	18	F.	Isaiah 5:13-17	*God's Judgment Is Just*
Aug.	19	S.	Isaiah 5:18-23	*Judgment on Arrogant Immortality*
Aug.	20	S.	Isaiah 5:24-30	*Destruction Awaits the Wicked*

BACKGROUND

During the early part of the eighth century B.C., the northern kingdom enjoyed a period of prosperity. Under King Jeroboam II, Israel had grabbed back territories in Transjordan and took some of Judah's lands. Wealth flowed into Samaria, Israel's great capital. However, as Amos and Hosea proclaimed, Israel was doomed. These perceptive prophets and other godly figures knew that greed, injustice, and corruption, like moral dryrot, were destroying the nation. Israel had repudiated its covenant with the Lord.

Following Jeroboam's death, the stability and prosperity came to an end. During the following thirty years leading to the fall of Samaria, six kings held the throne. In the meantime, Assyrian might was growing. Ambitious Assyrian emperors tightened the pressure on all the small nations in the Middle East to become vassal states. The kings of Israel faced demands for heavy payments of tribute money to Assyria at the risk of cruel treatment by Assyrian storm troopers. When Tiglath Pileser III of Assyria died and Shalmaneser V took the throne, Israel recklessly revolted. Assyria quickly invaded. After a three-year siege, Samaria fell.

In the southern nation of Judah, Isaiah used the fall of Israel as a warning that God could also allow devastation to come to Jerusalem if the people persisted in rejecting God's law. With unsparing frankness, the prophet condemned those whose greed for additional land was victimizing the poor and those whose heavy partying and drunken debauchery were making them insensitive to the Lord's way. Isaiah thundered that those perpetuating injustice should not complain about the Lord's response in the time to come. With the insight that only a person close to God can have, Isaiah told his fellow citizens that they were substituting their own desires for God's standards of morality.

In the time when nearly everyone was certain that the greatest danger to Judah was the Assyrians, Isaiah persistently warned that the greatest threat to Jerusalem was not the Assyrians but Judah's continuing rejection of God. National sin, not Assyrian might, threatened Judah's existence.

NOTES ON THE PRINTED TEXT

The "woe" form found in today's lesson was used by practically all the prophets. A most elaborate example comes in this lesson from Isaiah. The prophet's message was clear: Israel faced God's judgment for the uncaring way it was living, disregarding God's commands.

Woe to those who join house to house, who add field to field, until there is no more room, and you are made to dwell alone in the midst of the land

(5:8). Isaiah condemned the greedy for acquiring land in ways that victimized the poor. Traditionally, land was viewed as God's. Since no human ultimately owned the land, it could not be sold. People were stewards of the land. This provided a social structure whereby everyone had property and access to food.

With the growing economy, money was available. The rich bought up huge amounts of land and built house after house. These property owners became rich landlords, and the gulf between the poor and rich widened. Isaiah was concerned about the poor and prophesied doom to the wealthy.

Archaeology has provided a unique insight into Isaiah's words. In the early days of Israel's kings, most homes were fairly uniform in size and structure, reflecting a society that had little social stratification. However, by Isaiah's time, things had changed. At Tirzah, for example, large homes with well-dressed facings on both sides and well-joined corners were unearthed. These were the homes of the wealthy. They were separated from the poor citizens' quarter by a long, straight wall. These homes were small and closely packed together; they had thin, rough walls.

Surely many houses shall be desolate, large and beautiful houses, without inhabitant (5:9). All of the new, lavish homes built by the rich were doomed to destruction and desertion. In addition, all of the wealthy people's expectations of a good harvest were shattered. The harvest would be a failure. Instead of a blessing, those inhabitants remaining would experience judgment. Ten acres of vineyards would produce only six gallons of wine. Six bushels of seed planted would produce less than one bushel of grain. *Ten acres of vineyard shall yield but one bath, and a homer of seed shall yield but an ephah* (5:10).

Two of Isaiah's seven woes upon Israel had to do with alcoholism. The first woe pictured the lives of the men in the ruling class who lived only to satisfy their own pleasures. They rose early in the morning to drink and party and carouse all day until late into the evening. *Woe to those who rise early in the morning, that they may run after strong drink, who tarry late into the evening till wine inflames them!* (5:11). As long as they had music and wine, they cared nothing about God or His way. *They have lyre and harp, timbrel and flute and wine at their feasts; but they do not regard the deeds of the Lord, or see the work of his hands* (5:12).

Isaiah condemned those who purposefully ignored God's demands with contempt. He likened these people to a farmer dragging a bullock. They pulled their sin and guilt like a cow on a lead rope. *Woe to those who draw iniquity with cords of falsehood, who draw sin as with cart ropes* (5:18). These people simply would not believe in God's coming judgment. Indifferently they replied that if God was the Holy One of Israel, then He would punish them, but they would not believe Isaiah or God without proof. *Let him make haste, let him speed his work that we may see it; let the purpose of the Holy One of Israel draw near, and let it come, that we may know it!* (5:19).

Isaiah condemned those who perverted the truth. These people perverted all the moral standards in their pursuit of pleasure. "If it feels good, do it!" these people preached. *Woe to those who call evil good and good evil* (5:20).

Isaiah warned against trusting human wisdom and having no fear of the Lord. *Woe to those who are wise in their own eyes, and shrewd in their own sight!* (5:21).

Isaiah condemned all those who perpetuated injustice. Those who were professional judges and those who were to sit in the local courts and maintain the law were warned that God would judge them. Instead of being legal experts, they had become experts in wine. *Woe to those who acquit the guilty for a bribe, and deprive the innocent of his right!* (5:23).

As Israel had fallen, so would Judah. God would allow the same devastation to come if the nation continued to reject God's law.

SUGGESTIONS TO TEACHERS

Some mistakenly think that the Christian faith has to do only with private or personal behavior. The Bible's message, however, clearly states that God is also Lord of the nations.

God's judgment finally came to Israel. The list continues through history, with the Soviet Union's collapse as perhaps the best recent example of the downfall of a nation because of idolatry and injustice. But the point of the lesson is not to point our fingers at ancient Israel or any modern government. The lesson should help us reflect on how we in our nation bear responsibility to the God of all nations.

1. LESSON FROM HISTORY. Isaiah pointed to the defeat and end of Israel as an object lesson for his country of Judah. The continued wickedness of the Israelites, encouraged by deceitful religious leaders, undermined the foundations of that nation. Unless repentance comes from stubborn pride, Isaiah warned, Judah would suffer the same inglorious ending. (Later, in 587 B.C., Judah's turn came when the Babylonians destroyed Jerusalem.) Invite your students to comment on the modern-day relevance of Israel's experience.

2. LEGALITY OF OPPRESSION. Isaiah spelled out in detail the problems with Judah. Lawmakers, in league with wealthy landowners, wrote legislation permitting breaks for the rich. Judges, often bribed by the well-to-do, handed down rulings that brought hardship to the underclass. The upper classes, already comfortable with ample holdings, were able to use the legal system to grab more land, thereby causing widespread homelessness and poverty. Isaiah warned that social justice must be a national policy as well as a religious priority.

3. LAMENT FOR NATIONAL FAILURE. Study the poetic indictment of Judah that Isaiah presented (5:1-7). What does the Song of the Vineyard suggest about us, God's community today?

4. LIST OF OFFENDERS. Examine the catalog of types of persons whose acts and life-styles were weakening the moral fiber of Judah. Have your students pick out various kinds of wrongdoers: the covetous schemers plotting takeovers of helpless peasants' properties, drunken libertines, conceited carousers, those practicing and encouraging acts of moral depravity, those accepting bribes, and others mocking God. The list sounds as if it comes from this week's newsmagazine, doesn't it? How does God react to such behavior in our culture?

5. LOSS OF INDEPENDENCE AND IDENTITY. Isaiah calmly announced that the Lord of history would institute a time of reckoning also for Judah. God would bring this about in His own time and in His

own way, unless the nation repented. Does God also pronounce judgment on nations today?

TOPIC FOR ADULTS
FAIR WARNING

Warning. The American Dental Society placed signs on highways in some parts of the country. The signs stated: "Ignore your teeth and they will go away." The message reminded readers to take care of their teeth, with the subtle warning that neglecting them could prove costly and painful. Preventive dental care is vital.

It's even more important to remember God. Signs of spiritual warning could well be posted in the offices of every local, state, and national leader. King Ahaz and Judah's leaders ignored their faith and allowed their country to become a satellite nation to Assyria.

Lest We Forget. At the end of the nineteenth century, the British Empire stood at its zenith. One quarter of the globe was colored in red, depicting British possession. English schoolchildren were taught that the sun never sets on the British Empire. Nearly everyone in Great Britain assumed that its nation's wealth and power would continue indefinitely. Proud of its preeminent position in the world, the British government planned an extravagant event on the occasion of Queen Victoria's Diamond Jubilee in 1897 to celebrate the mighty Empire.

Rudyard Kipling, the best-known poet, was asked to write a suitable poem. Those preparing the gala affair expected verses glorifying the conquests and prestige of the world's greatest power at that time. Instead, Kipling took his ideas from the Bible. He recalled the perils of national pride in empires of the past, such as Tyre and Assyria. To the disgust and disappointment of many in 1897, Kipling did not pen a poem boasting of global dominance. Instead, he wrote the memorable lines of "Recessional," pointing out the dangers of national preening and parading, and concluding each stanza, "Lest We Forget."

The poet, like the prophets of old, warned his countrymen of the dangers of national conceit. Although criticized for not producing a poem extolling British might, Kipling could see that the seeds of decay were already at work. Kipling was proven right a few years later when World War I ended, leaving Britain broken and humbled.

Kipling's poem is actually a hymn, and could well be sung on every national occasion in every country.

Fair Warning. Following World War II, chemical pesticides were used widely in agriculture. The late 1940s and the 1950s saw DDT and other powerful toxins sprayed indiscriminately on fields, lawns, and woodlands in enormous quantities. Crop-dusting planes and tank trucks continued to rain deadly clouds even on the few who protested the dangerous practice. "Experts" claimed the chemicals were harmless.

Rachel Carson, a modest naturalist and writer, observed that birds and fish were dying, and that many survivors were not reproducing. She raised questions, noting the link between the deadly poisons polluting the food chain and the absence of songbirds in certain areas in spring. Although DDT killed insects, the chemicals also killed wildlife. And, Carson suspected, the stuff would also kill human life, too.

Rachel Carson began to collect data. As a trained scientist, she painstakingly built her case. The chemical industry attacked her, slandering her personally as an incompetent woman and belittling her methods. The big chemical companies with powerful public relations techniques dismissed her findings as exaggerated and irrelevant. Various spokesmen for the vested interests claimed that humans were meant to tame and exploit nature for their own use, and if that meant using pesticides, that was the way things were intended.

Carson worked on. The accusations that she was a crackpot and silly bird-watcher stung, but she realized the threat to human life if reckless pesticide use was not stopped. Even while suffering from a painful, debilitating illness, Carson spent two years meticulously checking her data. She published her initial findings in a series of three articles in the *New Yorker*, then in a book, *Silent Spring*, in 1962 (New York: Houghton-Mifflin).

Like a prophet who was vilified, Carson fearlessly proclaimed her warnings about the dangers of careless use of DDT and other lethal pesticides. Fortunately, her book finally convinced Congress to pass bills curtailing the use of these harmful chemicals. Thanks to Rachel Carson, this past spring was not silent but filled with the songs of birds. And thanks to this quiet, caring woman, the human race will not poison itself with deadly sprays and powders.

Questions for Students on the Next Lesson. 1. Who were the Assyrians, and why were they dreaded? 2. What did the Assyrians do to Samaria and its inhabitants? 3. How did the prophets interpret this event? 4. What practices in our society do you believe may have disastrous consequences for us and our children? 5. Is it possible to put loyalty to nation on the same level as loyalty to God?

TOPIC FOR YOUTH
FAIR WARNING

Warning about Slavery. Many people believe that slavery no longer exists. However, despite international laws against forced labor, millions of people are still in bondage, according to a report by the International Labor Organization. *AntiSlavery International* estimates that 200 million people, many of them children, are slaves. In Thailand, "child catchers" roam the rural countryside, either buying or stealing children from poor families to be put on sale for work in private households, factories, brothels, and restaurants. In Haiti, "searchers" roam the interior searching for children to be shipped off to the Dominican Republic for labor on the sugar plantations. In Brazil, "cats" prowl rural villages for children to labor in the large metropolitan areas. Sadly, even today slavery's chains still exist.

Isaiah condemned this practice and other injustices that existed within his nation. His warning to his listeners was that they should not be complacent. God would act against such injustice. Listen to Isaiah's warning.

Warning about Cheating. Mary was a teenager enduring Latin class in high school. One day, she was taking an exam when she had some difficulty with some questions. She gave in to the temptation to cheat and looked at some of the answers on another person's exam paper. When she smugly turned in her exam, she felt that she had done fairly well.

She had indeed done well on her exam. It was so good, in fact, that she won the honor of representing her high school in the statewide Latin contest. She carried her shock, guilt, and fear into the contest. She was miserable because she had not qualified honestly. Her miserable feelings were confirmed by her dismal performance.

Isaiah warned his people that judgment would come. Those who rejected God's warnings were punished.

Warning about Alcoholism. The United States Department of Health and Human Services and the Department of Education have issued reports to young people about drugs and alcohol. One report stated that 4.6 million teens have a drinking problem and that 4 percent of high school seniors drink every day.

These reports also stated that a young person does not have to drink every day to be an alcoholic or to have a problem with alcohol. For example, ten thousand young people were killed and forty thousand were seriously injured in alcohol-related automobile crashes, drownings, and suicides. In fact, alcohol-related accidents are the leading cause of death among young people fifteen to twenty-four years of age. Half of all drownings, fires, homicides, and suicides are alcohol related. Shockingly, 25 percent of hospital admissions for young people are alcohol-related.

The public health service simply wanted to provide fair warning to teens and young people. However, long before this report was issued, Isaiah issued a similar warning. Listen to his words.

Questions for Students on the Next Lesson. 1. How did Israel specifically disregard God? 2. What was the result of Israel's sin? 3. Does evil always bring God's judgment? 4. How does God punish a whole nation? 5. In what ways are individuals to be responsible for their actions?

LESSON 13—AUGUST 27

THE END OF A NATION

Background Scripture: II Kings 17:1-23
Devotional Reading: Deuteronomy 8:11-20

KING JAMES VERSION

II KINGS 17:6 In the ninth year of Hoshea the king of Assyria took Samaria, and carried Israel away into Assyria, and placed them in Halah and in Habor by the river of Gozan, and in the cities of the Medes.

7 For so it was, that the children of Israel had sinned against the Lord their God, which had brought them up out of the land of Egypt, from under the hand of Pharaoh king of Egypt, and had feared other gods,

8 And walked in the statutes of the heathen, whom the Lord cast out from before the children of Israel, and of the kings of Israel, which they had made.

9 And the children of Israel did secretly those things that were not right against the Lord their God, and they built them high places in all their cities, from the tower of the watchmen to the fenced city.

10 And they set them up images and groves in every high hill, and under every green tree:

11 And there they burnt incense in all the high places, as did the heathen whom the Lord carried away before them; and wrought wicked things to provoke the Lord to anger:

12 For they served idols, whereof the Lord had said unto them, Ye shall not do this thing.

13 Yet the Lord testified against Israel, and against Judah, by all the prophets, and by all the seers, saying, Turn ye from your evil ways, and keep my commandments and my statutes, according to all the law which I commanded your fathers, and which I sent to you by my servants the prophets.

14 Notwithstanding they would not hear, but hardened their necks, like to the neck of their fathers, that did not believe in the Lord their God.

REVISED STANDARD VERSION

II KINGS 17:6 In the ninth year of Hoshea the king of Assyria captured Samaria, and he carried the Israelites away to Assyria, and placed them in Halah, and on the Habor, the river of Gozan, and in the cities of the Medes.

7 And this was so, because the people of Israel had sinned against the Lord their God, who had brought them up out of the land of Egypt from under the hand of Pharaoh king of Egypt, and had feared other gods 8 and walked in the customs of the nations whom the Lord drove out before the people of Israel, and in the customs which the kings of Israel had introduced. 9 And the people of Israel did secretly against the Lord their God things that were not right. They built for themselves high places at all their towns, from watchtower to fortified city; 10 they set up for themselves pillars and Asherim on every high hill and under every green tree; 11 and there they burned incense on all the high places, as the nations did whom the Lord carried away before them. And they did wicked things, provoking the Lord to anger, 12 and they served idols, of which the Lord had said to them, "You shall not do this." 13 Yet the Lord warned Israel and Judah by every prophet and every seer, saying, "Turn from your evil ways and keep my commandments and my statutes, in accordance with all the law which I commanded your fathers, and which I sent to you by my servants the prophets." 14 But they would not listen, but were stubborn, as their fathers had been, who did not believe in the Lord their God.

KEY VERSE: *The Lord warned Israel and Judah by every prophet and every seer, saying, "Turn from your evil ways and keep my commandments and my statutes." II Kings 17:13a.*

HOME DAILY BIBLE READINGS

Aug.	21	M.	Deuteronomy 8:11-20	A Warning to Keep God's Commandments
Aug.	22	T.	II Kings 17:1-6	Israel Falls, the People Are Deported
Aug.	23	W.	II Kings 17:7-12	Israel's Sins Caused Its Fall
Aug.	24	T.	II Kings 17:13-18	Israel Scorned God and Worshiped Idols
Aug.	25	F.	II Kings 17:19-23	Jeroboam's Leadership Started Israel's Decline
Aug.	26	S.	II Kings 17:24-28	The Land Resettled with Other Peoples
Aug.	27	S.	II Kings 17:29-34	Both God and Idols Worshiped

BACKGROUND

The Assyrian's armored columns were the terror of the ancient world. Under cunningly ingenious military leaders, Assyria perfected tactics to intimidate opponents. Assyrian treatment of captured cities was brief and brutal; soldiers carried out a scorched earth policy, leveling the walls and buildings, slaughtering indiscriminately, and deporting the survivors as slave labor. Usually the Assyrians uprooted the local surviving population, marched it to a distant part of the empire, and replaced the displaced people with a group forcibly brought from another area.

Tiglath Pileser III had put his own puppet king in place in Israel and taken heavy tribute payments. Upon Tiglath Pileser's death, Israel rebelled against his successor, Shalmaneser V, who promptly sent the most powerful army of the time to seize Samaria. The city of Samaria, Israel's capital, held on for three long, terrible years, but the siege finally succeeded in 722 B.C. Israel ceased to exist. Most of the ten tribes taken into captivity simply disappeared by being absorbed into the cultures of the distant areas where they were forcibly relocated.

The prophets saw God's hand in all these events. The fall of Israel was not merely the result of flawed diplomacy, according to the spokesmen for the Lord. Nor could the capture of Samaria be credited merely to superior Assyrian military power. The end of the northern nation was blamed on the idolatry of the kings and the people. Although God had sent a series of prophets warning them to keep the covenant of faithfulness that their ancestors had made, the Israelites had refused to listen. Inevitably, the prophets lamented, the nation's disobedience brought destruction.

NOTES ON THE PRINTED TEXT

Hoshea, Israel's last king, made a foolish attempt to gain independence in 724 B.C. He had already occasionally withheld tribute, and the Assyrian king finally had had enough of this annoyance. Assyria's plume-helmeted soldiers moved into the whole northern countryside. They overran villages, towns, and cities and laid waste to everything. Then Shalmaneser, Assyria's king, besieged Samaria, Israel's capital city. The heavily fortified city held out for over two years until 721 B.C., when it fell to the new king, Sargon II.

In the ninth year of Hoshea the king of Assyria captured Samaria, and he carried the Israelites away to Assyria (17:6). Archaeological excavations at Samaria show that the city was totally destroyed. Thick layers of ashes give evidence of burning. Broken ivories attest to looting. The city was quite literally leveled.

Excavations at Khorsabad, the great Assyrian city, have yielded stone slabs stating that fifty Israelite chariots were captured, and 27,290 inhabitants were deported to distant cities of the Assyrian Empire. Likely this number represented the population of Samaria as well as those who fled to the city for safety. These people and their leaders were deported and replaced with the same sort of people from another area of the empire.

This was so, because the people of Israel had sinned against the Lord (17:7). The fall of Israel was a punishment. The general indictment against the nation was that it had sinned and angered the Lord. Even though God had delivered Israel out of Egypt during the Exodus, the nation broke the covenant and served and *feared other gods* (17:7). Israel *walked in the customs of the nations whom the Lord drove out before the people of Israel, and in the customs which the kings of Israel had introduced* (17:8). Called to be a unique chosen people, Israel instead copied the Canaanites. Part of Israel's sin was even introduced by royal decrees.

The nation's sins were detailed. *The people of Israel did secretly against the Lord their God things that were not right. They built for themselves high places at all their towns, from watchtower to fortified city* (17:9). Israel worshiped God improperly and *burned incense* (17:11) at high places. In addition, the nation worshiped alien gods and idols. The worship of these gods also involved child sacrifice. *They set up for themselves pillars and Asherim on every high hill and under every green tree* (17:10). Israel involved itself with the rites of the fertility cult of Baal. The pillars symbolized Baal and the mother goddess Asherah. Hordes of clay figurines were found in Israel, even on the temple mount, attesting to the fertility cult's influence. Often the fertility rites took place under a tree in a sacred forest.

Israel deliberately broke another commandment and served idols. *They served idols, of which the Lord had said to them, "You shall not do this"* (17:12).

Israel had been repeatedly warned by the prophets to repent and to keep God's law. God had sent prophets to remind the nation to keep the covenant its ancestors had made with God. *Yet the Lord warned Israel and Judah by every prophet and every seer, saying, "Turn from your evil ways and keep my commandments and my statutes, in accordance with all the law which I commanded your fathers, and which I sent to you by my servants the prophets"* (17:13).

The people refused to listen to God's warning. The nation continued to follow the worthless idols, lacking any faith in the true God. *They would not listen, but were stubborn, as their fathers had been, who did not believe in the Lord their God* (17:14).

SUGGESTIONS TO TEACHERS

Ten years ago, who would have foreseen the collapse of the Soviet Empire or the disintegration of Yugoslavia? The people of Judah, you may remind your class, were just as startled to hear about the fall of Israel.

Just as various experts have been presenting reasons for the end of the Soviet Union and Yugoslavia, Isaiah and the prophets examined the causes for Israel's downfall. Their analysis has relevance for us in our culture.

1. COLLAPSE OF A COUNTRY. The immediate cause of Israel's fall was the evil and foolish king of Israel, who presumed he could outsmart the Assyrians by his clever maneuvering. The problem was that the rulers of Israel insisted on relying on their own human wisdom instead of seeking divine guidance. Some went through the pretense of listening to the Lord, never hearing God's call for repentance and justice.

2. CAUSE OF THE CATASTROPHE. The deeper reason behind Israel's end was that the people had "sinned against the Lord their God . . . feared other gods and walked in the customs of the nations . . . [and] did secretly against the Lord their God things that were not right" (Kings 17:7-9). Persistent disloyalty to God, putting pure self-interest ahead of the Lord, is a form of idolatry. The Israelites ignored the sacred covenant relationship, breaking trust by descending to disgusting acts of depravity in the name of pagan cults. The Scriptures refer to them as selling themselves to evil (17:17). In other words, the Israelites sold themselves as slaves to destructive practices. Talk with your class members about how sin can enslave us to evil.

3. CONDITIONS OF CONTINUITY. The only way a community of any kind may survive is to have standards for moral behavior and a concern for justice. This is true whether the community is a family, a town, a congregation, a country, or the world.

TOPIC FOR ADULTS
DISOBEDIENCE BRINGS DESTRUCTION

Death by Armed Cult. The world gasped in February, 1993, when a cult near Waco, Texas, known as the Branch Davidians, opened fire on investigating law officers, killing four federal agents and wounding fifteen more. Led by a man named Vernon Howell (who had taken the name of David Koresh), the group of about eighty faithful fanatically believed Koresh's claims to be the Christ.

Koresh presented a bizarre, distorted picture of the Jesus Christ of Scripture. According to court records, statements to law enforcement officers, and interviews with former cult members, the self-styled messiah of the Branch Davidians had abused children physically and psychologically, boasted of having sex with underage girls in the cult, claimed the right to take every man's wife, had at least fifteen so-called "wives," and carried a 9mm Glock pistol.

Koresh had established a compound ten miles from Waco and stockpiled it with weapons, including .50-caliber machine guns, AK-47s, AR-15s, Israeli assault rifles, and at least one starlight filter for night patrol. Neighbors complained of the weapons being fired, and former disciples of Koresh reported many immoral practices by the man posing as "Jesus Christ." When Federal Alcohol, Tobacco and Firearms marshals attempted to serve arrest and search warrants on Koresh, they were met with an unexpected murderous fusillade of gunfire on February 28, 1993, resulting in the deaths of six people. Disobedience to God brings destruction.

Ignored Guidelines. News organizations claim to have high ethical standards. Journalists, though, have no licensing procedures, no code of behavior, and no disciplinary panels.

Network news agencies do claim to have internal codes of conduct. NBC's document runs fifty pages. ABC's document is seventy-five pages long. However, senior news personnel and managers say these are mere guidelines.

Falsifying the facts is taboo, but there is disagreement over exactly what this means. Therefore, some pictures and stories may be intentionally misleading in order to promote reading or viewing. For example, *USA Today* ran a story on armed Los Angeles youth gangs ready to retaliate if the police officers who beat Rodney King were acquitted a second time. The photos were all mock shots created for effect. NBC was embarrassed when a story on unsafe General Motors Corporation trucks was proven to have used igniters to set the fuel in the fuel tanks on fire. In another case, a TV news reporter and the camera operator supplied alcohol to a minor for a story on teenage drinking.

No one seems quite sure what is defined as breaking the rules. Sometimes journalists do not know what it is to step over the line.

God did provide standards for His people. Repeatedly Israel's prophets summoned the people to follow the commandments. The story of Israel is that it refused. Ultimately, the nation's disobedience brought destruction.

Halloween Fun House. The leaders of the youth group at a Tennessee church hoped to scare youngsters into obeying Christ during a recent Halloween by setting up what they called "Judgment House." The trick-or-treaters visiting Judgment House encountered the story of a teenage couple in a fatal car accident where Billy, the obedient Christian, made it to heaven, while his disobedient girlfriend was consigned to hell. The youths would then proceed to a room heated to 140 degrees by construction heaters to simulate hell. According to some reports, kids laughed at the experience and thought it was "fun" going through Judgment House.

God's judgment is not a mock-up of the hereafter or a parody on Halloween's haunted houses. God holds each person responsible here and now and demands obedience. Disobedience brings inevitable destruction of character and of communities.

TOPIC FOR YOUTH
DISOBEDIENCE BRINGS DESTRUCTION

Dangers of Disobedience. In Germany a few years ago, children were repeatedly warned not to pick up any unexploded bullets, grenades, or munitions in a wooded area that had been the site of severe fighting during the closing days of World War II. Parents and school authorities lectured the youngsters that it was dangerous to handle anything found in the woods from the war and asked them to report any suspicious-looking objects.

Three boys found an old artillery shell. Instead of telling the police, they decided to hold on to their "souvenir." Curiosity got the better of them, and they determined to find out if the old shell was still live. Unfortunately, it was. Two boys were killed, and the third was terribly maimed. Their disobedience cost dearly. Likewise, disobedience to God eventually exacts a grim price, as Israel and Judah both learned.

For God and Country? Burislav Herak was a twenty-one-year-old laborer from Sarajevo. The young Serb was held and tried for war crimes that he committed in Bosnia. He admitted to raping seven Muslim women and murdering eighteen others.

The young Serb defended his actions, saying that he was ordered to commit the crimes. He felt that he and others' behavior should be excused on the ground that there was a war and that there was no law or order.

The young man felt he was being noble and loyal to his religion and his nation. He was Eastern Orthodox and opposed to both Muslims and Roman Catholics. In reality, he was loyal to neither. For his crimes, Herak was found guilty and ordered to be executed by a firing squad.

Israel, too, felt it was being loyal to God and country. However, it was not, and disobedience brought the same judgment and destruction.

No Shortcuts. Bodybuilding competitions are held in many places in North America. Competitors who have gone through the disciplined training for years to develop their arms, chests, and legs through regular workouts in the weight rooms know that achieving an impressive physique takes time and effort.

Unfortunately, however, some would-be competitors have tried a shortcut. Using a group of substances known as anabolic steroids, which artificially enhance muscular bulk, these cheaters have thought they could develop an impressive physique without hard work. They invariably get disqualified from competing when drug testing shows what they have done. Worse, these bodybuilders seeking shortcuts are potentially harming their bodies. Scientifically conducted tests reveal that steroids can cause cancer and mental problems, for instance. However, some athletes ignore the potential harm in an effort to gain the advantage quickly and easily.

Bodybuilders are not the only people looking for quick and easy answers. Nations sometimes take shortcuts. Israel's history is the story of a nation that sometimes looked for a quick answer. Do not make the same mistake.